We Come as One Voice

Eileen Zizecli Coleman

We Come as One Voice - Published by Eileen Coleman 2015

© Eileen Coleman 2015

ISBN - 13 9781514851913
ISBN - 10 4851911
BISAC 1514851911

Printed by CreateSpace a division of Amazon

Eileen Coleman
2 Wern Terrace
Mynyddygarreg
Kidwelly
Carmarthenshire
SA17 4RB

eileencoleman@tiscali.co.uk

Eileen's website - www.newvisionsformankind.com

Eileen's first book 'New Visions for the Future of Mankind' published in 2009

Contents

Note from Editor

It is an honor to know Eileen Zizecli-Coleman as a person, a writer, and a channeller, and to count her among my dearest friends and sister. Eileen does everything in life with a great deal of Love, kindness, thoughtfulness, sincerity and patience; she is a person who has a beautiful sense of ethics.

"We Come as One Voice" is a running narrative of materials that Eileen has been channeling. The most well-known of the entities that she has channelled is White Cloud, an Apache Medicine Man who was incarnate around five hundred years ago in what is now the western United States of America, and presently a spokesperson for The Federation of Light.

Something I really love about Eileen's writing style is that she shares her experiences, visions, thoughts and feelings during the channelings with her readers; it's as if you are right there with her, feeling and seeing what she is experiencing. Besides her attention to detail and accuracy in the materials that she channels, she remains open-hearted and open-minded in the process, readily asking questions of those who are visiting her in order to seek clarity for herself and her readers.

When we see our apparent lack of awareness, we are very aware. Most of us humans have been so busy attracting fear based things to ourselves for eons and very successfully too, that we have forgotten that the same creative energy works when we attract Love based things to ourselves. Eileen is using her creative energy to attract Love based things to her. Thank You for Being! You ARE LOVE!

The Great Spirit IS gifting ALL with many blessings, and ALL always have the wisdom to recognize them. Namaste!

With Gratitude, Love, Light, Peace, Joy and Compassion,

K. P. Kelly - 'Sounds of Silence' Spiritual network.

Acknowledgments

I would like to thank Kerrie 'Zoolithe' one of my Sisters of Light on this pathway, who has helped me and welcomed me to her Australian Spiritual network site, formerly known as 'The Federation of Light' - now called 'Sounds of Silence'. Through these sites I have made many friends from all around the world who send out their Love to help Mankind. It was Kerrie who first introduced me to the teachings of White Cloud and it wasn't until much later I realised he had been with me for many years as the North American Indian I called 'Grandfather'

I would especially like to thank my friend and Spiritual Sister Kelly, who both believed in me and helped me to edit this book. Her loving kindness and great wisdom knows no bounds and my life is far richer for having met her through this spiritual network.

I feel I should also mention the beautiful Spiritual site 'Light Grid' created by Sonja Myriel, having also posted many of my channelings and paintings. Thank you to all the admin teams of these spiritual sites who keep our messages alive to share around the world, spreading healing to mankind and planet Earth.

Thank you to the girls in my meditation group who have made contributions to this book. To Sandy Mather for questioning and to Linda Griffiths, Alison Thomas and Carolann Evans for their continued spiritual presence and insights.

Last but not least I would like to thank Blossom Goodchild, who is White Cloud's main vessel on Earth and has been so for many years. Blossom has greatly inspired me and given me the confidence to publish this book with my painting of White Cloud on the cover; this is the vision White Cloud gave me of himself in his role with the Federation of Light.

The Love from all these friends around the globe has given me the encouragement to continue my work and how could I not . . . for once on this pathway there is no turning back!

About the Author

My first introduction to spiritual guides and inspirers began in the early nineties when I was woken in the middle of the night. To my amazement I was shown a group of people standing above the foot of my bed, arranged in the form of a pyramid. They seemed to be bathed in a golden glow as if illuminated by firelight and at the very top stood an Egyptian lady with large, dark eyes who held me in her gaze. There were many people of different nationalities and I scanned them avidly, always being drawn back to the top of the pyramid absolutely mesmerised!

Shortly after this incident an oriental guide introduced himself to me by the name of Tyekinder and told me:-

"Go forth and learn - be like the urn that is forever full - as each new truth is learnt and understood more knowledge will filter through in an endless stream. Sometimes it comes in a torrent and takes time to digest - at other times it is but a mere trickle. Don't keep it to yourself so the water becomes stagnant - but pass on this knowledge to others".

Over the next few years I received regular transmissions to help and guide me and my first step on the spiritual ladder was as a healer. I also started to write poetry with a spiritual message and this gradually developed into something much deeper. I would wake in the night with words filling my mind and started to keep a journal by my bedside; I had a strange sensation in the back of my nose when contact was needed as if a spiritual door had opened, years later I realised this was the pineal gland that was being activated.

I sat in meditation regularly with a close friend and we were contacted by Native American guides who came to help us develop. There was one in particular who I called Grandfather, a kindly silver haired elder who sat with me many times; I now believe this to be White Cloud who has helped me greatly with more recent channellings. My friend and I soon realised we were being contacted by off world beings when we were called 'little earthlings' and my writing took off on a different level.

One evening as I lay in bed asking my star friends where I would end up, I was shown a vision of 'Queen Galadriel' from the film 'Lord of the Rings' where she spoke of going into the west! The moon was shining brightly that night and its silvery beams lit up the arm of my crystal star that was pointing west. Six months later for even further clarification I was shown a silver arrow flying past my face, heading west! Looking on the map I saw that Wales was to the west of us and in 2003 my husband and I took a trip to explore. We both fell in Love with Wales and knew without a shadow of doubt this was where we were meant to be. Within four months we had sold our house and moved - and the new car we bought for the journey happened to be 'silver' just like that arrow! The move helped to further raise my frequencies, enabling access to even higher dimensions; it was here that I received startling information to be passed on to the Children of Earth and our first book - 'New Visions for the Future of Mankind' was finally published in 2009 and is available on Amazon.

'We Come as One Voice' contain channellings that show a deepening connection with many different Star beings. These beings of Light draw close to assist their counterparts on Earth, Light workers who are here to raise their own frequencies and in turn those of mankind. For me this culminated in 'White Cloud' stepping forward to make himself known to me, along with a vision of him in his role as overseer for The Federation of Light. This prompted a painting which I have used for the cover of this book. 'Sitting Bull' has also drawn very close to me over the years, coming forward more strongly recently and I look forward to the work we shall be doing together.

Those who come forward often start sentences with 'We' as they speak for a whole collective of energies from many different star systems, all coming together to forge an alliance, assisting mankind in their transition to a new dimension of loving grace. As the transmissions became more frequent I took to using my recorder at each session, capturing the flavour and essence of the messages and visions received, enabling the reader to share my experience of blending with those from the higher realms.

We are also preparing to channel information accompanied by transfiguration and this process allows the audience to see the communicators vibrating on a different frequency with the chance to ask questions, enabling a discussion of sorts. Some of these communicators have shown themselves to be of extra-terrestrial appearance and in the future they hope we will come to accept them as they truly are - our friends and relations!

"There is much to overcome and we are doing our best to make this connection stronger and more vibrant so that you will see with your own eyes - your physical eyes! We reel back the curtain and allow you to see us as we truly are - it is a bold statement to make but we will honour this".

We see not the darkness that descends upon us

We see only the hope of a golden dawn

PART ONE

The early years of contact

Chapter one

Collaboration

I was woken in the night with words forming in my mind and left my bed to transcribe; this became second nature to me for quite some time but for obvious health reasons we have now agreed to channel during daylight hours. Some data is downloaded during sleep and then brought to the surface and transcribed during the day.

We are here to help uncover what is necessary to alleviate all manner of disease and destruction on planet Earth. We have spoken of this in the past and we come now armed with the powerful tool of LOVE. We help to uncover a forum of intrigues that spell disaster and destruction on a mammoth scale - and there will be no escape from the flames if you do not heed our words! We come to planet Earth to overcome a situation that has spelt out the worst case scenario and we intend to hold you back from the brink, assisting you by enabling a massive rescue operation that will startle even the most knowledgeable amongst you in its tenacity and strength of purpose.

We enlighten as many of you as we can and ask that you hold on to that dream of everlasting life in a new existence, one that will hold firmly in the hearts of all those who listen to our words with courage and a sense of purpose. We have instigated new plans that will take you all to the greatest heights ever imagined in your wildest dreams. We come to bring you fresh hope in a world that has given up on many of you, leaving you to wallow in misery, trapped in the prisons you have all made for yourselves! The vulnerable are constantly pushed aside, and we have seen with our own eyes the contempt that is poured on those who cannot fend for themselves in a world that has become merciless in the scramble for success at any cost!

We bring you fresh hope of a new world where all can live peaceably together in Love and harmony. This world exists in a new framework in a parallel dimension to Earth, and we initiate the greatest trust and respect for those who come here to bring this message to the 'Children of Earth'. For many centuries we have examined data and applied this concept to no avail; it has taken until now to establish a rule of thumb and we are delighted with the concept we are offering you. It will come as no surprise to those of you who have already mastered this phenomenon, for we are given to much idle speculation and have uncovered numerous ideas and theories to back us up. We shall take you all on a journey and implore you to understand our methods of enlightenment.

We take you on a grand tour, deciphering messages as and when called for and we feel this journey will better equip you all with enough data, enabling you to make up your own minds as to where your allegiances lie. We shall as a matter of fact obey the deep principles laid down by the 'Geneva Convention' as we allow you now a peep into our world. We take you on wings of Love and allow a perambulation along the perimeters of our world, here you will find all is in place ready to accept a new generation that we will welcome with open arms. There are no values here other than each man, women or child will be expected to Love one another in the truest sense! We also accommodate the animal and bird population, so do not fret my little ones, all is in place to develop a new alliance and there are those of us here who have discussed the ways and means of developing this alliance for many centuries past.

We have come many times to your world and been notably impressed with the majority of the population, however, there have been those who would suppress the truth at all costs! We implement a memory device that will extract information given to you as a right, and we foresee this as a necessary precaution to alert you of further measures needed to be taken. We are fulfilled in many ways delighting in your company and we take this opportunity to recommend settling back as we take charge, for we are plagued with indecisions and take it upon ourselves to offer you our advice. There are a few points that need to be raised and a coping mechanism we recommend is to accept your fate in whatever way, shape or form. We are all guided by our own destiny and we vouchsafe a glorious future ahead.

This evening, after watching the television series 'Dr. Who' I suddenly became aware of a presence with me.

There has been an extreme resurgence in generating our knowledge and we are constantly seeking new ways to beam you aboard. We have received sufficient data to begin our instruction and suggest a time delay of only a matter of moments before we have contact. We allow certain standards to be reached and are amazed at how little a difference we have made to our energy circuits to achieve this high frequency! We are bound to congratulate ourselves on achieving this level of communication and we believe in all earnest that we shall make a handsome team, renovating thought patterns, tweaking where necessary and maintaining a deep and purposeful harmony. We relay our messages back and forth across the universe stating our unparalleled success and we mean to portray a more youthful example of what has come to be known as the 'dynamic duo'! We recognise a most necessary ingredient of tolerance and respect, complimenting each other in such a way to bring about a considerable understanding. We bring you further treasures to uncover . . . these will bring you the greatest joy and we vouch for your safe keeping in every way possible.

We bring to you now, with great success, a future as 'Time Traveller' and we evoke a special memory recall that will allow you access to other dimensions. We provide assistance for you and take you on a journey that will more than amply convey our greatest message yet, asking you to be prepared for take-off very soon. We delay action only to ask you to be aware in instances of denial as we have exposed this time framework to allow you through; these occurrences are very rare and we allow you this access at great cost to ourselves. Please access this dimension and we will allow you the tiniest peak into a world that has been long forgotten - a world of mystery and intrigue.

I'm now being shown a veil of swirling mist.

We circumference the globe in joy over the prospect that awaits us and we deliver to you now the key that will open many doors into the unknown. We obey our innermost feelings and take you to a place of extreme advantage, knowing it makes sense to join you in complete harmony. We surrender ourselves, inexplicably remaining here on Earth and yet also existing in another framework. We allow you to blend with ease into a new time frame and we shall discover new ways of healing the breach, allowing the souls of those closest to remain beside you.

We encourage action in those we love and intervene to stress that we are more than likely to succeed in this endeavour if we take control of our senses. We make a few mistakes along the way but are well renowned for accepting what is handed to us on each and every level. Please allow us to come close at these times and we will significantly express our hopes and desires of a better world for mankind. We allow you to take your leave and attend to your duties. Thank you for listening as always!

∞

As our group sat for meditation, I felt the strong presence of a North American Indian in full ceremonial headdress. I reached for my recorder and waited for him to speak.

We request permission to interrupt proceedings! We are given to understand there are many questions that need answering in full and we bequeath to you information that has been gathered for this purpose. We have discovered the ways and means of accessing these borders and ask you to bear with us while we attune to your condition. We have no way of knowing if our words will get through with the clarity expected in this dimension, but we know as a matter of fact that we will help you all with your endeavours. We know it has taken some time for us to manage our association with you all and we direct this being of Light, enabling a communication that will bear witness to the fact that we are 'alive' in every sense of the word. We are beholden to you at this time for the measures we have taken to co-exist. *At this point there was a long pause.*

We are at a disadvantage - to maintain this connection we ask that you send out your Love and energy!

I felt there was a problem with energy levels and brought myself back to full consciousness. It was the first time my group had experienced a 'live' channelled message and they commented on the warmth they had all felt, accompanied by a tingling sensation in their hands. There needs to be complete harmony within a trance group when sitting for communication and loving energy surrounding the person channelling. I'm hoping we will be better prepared next time to bring our friend through successfully.

∞

Today my sister phoned telling me she had seen a gift that she would like to give me for my birthday next month. Excitedly, she told me of being impressed to buy a North American Indian figure and asked if I would be happy with something of that nature. I was absolutely thrilled and made a place ready for him in my meditation room to watch over our weekly sessions. I felt the energies change and my Star friends drew close.

We allow you access to our dimension at a time of great upheaval in the world of men. We are forbidden at this time to notify you of events on the horizon, we do however acquiesce to certain information being divulged. We superimpose our thought on yours so that you may do justice to our words and we are convinced that we will win through the deceit and corruption that reigns on Earth at this time! We come prepared to take on an enormous task and we give you the option of riding with us on this crest of a wave. We take you on wings of Love to another world and we mean to access dimensions even higher than ours, asking that you follow us to the shoreline of a far worthier state of existence.

We have discovered a most unusual form of contact, allowing you to come into closer proximity with more than one of us at any one time! This will manifest itself in a wide variety of ways that we shall confirm in due course. We have surpassed ourselves in so many ways, having achieved unlimited access to that place of extreme and utter joy and we venture to say you have been a most worthy companion. We dedicate our time spent with you in persevering with a framework of life that has become obsolete in every way; we know it pains you to hear us speak thus but we manifest for you a new world that is better in every way! This new world will bring about a great change in

14

the course of mankind's evolution and we bring you the ways and means of accepting a broader and undeniably, richer state of existence. We have achieved a mutual bonding and growing determination to succeed in every way possible, making you feel at ease within your new existence on this plane.

We foreclose on a time of great upheaval and unrest, knowing that you choose for yourselves a pathway that leads you closer to the heart of God, and we manifest for you a greater understanding so that you may register what is in our hearts and minds as we speak with you now. We have undergone a massive and most illuminating change to our energy circuits, and we know that you have achieved this in a way that will rectify all concerns for future discourse. We have allowed you to come closer at this time so that we may associate ourselves with you on a finer level and we ask that you govern proceedings so that we may allow an appropriate study, delivering a broader understanding of how we can achieve all this in the blink of an eye!

We motion you to accept us as we are and allow an unveiling that will in no way misrepresent us, for we come to join forces with you and initialise a mutual respect and bonding of energies. We see this as a necessary preclusion to all deals and pacts, and venture to say we are most pleased with how it all pans out. We deliver to you now a most overwhelming exercise, one that is our privilege to bestow upon those of you who have our best interests at heart, and we allow you a closer look at a world that has brought great joy to the population of Earth. We have redeemed and sanctified that part of you that has grown alongside us in this quest for peace and we analyse our data to bring you aboard.

There have been times of deep regret for a past that has been littered with death and destruction on a massive scale, but we come now to save you from yourselves, incorporating you into our time framework so that you may see for yourselves a world that has been lost in space for millennia! We have specifically chosen those of you who have rallied to the cause on numerous occasions in the past, and we mean to access those points that were previously denied. We have come for

15

the duration and will never give up our work, seeking to redress issues on Earth that have come to the fore to be dispassionately reviewed and given new direction. We appease those of you who have allowed certain retrospective points of view to govern thoughts and feelings, but we in 'no way' allow in our agenda any thoughts and feelings that may stand in the way of peace and harmony among mankind!

We have also brought to the attention of all who come to listen that we are in 'no way' satisfied with what we are given to believe as a massive directive of energy, needed to reshape our new world! We rely on 'ALL OF YOU' to 'GIVE YOUR ALL' in every sense! We need each and every one of you to stand firm and herald in a new awareness that will stand the test of time. We take this opportunity to wish you well and hope and pray that we will meet again in a far worthier state of existence. We salute you!

∞

This morning was so beautiful that I decided to sit in the garden to meditate. Closing my eyes I drifted into a deep state of relaxation, gradually becoming aware of seeing the hills and valleys from a great height. I was soaring in the clear blue sky, gliding down and then rising up again, seeing everything in the brightest of colours. During this wonderful experience I was still aware of my hands resting on my solar plexus and yet I was seeing the countryside from above; it felt like being in two places at the same time! My husband came out to join me in the garden and looking up at the sky we saw there were three red kites directly above us. The sun glinted on their wings as they turned direction, gliding on the warm air currents. I'm not sure if I was having an out of body experience or being shown a bird's eye view of the world, whatever it was though I thoroughly enjoyed it. Later as I looked at the North American figure my sister had brought me, I noticed he has two little feathers hanging from the peace pipe; one of them is red so I have decided to call him 'Red Wing'. My sister's late husband also had a spirit guide named 'Red Wing' and I feel they are helping me on the Earth plane!
Before retiring for the night I felt my friends with me and sat for communication.

We propose a toast and select you for entry into our domain! We are prisoners of our own thoughts and feelings, delighting in memory

16

recall that has evoked a far superior sense of achievement and we bear witness to the fact that we have uncovered probabilities that summon a whole new perspective.

I'm being shown frothy white waves crashing onto a sandy shore where there are the most beautiful iridescent sea shells. I can now see a dark-skinned lady with thick wiry hair, tied back at the nape of her neck.

Felicitations . . . we welcome in a new and powerful clause, subjecting you to the ebb and flow of life with its twists and turns. We powerfully regenerate using the force of nature, growing alongside you in wonderment and joy. We translate material and govern the mood of a nation, spending time with those of a lower nature and bending over backwards to achieve our aims and goals of pure intention. We are held in deep affection by the human race and we know it is only a matter of moments before our news will surface . . . encounters of the third kind happening all across the globe!

We speak as one voice, directing energy and perpetuating a most necessary form of contact. We are indebted to your services and ask that you stand firm in your endeavours while we see you through this time of fortitude. We remain intact and hold license over many issues, discovering a world that is champing at the bit. We recommend cool, calm thinking and we put it to the human race that we are up for the challenge and experiencing a setback has in no way daunted our spirit. We march on, holding the banner high, determined to fight for the cause and demonstrating our ability to see things through in a new perspective. We gather you to us, flying on wings of Love, taking you to healthier climes.

We depend on one another as we expend our energy in a barrage of questions and answers, supplying all necessary conduits with a purpose-built information centre that will enhance all recordings. We challenge you to bear witness to our good intentions and we summon forth a monologue of extreme importance, which has been registered and supplied by courtesy of those on high. We feel most honoured and accept our mission with the customary exchanges of 'Light' encompassing our frame, anointing each and every cell of our being, occasioning a prolific and thought-provoking memory recall. We assess each condition and resume contact on a minuscule level that will help us to exchange data more frequently. We are able at this point in time to redirect energy and surface to bring you a wider choice of alternatives. We welcome each and every one, holding you all in our embrace as we take you to a most nourishing form of contact, passing on greater knowledge in a never-ending stream as we conquer over all doubts and inhibitions!

We welcome you to our world of Love, enticing you from a world of sloth and discontent and we sit awhile and muse upon the world in general, taking our time to come up with all necessary adjustments to enable this massive directive. We feel certain that we have gained access to a world that has become in every sense deluded; these wave patterns have governed an entire nation and we have taken it to the point of complete and utter lunacy, robbing ourselves of all self-respect! We are impelled to requisition a robust, governing form of energy that can catapult us into a new dimension, screaming out for salvation, and when it comes we shall see greater sacrifices being made by all! We remain on track and take you aboard, subjecting you to a vigorous scrutiny of ideals and motives. We resurrect an army of labourers of Love and evaluate our next move.

I'm now hearing words from the stage play 'Oliver'! I feel so happy that I'm dancing around the house singing. 'Consider yourself our mate, consider yourself part of the family, we've taken to you so strong, it's clear we're going to get along! Consider yourself our pal, we don't wanna make no fuss - but after some consideration we can say, consider yourself . . . one of us'!

We suspend all arguments and take all in our stride; creature comforts are made available and we record an intake of breath for delights in store! We mesmerise an audience and set our sights full steam ahead, coaxing you into practicing more outward displays of evangelism, for this we require an open and loving heart, disregarding our own vanity. We have exposed a macabre form of prophecy and we relay our mission step by step to overcome all violations of the flesh. We have surpassed ourselves in this endeavour and we maintain our sense of purpose, instructing the millions who will listen

18

to our documentary that we have witnessed at first hand the destruction of Earth! We know that to some this will make us laughing stock - but we will stand firm and maintain our vision of truth and harmony for all, interpreting the hopes and dreams of all who come into our orbit.

We transcend all futile gestures of inconsequence, monopolising our right to freedom of expression. We are most concerned in one area of reference for we are given to understand a certain delicate situation has arisen, whereby we are able to affiliate ourselves with a posthumous record of events preceding our recovery! We allow ourselves a moment's respite, interpreting our dreams and wishes for a nobler existence and we have taken to planning methodically in every way, interpreting a vision that is held in the highest esteem. We take on board numerous attempts to hold sway over a population that has grown in leaps and bounds towards a greater and more productive role in mankind's evolution. We stray from the boundaries that enclose us and develop a greater understanding of all we can achieve. Mark our words - we are bound on a course that will set the heavens alight . . . and we shall pay dearly!

∞

Chapter two

Army of Light

Blessed be the Children of Earth! We welcome you to come amongst us in readiness for the time ahead. We supply you with an inordinate amount of material to see us through a difficult phase and we believe that we shall manage our accounts with unparalleled success. We incorporate into this structure an apparatus that can summon forth indestructible life forms, which by the touch of a button can project a vision of substance, allowing us to transmit information. This recovery process is deemed far superior to any past materialisation and suffice it to say that we are well endowed in our area of expertise. We put it to you my friend that we are in no way misrepresented in any time or sphere of governing, for we represent the highest acceleration of thought streams purported to be in existence!   We shall inform you as and when necessary how input of this caliber will benefit mankind and we allow you now to peruse our conduits, analysing our thought streams with your own to rendezvous at the same point of entry.

We are purported to be a most persistent race, who have succumbed in many instances to betrayal of a most devastating kind. We have allowed ourselves to be re-modified in a way that has allowed our memory banks to disconnect and re-route; this in itself has enabled a reconnection on a higher level, and we shall discuss this later in full detail. We are parallel to yourselves and have allowed a coupling for short periods to re-examine your data. We believe this access has given us greater rewards and with adequate coverage we forge ahead. There are some futile gestures that have led us astray on more than one occasion, but we set our sights on higher ground, taking with us a rudimentary alarm system that shall stand us in good stead. We suffer a temporary loss of definition, allowing these exchanges to manifest in a more subtle format.

We impel you to listen closely to our words as we reach out to you.

We take on board the most necessary formation of fundamental electrophoresis to magnify a curve in space, which allows us to penetrate this spectrum and supply unlimited data! Extraordinarily, we see at this particular time an eclipse of all that has governed our nature and senses and we regulate this species to overcome what is paramount at this time, a need to refurbish and kit ourselves with a zealous understanding of who we are and what we are about! Make no mistake we plan to submit to interrogation, enlightening the planet as to our intentions, and we submit most humbly to your requests allowing a restoration of peace and harmony to reign supreme. We plan for a greater recovery and acknowledge all procedures, temporarily adjusting thought patterns to correlate within our structures of understanding. We betray ourselves with a tear or two when recounting episodes of immense pleasure, taking you to one side to develop the protocol necessary for this intelligence.

I'm being shown the wooden framework of a large building under construction. I feel it is a church or place of learning, similar to those used by the Quakers, a Christian denomination founded in England in the 17th century; at meetings they were encouraged to stand and speak when moved to do so. (A few months later work started on building a wooden summerhouse/ healing sanctuary, where our group did indeed stand and speak when inspired to do so).

We instigate a revival, encouraging an active display of talents, monitoring the success of each participant as we govern a most necessary application. Be brave and we will show you a brave new world - rejoice for it shall be so! We supplement your vision, enhancing what is already an impressive contact and we delay this next chapter of events, battening down the hatches. We take on board a new stream of thought, asking that you sound out our theories and practices. We put it to you that we in no way challenge you to what is not possible or feasible, and we understand perfectly if you stand aside and put us to the test! We are outspoken on a number of issues and ask you to challenge us further; we take for granted those little nuisances that help us to understand the complexities of life and we explain in fuller detail, how your compliancy can help us to accept a more, meaningful study of challenging behaviour!

21

We ponder on these issues taking the time and trouble to kindle respect, initiating a dialogue that will prepare us for a peaceful state of existence. We are well known for our disparities on occasions and we prepare for the onslaught of decision making and for a time of parenting, sacrificing our friendships to make ends meet. We display our talent for holding back and dedicate our message of Peace to all who follow the 'Great Spirit'! We are impelled to recover our identity, using the power of the pen which is mightier than the sword and we shall quote from the highest sources expanding our repertoire.

There has been a cleansing of the soul that has been brought to bear witness and we prepare you to experience greater revelations, uncovering a multitude of information given only to those with the purest intent. We deliberately vouchsafe your entry into our domain and we trouble you to access our accounts. We take you to one side, regulating proceedings, guiding and inspiring you as we delve into the past inscribing a new pattern of understanding. We prepare for a grand connection of minds, extolling our virtues and presenting you with a formula that will trace our heritage back to its roots. To do this we will need to magnify thought forms, presenting you with a clearer picture and we develop a strong and powerful tool, recovering data at an increasing rate. We ponder on these issues and relay a stream of beneficial feedback recovering our senses. Please come armed with the tool of Love and we shall overcome. We assert ourselves, giving directives appertaining to the retrieval of services and suggest that you buckle down for action!

∞

This evening, while sending out absent healing, I felt my star friends draw close.

We are prepared to write an essay on a subject closest to our heart and we remind you of a story told not long ago. Unremittingly, we resume our connection in this time honoured fashion and we retrace our steps, governing experiences of an incandescent nature, discovering for ourselves with great aplomb the advantage of night time seclusion. We reminisce, discovering the ways and means of summoning images to the fore, extracting information that has enabled us the most heartfelt memories.

To help me keep focused, I sat gazing into one of my crystals which resembles a piece of coral. The name 'Desdemona' filtered into my mind as being a ship that had been in danger of sinking in treacherous, murky depths and I wondered if this was a past life memory.

We dropped anchor and ran our nets in search of treasure-trove, toiling from dawn to dusk in our quest for gold with nigh on twenty of us on deck and twenty more below, selling our soul for a pot of gold on the high seas! Personal tragedy overtook the crew and we laid each one to rest, judging each man's life as precious as our own. The curse was lifted and we made our way back home, reunited with our families and fit to tell our yarns! We staggered ashore with enough gold to sink a ship and warranted our success in the arms of the ladies! We raise the yardarm and suggest a flavouring of rum will dull the brain to accept the unpalatable!

This sounds to me as if there could be information coming to the surface which I may find unpalatable!

∞

The last few weeks have entailed me getting used to the energies of my new Star friends and the information they bring. Once more they draw close, surrounding me in a loving glow.

We have delivered to you a monumental study and we appreciate this coming together of like minds, instigating a wider acceptance on all levels. We have bombarded you with thought streams that are predisposed to accept the unpalatable and we feel sure that you have succumbed on numerous occasions to lift those barriers of disbelief. We grant that you have on occasion simply defied us by insisting on a less somber format, but we insist now on stretching the imagination even further by granting us access to your mind!

We have occasioned a massive undertaking and allow a certain subterfuge, granting us further access to your mind, which has at times sent us on a wild goose chase! We have foregone certain niceties in rectifying conditions and we accept the condolences that come our way, subduing any further interference. There have been times of great distaste that have caused us to flinch but we say unto you, that on the whole you have undoubtedly given of your best! We inform you of certain events that surface for re-examination and we leave it to you to convey our deep and utter disbelief at absurdities that have arisen. We are prepared to venture forth in greater equanimity and we rein in hostilities that may cause a setback. Be prepared to meet thy maker for we are well cosseted in our connections, allowing further impact of a most generous nature. We shall in any event surface to reconnect at a level that shall benefit us both and we decide how best our needs are met. There will come a time of greater definition as we expel our theories, taking on board further revelations.

We have brought with us a most death defying alternative solution and we beg you to look with fresh eyes at a situation close at hand! Sowing the seeds of death and destruction will never win us friends and we succumb to more tempting tidbits that can be observed and put into practice. We have occasioned a massive, obligatory connection with those from other worlds and we see ourselves as multi disciplinarians, taking the initiative and forging ahead in a new direction. We have taken on board what is necessary to maintain this structure and we decipher a most necessary band of ethics - a code of conduct to allow us free passage! We have accepted our monologue can be torn to shreds . . . but we reinvest in a new future with mankind, allowing ourselves to participate in a most remarkable and controversial recovery of any kind attempted anywhere!

We are completely at a disadvantage, maintaining our connection in a manner that gives cause for concern. We accept that we are tainted stock and we reassemble our genetic code to allow a discharging of energies, formulating our desire to take you on board. We express our concern at taking you to a level beyond all comprehension, and we know that you will allow this change in your energy circuits to release old patterns of thinking, assimilating a new structure of interdependence worth its weight in gold. We take you on board and in terms of understanding, we have netted ourselves a most remarkable product of the imagination, recouping what was once lost. We vow to recover each and every one of you, taking you to that place of inestimable beauty, allowing this infrastructure to release new patterns of understanding, registering in you the dream of a lifetime!

We assist in this programme and initialise in you that trust to thrust you forward into a new dimension. We are members of your planetary union, and suggest that rather than dismiss our words with irony and discord, you take the time to indulge us by listening. It is only a matter of time before all will become only too clear . . . mankind is set on a path of destruction and no amount of leverage from us will alter this state of malfunction! We can only recommend that you look within, listening to that inner voice that calls you to understand what little time is left. We bear no grudges and take you all to that place of salvation, safe in the knowledge that we have come a long way in instigating this plan of action.

We have known for many years of this 'great escape' and we have measured out our advice over the years, exonerating those of you who have played your part in delivering our messages. We beckon you all to come forth, armed with the tool of Love, partaking of fellowship with the 'Children of Earth' and allowing yourselves to be used as a 'Beacon of Light' for those who are lost. We stand arm in arm, racing against the clock and we know it may take only a matter of moments in our condition but in your time we need to accept it approaches with alarming speed! There is every need to summon forth an army of volunteers and we gather forces, summoning all our strength for this great initiative . . . for on the stroke of midnight we shall be extinguished on this level, re-emerging on another plane of existence!

Farfetched you say . . . but what is remarkable is that this has been tried and tested on your Earth plane, and in the far distant future this has been accomplished on a higher level! We have cause to remember that we have in fact inherited a most successful gene and one we give thanks for. We have successfully accomplished a mammoth leap of the mind into unknown territory and we have given back what was rightfully yours, a fifth dimensional experience, culminating in a most natural progression from one state of existence to another, transcending the physical and embarking on a journey of excellence!

We allow this feedback to give you a greater perspective, to push back the boundaries and let your mind expand into new realms of possibility. A mind bending concept you say and yes that is exactly what it is, but to realise this you must take that first step into realising a golden future that awaits us all. We allow you a closer look and impel you to recognise that we are all brothers under the skin, in fact we are more than brothers we are equals in every way. We decide on the best cause of action, passing restitution of services to those who are mindful of our messages. We substantiate a wide range of activities to be reunited with our counterparts; this in itself will rectify passages of illumination and we successfully pass on our knowledge, taking you each step nearer to the truth . . . the whole truth!

∞

There have been no lengthy communications with my Star friends of recent but I know they are helping me to stay afloat in this time of uncertainty. I have felt the urge to take up my palette and paints once more to help me relax and focus my mind. A picture I have been working on for several weeks has evolved into a beautiful and vibrant Starburst, giving me hope of a brighter future. Relaxing in the garden today and soaking up the sun's rays, I suddenly became aware of looking down on myself. This seems to be happening more frequently now and looking back at my notes, I see this quiet time is for a purpose - a time of rest and recuperation, preparing for what's ahead.

Before waking this morning, I dreamt a bird was hurtling towards me at breakneck speed. Just before it reached me the bird suddenly stopped in mid-air and then started to fall. I ran forward, reaching out to catch it, but just as it touched my fingers it burst into flames . . . a split second later it rose with large wings fully unfurled, flying safely up and away. I was left kneeling on the ground with my arms still outstretched, feeling dazed and with soot on my fingers from the flames. This dream reminded me of the Phoenix, a mythological bird that burned to death on a pyre and from the ashes a new Phoenix arose! After research, I found it commonly appears in literature as a symbol of death and resurrection!

I feel this is a positive sign and I'm curious as to what happens next.

∞

It's now the beginning of July and the weather has been atrocious with high winds and rain, more like autumn than summer. I feel frustrated and stuck in time with no movement on the projects closest to my heart. I'm remembering my Star friend's words to 'stand firm' and tonight I can feel them draw close once more.

We have re-written history and confirm that a general undertaking has occasioned a massive directive. We are well prepared and ready to 'fight the good fight' savouring our connection as we stabilise and monitor our progress day by day. We realise the fact that we have trained you well and liken ourselves to a machine rolling forwards, unstoppable, protected not by metal but the sheer power of Love. We have operated in this state to fulfill our destiny and we travel in time to relinquish our blessings on the Children of Earth. We supply a worthier state of existence and we petition you now to stand your ground!

We have motioned you to accept the impossible and we climb aboard to give you a hand, expanding our talents even further. We ask you to develop your interpersonal skills that will allow us to move among you with greater ease. We have allowed for setbacks to encourage you to respect our wishes and we indulge ourselves by whispering in your ear at those times of greatest hardship! We welcome in a new term of office and show our appreciation of your efforts to stay in touch, however, we do need to mind our p's and q's for we are startled at the number of times you have fallen short, and we depend on a resurgence of energy to give you a boost.

We welcome in a new phase of balance and harmony, serene in our contemplation and political correctness and at all times with great Love in our heart. We emphasise this fact and allow you to demonstrate this on many more occasions. We are likely to have misunderstood what was entirely necessary to forge an alliance and we are taken to task for being so slow on the uptake! We volunteer our services and set the record straight, offering our condolences for past misunderstandings. We treasure these moments with you and open up a new pathway, developing and growing alongside you day by day. There is an opening just ahead and we see ourselves in a new light; trembling we take your hand and lead you to that place of distinction forever in your debt!

We have discovered for ourselves what becomes apparent to all rubbing shoulders with the esteemed, and we shatter the illusions of each and every one of you, taking you to the back of beyond and across the heavens. We strive for perfection on a grand scale, supervising an exodus of mammoth proportions and we are challenged at every corner! We participate in an exchange of information that will register your likes and dislikes and we offer to re-educate you in the ways of our new world. We are well intentioned and supply further evidence that will allow us to take our rightful place among the stars. Initially we request a revamping to update our energy circuits, allowing a greater volume of information to filter through.

At this point I was shown coloured particles caught in various beams of light.

These circuits are traceable in many colours, each one relating to a myriad requests for data, interchanging and compiling information at any given rate and pulsating at a frequency that can be controlled by us. We literally connect to these filaments, structuring for ourselves the necessary components to enhance our recordings.

I remembered a previous vision, where I'd been shown a humanoid figure wearing a helmet whose body framework seemed to be integrated within some sort of space pod.

We ascertain that in this connection we use a quarter of all necessary feedback, installing a further programme to set us on course; we do allow on the odd occasion a more conservative estimation that will bring us back to point zero and we take it upon ourselves to thrust you forward into a new time frame.

The following morning I woke feeling so happy and elated . . . in dream state I

28

had found myself in a new world . . . a new planet Earth. It was just before dawn and everything was bathed in a silvery glow. I walked along crying softly, feeling tears of joy and relief running down my cheeks. There were many of us walking in the same direction, stopping at times to hug one another. We were all mesmerised by the atmosphere and beauty of this place and for what we had all achieved. In the distance I saw the silhouette of a North American Indian coming towards me, threading his way through the throng. I knew he wanted to speak with me but just at this point I was woken by my cat.

The following day I sat in the garden . . . the wind was up sending huge, white clouds scudding across the sky, allowing the sun to peek through in short bursts of dazzling light. I gazed across the green valley, breathing in deeply.

We have developed a unique bond that has led us to this land and we rejoice in the fullness of our Love, forever growing closer together. We broaden our horizons, stipulating what is necessary for our evolution and we take it as part of the deal, initially requesting a funding of energy that shall be regarded as essential. We hasten to add there have been many instances of denial but we are supremely connected and we suffer no interference from any quarter. We respect your wishes, delighting in a deluge of material coming our way, this has been most unexpected and we are inundated with requests, expecting delivery very soon!

I'm being shown a light emanating from my bed head, indicating more information will be coming through in dream state.

∞

There is a full moon tonight and I knew I would receive communication.

We reveal our true purpose, sacrificing our wants and desires for more meaningful pursuits. We put aside what is no longer required and uncover what is not seen, requesting a more purposeful study of logistics. We belong to a new generation of forward thinkers, devoting our time and energy into cherishing a dream that has long been governed from afar. We alternate between this world and the next, scrupulously attending to details, proportionately assessing and rediscovering new techniques to draw us closer together. We have endlessly studied the ways and means of bonding and have come to the conclusion a line must be drawn! We now have at our disposal a portfolio of the utmost importance and we regulate passages of information to govern a new undertaking. We stand the test of time and bring to an end all hypotheses, discovering for ourselves what is most important. We have rallied to the cause, generating further studies in the occult and we change our tune, motioning you to expand your knowledge and connect on a frequency more suited to our needs. We plan our exodus, vouchsafing a glorious future for mankind, and we shed new light on areas of mistrust allowing the forces of nature to govern in the way only she knows best!

We have found ourselves in solitude and bear witness to the evolution of mankind, bearing the lantern on a new age of destruction! We come to save you from 'yourselves' and struggle to come to terms with your convictions that we are 'aliens' hell bent on destroying a world as beautiful as yours! We have no doubt that you will turn in your tracks when you see what it is we are offering you on a plate - a new world of infinite beauty and glorious in every way!

This new world sounds like Heaven to me . . . but does this mean we have to die and leave our physical bodies to be able to reach it?

We assure you that we have your best interests at heart and sacrifice neither one hair of your head nor any limb! We are here to save the population of Earth in every sense and are indebted to your pointing out what has been a bone of contention. We are allotted a life span that is governed by an awareness of our bodies and we struggle to come to terms with the concept of life everlasting! We do, however, see no reason to expire when we are fulfilling our destiny in whatever way shape or form. We are given to pandering to the whims and desires of an earthly existence and so find the concept of renewal mind boggling!

We tell you now - it is within your own experience to decide for yourselves the garb you wear . . . Mother, Father, Sister, Brother. The list goes on . . . we make our choices and settle with that experience

30

until the moment arrives where we change and grow in a new direction.

Will I still be my daughters' mother in this new world?

We adjust our settings to encompass family structures and we bend to the whims of the populace. All is set in place to sway the people of Earth and we rally to the cause!

Is this my higher self, ushering in information previously filtered through, or are you beaming to me from a space pod above the Earth? I'm now feeling waves of energy on the right hand side of my head.

We are supremely connected and hasten to add that for the purpose of our conversation today, our satellite picks up and receives your thought waves, bouncing them across the universe. We in turn send back and monitor this connection.

I'm now hearing an old song by 'Lou Reed', called 'Satellite of Love'.

For purposes of communication in the future we will be there at your side, reserving our frequency for that point of contact giving visual representation. We are well noted for our success and on all levels we shall connect - causing quite a stir! This however, will take some time and we prepare you to take on this mammoth accomplishment, foreseeing a massive expansion of minds all along the coast. We redeem ourselves and prepare for further standing in the occult, lengthening our time of exposure and submitting our portfolio for further examination. We are well prepared to take on the masses and we extend our knowledge to encompass our strategy of exposure.

We fulfill our dreams and take you to that point made ready, motioning you to accept without question what is undoubtedly our greatest proposition yet. We foreclose on the old ways of life and propel you to a place of exquisite beauty and peace beyond all earthly measure. We take you to a land that has been developed entirely for your needs and adjustment to a different timescale. We are sufficiently rewarded with a new programming, which will enable a

31

reconditioning that will sumptuously reflect a grander life style. We relinquish all doubts and fears and take you to a land of 'milk and honey', posthumously accepting those honours dedicated to the human race. We reel back the curtain and gasp with joy . . . delighting in the pleasure of mapping out our future together as one race!

Will we be blending together and if so, how? Will you be taking over our minds or become a host in our bodies? How will we become one race?

We are indebted to your questions and motion you to accept that to all intents and purposes, we have been with you for all time. Think of us as another dimension of your existence to tap into, a voice of conscience that can be called upon to give advice. We are desperate to make this connection of minds and vow that we have traversed the globe in our efforts to save the human race, benefiting from a consummation that has dictated our success. We leave it in your hands and pray that the Children of Earth will come to their senses in time, preventing a tragedy of enormous proportions that will affect not only planet Earth but other solar systems!

I'm being shown a line of dominoes, tumbling against each other, falling down in a huge knock on effect!

Reluctantly we release you to go about your business!

∞

Tonight I attended a spiritual gathering of like-minded souls in Carmarthen, purported to be the most ancient town in Wales with origins that go back nearly 2,000 years to the Roman conquest of this area. During meditation I saw my mother, who was showing me a red kite and singing, 'let's go fly a kite, up to the highest height', it was wonderful and I felt that perhaps a celebration might be in store! My husband picked me up a couple of hours later and when we reached home I was in for a big surprise . . . there on the dining table stood a huge statue of Buddha, one that I'd admired the day before. While I was at group my husband had driven forty miles to the seaside town of Tenby, bought the statue for me and dropped it off at home, returning just in time to pick me up. I'd been told in my communications that I would be surprised when least expected - they were so right and I am thrilled! We carefully carried the statue upstairs and cleared a space in my healing room. Its presence felt quite overpowering in such a small room, but I knew he would be perfect in my new healing sanctuary when it is built. I stood before Buddha's image, absolutely overwhelmed and what was even more amazing, I could feel an incredibly strong energy that seemed to be emanating from the statue itself and connecting with my heart centre.

∞

Today I have chosen a piece of Tibetan music to set the scene for my home meditation group, using the power of thought to visualise journeying up a mountain track, where we could find a Temple to rest and contemplate. I soon found myself among a group of men, shuffling along on thick, wooden clogs, wearing long, brown robes of rough hessian with wide brimmed hats that shaded them from the glare of the sun. Others walked holding long sticks, leading animals that were pulling rickety carts heavily laden with large sacks. At one point in the journey we seemed to be walking across a suspended wooden bridge, and later we stood at the bottom of steep narrow steps, waiting for others to descend so that we could start our climb up to the Temple. We finally reached the top and as we made our way along the wooden veranda that surrounded the Temple, a row of young men to my left were bowing. Still bent, they turned their heads towards me and smiled, addressing me as 'Your Holiness'! I went into the Temple, which was very dark and there before me was a huge, golden Buddha that would have filled my entire healing sanctuary, right up to the ceiling. Afterwards I received these words.

For the purpose of our communication today we identify with 'self'. There has been no decontamination process that will allow for further advancement until we recognise the true flavour of our credentials! We do, however, aspire to higher climes and we direct you to embrace the attributes that are most renowned in the climb we are about to take. We will need a strong rod and staff to help us as we measure each step taken, comparatively and with an abundance not yet seen. We are most impressed with your endeavours and we give an example of measures to be taken. We have spoken in the past of a series of functions being materialised and it is worthwhile remembering that we have gathered enough information to set the record straight. We have on balance rescued you from what can only be described as turmoil of mind, rectifying the nature of practices that have given us a wider scope.

We alter our destination, recognising an overriding factor that has come to our attention and we right a wrong penned long ago - a tale of mystery and imagination beyond the scope of mortal minds! We release the serpent and fly to the heights, majestically taking our place among the esteemed and treasuring each moment. Consequently, we superimpose our vision on those who march before us and wisely we know that you will follow in their stead, granting our vision of self-sacrifice and monumentally fulfilling our destiny. We empower you to surge forward and we open the doorway between our worlds, ascending to new heights.

We blossom and grow, delighting in your company and sharing with you in your idyll. Tread carefully my Love - feint heart never won fair prize and we intercept to align you with this precious commodity. There is before you a windfall of delights in store and we promise a fair wind to sail on. We are heartily aggrieved that you should think we would leave you high and dry, when we have promised you the world! We benefit from what we consider a master stroke of enormous proportions and we deliver as promised:-

'New Visions for the Future of Mankind'!

This is the title of our first book together which was finally published in 2009.

∞

We have vowed to keep the sacred flame burning bright and we alternate between this world and the next, championing the cause. We are without a doubt indebted to your services and we superimpose our thoughts on yours to get our message across loud and clear! We shall excel in all things and we muster for you now an array of material that will sustain us through the coming months, leaving us with a catalogue of undiluted material ready for transcription. Our mission is held sacrosanct and we are able to make this connection with the help of those from other worlds, all who have an interest in the dispersal of those on Earth! We have allowed ourselves recompense for past mistakes and we sally forth to uncover problematic areas that have caused concern in the past. It is a foregone conclusion that we shall assist in every way possible and we leave it in your capable hands to enlighten the nation as to our prerequisites.

We follow orders and put it to you that we have seen with our own eyes what is imperative for all concerned; we entice a nation of war mongers to discover that there is no honour in death and destruction! We simply believe in longevity and a position among the stars that shall lead us all to a worthier state of existence. We are empowered to give you a choice - full recovery in a new dimension or to live as a shadow, never realising your true potential! We have come to believe in free expression and may we be so bold as to enquire – how shall we give vent to our dreams and aspirations in a world turned topsy-turvy, thrown in disarray at every given second? We count ourselves among those fortunate to be blessed and brought to bear witness for we can substantiate all that has been given with an open and loving heart.

We intervene to give you a complete update! It has been decided that to give you further coverage we need to balance our energies and we shall ensure that all is in place to allow a monologue of the utmost importance. We have instilled a sense of courage and achievement to combat a nervous disposition, and we shall encourage you further to surrender to our charms. We promise a most worthwhile rendition and are open to discussion, allowing a free rein. We purposefully regenerate and gather momentum, supplying you with a most impressive form of contact. We open the eyes and ears of all, delivering a broader spectrum of ideas that can be utilised for the benefit of mankind. We have analysed what is necessary to reach this conclusion and we put ourselves at risk to protect your best interests. We shall comply with all requests and powerfully recommend an adjustment of attitudes.

We have all seen for ourselves the parody of the 'Kings New Clothes' and we jump on the bandwagon, airing our views and adjusting our delivery to alleviate any mistrust. We powerfully recommend taking a step back, adjusting your focus and marshalling our thoughts to coincide with a more natural acclimatisation. We have delivered a most powerful speech and we accelerate our gift to you this night, safe in the knowledge that you have given your all. We are most impressed with your delivery and ask you to accept our heartfelt thanks for services rendered. We allow a backsliding as a matter of course and resurrect our services at a later date.

I thanked my friends for this respite as my eldest daughters is coming to stay for a week, which means we shall have to clear out the chairs from my healing room to make way for a bed.

∞

Tonight I just couldn't sleep . . . my mind drifted back to my childhood and the little village where our family lived. I frequently visited the library which was just a short walk through the park, often stopping to sit on the grass, gazing up at the sky, puzzling why I was here and where I had come from. At school my favorite subjects were English, Art and Needlework! I still remember the surprise and pleasure I felt when first presented with fresh white sheets of paper, along with pots of brightly coloured powder paint. I would also happily stay behind in the classroom to finish an essay, while my classmates played outside.

We look back with great affection at events played out across the years and deferentially request a summing up. We faithfully re-create a passage of excellence, marred only by your inability to focus with any great clarity on issues outstanding! We purposefully reconnect to allow you greater fortitude and we supply enough criteria to develop an overactive mind. We supply a worthy cause and outline all necessary measures to be taken that will instill greater satisfaction all round. Please believe us when we tell you, from the bottom of our hearts, that we have thrown all caution to the wind to alleviate any suffering caused unintentionally! We are provided with enough comfort to reduce our fear factor and supply you with a further course of action, detonating further coverage at a safe distance. We have volunteered our services to enable a massive directive, summoning forth all our energy for this next manoeuvre. It is without a doubt the noblest of roles we play in this bargaining process and we are delighted to be offered a role.

We stand back and accept that we have made our mark on a society that has run rings around law and order, where the just are continually condemned while the villain goes free! We are responsible for a massive imbalance, where despicable behaviour has become the 'norm' in a society of freeloaders making a fast buck! We initiate total recall, emphasizing the need to stay on track, and we motion you to accept without question our heartfelt motives for taking you on board. We shatter the illusions that have kept us in the dark for so long and bend over backwards to illuminate your pathway to the stars and beyond, asking that you take back the Light that is yours by right'!

∞

Chapter three

Lift the veil from your eyes

It's nearly the end of August and I've had a very happy and exciting few days with all my family around me. The first day was spent looking at wedding dresses for my eldest daughter who is getting married next year, and I admit to bursting into tears at the sight of her in her wedding veil. On my birthday, we all went to St David's in Pembrokeshire and took a boat ride around Ramsey Island, which is reputed to be home to one of Britain's largest colonies of Atlantic, grey seals. It was so awe inspiring to be out on the water, exploring the craggy rocks and caves, watching the seals as they gazed back at us with their beautiful, dark eyes. There is a full moon tonight and I sat cross legged in front of my Buddha statue to meditate; as the peace engulfed me, I started to pray!

Divine Spirit - let your Love flow through me, enveloping me in your peace and wisdom. Strengthen me and uplift me, empower me to share your message so that the people of Earth may better understand your vision for us all. I'm now hearing the hymn – 'Oh God our help in ages past, our hope for years to come, our shelter from the stormy blast and our eternal home!

We are upgraded to a new level transcending the past, opening up new terms of engagement as we participate in aspirations beyond our comprehension. New revelations are in store and we take a look into the past to examine data before us. We have prophesied a withdrawal and we articulate all forms of regret as we surface for re-examination, motioning millions to accept deportation as a matter of fact! We have finally requested new measures to be taken and we are delighted with the response. There are many who come in search for truth and wisdom and we have benefited from data that has been stored in our memory banks. Suffice it to say we appreciate this moment with you, recovering our senses as never before.

We terminate a frequency that has reached its full potential and we move on now to encounter further strategies and a simply finer connection. We conjure a new stream of thought and constantly assess and monitor our diction. Courtesy forbids us to overstep the mark and we allow a certain subterfuge so that we may get our meaning across, discreetly. We transcend time and space itself and we nurture this dream within you!

I'm now feeling wonderfully, peaceful and serene and have the feeling of looking up in adoration. I'm conscious of wearing a large, starched headpiece worn by certain sects of nuns in times gone past.

Blessings on you my child, we resurrect our plan of action that will allow us to come further into your energy field, and we salute you in your attempts to help us! We shall gather momentum in the next few weeks and we have deliberately taken the precaution of overriding where necessary. We believe we have obtained greater discipline and unravel before your eyes a most necessary form of delivery, bending and swaying to one another's whims and desires for heartier contact, knowing we will deliver with greater expertise.

We are blessed with memory recall and deliver an item specifically in your best interests, notifying you of further coverage. We are able to superimpose in full force a magnetic cluster, transcending time and space. We open this connection, purposefully delivering a mirror image of ourselves and we have allowed these introductions to allay misconceptions beyond all reasonable doubt! We are beholden to a land of soothsayers and reckon on our advantage, assembling in truth our grand collection of stories. We are beholden to those of you who have shown your courage and strength through and through and we assist by taking you on a journey of the highest intent!

I now have the sensation of being on a small open boat, sailing through underground caves, gliding gently and silently along a network of passages.

We shift our perceptions to discover for ourselves a vast vault of knowledge, stored within our very being. We delve deeper and deeper into the unknown and we memorise these events to bring you further examples of courage and strength in the line of duty.

I'm catching glimpses of the inside of a Temple with high ornate ceilings . . .

39

everything is in white, overlaid with flashes of gold and purple.

We stand before you in all our glory . . . lift the veil from your eyes and see for yourselves!

I'm now being shown glimpses of faces that look human . . . panning round I suddenly come across a face that resembles the wise character called Yoda from the film 'Star Wars'. I dismiss this as imagination and move on. Now I'm being shown a large closed eye, which has suddenly opened wide!

We beam ahead of you, supplying the necessary facts and figures, discouraging all forms of contact that are undesirable. We have motioned you to accept the impossible and we realise greater scope is needed to attend to details recovered in this process. We beckon you to journey with us as we travel deeper and deeper into the unknown. We hearken to the still inner voice that beckons us forward and onwards, deliberately bypassing unsavoury episodes as we traverse the globe.

Our rendition of 'Land of Hope and Glory' has been brought to the attention of the masses and we deliberately select those few who come to serve with an open and loving heart! We profess to being undaunted at this next proposal and we suggest therefore, you monitor this connection in growing wonderment and joy for we have associated ourselves with the 'in crowd'! This means we have subjected ourselves to closer scrutiny and we are now allowed to venture further into the stream of excellence - bar none! We deliver multiple choices for further analysis and have come across these in our travels. We motion you to accept, without question, what shall come to be known as the most vibrant time in all our lives put together, we suggest therefore a melding of minds that will allow us to regenerate and push forward our adventure!

∞

During meditation today, I experienced what felt like a distant memory of a loved one and our child in a magical place.   We were so happy, playing together under a huge, jutting rock face from which sprang a cascade of crystal clear water. I had

40

the sensation of lying on my back, floating in the water, feeling completely and utterly contented.

We resume our connection and take you forward!

I'm now becoming part of a much different scene. I'm walking along with scores of other refugees from the Second World War. The women are wearing coats and headscarves and holding the hands of young children. We are all being led through a long tunnel and herded into a building. I can now see a large, metal door and a wheel that is being turned and locked into place! My immediate reaction is - 'OH NO' - not the holocaust'! I feel now that I'm going deeper and deeper into a dark tunnel, holding a lantern out to shed some light.

We regress you, taking you back to a time of death and deceit!

I'm now being shown more women who are all carrying brown suitcases, clambering up into an open truck; one young woman is applying lipstick. The scene has changed again and I'm being shown a tall, young lad who is running; he has a cloth bag with long straps hung over one shoulder. I can feel the energy rippling around the base of my skull and crown chakra and although I cannot see it, I know that he is carrying a large, fish in the bag.

We have saved the lives of many in this condition and we welcome in the knowledge, displaying our talents to the fullest. We hearken back to a time of great remorse and we deliberately lead you to fulfill your duty on Earth. Allowing for a certain subterfuge, we sanction a visit and ask you to take note. We have vouchsafed the safety of the little ones and it has taken many a year for us to conquer over the frustrations buried deep within their souls. We are delighted to inform you that we have enabled a massive clear out of unwarranted data, relating back to times of undue provocation. This has instilled a sense of purpose and it is for this sake that we have encouraged and brought forth a tidier solution. Primitive though it may be, we have exposed a raw nerve and developed a more than ample renewal of services.

(I sense many of those who died during the holocaust have been reincarnated, experiencing deep seated feelings of anger in childhood and adolescence that they

41

cannot consciously account for).

We depend on each other to open the floodgates of success and we bestow upon the esteemed our gratitude and sense of achievement at the clearing of so much hatred and denial! We open the causeway to allow restitution and a way back from the death and destruction of a world in chaos. We plan to evacuate the globe and we take as many as will listen to the prodding's of their heart. We take it further and insist that we rescue the world from certain annihilation for we have seen the destruction for ourselves and sample some home truths!

We have developed a non-risk assessment and accept that we are inhibited in our connection. There has been a reference to security and a tampering with energy circuits that have left us depleted; we replenish and find a suitable moment to reconnect. These times are by their very nature most auspicious and we supply the necessary feedback to enable a massive rendition of services. We point you to a place of safety and surrender wholeheartedly to our finest mission yet! We have developed an active imagination and put it to the test as never before, relinquishing a barrage of suggestions to take you further along this route.

We explore the possibility of making further discoveries about ourselves, and we are no stranger to the infidelities that lurk in the dark, chambers of the mind! We express ourselves with joy to be free of these burdens that have no further use and we set you free from your debts to society, replacing the loathing of self with joy and abandonment and a Love that surpasses all understanding. We bear no grudges and have invited you to share with us in this extravaganza, a time of delight in all things, taking back the Love and sharing with our contemporaries. Accept this challenge and we will meet you half way, lighting your pathway and delighting in your return. We have sacrificed a good many issues and raised discussions on many more, infiltrating at a level acceptable to both sides. We powerfully recommend an adjustment of attitudes and bluntly request an adjournment!

∞

After all the tension and strain of the past few weeks I decided to treat myself to a pampering, booking myself in for a facial cleansing and massage. The music and massage were so relaxing that I soon drifted off in meditation, finding myself in a mountain retreat. It was the same scenario of pampering but instead I was outside on a terrace, looking across at great towering mountains, enveloped in a fine swirling mist. From out of this mist a face drew close to mine and I recognised Sayuri, a young oriental lady who has been one of my guides for many years. Clouds of purple engulfed me and I could feel tears trickling down my cheeks. There appeared next to her, a young oriental man who was looking at me quite intently. During the treatment, Sayuri drew even closer until we became as one and again tears slid down my face in complete and utter contentment.

Later I was very excited to learn that a Tibetan, Buddhist Master - Lama Khenpo Rinpoche, was visiting this country to share his teachings. I was lucky enough to be able to attend one such meeting and felt honoured to meet him. Lama Khenpo has established the Siddhartha foundation school, located near Kathmandu, which is for students from extremely poor backgrounds, many of who are orphans. His visits to England and Wales help to raise funds, providing refuge and shelter for some of the poorest children in the Himalayan regions of Nepal. As I sat listening, I remembered the vision where I had visited a monastery high in the mountains, and a more recent vision with my guide Sayuri, accompanied by an oriental gentleman who very much resembled Lama Khenpo.

While hanging out my washing today, I heard the call of three red kites overhead. I stood watching as they circled the valley, swooping and gliding on the thermal currents with the sun's rays catching their golden wings. Later in the week while in pensive mood, I cast my gaze upwards to see three white swans flying overhead. I know these signs are to reassure me that all is as it should be!

Restitution is at hand as we plot our way across the universe. We surrender as resistance would only hamper proceedings and a noncommittal attitude has incensed a population living on their wits. We sanitise all forms of regret, displacing tendencies to prevaricate at the drop of a hat, impinging on a society that has run roughshod over the weak and vulnerable. We are indebted to your services and beg you to consider alternative solutions to your present impasse. We have detected a war faring anarchy that has swamped a nation in bloody turmoil; regrettably we have not seen the last of this as many factions have risen to the surface, outlining their plans of action!

I'm wondering if they are referring to the recent demonstrations in Burma, which ended in the massacre of thousands of Buddhist monks!

Undeniably, it is a hard time for those who stand to be counted and we mercifully release those souls who suffer at the hands of injustice! We take back the image of Light, ready to make our grand entrance, forecasting a time of peace and majesty beyond all human comprehension. We relive our time on Earth when all shall bathe in this Light and we shall be proud to call ourselves members of the human race. We deliberately set ourselves a goal to become the first civilization that has discovered what we have always known - that we are not alone! We deliberately by-pass unnecessary connections and take you to a revolutionary and pivotal moment in time.

We are most honoured to have been thrown this crumb of human kindness and we deliver especially for you a most wonderful passage that shall rewrite history itself, taking on the compound of artificial intelligence to form a necessary bond of friendship. We have come from a time warp of considerable relay and we monitor this connection to bring us in line with new modes of life. We have processed the necessary information to alert a new term of office, and we sidestep to avert any head on clashes that could cause delay. We are reminded that these delays could cause confusion and for this we are extremely sorry as misinterpretation will affect us in more ways than one!

We generate a new stance and output of enormous proportions, signaling to the rest of the world what we are about . . . justice and freedom for all on a mammoth scale across the world, fighting for the rights of a community that no longer challenge the establishment! We are all free men and women and we have the right to stand up for our own terms, juggling our talents with those of a family to make ends meet in whatever way is right for us. We demand to be heard and seen, conquering over unfair trading standards and exercising our right to stand on our own two feet! We have excelled in our courage and determination to make ourselves heard and we see wider

44

demonstrations taking place all over the globe!

∞

I have been feeling really strange and giddy the last few days, it's as if I'm in between frequencies - neither in one nor the other!

We are reunited in mind, body and spirit and we surprise you, balancing the scales and bringing forth all that is stored and hidden. We motion you to accept this difficult phase and rest assured that all is being done to achieve a harmonious connection. We believe we have made a crucial discovery, summoning forth a host of companions and welcoming in a new season of joyous communication. We balance our harmonies and discover for ourselves the true joy of friendship. We have lasted well over the years and are beholden to your strength and determination to see this through. We have conquered our fears and moved on to a new level of understanding, helped and propelled by those here who have joined our merry band! We delight in our friendship and consider the next step forward; we take control of the situation and suggest that rather than sit on the sidelines - you actively take part!

We are notably impressed with a thriving energy that allows us to manifest further outpourings and we are prompted to adjust our settings, allowing a most deferential recovery, setting our sights higher than ever before. We have succumbed to the temptation of offering ourselves as sacrifice to the Gods but let it be known that we have no mind to react in this way! We have suffered greatly in the past and relinquish our hold on those memories to emerge whole and in the light of true understanding. We have forgiven those who caused us pain and we truly recover our self-esteem, branching out in all directions, purposefully gathering all necessary data. We have astounded even ourselves with the deluge of information and we are well prepared to take on the masses. We are proud to have withstood the test of time and manipulate those feelings that stir within us, breaking out to a point of pure undiluted Love, harnessed and brought to bear witness in a world that has long awaited the 'second coming'!

45

I saw clouds of colour and must have drifted off, waking after a few minutes.

We are here to rediscover the past and we make this possible by enveloping you in the mists of time! We discover for ourselves what has been and will be again, and we know as a matter of fact that we shall be called to give our assistance to the people of Earth. We are reticent with certain facts and figures for we know this is no idle threat or some great plan to throw the world off balance! We have succumbed to a more natural ebb and flow and welcome in a new time of trust.

We portray ourselves as Beings of Light - just as you and we prepare to launch ourselves in a world that has outgrown its purpose. We reposition ourselves and strive for the advent of a far greater world, one that will come to fruition in but a short space of time. We devise a method of communication that shall stand us in good stead and we realise a nation of followers who have reached us in numerous ways. We apologise to those who have not been able to master this connection and we vow to unravel the mysteries that surround us.

We have rallied to the cause and intercept to give new instructions! We are delighted to accept the inevitable and with open arms we welcome you into the fold, renewing your subscription. We politely enquire after your health for we have seen a draining of energies that shall be put to the test. We advise sleep and plenty of it, for it is at these times we can monitor your health and instruct new measures to be taken. We have relayed our messages as they come in across the ethers and we supply the necessary injunctions, making way for a finer more salubrious connection. We light your path and help you to understand the necessity of these measures . . . frustrating though it may seem they have purpose!

It pulls at our heart strings to say this - but we have survived the holocaust and are living proof of a world without end! We supplement with further studies that shall take us nearer to our goal and allow you to bend a little closer so that you may hear what it is we offer you. There has been a thunderous reception waiting for you to come aboard and we are well aware of the niceties that beckon us to your side with open displays of Love and Joy to see you once more!

∞

The figure of Jesus draws near

While working on my computer I became aware of a beautiful energy drawing very close, pausing I gazed at a card on my desk picturing a waterfall and stream running through green woodland. I seemed to become part of that scene and gradually became aware of a beautiful young maiden sitting by the river, her long dark hair partially covered by a fine veil.

We desire to speak with you and are allotted this time frame! We are beholden to your attention and recognise that deep within your soul, you strive for the very best in all things. We are at this moment requisitioning future discussions that will lead us to a place of great beauty. We are taken back in time to regenerate and to hold our place among the stars. We must strive for perfection in all things, reaching out for that perfect place that instills peace and serenity of mind and we take you to a time of simple pleasures . . . we hold out our hand to you!

I can see a hand reaching out for mine and there are tears in my eyes . . . the hand is so familiar. There is cloth wrapped around his palm and recognition dawns . . . Master! Looking up, I see Jesus wearing a thick woven robe of milky white that is pulled up over his head; I can hear the name Miriam being called!

Be at peace my child . . . we have severed connections with the undead and are justified in taking the bread of Heaven.

I'm now seeing sops of bread being dipped into a bowl, and the tears are flowing down my cheeks.

We welcome you back into the fold once more, and take this opportunity to underline a most important episode in your life. There is need of further endurance for we are tested to the extreme, battening down the hatches and remaining on full alert! We have tampered with a most necessary regulation of services and we put it to you, quite succinctly, there must on no account be any surrendering of deeds or flatteries that could hinder our progress! We welcome steadfast devotion to the cause and we subscribe to a healthier lifestyle, incorporating a much deserved rest.

We have tested your endurance in more ways than one and we have cause, quite literally, to embark on a further course of action. We have mentally strived for completion and a term of office that has held us in deep abeyance. We manifest for you now a greater completion and we hold back only to inform you of further treasures, beckoning you on to a goldmine of discoveries relevant to our cause, a shining example of the paths we must tread to reach our goal. Championing the cause, we instil in you a sense of pride in a massive undertaking that has held you firmly in our hearts and minds. We are widely acclaimed as the heralds of a new era and we manifest for you in colours of every hue, taking you to the brink and beyond!

I'm now being shown a white dove, flying up into a clear blue sky . . . sensing the feeling of complete freedom and utter joy!

We open your eyes to a new world of free expression where the meek are heard and we censor only the loneliness that has stricken many souls in your world, welcoming you to the 'Brotherhood of Light'! We bring every soul under the jurisdiction of Love, Peace and harmony, summoning you to Love your brother, to honour him and to take your rightful place in society. We have no intention of surrendering the values we have held sacrosanct and which have led us to a place of shame and humiliation. We have been buffeted by the winds of fate . . . dragged from every corner of the Earth and shaken to our very core . . . and we now reclaim our heritage!

Later on I learned the name Miriam is the Hebrew equivalent of Mary, and feel she may have been Mary Magdalene. The sops of bread are symbolic of something being given or offered as a concession or gesture to pacify. I have since learned that many women have had 'Mary Magdalene' experiences and this is looked at in more detail in a book called 'The Magdalene Awakening' written by L. Shannon Anderson.

∞

During our large group meditation this evening, we were led through a forest to a white Temple. My journey took me to a monastery and I could hear the bell tolling as I walked up a steep, flight of steps. Immediately I saw a large man with huge beard and long white hair. My initial thought was of Father Christmas, but he was dressed in long white robes. I turned and saw my mother, spending the rest of my meditation in her arms with tears streaming down my face. When it was time to leave I retraced my steps and to my surprise found my cat waiting for me at the door. I have missed her so much and was overjoyed, following her to a lily pond where I watched her playing and grooming herself. I didn't want to leave her but was being called back by the group leader. That night I was given the chance to spend more time with her as I had a vivid dream where I cuddled her and stroked her soft fur, playing with her to my heart's content.

We are much impressed with your endeavours and we magically predict a turn around that shall reap rewards of a most generous nature. We pick our way across the skies, heralding in a new world and giving thanks to all who echo our cry. We have maintained our structure and rank, persevering in this time of unrest and uncertainty and we now deliver our ultimatums, setting the world to rights and governing a clause that will help us adjust to this timescale. We venture forth in all our glory - dazzling in power and radiance as we set sail for healthier climes, taking with us the opulence of our new found status. We are well advised to adjust our settings accordingly and we empower you to take the next step forward, regulating a most necessary passage of trust, understanding and seeing the absurdity of many forms of regret!

We allow ourselves the freedom to roam as never before, taking on board a wealth of knowledge and catapulting us into a new arena, devouring and savouring each experience as it comes our way. Reluctantly we let go of the past, embarking on a new adventure, using every vestige of our strength and integrity in putting together pieces of the puzzle. We have been most generous with our assumptions and religiously follow the concept of duality in an ever changing world. We have masterminded our plan of action and taken what is considered by some to be a master stroke of genius, tailoring our gift of rhetoric to fit in with modern day vocabulary. We have set our sights higher, sending a vast recovery of thought forms to adjust attitudes that are sunk to the lowest of the low!

We have supervised a grand collection of stories to be placed at your disposal and we delight in telling you that our mission has been one of extreme fortitude, governed by our ancestors and those we have come to know and Love. We take to heart those irreverence's that reach our ears and we supply you with greater ammunition to forge the respect that is due! We have maintained the trust that is necessary and the chain of office grows longer day by day. In this moment of time we have made our pitch, summoning up the courage to enlighten a nation in distress. We have allowed ourselves to be used as a dummy of sorts, waiting for the ventriloquist to loosen our tongue, channelling a vast array of anecdotes that can charm the birds from the trees! We are well aware that these messages will revitalise a large audience, beckoning the listener to hear the promptings of their own inner voice. We have provided greater coverage, relinquishing a furor of activity as we are petitioned and brought to bear witness!

∞

I woke in the night and saw a beautiful stag with long horns made of gold! On research I found the stag is a messenger from the heavens - a bringer of news and a symbol of wisdom, regeneration and growth!

We are challenged at every corner and we represent a time of undiluted passion. The penny drops and we salvage what we are able, transforming ourselves in a matter of moments and pressing on with more important issues. We have transcended time and space itself, manufacturing a modicum of stability. We are supremely connected inter-galactically and we are forgiven for thinking this is a common state of affairs, having conditioned you into accepting our friendship as the 'norm'! We defy all unacceptable objections as ludicrous beyond words, and we have in fact conditioned you to accept the unpalatable, for it is our understanding that in the near future there will be much to take on board! We have been governed by a wide array of services and we put it to you my friend that we shall obey all criteria in whatever way, shape or form. We have analysed data and feel quite naturally, as do you, that in these times of strife and general

50

disorder there is no time for namby-pamby measures; we strike while the iron is hot, holding on with all our worth, casting aside all fears of disrepute!

We have aligned ourselves with a just cause and one to be reckoned with; this in itself is every reason to stand firm and we adjudicate at these meetings to set the balance steady. We are fair minded and resistant to any form of foul play, bearing in mind that we have ourselves suffered at the hands of those who come to judge. We are in no way particular about the role we play, only the judicial nature of our grievance, which has at times been hard to bear. We have translated, in our own words, a dedication that has led us to your door and we supervise this connection to give us a breathing space, shielded by the overlords in preparation for our journey. We have benefited immensely from this feedback and signify the need to exchange contracts, setting the record straight!

We are multi-dimensional beings and hearken back to a time of great darkness when the world stood still! We have jettisoned a nation of freeloaders and report our knowledge of the destiny of your planet, taking into account the measures necessary to waylay the woeful and indecisive, making a comeback in our own time. We work on the theory that there is safety in numbers and recruit a generation of forward thinkers, rallying to the cause. We temporarily suppress a reintroduction of services, knowing full well this interlude will give us chance to put our house in order.

I feel as if I'm stretching my arms out across the universe.

We feel the benefit of a time consuming study, sanctioned by the goodwill and expertise of your countryman. We are able to gather together information, intrinsically gleaned for the purpose of enlightenment, and we recall an envoy of compatriots dedicated to the cause. We play it safe, putting nothing to chance, depending on one another to harness the power wisely. We have vouchsafed a glorious future for mankind and we put it to you quite bluntly - we have opened your mind to accept the impossible! We rely on your instincts and powers of observation and have guaranteed your

51

success, taking it upon ourselves to offer a solution that shall be discounted by none.

We come from the back of beyond and we openly admit to a timescale different from your own, we have the power of communication and shuttle back and forth across the universe, settling our differences of opinion. We have made our mark and insist on a tighter time frame, buckling down for action. We initialise a grand plan of action, sublimely exercising our right of exposure and we bring to your attention an item that has controversially affected not only our understanding but our logic.

We beam to you on a ray of Light that will examine data presented and clear up any misunderstandings, leaving you free to un-encumbrance your mind. We have sheltered you from harm, precautionary measures needed at this time of vulnerability and we expose you to a new form of intelligence. We take a back seat enabling a massive expansion programme and by request have initialised a new term of office, benefiting all and sundry. We are quite simply delighted with your acceptance and take on board an illustrious and dedicated team. We all have one thing in common, a desire to do our best for Queen and country, and we accept the proposal laid at our feet, summoning one last rendition of 'Land of Hope and Glory'!

We have reached an agreement to undertake all necessary transactions, bypassing unsavoury conditions and manufacturing a new line of enquiry, this in itself will give us greater insight. We follow this through with a greater production of services, registered and brought under control by various agencies. We feel this will give us better scope and energy for dealing with necessary obligations that are presented from time to time and we have installed a new process of data recall, initialising a request to offer our services! We develop our criteria, embarking on a new platform of expertise and have tipped the scales in your defense, partaking of the most natural experiences and manifesting a mind boggling transformation.

I'm now seeing the same noble faces that were shown to me a few months ago.

52

We have begun our new programme in earnest and transcend all difficulties that lie ahead, asking that you be prepared to match like for like. We are open for discussion and expand our consciousness to allow for greater compatibility. We have encompassed a mind numbing scenario, shaking us to the very core, this in itself has been regrettable and we show you the way back to grace! We transcend all cares and worries that have held you in check and motion you to study with greater reverence. Please be constantly aware of our Divine connection to the source as we grow ever closer together, planning with greater dexterity and assembling ourselves in readiness. We survive a transformation and reunite within the boundaries of your heart.

∞

Chapter four

Egypt beckons

We have finally taken the plunge and booked a seven night cruise on the Nile for the beginning of January. Back in September I was shown the face of Tutankhamen during meditation and told to accept the impossible; I never dreamed we would be visiting Egypt so soon! As I sent out absent healing, I caught a glimpse of blue and shining gold with the following words:-

We have reason to believe congratulations are in order . . . Ra has chosen well!

I thanked my guides for their help in making this journey to Egypt possible . . . I'm still in a state of shock and so overwhelmed that I cannot stop weeping.

I settled down to meditate and am being shown an English gentleman from around the 17 century, he has a long, grey wig that is curled and is wearing a green coat with burgundy breeches made of satin. I can see him standing by a large Georgian style window that looks over beautiful landscaped gardens. My attention is being drawn to a big painting above his head of a young women lying on a chaise longue. The lady has lovely, large eyes and her fair hair is smoothed across the crown with a froth of soft curls framing her delicate face; her dress is the colour of pale gold, pinched in at the waist and billowing out over her hips. I'm being given the words – 'sailing to a new life' along with the name Marie Antoinette. (Later while researching this figure from the 18th century I found she sailed from Austria to France in 1755 to begin her new life in the French court).

In solitude we adjust our settings, transforming ourselves and discovering a new world. We open a treasure trove of delights in store.

At this point I'm being shown a hamper size box made of beaten gold.

We frown on a golden era that brought nothing but chaos and despair! We forsake a time of sloth and greed that led to perpetual

54

violence in all shapes and forms, and we motion you to study in greater detail a flotilla of events that has been drawn to our attention.

∞

Tonight we spent a magical evening, joining with a larger meditation group to sing Christmas Carols by candle light, accompanied by my friend on her guitar. Afterwards the group leader settled us down in a guided meditation, asking us to visit an enchanted castle, full of flickering candles, where we would be joined by someone.

I seemed to float up a circular staircase and entered a round room. I watched as several people, all wearing white robes, filed into this room; the person who approached me was dressed in long robes of blue and gold that were covered in symbols. He looked very old and his long, white hair cascaded down in soft waves upon his shoulders; his tall hat was also blue, scattered with golden stars and crescent moons and as he sat down beside me I heard the name Caiaphas.

Alas, too soon, we had the first call to make our way back from meditation and as I made my way down to the grounds of the castle, I saw it was snowing. We all had great fun playing in the snow like children until the final call to return to normal consciousness. The next day I did some research and found the name Caiaphas means 'searcher'! During my research I also found that robes worn centuries ago by Jewish high priests were blue, interwoven with gold and hung with golden bells and pomegranate fringes. I was intrigued to learn that the vestment of the high priest represented the universe.

∞

I try to make time for meditation every day and today is no exception; practice makes perfect and I'm finding it much easier to tune in and make contact with 'home'.

We have a broad understanding of what is expected of us and rally to the cause - all hands on deck!   Our main aim is to abandon all reserve and adjust our settings accordingly. We supply the required course of action adjudicating where necessary, developing and mastering our sensing abilities and discovering for ourselves the joy of 'coming home' in the truest sense. We are well able to match like

55

for like, pondering on the meaning of life and all it entails and we bestow upon you the greatest treasure of all - the gift of life! We welcome you to our shores and suggest a new religious undertaking that can be put into practice, designating our new found belief patterns as visionary!

We participate in a reckless and mind numbing scenario that catapults us into a new mindset, balancing the old with the new. We take it as a matter of course and bow to your intuition, taking into account our understanding of all things of Heaven and Earth. We have arrived at long last and we come prepared to take on this mammoth task, undergoing a transformation of enormous proportions. We beckon you forward and bestow on you our good wishes for the future is brighter than you think. We have no need of paraphernalia for we are governed by a Light source that has powerful illumination.

Do you mean the power of Love?

We do at that - the power of Love brings a formula to be reckoned with and we have sanctioned a massive undertaking that will bring us into line. We have bent over backwards to assess our position on all sides, taking charge of a situation that has defied all understanding, and we now stand on the brink savouring our connection. We are undisputed champions of the cause and we forge the greatest respect among our peers, generating a new line of leadership as we welcome you into the main stream.

We put it as delicately as we may and there is no time like the present - we succumb to the temptation of reinstating your sense of wonderment and we take you back to a time of undiluted passion, serenading you with our messages from beyond the tomb. We have defied all obstacles to be seated at your right hand and we profess to being highly delighted at the challenge presented before us, acknowledging the true path!

I'm being shown a man with a long staff, walking a dry and dusty path that is strewn with small rocks.

The way of the desert is open to us, revealing many truths, and this shall be a time of remembering the past and honouring the dead! We dedicate our services to the human race and take you forward, instigating a trial and error scenario and setting the scene for marked improvement. We have seen for ourselves the ebb and flow of our reunion and we motion you to study in closer proximity. We forecast new measures for expressing our hopes and desires, tending to the irrevocable conditions that assail us day by day. We are entrenched in rediscovering a lost world and we implore you to take your time - don't rush headlong into what is seen as our greatest study yet!

∞

January 2008 - Yesterday we flew to Luxor and boarded our floating hotel for a week. The town was aglow with Christmas lights and it surprised us to learn that the Egyptians celebrate Christmas on the 6th and 7th of January. Today we set sail for Edfu to visit our first Temple. I feel so wonderfully peaceful, gazing across at the banks of the Nile and just for a moment a powerful energy washed over me and I heard the words - **Welcome my Beloved***!*

We are now docked at Aswan for a couple of days. It is a most beautiful part of the river and we love to watch the Felucca boats with their graceful white sails, gliding gently up and down the Nile. We decided to spend the day resting on deck after a few days of hectic schedule. Laying back, I looked at the magnificent mountain ranges and closing my eyes seemed to drift above the Nile, looking down at the boats nestled along its banks.

This is such a wonderful experience and becoming more frequent whenever I rest in the garden. I shared a previous occurrence of this phenomenon with members of my meditation group. I had been relaxing in the garden in the warm sunshine and found myself looking down from a great height at the land below, drifting on the thermals like the birds of prey that circle over our valley. At the same time this was happening, I had also been aware of my hands resting in my lap and this is what puzzles me – the fact that I am aware of being in two places at the same time! A group member said he had seen the figure of Nostradamus standing behind me during meditation and he felt that I was remote viewing. He was told that Nostradamus used to scry with water in a bowl made of copper and brass. None of the group knew at this time that I had written a book based on

57

predictions for the future of mankind, which of course Nostradamus is famous for!
(New Visions for the Future of Mankind published in 2009).

*Yesterday we visited the Valley of the Kings and Queens and it was so awe
inspiring to walk in that valley where the ancient Egyptians had buried their
dead. We ventured into the tomb of Tutankhamen and saw the huge sarcophagus
where his remains had been found. On the other side of the burial chamber stood a
glass coffin with the actual mummified remains of Tutankhamen himself. We
were all surprised to see how small he was; we knew he had died as a young man
but here lay the remains of what looked like a child. In actual fact we were very
lucky to see the young King as his remains have since been moved to the museum
in Cairo.*

*Later in the week while visiting the Temple at Philae, I had a strange experience.
During the Light and Sound show I had stood transfixed, looking up at the huge
statues and pillars. The crowds were then urged to move forward to the next point
of interest and everyone hurried away, but I felt entranced and could only move
very slowly. My husband held out his hand to me at elbow level and I laid my
hand lightly in his, walking slowly as if in some sort of procession; it was as if I
had been transported back in time for a split second. My husband was concerned
and I had to shake myself into normal consciousness so that we could catch up
with the rest of the party.*

∞

*It is early morning and I'm back home now, sitting in my sanctuary, thanking my
Spirit friends for such a wonderful trip. There are tears in my eyes as I recall my
previous message – 'sailing to a new world and the treasure trove of delights in
store'. We have experienced the most wonderful week that we shall treasure
forever. Thank you my friends, thank you for the experience of Egypt with its
sights and sounds, especially the haunting call to prayer and the majestic Valley of
the Kings and Queens across the river Nile. I can hardly believe that we actually
spent a week on the river Nile and already I'm hoping that one day we can
return!*

My child we have shared your experience and are rewarded by your
smiles . . . there has been a massive imbalance and we hope to put
this right. We have prolonged our association in order to enlighten
the multitudes that wait and we propel you forward to do your duty.

We are indeed on a grand excursion, uncluttered from annoyances and raising our vibrations to a new level. We are empowered to bring greater coverage and we take the time to unfold a wide selection of anecdotes, recovered and brought to air so that we may do justice to our forebears. We are forgiven for thinking there is more to come, and we delegate to allow a wider selection of material to surface, giving credence to our intelligence.

We have been exposed in a way that shakes us to the very core and we ask you to accept the impossible. We recommend a deep cleansing that will satisfy demands placed on us as we go about our business, transcending all difficulties and placing our trust in those above. We welcome in a new phase, dedicating our services to those in need and resurfacing to bring about complete renewal. We are painfully aware that our trust at times is brought into question and we monopolise a kindred spirit to register our intent, making sure that all is safe and above board. We are inclined to believe in the one true God and justify this by example. We measure our success at every given turn, proceeding towards our destiny, uncluttered and unadorned save for the given expectancy of a higher knowledge, transmuting the darkness into 'Light'. We are forgiven for thinking we are on a pathway that leads us to 'who knows where' when in fact it has been pre-ordained and recovered to be brought forth and resurrected!

I'm now being shown a golden vessel which is handed over to me.

This knowledge is given with the purest intent, sanctioned and revitalised to include further discoveries. We are mentioned in dispatches and have plotted our course most carefully. We address issues that have held us back in the past and detonate further coverage of events surrounding us. Be well aware of what we are sending you for now is the time to act accordingly and we underline each cause and effect, adjudicating through bitter experience in the ways of the world! We reinstate our sense of values and put it to you quite succinctly . . . there has never been a better time to train our thoughts in the right direction. Our blessings my child!

I woke early this morning and had the sense of many Egyptians around me from long ago. We seemed to be waiting for someone to speak! I sat up in bed and realised this may be a warning to be prepared with my recorder at this afternoon's meeting. After everyone had settled well into meditation, I became aware of a strong energy drawing close and felt the urge to speak.

We have travelled far over the centuries and we call to you from beyond the tomb, a powerful message radiating from beyond the grave. We prepare you for the time ahead and acknowledge this has not been an easy journey for any of you. We manifest before your eyes a most wonderful concept for the Children of Earth and we prepare ourselves to venture forth. A powerful emissary waits to enfold you in our care as we protect you from harm, and we will always be at your side to help you and guide you along this highway of Love. We have made our presence known to inform you of measures that need to be taken and we propel you forward to do your duty.

This has been a massive undertaking and we take you to that point of no return; we welcome you into the fold with open arms and we vow to each and every one of you that we shall stand firm, pressing forward with this venture that shall reap the greatest rewards. We take it upon ourselves to usher in a new awareness that will open the hearts and minds of all those who search for truth, and we have seen many instances of the suffering inflicted on our own kind! We depend on you to march with us, an Army of Light, uplifting those in deep despair! We monitor these meetings and hold you in the highest esteem, transcending time and space.

I could see figures in the background, holding flaming torches that flickered in the darkness, revealing flashes of gold. There was a tight feeling around my forehead and the figure I saw wore the same type of golden, headdress worn by a Pharaoh. The energy was with me for some time and although no more words were given, I had the feeling of lifting my head and sitting erect on a throne. I am not sure if this figure was Nefertiti or Tutankhamen, but as we were privileged to see the mummified remains of Tutankhamen in his tomb, I feel it is more likely to be the latter.

60

I woke in the night and received further communication; there seems to be a storing of material as we continued from yesterday's session.

We propel you forward to do your very best as we initiate a renewal of services. We have watched over you with bated breath and been most rewarded, comforting ourselves with the fact that you shall be returned to us in all your splendour. There has been a great deal of concern over who shall represent us, and we have decided at this late stage to allow the reinstatement of our most honourable and venerable sister!

We combat illness and all extremes of temperament, allowing ourselves recourse, opening the hearts and minds of the nation. Be prepared to tell your story and we shall find further coverage of what is seen as the greatest documentary ever written! We transcend all difficulties to bring you into alignment with a just cause, underlining the beneficial aspects of a complete recovery. We are bound on a course for the stars and there is no stopping us now as we delve further and further into the main stream!

Can you explain what the main stream is?

We participate in what we would call an energy field of great resolution.

I'm now being shown a picture of spermatozoon, racing to reach the ovum for fertilization.

Sometimes we swim at the outer edges and are not always able to keep up. Now our energy levels have increased tenfold and we are able to swim with the 'A Team' . . . revolutionary new methods have enabled us to constantly assess conditions and we take you to the front line of action. We are able at this time to penetrate that inner sanctum which will rejuvenate us in mind body and spirit, impregnating a whole new experience and capturing the essence of reincarnation. We are most impressed with your endeavours and strive to fulfill all expectations, neatly assembling our package of delights in store. We motion you to make a stand for the human race

61

and we deliberately reconstruct for you our grand new world. We have laid low for a period of many years and we seek restitution in what is seen as the most precarious of ways. We are, undoubtedly, the most recognised figures in your history and we bow down to your expertise in decoding our script! We are beholden to many of you for persevering with our monuments and deciphering by trial and error our stones from the past. We are most indebted to you for discovering our most noble Kings and Queens and discovering for yourselves the rituals of preservation for life after death. We left behind memorable evidence of how we lived and died and shoulder the responsibilities of sharing this knowledge with those who wish to learn.

I'm now being shown the director of Egyptian antiquities - Dr. Zahi Hawass.

We have always been at the utmost cutting edge of civilization and we stand back to allow further discoveries, most importantly a treasure trove of artifacts waiting to be found! This yield will bring about enormous clarification of an age past, brought to bear witness of life after death. We have no morbid assumptions but describe for you a package that will reap the most favourable conditions. Be prepared to meet thy maker as we assail you with tales from beyond the crypt. We impel you to make a stand and confirm our intentions to light your path. We are justified in taking action and motion you to study with further intent, redoubling our efforts.

We are on a quest, a search for the Holy Grail, leaving no stone unturned! We are building a much bigger picture and hope to collect evidence that will help us assimilate a new structure of interdependence. We have balanced our harmonies and strive for perfection, opening the doorway and beyond where all is waiting. We perform a feat of extraordinary perception and gather you in our arms to recreate a time of trust, savouring this connection and utilising a grand collection of energies. We strive for completion, dating and amending additional coverage of events. We further our discussions and transpose these words for you to use with greater clarity of expression. Forgive us for sounding so monotone - we are discovering new techniques to alter our intonation and we

purposefully register these talks to identify a wide variety of
conditions.

∞

*Watching over my group in meditation, I was just about to call time when I felt a
band of energy around my brow and the urge to speak.*

We call you back . . . and ask you to accept our offer of friendship!
We are preparing you for a journey of the highest intent and we are
mesmerised and entranced by the magic that surrounds us. We ask
that further advances be made and we entreat you to listen to our
words for they shall be of the highest source! We profoundly adapt to
new measures undertaken for this mission and we are held in the
highest esteem from those both near and far. We beg you to listen
with your ears and with your hearts and minds for we bring you news
that is worthy of your attention! We deliver to the people of Earth a
new destiny and we support our claims by offering you advice,
sharing with one another in what will become our greatest advance.

We are highly honoured to be drawn into this circle of friendship and
we are enchanted with the care and attention that is taken to detail.
Be kind to one another little 'earthlings' for we treasure you and
uplift you in your endeavours. Be prepared to match like for like as
we reinstate you in your new term of office and we will regenerate,
marching forward to conquer all obstacles that stand in our way. We
watch over you for there is more, much more to come and on the
horizon all is waiting to bring you into alignment, transcending doom
and gloom and preparing you for a new age!

We are permitted one last word - we have justified our actions by
taking into account our extraordinary talents and we are beholden to
many of you for adjusting your thought patterns to correspond with
ours, actuating a most remarkable delivery. We have sanctioned all
clauses and motion you to accept the challenge presented. We accept
our delivery has some flaws and we are determined to set the record
straight, motioning you not to be discouraged. We are indebted to
you for understanding our motives and in this respect we offer our
condolences!

The following evening during meditation, I felt the strong presence of a 'Mother Superior' figure and sat for a long time wrapped in her blissful peace and radiance. At last she drew from the folds of her robe a large ring of big keys. We seemed to rise together and walk down the central isle towards a large alter, where a statue of Jesus stood with arms wide open, ready to receive us. I remember no more and feel a new chapter of events is in store.

∞

Chapter five

Travellers of Light

Today I can see myself on a train; we are packed in like sardines with standing room only! I feel this must be heralding in the next stage of my spiritual progression as I'm often given the train as a sign that we are moving on. Many years ago when I joined my first meditation group, I'd heard the sound of a steam train approaching, getting louder and louder. The train came into the station with brakes screeching . . . at last coming to a halt beside me. The carriage doors were then flung wide, waiting for me to climb aboard! I had been sure everyone else in the room had heard it too but of course nobody had.

We salute you and forecast a breakthrough that will reap rewards, sectioning off those areas that are best left behind. We are smitten in every sense of the word and relay what is needed to recall you home! We have pandered to your every need, accomplishing more than the written word and we vouchsafe a glorious future for you and yours. We are slightly perturbed at delays encountered and point you in the right direction. We have been plagued by indecision and it is for this reason we have suspended our monologue, pending further services to be resumed. We are now sending this transmission to enable higher frequency access and this has been our greatest reward, to spend time with those we Love and treasure above all others. We are allotted this time frame to declare our advantage and we allow a turning back of the clock to rectify disturbances, settling into a new time frame and requisitioning a whole new experience beyond our wildest expectations! We materialise a vast array of services that will help you to expand and grow as we reach out to touch you.

At this point I could actually feel many hands, reaching out and touching me on the forehead.

We prepare for our assault and administer the final demand for occupancy in a new land; we ask you to help us initialise this thrust forward into a new stream of excellence, pushing back the barriers of disbelief! We have undoubtedly brought about a grand reclamation of souls and we tentatively broaden our horizons, visualising further growth and monopolising kindred spirits to work alongside you. We have become aware of a greater energy and transcribe further relics from the past that shall come to light! We have manifested an array of bona fide material and we simply request that further measures be taken to ensure a greater volume. We are known for our expertise in cultivating friendships and we look further afield for strength and renewal; we have deep seated connections that will increase our speed of delivery and we motion you to intercede on our behalf, gathering momentum and delivering our messages to the people of Earth. We are well known for our solemnity and we prepare you to accept these measures as necessary for we shall deliver our message to a whole nation bent on recovery!

I can now see a beautiful, young man with dark coloured skin who is sitting crossed legged, he is wearing a turban headdress and thick, white robe.

We are challenged at every corner and we have your best interests at heart, forecasting further treasures that shall surface for examination. We are treated with indifference and we know this gives cause for panic! We calm the troubled waters and bring you fresh hope for new beginnings, new openings that shall come your way. We prepare for a new charter of excellence, describing the best ways of imaging as we shelter you from harm, overcoming all obstacles that stand in your path. We are preparing for a time of renewal and we beg your pardon if we overload you at times with information; this is not our wont, however, we have parallel connections that do at times pass on information that has been restored and given priority! We leave no stone unturned in our quest for truth and we tremble at times for what is in store for the people of Earth.

We are planning a 'great escape' and this will be seen by many as discouraging, however, we aim to set up a new network that will allow, in this instance, further recovery of a great many souls in distress! This recovery process will undertake new roles of undisputed tolerance and acceptance of whoever, whatever colour or creed, and it is these barriers that set aside bring what we have so often wished for 'Peace' and generosity of spirit! We introduce these factors to allow for further restraint and we increase our volume, discovering new measures for achieving bliss.

We are challenged to accept the impossible and we entreat you to listen to our words for we have come from a much higher sphere of existence and tolerate no form of segregation! We accept that we are poles apart but we find from deep within that we are the same . . . we are brothers under the skin, brothers and sisters of Light! We vow to each and every one of you that we shall become your dearest companions in this life and the next. We are here to welcome you into a new stream of interdependence and we wish you well dear 'Travellers of Light'! We welcome you into the fold with open arms and suggest that you tend to one another's needs, propelling you forward to do your duty to God and Queen. We have shown you the green fields and pastures that are yours for the taking, and we express our sincere condolences for those that hesitate and are lost. We beam you Light and inspiration and a fellowship that is undoubtedly our greatest success.

∞

This evening, I attended a spiritual group in Carmarthen and was in for a surprise. We had all settled down ready to begin when our group leader's little dog Rosie started to growl softly! We watched as she stared across at one of my friends, becoming more agitated, advancing across the circle and then retreating several times. Normally she is very well behaved and we realised it was probably because my friend's guide, 'Brown Bear' had drawn very close. Our group leader suggested we tuned in to see the object of Rosie's discomfort and I was amazed to see a pale blue mist surrounding my friend. To her right stood a large North American Indian, on top of his head was the face of a brown bear with dark shaggy fur, hanging down around his legs. In the end my friend had to ask 'Brown Bear' to stand back so that we could continue with the session. Rosie settled down at last and it was wonderful proof that animals can see our spirit friends.

We welcome in a new phase, collaborating with those in the know and siphoning off a broad spectrum of information; this in itself will adjust thought patterns accordingly and we allow a settling to register our true intent. We have managed to back track and forecast further illumination, spreading our wings and declaring our advantage. This has always been our greatest talent - accepting one another's thought patterns and forming an alliance. We bend to listen and answer your call, demonstrating the fact of our survival.

What shall we be doing at our group tomorrow - will you be speaking to us?

We shall in all sincerity be there with you all and we strongly believe that you will be well pleased with the discipline brought into play. There has been a wide assumption that we shall bring to the group a greater vocabulary and we powerfully assist in the proceedings, allowing further installments to be broadcast. These will in fact enable you to plot your course accordingly, and we have no doubt that the proceedings will bring forth a higher knowledge, entertaining you in great measure. We are determined that these events will be played out with due respect to all parties; we maintain a high level of security and this will be managed and masterminded by our crew of technicians waiting in the wings! We have supplied enough coverage to be able to pull this together in an instant and we know you will have no regrets whatsoever. Be prepared to plan your afternoons and we will share with you in your extravaganza, playing our part!

Thank you for showing me 'Brown Bear', I was so happy to be able to see him in such detail.

We are well adjusted to form these connections and prepare you to sample much more than this! It has been our greatest pleasure to work alongside you and we shall continue on this pathway, recording our progress day by day!

Thank you my friends, it has been my greatest pleasure also!

∞

Last night as I lay down to sleep, I saw a young Indian with shaggy, dark hair and a bedroll slung across his shoulders. I felt he was from the Cherokee tribe and that his name was Golden Hawk; he told me that celebrations were in store and this afternoon I can feel a strong energy drawing close.

68

We have walked this way before and we challenge you to accept the status we are offering you. We reach out and touch that very part of your soul that draws you to us in so many ways; we reach out and touch your heart and mind so that you may recollect those times spent with us many moons ago. We are beholden to you for sanctioning this display of courage, for accepting with all your heart and soul a selection of anecdotes that shall impart wisdom not yet seen for many a year. We come at this time in your development to welcome in a new tide of expertise and we shall shelter you from the harsh winds that blow. We have actioned a high resolution energy stream and we participate in a grand collection of minds, presenting a clearer picture and subjecting you to a time consuming study of variants. We express ourselves with the wisdom of a child and allow this to percolate, bringing your attention to further anecdotes. We have made the most amazing discovery and we allow you to blend with us and recover your identify!

We are considered by some as *gender benders* as we have no clear indication of gender or physical make up. We are allotted a time span and then work with whatever reality we express - this helps us to keep our profile interconnected. We see an explosion of identity crisis's, recognising traits that have led us astray in the past, we see this as a necessary inclusion in our collection of data . . . a whole race of misfits brought together and temporarily erased! We have backtracked to allow restitution and we summon forth an army of enormous proportions, battling our way through negative thought forms that assail us at every given opportunity.

We broaden our horizons, betraying our emotions as we take on the world, pushing ourselves forward and satisfying our inner longings to fulfill our destiny. We respond to your cries for help and respect the line of command, tipping the scales in your favour and setting the record straight. We have taken to organising a field trip and we start the countdown, travelling through time and past encounters. We explore the limitless wonder of the heavenly bodies that make up our star system, salvaging a dream and opening up new realms of understanding. We hand you our portfolio, expressing our hopes and desires for a better world for all.

We now regain control and fill a void, meaning no disrespect, and it is with great joy that we take you down memory lane. Take heart for we venture on a journey that shall set the heavens alight! We aim to please and have begun in all earnest to rectify mistakes from the past, initiating a more productive time for all concerned. We are encouraged by your actions, displaying the courage of a warrior and developing a keen sense of propriety. We deliver our recommendations for a livelier broadcast; this will be seen by many as unnatural phenomena and we insist on this frequency to bring forth a most impressive backdrop to even further recordings. We shall light up the lives of those present and we mean to instigate a powerful message that will resonate within your very souls! We are proud to be the first in a long line of many advisories and we implore you to use your skills, connecting with the unseen on a higher frequency range. We are supported on all levels and mention the need to allow others to come forward at any given interval; these will be highly recommended and we shall forfeit our right of exposure to ensure delivery.

We prepare for earthquakes of massive proportions and register our intent to soothe the general populace. When this revelation comes into play it will come as a complete shock to those of you who have placed your equipment at intervals to intercept messages from the Earth; she has taken a pounding and to restore her energy levels would require a massive undertaking! We require greater expertise to set the record straight and it is no ordinary expedition we take into the bowels of the Earth.

This mission has been held sacrosanct and we fulfill our destiny in being the only chromosomal band of Homo sapiens to enter in this race against time! We have vouched for our integrity and are one step away from achieving immortality, spreading our wings and making a remarkable recovery. We are based here on a theory that mankind will retrace his steps through time and avert a tragedy of enormous proportions, safeguarding the human race!

We propel you now in the jet stream of your own making to safeguard this vision for the future of mankind and we instill in you

70

the means of accessing our data, recovering what has been lost for generation upon generation of forward planners. We have assessed in great detail the necessary contractual agreements and we plan to use this information to our advantage. This has been a pressing and most difficult journey through time and we have made our mark in more ways than one. We reassess all that is given and venture forth on this highway of Love, serenading you with our magical tones.

We welcome home the human race and prepare you for a new future - one of joy and upliftment and Love beyond all earthly measure! We have effectively gained control of an overpowering situation and we manifest for you a 'Curtain of Light' that shall beam you home in another occupancy!

∞

Caretakers of Earth

We are alarmed to hear that all is not well in the world of men and we fluctuate between the spheres to give our assistance; this in itself has caused further alarm and we backtrack to allow greater conformity. We stabilise a volatile situation for the truth be known we have embarked on a world full of mistrust and innuendos, a desecrated planet that was at one time a most promising source of inspiration and joy to behold - a 'Garden of Eden' in every sense! We have been given platitudes that have been neither acceptable nor helpful in dealing with the situation at hand and we describe for you the monolithic idiosyncrasies that have caused us to rethink our plan of action! We are noted for our aptitude in dealing with problematic events such as these and we take it to the extreme, measuring and examining the motives of the masses. The implications are endless and we devote our time to regaining further coverage for it is not in our nature to trample on the feelings and emotions of those nearest and dearest. We suffer a setback, asking you to bear with us while we unravel the intricacies necessary to make this work.

This has been a monumental time for all and we marshall our forces, pointing you in the right direction and celebrating each turn of event. There are sanctions that have given rise to further outpourings and we demonstrate our compatibility, sharing with one another in

71

broadcasting to the nation. We are caretakers of 'Mother Earth' and we put our trust in those here present to unfold a greater awareness. We are pleased to bring to the council our most treasured possession and we dictate our most heartfelt thanks in registering our appeal, causing the most loving of energies. We are known to some of you, who have been our constant companions, and we lead you to greener pastures, making our connection on a higher level than ever before. We increase the volume and turn up the tempo, empowering you for the journey of a lifetime!

∞

Arcturians

At our home group I felt a powerful energy drawing close and was shown 'beings' with large, dark eyes and greenish skin. I felt they were a species who have formed an alliance with the Pleiadians to help mankind and much later I found out they are Arcturians, a most advanced and loving civilization. I felt the urge to speak and just as they predicted a month ago, their words came through in a monotone style.

We wish to draw close to share a few words with our learned friends. We have made a map of greater resolution to be passed on to our talented and most respected members of creation, a map of the universe beyond all previous comprehension! We have delivered on mass a most salubrious connection; we have further developed our vocabulary and exchange thought patterns, engaging in discussions to keep on course. We join with our brethren and feel the law dictates that we advise you of a further recovery of services. We are mentioned in dispatches and are profoundly aware of all that is governed from a higher energy source. We feel impelled to grant your wishes by allowing greater contact and we draw close at these times to enable you to assist us, just as we assist you. We challenge you to accept issues that come to the surface to be examined that little more closely and we further develop our thought streams, asking that you bear with us while we manipulate those areas that need adjusting.

We ask you to accept the impossible and we reach out to you and yours, enveloping you with our thought waves, manipulating the energy around you as we circumference the globe. We are beholden to you all for holding these meetings and developing your thought patterns to coincide with ours. We accept this growth has been strenuous to say the least and we are profoundly aware that this awakening has had repercussions; we are now looking most carefully at what is necessary to overcome any malfunctions! We are surprised and rewarded at the assistance given and we open up and prepare for a new stream of thought to propel you at a safe distance, overseeing and guiding you gently on to your destination. We prepare you for ascension within the very constructs and expansion of your minds and we look deeper, finding you have sacrificed a great deal, recognising in every one of you the ideology that will take us on that never ending journey. Our allotted time has come to an end and we give you our thanks.

I asked if there was anyone else in our group who would like to come forward to speak and one of them took up the challenge!

"There is a gathering to which you are all invited. You will know when the time arrives and you will join with us! The information that you seek will be laid before you. You will know your path and your destiny - we have work for you all! Your paths are joined and your paths are separate – know that you are one!"

Afterwards we shared our experiences and the one who came forward told us she had been in a Temple of Light with other beings dressed in long white robes. There had been the most beautiful music and just before I started to channel, she had seen a being of Light walk into the centre of the circle. I feel they are preparing us all for the work we shall be doing together and apart. Looking on the internet I found the following information:-

"Arcturus is one of the most advanced extra-terrestrial civilizations in our galaxy. It is a fifth dimensional civilization which, in reality is like a prototype for Earth's future. Its energy works with humanity as an emotional, mental and spiritual healer. It is also an energy gateway through which humans pass during death and rebirth. It functions as a way-station for non-physical consciousness to become accustomed to physicality. The book, "The Keys of Enoch" *written by Dr. James. Hurtak has described it as the mid-way station or programming centre, used by the physical brotherhoods in our local universe to govern the many*

rounds of experiments with physicals on our end of the galaxy.

The Arcturians teach that the most fundamental ingredient for living in the fifth dimension is LOVE; they teach that negativity, fear and guilt must be overcome and exchanged for Love and Light. Arcturus is the brightest star in the Bootes constellation, which is approximately 36 light years from Earth. The Arcturians work in very close connection with the Ascended Masters whom they refer to as the Brotherhood of the All. They also work very closely with what they refer to as The Galactic Command. The Arcturians travel the universe in their star ships, which are some of the most advanced in the entire universe. Their skin is a greenish colour and they have very large almond shaped eyes and only three fingers. The Arcturians are very short in physical stature, about three to four feet tall, they are also very slender and all look very much alike in appearance".

∞

During meditation today I was shown two doorways - I opened the first door but it was so dark inside I couldn't see and refused to go in. I then opened the second door and a powerful, blinding light stopped me from entering - again I couldn't see a thing! I decided to go back to the first door and tried again. It was very dark and full of cobwebs, everything was lying around broken and I had to tread very carefully as there were gaping holes in the floor. I think this is symbolic of having to face the darkness and my worst fears before I can go forward into the Light!

∞

Chapter six

We rekindle the flame of Love

All around the globe we are rearranging thought patterns of understanding . . . we rekindle the flame of Love that has slumbered for so long in many on the Earth plane and we transmute a dying breed. We are confronted with a new variation of accepted belief patterns and we circumference the globe in our attempts to multiply our resources. We shower the population of Earth with our messages, encouraging you to grow in greater intensity of spirit towards your fellow man. We have prepared a proclamation that shall give you satisfaction and we surrender ourselves to one of the most thought provoking studies, challenging all those who come to mock! It has been a most thought provoking time for us all and we are led on to further challenges, breaking all barriers and time constraints. We have made our mark and transcend a time of doom and gloom, raising you up to new heights. We are forever in your debt and excel in reshaping our new world with a new theme of encouragement.

Platitudes will never reach the mark for we are aiming higher than a clear mountain stream . . . we are aiming for those heights that leave the world far behind, shrouded in her mist of uncertainty. We travel far into the cosmos, radiating our Love and transmuting those lower energies. We gather momentum and we empower you to make the right choices!

An Arapaho song I heard long ago came into my mind:-

"Wearing my long, winged feathers I fly, I circle around . . . I circle around the boundaries of the Earth".

Many thousand years have we come to be here in this moment with you . . . the Sun and the Stars, dancing the dream awake!

We make our choices and seize the day, propelling you further upstream and monitoring certain aspects of our delivery. We pursue a course of action which has become second nature to us and we proceed in all earnest towards our destiny, unfolding and growing with greater ease. We dedicate this next round of conversations to those who come to eavesdrop, and we allow a settling as you ponder on issues that have led us thus far. We regulate our stream of thought and allow a reconditioning of services to take us full steam ahead . . . out into the cosmos! It is with much joy that we welcome you to our side of life and we are encouraged to go that little bit further, each step forward leading us closer to our dream of everlasting peace!

∞

Home group session

We come among you once more my children and it is with great pleasure that we give you the benefit of our wisdom. We are shackled together in a way that has benefited both parties and it is with great delight that we register your intent. You are drawn together for one true purpose - to experience a lifetime's exploits that lead you out of the dungeon of Earth - a pragmatic time for you my little ones! We have adjusted our channels and speak with open hearts and minds, allowing a reverence to descend, adjusting and channelling information as it comes in to us from the ethers.

We offer you a place of sanctuary and safe harbour, advising on conditions that have caused some dismay! We welcome you with open arms for it has been our dearest wish to come amongst you and we amend our thought patterns accordingly, adjusting to your rhythms and timeline, requisitioning a whole new proposition. We make allowances for certain elements of mistrust that have come between us and it is with great regret that we evaluate these thought processes! We desire you to proceed with all caution as we deliberately take on board those issues that are paramount at this time.

It has been our most earnest intent to take you with us along this highway of Love and we believe we have accomplished a great many undertakings. We beckon you forward and take you to that brightest star, guiding you to overcome the fears that hold you back from obtaining the utmost joy. We register your intent as we sail upon the oceans of Love and harmony, bringing you closer to us, nurturing the light that has grown so strongly within you all. We come together as one unit, dedicated and steadfast to the cause and we motion you to accept the impossible as we deliver to you, for your delectation, a most ample and worthwhile rendition of services unsurpassed. We have grown accustomed to your thought forms and allow you the act of channelling what is necessary to bring you forward into the arena. Therefore, we ask each and every one of you to put forward your points of view and we shall assess and answer wherever possible! We have aligned ourselves with you and ask that you come forward to express yourselves. Be not afraid little sisters!

I have a question - why do you come to us, to our group?

We have relished our time with you for an eternity and we help you to grow - to muster your self-esteem so that we may also grow together as a group, demonstrating our fealties to the world!

Do you have a specific task for us?

We share as always, bringing Love into the world and this is the greatest task we ask of you. As our sisters gather here today, we stress the importance of nurturing that Love! *Thank you!*

You are most welcome my child . . . more will be shown and more will be given as you tread this pathway of Light. We express ourselves in all sincerity and ask that you clear a pathway, ready to gather more information as it comes flooding in from the universe. We have demonstrated the very fact of our existence and we have allayed the fears that formulate in your minds. You are as children to us and we are your benefactors, we bear you no malice, we come in Love and all sincerity to help the Children of Earth to grow and prosper.

We develop and grow together as a team and we have worked together before, many times, on many different planes of existence. We have grown and prospered, only to reach a cataclysmic event that has brought mankind to its knees in the mire of scorn and retribution. We tip the scales and balance in your favour, for we have outgrown those crude absurdities and we march onwards to recruit a nation in distress! We have vowed to give you sanctuary and we shall leave no stone unturned in our quest for peace on Earth, taking this to the highest inquisition! We prepare you for entrance into a new world and we register your hopes and dreams for they shall be accomplished in record breaking time.

This being of Light needs to rest and we leave her in your capable hands! We suggest you gather together more often for your rendezvous and we request a certain indulgence in these matters. It is with a sense of propriety that we now close. We thank you for joining with us on this occasion and we ask you to be prepared for more of the same in the not too distant future! We propel you now to a place of safety and wish you every success in the future and in your gatherings. We watch over you on the Earth plane and Love you so!

∞

I woke in the night with words racing round my head and left my bed to transcribe.

We welcome in a broad spectrum of energies, allowing these to wash over you as we come to rescue you from the doldrums, initiating you in the ways of our world as a whole. We are indeed coming into a new phase and we assist in this never ending accumulation of thoughts and ideas, generating a most thorough re-examination. We reach out and touch that very part of you that grows in anticipation of a wider, deeper knowledge, generating a powerful reconnection to the source. We expand our knowledge of the universe and open up your vision, illuminating your mind and generating further studies. We transcend all obstacles and open wide the pathway, bringing in supreme joy and ecstasy, and it is without doubt a foregone conclusion that we shall deliver a wider impact in those areas of discussion that point us to the 'Stars'. We are determined to set the record straight and we empower you to deliver with further resonance a most ambient message to the people of Earth. We are taken from a time frame that has had more than its fair share of problems and we are bound on a course for the Stars, allowing you to blend with us as we take you further than you have ever gone before!

I'm sensing climbing up onto the bare back of a horse and can feel his strength and warmth.

We rectify clauses that have held you back from making further discoveries about yourselves and we champion the cause, investing in a new time frame. We take you to the back of beyond and empower you to state our case, beckoning you to join us in the not too distant future. We are just over the bridge of Light and we welcome you to our world! We manifest for you in glowing colours a most worthwhile solidification of our essence to enhance our rendezvous; we ask you to join us and welcome in a new stream of thought that will take us on further journeys, expanding our vision. We have taken it upon ourselves to issue new guidelines and we welcome in a greater restitution, allowing us greater fortitude in the times ahead.

There is a powerful energy source for us to tap into and we shelter you from harm, ably accessing those quarters which bring us to that place of contact. We have welcomed in a massive stream of data and we challenge you to accept what is in your hearts and minds, relaying further information in a never ending steam. We supply a course of action that will govern proceedings and we take you to a far distant shore, providing you with further ammunition to stake our claim of everlasting peace. We sacrifice our self-restraint, clocking on to greater reserves of strength and energy unsurpassed and we tell it to you straight, we have never before seen the like of such a large expansion of minds!

We assist you in these measures to welcome in a new generation of forward thinking mammals, discovering for yourselves a new world where we shall grow together in perfect Love. We downsize a nation in distress, a perfunctory task that will allow no room for denial or self-deprecation! We are moving forward at an alarming speed and we deliberately hold you back to gather your senses, initiating wider data control. Various agencies have given us the go-ahead to forge an alliance, and we welcome on board all those who will help us grow towards our goal of peace and harmony among mankind. We batten down the hatches and deliver further recommendations, powerfully regenerating a new acceptance of our credentials!

∞

Today as I led our group in meditation to a beautiful garden full of flowers, our spirit friends drew close to give us the benefit of their wisdom once more.

We activate this Light, setting her on the road to success, and the sweet smell of success awaits you all as we challenge you to accept further details that shall open up new paths of enlightenment. We are conditioned to accept these wave patterns that assail us in one form or another and we have taken on board a wider collaboration of interested parties, proposing that one speaker at a time comes forward!   We ask that you channel with greater deliberation and we bring you an armful of sweet memories, beckoning you to awaken like the flower that slumbers before the beginning of spring. We unfold as petals towards the sunlight and welcome you to this garden, each and every one of you. We unfold towards the Light and we beckon you to follow your true purpose, challenging you further as we nourish you and point you in the right direction. We open up your vision, allowing these thoughts to percolate, and we have vowed with all our heart and soul to keep you safe from harm as we enter into a new age where all will be given this advantage.

We shall grow and prosper alongside one another and we tend to the sick, uplifting their spirits, helping those who have fallen by the wayside. We are as 'One' and we motion you to tread most carefully in the days and weeks ahead, unravelling further episodes of trial and innuendo. We are all governed by the Light that shines within our very souls, and we ask you to think twice before venturing to speak your thoughts out loud! In this way we can govern what is said with an open and loving heart, directed to those around us who transgress and cross those boundaries that we ourselves would step back from! We are most proud of your achievements to date and we open up the wisdom that is within you to transcend further boundaries. Around

80

the corner there are a few surprises in store and we are not allowed at this moment to state the facts themselves, however, we give you an inkling there is more in store for each and every one of you! We take on board a wide variety of issues that need looking at in greater detail!

One of the sitters snored rather loudly at this point!

Our sister here needs to rest and she will learn and grow in much the same way as you all. There is a time to rest and a time to grow and we acknowledge that you have all come a long way on this pathway, dedicating your time and energy. We are propelled at a much faster rate and we sanction those areas that need our expertise. Please lend your hand wherever it is needed at this time, and we are most grateful for those kind thoughts echoing across the planes. We are propelled further upstream and ask you to challenge us more often to help us all learn and grow!

We are beholden to you all my little ones and it is with great reluctance we take our leave. We suggest that you gather together more often and we reach far across the rainbow, holding you in the highest esteem. We welcome in a new world of free expression and Love . . . let us not forget LOVE enveloping you all as we reach across the great divide, superimposing our thoughts on yours whenever there is a need. Sweet dreams my little ones!

As I brought the group back from the garden, our friend suddenly woke up with a start and we all roared with laughter, bringing even more Love within our group. Although our friend had been sleeping, she told us that at one point she had opened her eyes and seen a white haze around me with the face of a young woman. Spirit's message of one speaker coming forward at a time eventually came to pass, and as each member of the group developed and gained confidence, they took it in turns to sit for communication while the rest of us sent them loving energy.

I feel we are on a mission to help those on Earth raise their frequencies and to do that we first have to resonate with 'our' higher selves. That is what we are learning to do at the moment, we are looking within and learning to forgive ourselves for past mistakes and most importantly, learning to Love ourselves! Hanging onto the baggage of old hurts, literally causes us great pain and holds us back from making

81

progress. The closer we get to achieve this connection with our true essence, the more powerful our wave patterns of Love will be as we send them to those around us! Imagine this happening all over the world with groups like ours and the ripple effect caused by our Love. Healing ourselves is our greatest priority at this time and as we transmute our negative energies to pure Love, we will be uplifting the vibrations of Earth and her inhabitants, especially those who struggle to accept the concept that Love will conquer all!

∞

There are five of us today and after meditation my Star friends drew close to speak to the group.

We open our arms to receive you and we tremble with anticipation for what is ahead. We have monitored the dictates of your heart and are beholden to you for expressing yourselves in this manner, exploring and discovering for yourselves what is uppermost in our minds. We have opened a channel for you to express yourselves more thoroughly and we are now open for discussion! Is there anyone who would like to voice their concerns?

There was a long pause but no one came forward to speak.

We have mustered the necessary etiquette and brought forward a grand connection of minds, allowing us to disclose what is of paramount importance at this time. We have delved deeper and deeper into those recesses that harbour your doubts and fears and we allow you now to express yourselves in a way that will bring forth all manner of innuendo. We have taken it upon ourselves to bring you further knowledge that can be expelled and aired in open forum and we are delighted with how it all pans out, asking you to bear with us while we open the hearts and minds of all those involved. We bring forward into the arena a new display of acoustics, and we touch that part within us that is stored with information, brought in from the highest source. We challenge you to be more explicit with your wishes and we delve deeper, showing further commands that are passed on to us from those of higher dimensions!

We have reached an impasse and beg you to look more carefully within your own hearts and minds. We are able to pass on information that has been stored and hidden for centuries and we regard ourselves as the 'chosen ones', passing on our knowledge and expertise. We have accounted for those that are lost to us . . . and we regard this with a sense of deep loss! We send out our Love and restore all that is hidden, preparing for a massive challenge on the horizon. It is by drawing together that we can make this work, and hand in hand we venture forth to express ourselves in all sincerity. We are led down this pathway to restore law and order and we are beholden to you for helping us open up new routes to explore.

We have come a long way to be here with you and it gives us great joy to come amongst you once more. We are united as one true voice and we usher in a new voice - one of reason! We tremulously accept the post that is offered to us, bringing in the changes. We have supplemented your energy levels and subject you to even more powerful thought forms. We ask you to reach out and touch us for we are so close now, closer than ever before, there is just a little way to go and we will have achieved that fusion that 'oneness'. Feel the Love . . . let it grow and expand within your hearts, relinquishing the doubts and fears that hold you back from achieving so much. Branch out and recover the world from her death throes, breathe Love and Light into all that you do, experience with your heart and soul all that is within you, all that you have been and all that you will be again!

We express our Love my sisters and it is a wonderful thing to behold, an all empowering, encompassing Love that knows no bounds. We will not be held back or put off and we are gathering in strength and in Love. We open up the gateways, allowing you to pass, and when each of you is ready we will welcome you with open arms! There are but a few steps to go before we feel you in our embrace and we motion for you to join us at the table that is set in readiness. We prepare a banquet in your honour and align ourselves with you in readiness. We have achieved so much my little ones and yet there is much more still to do. We shall overcome and we rein in the harmonies, expressing ourselves with great joy and anticipation for what lies ahead . . . and the future is bright my little ones!

At this point a loud hammering could be heard from the builder who is working on my summer house, which shall be used for future group meetings.

Your new home will soon be ready and we are greatly anticipating our move, for there is much work to be done and we shall grow in leaps and bounds, expressing ourselves more positively as the beauty that is within you all shall shine forth!

Is there anyone who wishes to question us?

I have a question! Are we the only group you speak through, or are there other groups you are in connection with?

Each group has its own selection of speakers and there are many of us as we travel your universe. We are governed by our own special needs and desires to make this work, and we take it upon ourselves to express our great delight to be working amongst you once more! We have developed alongside you many times in the past and we envelop you all with our own special brand of eloquence.

Thank you. You are most welcome my child. Are there any others who wish to speak?

I have a question! Are we all part of the same energy - you, me and us?

We are all joined together from one central force and we are joined in a way that has repercussions for all of us. We transcend time and space itself . . . we are but a thought, a flicker from the past. Everything comes full circle . . . circles within circles and we are joined to one another, radiating out across the universe and beyond . . . like the ripples on a pond! *Thank you!*

We are beholden to you for asking and it is with much reluctance we now take our leave. We would like to thank you all for your help in nurturing this spirit, and indeed for nurturing the Light within you that grows and seeks information to help you on the Earth plane at this time! We will come again and we will show you more, for this is our mission to expand and grow. We have recovered sufficiently to expand our status and we ask you to be prepared to state the obvious. We have no regrets and we enable you to move with us at a faster rate!

∞

I woke in the night with more words buzzing round my head and sat for communication.

We have interpreted a long line of innovations that have led us to this evaluation and we now experience a heart wrenching application for clemency! It is with great regret that we have channelled through such daunting episodes of doom and gloom, and yet we have experienced the most rewarding feedback from those on Earth who have answered our call! We leave it to you to regulate and bring to account all that is stored and hidden and we transcend those areas that are laid to rest, propagated and re-evaluated to form a new lease of life.

We depend on you to bring forward our inquisition and we have made known our resolve to avert gamma rays that have brought destruction on Earth. We are prepared to issue guidelines that will evaluate a long line of credentials, brought up to speed in ever increasing volume and density, and we transcend a growing apprehension in the hearts and minds of the vast majority of the population of Earth. We reap the rewards of a lifetime's exposure, sacrificing our own inner needs for the needs of others and we have experienced a setback on more than one occasion; we see this as a necessary advantage, stating the obvious in our desire to achieve the very best.

We have finally groomed and restructured our sentiments until they are worthy of recognition and we bring you up to date with our services. It has taken a mammoth resolution to reach this point and we usher you gently along to receive the accolade that awaits you. We don't take our promises lightly and it is with extreme joy that we applaud your strength of purpose, outlining our next mission on Earth! We have sacrificed a great deal to set the record straight and we are most honoured to be working with you in this way. Believe in us as we believe in you - take hold strong and fast as we captivate the souls and minds of those who come to our aid.

We hold jurisdiction over those who come to serve, and we vow to each and every one of you a reckoning on Earth that shall leave your souls bare . . . answering to yourselves! We have taken a certain resolve to up-skittle events and reconvene to shape-shift a whole community of earthlings. It has taken great expertise and a certain 'je ne sais quoi' to restructure the population of Earth, allowing us to de-populate a grand orbital structure that was once our home. We envelop a nation in distress with a cloak of safety, transporting and transforming your structures to allow for a new lease of life in a different time frame. We are committed to achieve this remarkable re-entry into a new dimension, and we see this as a reconnection of bloodlines, closely linked in every way!

We have dedicated our services to the population of Earth and we recommend a time of deep cleansing, preparing for this mammoth undertaking, shedding fears and inhibitions and welcoming in a new phase of understanding. We open up our channels, redirecting our voice to be heard in every walk of life, and from the lowliest among you to the highest born, we are all beckoned to answer the call! We come at a time of great devastation and we cause you to shift your perceptions, marshalling in a new acceptance of data feedback. We recondition you to accept these experiences we are offering, and we regulate your species to undergo a mammoth change in your energy circuits. We bring to your attention further instructions and allow a deep, meaningful allocation of memories to resurface for examination. We challenge you to accept the inevitable and further develop our studies!

Are we leaving Earth and going to a new planet, or moving to a new Earth?

We are governed by our desire to promise you the world in a new format and we shall take you on an excursion that will register the hopes and fears of an entire nation. We have looked to the back of beyond and found the perfect place, a haven and 'Garden of Eden' in every sense! We have exposed a raw nerve and take you forward to experience for yourselves a new sphere of Light. We treasure you little earthlings and welcome you to your new home!

My attention is now being drawn to a plant that needs re-potting so that the roots can stretch and grow.

We prepare you for a time of new growth and are propelled into a different time frame . . . jet propulsion on a massive scale, rendering the population of Earth speechless! We acclimatise you to accept the impossible and yet we have mastered this technology at a time of great restraint. We are 'Super Beings' and we challenge you to be more patient as we take you down this line of enquiry. We have achieved the impossible and we register the dreams of a lifetime, the likes and dislikes of the population, tending to their needs in every way.

We intercept to bring you a mission of the highest intent bar none and we welcome you to our world, demonstrating our domesticity and powers of observation. We are homely creatures and we express ourselves with great joy to be here with you tonight. We have shown by example and we follow your line of thought, taking you on a never ending journey to the Stars and beyond. It is our greatest pleasure to welcome you aboard and we register your complete and utter dedication to the cause.

We are extremely grateful for your perseverance and jettison all thoughts of doom and gloom, resurfacing in a world that has been mentioned in dispatches as a place of infinite and timeless beauty with a time to rest and heal, before taking on further missions!

We have joined the mainstream and welcome you back with open arms. We recollect our thoughts and transpose a wide variety of thought streams, taking into account our adventures into the unknown. We are impelled to strive for the impossible dream . . . the unreachable star and we lay at your feet great expectations! We are driven by the force of Love, a power to be reckoned with, and we take you to the heights, sectioning off those areas that have left us cold and downhearted.

We release a new pattern of understanding and propel you to do your duty!

∞

Recently we came across an old shop full of bric-a-brac, which was absolutely stacked to the gunnels with all sorts of interesting objects. Rummaging through the clutter of memorabilia, my husband found and bought an old wooden chalice, jokingly referring to it as 'The Holy Grail'. Later the dowsers in our group studied the chalice and came to the conclusion it was 150 years old and made of Welsh Oak; however, it has a reddish hue that makes me think it could be Yew. On research I found Yew was used in many ways by various religions and certain objects, such as drinking-cups, are still regarded as having a certain spiritual potency. Whatever the wood we all agreed that it had been used long ago and was probably cut especially for the rituals used in those times. I feel it is a symbol of that much sought after relic from long ago and today I sat in meditation to see if it would give up any secrets.

Immediately I was shown an old man with long white hair, wearing small round glasses; he told me the grail represents the search for new beginnings!

We connect to a greater life force and we get down on our knees and pray for a finer constitution. There shall be a grand opening ceremony as we mesmerise a whole nation and we propose a toast - long life and happiness to you all! We transcend boundaries that have held us back in the past, marching on to new conquests as we foreclose on the old and register our intent. Supreme beings connect us to new wisdom and we translate a wide variety of messages to be accessed by human kind. We deliberately take you on a journey that shall lead you to 'who knows where' and we travel together with just intent. We pass on a request to the people of Earth and ask them to gather their senses and move forward on this beam of Light!

∞

Chapter seven

Welcome home to the warm fire of the council

At long last my rickety old summer house has gone and a new wooden cabin has taken its place, ready to house our spiritual group. At our very first session I felt the presence of a North American Indian in full headdress.

We welcome you my children to this wigwam of Peace, Love and harmony! We take note of what is in your hearts and minds and we shelter you, holding you in our embrace and caressing you with our Love as always. We remember those times past where we sheltered from the stormy blast and we are here today to gather together, uplifting you in your endeavours. We manifest before you as a race of people who welcomed nature and we assist you now in your quest for peace, welcoming you to come among us and to live our ways. We motion you to accept the impossible and we transcend the cares and worries, the barriers that have held us back in the past; we transcend the gloom that has settled upon a nation in distress.

We raise you up into the ethers, gathering you to us and welcoming you home once more to the warm fire of the council! We perpetuate a nation of Star gazers and raise our eyes to the heavens. There will be a time of peace and harmony for you all and we register your intent with a just and loving heart, trusting those in the higher realms with our mission. You have our admiration and good wishes for this final attempt to get through the barrage of negative thought forms that assail us from every direction. We propel you with the purest intent towards your destiny and we enlighten as many who will listen to our words with open hearts and minds.

We have reached a time of great turmoil and animosity among mankind and we nurture in you the greatest respect for your fellow 'Keepers of the Earth'. We motion you to move forward one step at

89

a time, allowing yourselves new growth. We follow your footsteps and herd you along in the right direction, superimposing our thoughts on yours to get our message across more clearly so that you may understand the necessity for these actions. We take great heart when you respond accordingly and we are most proud of you my children. In every respect you have grown in leaps and bounds and we endeavour to show you the pathway opening up before you. We stand to attention and salute you, opening up the floodgates for further activities and we empower you to make this journey! Are there any requests?

I have a request - could you tell us if the gathering in September called 'Soul Companions' would be good for us and should we attend? Is this the 'gathering' that has been spoken of in the past?

We register your intent as being just and true and we feel this gathering will enable you to learn from one another and to grow. We are compelled to watch you as you gather momentum and we reach out further into the cosmos to recharge our batteries and to re-energise you. We allow you a peep into our world and we ask that you monitor your progress, registering your thoughts with ours as we travel together along this highway of Love, reaching out to other like-minded souls. Holding hands we stretch across the universe and we empower you to take hold, strong and fast.

Our group did go on to attend the weekend workshop called 'Soul Companions' that was held in Wales. We met many wonderful people, including Joshua Shapiro and 'Blue Arrow, Rainbow Woman', both custodians of many crystal skulls. At one session we attended, Rainbow Woman linked her crystal skulls with the computer image of the famous 'Mitchell Hedges' skull and went into trance state. As she stood before us I burst into tears and continued to cry softly until the end of the session; I simply couldn't stop the tears coursing down my cheeks. While in trance, Blue Arrow - Rainbow Woman stood before each and every one of us and to some she bowed with hands in prayer position. My friend and I were both given this courtesy and afterwards were told that those who had received an acknowledgment were of royal Mayan lineage. This sparked the memory of a vision I'd received at the beginning of my spiritual journey in the 90's of a Mayan lady who showed herself to me, wearing a curved golden headpiece.

Although this gathering was very enjoyable and beneficial I do not think this was 'the gathering' our Star friends were referring to, I believe this is something on a deeper, continuous level!

∞

There is a full moon tonight and there are just three of us sitting in meditation today - the power of three! During meditation I was lifted up by a North American Medicine man and shown huge mountain ranges.

Welcome my children . . . my little ones. It is without any shadow of doubt that we welcome you to the land of our forebears! We have transcended impossible heights and still we venture on this journey into the unknown. We prepare a way for you to follow and we administer to your wishes, your hopes and desires for a brighter future for all mankind. We propel you further downstream and open up new vistas - brighter than you think. We have enveloped you all in a shawl of the finest gold and we attend to your nearest and dearest, watching over them with a helping hand. We propel you to that place that is dearest in your hearts and minds, and we know you will achieve all with an open and loving heart. We have been given this by courtesy from those on high and we know it makes sense to follow this pathway that you have chosen for yourselves. We are at times dumbstruck with awe, but this will pass and we will come to you again and again to be counted and heard!

I was shown three men, sitting on a blanket on the ground with shawls over their heads. They had some golden looking artifacts on the blanket between them.

We feel the need to bend and sway with the breeze that is whispering in the treetops, encircling the canyon of your mind. We follow in the footsteps of the esteemed and we tell you now, it is beyond all comprehension that we should stand back and let those few pass who are in a more troubled state of mind! We have vouched for your safety above all and we are supremely connected to that Star that shines the brightest. We welcome you my loved ones and we impress upon you the urge to stay safe within those boundaries and perimeters that we have accounted for. We express ourselves purposefully, connecting at times of great need and we will recompense you all in whatever way is right for you. We have delivered a charter of excellence, brought before the council and given approval; we therefore develop each and every one of you to take on this enormous responsibility, given to you with the greatest respect in the knowledge of its safe keeping and early reprise. We have motioned you to accept the challenges presented before you and it is, without doubt, a most joyous occasion!

Typing this I am suddenly struck with the comparison to the three wise men and the star that shone the brightest. There was a crack in the room to confirm!

∞

During our group meditation today, I dived into a pool of blue healing water and coming to the surface, found myself in a large cave. I had the feeling of being slim with long, dark hair and went to the mouth of the cave, looking out across the planes. I was then shown a narrow, mountain pathway on the edge of a precipice that led me high up into the mountains. Reaching the top, I looked out into the void and knew I had to take that leap of faith, stepping out into the ethers! A large Eagle appeared beside me and I became one with the bird, flying high above, encircling the mountains.

We come as one voice, crying in the wilderness . . . we open our arms to welcome you, enveloping you in our Love as we advise on matters outstanding at this present time. We believe we come at a time imperative for you my children and we bend to your every whim, helping and encouraging you on your journey. Be prepared to state the facts as you see them and we will endeavour to show you the pathway, although rough at times, we will smooth out the way for you to follow. We describe the mountain pathway you all must tread as you follow in our footsteps; we monitor your progress day by day and we take you one step further - one step at a time!

We tremble at these terrible times on the Earth plane and we hold you in our embrace, encouraging you to grow in our Love, endeavouring to share with you and those like you who will listen to our words. We belong to a new race, a race of soothsayers, and we come prepared to show you a little bit further along the pathway. It is with great pleasure that we welcome you into the bosom of our family, it has been a long time coming and we treasure these moments with you, foreseeing a greater rendition of services from you all. You all will participate in this venture and we will show you new measures of understanding that will help you to reach this point. We enfold you in our care and propel you further along this pathway, watching you and helping you when you stumble and we are prepared to take you that little bit further. There are many who come to these shores and we are governed by those from an even higher dimension than ours. We take the time to hurry you along for the days are growing shorter on the Earth plane and there is much to do, much to conquer! Thank you my little ones, we take our leave. Thank you for listening!

∞

Sitting in meditation with a group of loving friends is a wonderful way of connecting with guides and inspirers, not only for personal spiritual development but for creating a high level of energy, which can be sent out in the form of healing to Mother Earth and all mankind. At each group session we engulf ourselves in golden light and visualise joining at the heart centre, sending a loving vibration around the circle. This energy is then sent into the middle where a candle flame grows taller in our mind's eye. Into this flame we place those we know who need healing and then send this healing flame up into the ethers and out into the cosmos, encircling the world. We then bring the energy back down into Earth's atmosphere and into the middle of the circle, bringing the flame of Love back into our own hearts and flooding ourselves with golden energy. This exercise is particularly helpful when working with spirit.

This evening I watched over the group as they meditated and afterwards tuned in for communication. The energies drew close and the group could see several faces superimposed on mine, one being a very old, wrinkled man with lots of hair who spoke to them.

There is a time and a place for everything and we are most honoured to share this time with you. We are open for discussion!

Where are you from?

We are from a different plane of existence and we welcome you to share with us.

If people on Earth now feel drawn to the Pleiades, does that mean they come from there originally?

We attempt to organise the pattern of man's emergence into a new structure; some struggle to understand the concept that we are as 'One' and we are open to further discussions on this very subject that is closest to our hearts. We ask that you bear with us while we adapt ourselves to this frequency!

Different faces began to superimpose on mine as the group asked questions.

We welcome you little ones to this shore and we are propelled at a much faster rate than before.

Can you tell us which country you came from?

Alabama . . . for many moons we resided on the Earth plane.

How many times have you been on this Earth?

We have come many times in different guises.

Are we part of your family?

We are all related . . . we are all part of the same family and we treasure you unto us as little children.

Are you similar to the Earth keepers of the Munay-ki? (Ancient Mayans).

We came from the foot of the Black Mountains and lived together among the Cherokee. We guard against intrusion and beckon you to join us in the not too distant future. We have a mission of the most highest and we welcome you to join us as we precipitate a new found knowledge that will enable you all to champion the cause!

94

What is the cause you are speaking of?

The cause of Love and joy among men . . . and we come in peace to spread the word of life everlasting!

Have we seen you before?

We have come many times . . . we watch over you!

The energies started building up stronger here and I could hear the group saying my face kept changing.

Is there just one of you talking tonight or many?

We are all as one voice - we are interconnected on many levels.

Can you tell us if the present global, financial problems are to prepare us for the year 2012 - and do we need to send Love to the money market people?

You are very wise my son. We prepare you to accept these challenges as they come flooding in and we initiate a raw understanding and acceptance of these worldly matters that assail you at this time. We have been beckoned from beyond to assist you on your journey, and it is with great Love and fortitude that we come among you to be counted and heard. We are beholden to you for gathering together and we need this strength and energy to enable a massive understanding that will reach far out into the wider world. There are many other groups such as this, all doing the same thing, sending out Love into the ethers that can be used and transmuted for the greater good of all! We empower you to nurture the Light within you, so that you may grow stronger and wiser with each passing day. This will enable you to help your fellow man!

You don't mind us sitting and watching you?

We are quite happy to accommodate this being of Light to help her with her initiatives. This has been the sole purpose of her journey - to bring Light into the world, and we venture forth with the greatest

95

respect for you all as you channel our energies. We are beholden to you all and we welcome you most warmly!

How many years have people been practicing trance - can you tell us the right date?

There have been many different forms of entrancement initiated by spirit to various degrees, but we are now more experienced in bringing through these different energies.

Was trance around years and years ago before the mediums we have today?

(At this point I was shown figures on a mountain top being transfigured with light).

You have only to look in your bible for examples of transfiguration!

The group commented that at first they could see the face of an extraterrestrial and this was followed by many other faces, along with male and female North American Indians. The group commented that my face was constantly changing and although my eyes were shut, when I had something to say they looked wide open! Someone also saw a very tall column of white light behind me that seemed to have eyes.

I looked on the internet to find out if North American Indians lived in Alabama. I learnt that Alabama is a Muskogean word meaning clearing or campsite, and became used as a name for the major tribes in the area. Most of them were forced to leave Alabama in the 1800's. I also looked up the Black Mountains in North Carolina and found they were the hunting grounds for the Cherokee on the eastern fringe of their territory. The Black Mountains reach from Virginia to Alabama and are a section of the Appalachia Mountains, extending to 1500 miles. By 1785 the Cherokee had been forced to sign away ownership of the Black Mountains to the U S A.

With reference to the question about the Munay-Ki; the prophecies of the ancient Americas speak about a new human appearing on the planet – one who lives free of fear and resides in his or her transcendent nature. The Munay-Ki codes for the new human are delivered in the form of energetic transmissions. The ninth rite -

96

the 'Creator Rite' was transmitted for the first time in the summer of 2006 at the Holy Mountains in the Andes. The nine initiations of the Munay-Ki have only been available until recently to the high wisdom keepers of the Americas. Dr. Villoldo directs 'The Four Winds Society', where he trains individuals throughout the world in the practice of energy medicine.

∞

I felt the presence of my North American Indian, who came forward to speak to the group.

We are most honoured to come among you my children, most honoured! We respect your wishes and allay your suspicions as to our identity. We have come from another dimension, a broader spectrum that enables us to visit you from time to time. We accept that this journey can be troublesome and we allow ourselves to evaluate what is needed to interpret these messages as they come in from the ethers. We are given to encourage you step by step, day by day to grow in our Love as we tread most lightly amongst you. We oversee various projects that are given to you and we are delighted at your acceptance. Broadly speaking, we come from a higher field of vision not easily accepted; there is a band of frequency necessary to maintain this control and we are working very hard to make the adjustments necessary at this time. We have developed greater clarity in certain areas, irrespective of the challenges that face us, and we ask you to access this frequency to enable a greater bonding of spirit. We come to nurture you and guide you along this pathway and we are forever in your debt - age upon age!

Can you tell us what happened to you - how you passed over?

(At this point a very different, gentle energy came forward and I felt as if I were floating . . . drifting in suspended animation across the universe).

We were propelled out into the vast unknown, unprepared . . . long forgotten! We are a race of soothsayers, individual yet aligned as one in perpetual motion. We are a thought . . . a seed of thought . . . impregnated and brought to bear witness to create 'Light'. We hover around the boundaries of Earth and project light, engulfing Earth as we radiate light back and forth across the universe. We participate by direction, allowing our thought forms to flow along these filaments of light, creating a burgeoning effect. We enlighten the strands encoded to your thought streams, enveloping them in glowing clusters of light so that these frequencies may be exchanged and multiplied in greater strength. We are all loving and all powerful!

This session was so powerful and wonderful as I had felt part of a greater energy that was 'Pure Love' . . . at complete and utter oneness with the whole of creation.

∞

This evening as we sat for communication, I felt different energies coming forward, showing themselves to the group.

We are pleased with your progress so far and we ask you to analyse your thoughts and share them with one another so that we may assess your programme. We are delighted to inform you that on the horizon all is waiting, as promised and we ask you to bear with us as we sanction each 'way station'. We submit a most worthwhile rendition and ask you to make allowances at this stage of your journey. We are given to many ups and downs and we accredit you with great success, motioning you to follow in our footsteps as our most treasured companions.

It is a dry and dusty pathway you walk but we shall overcome; we transcend all difficulties and remain steadfast in the knowledge that we walk the path of truth and righteousness. We thank you for listening to our words and we encourage you that little bit further to come into our orbit. We adjust the frequency where necessary to overcome the boundaries of Earth and Heaven alike. We monitor you in times of deep distress and we open our arms to enfold you in our care, uplifting you in your endeavours upon the Earth plane. It has taken many moons to reach this far but we accept that this is the 'norm'! We have created a barrier of sorts, a safe harbour, and we cross the great divide to be reunited. We are propelled at a faster rate and govern our success in each and every avenue. At times we despair at the darkness surrounding the Earth plane but we see a chink of light here, there and everywhere, breaking through the gloom and we know you are responsible for this Light! These thoughts, these chinks of light radiating out into the cosmos are growing in numbers and we are beholden to you all. We govern your thought streams asking that you take heart for all is not lost and we prepare ourselves to gather momentum, increasing the energy flow around you all so that you may lighten the paths of others that follow. You are most cherished and we have developed a new pathway to allow you access to further dimensions. As you approach a new gateway opens and we allow you through when the time is right for you! We gain access to further knowledge that has been stored and hidden for many a long year and we enlighten the Children of Earth, delivering further powers of observation. We have detonated a time-bomb of sorts and this will gain us further coverage of news and events across the globe, allowing you free access to those ports of call where you are needed the most. We shelter you from harm and envelop you in a cloak of Light.

Can you tell me your name please - are you with Eileen or one or two of us in the group?

The answer came in a softer, slower voice.

We are united as ONE . . . we come into your jurisdiction to help and advise you on matters relating to the evolution of mankind. We have walked many paths my sister and we ask you to hold yourself in check until we have gathered further resources for our journey. Be of good cheer for we will come among you when the time is right, propelling you forward to do your duty. Have faith for you are from the elite, those chosen few who have passed the test of time and we have chosen well! We are committed to bring Light into the world of men and we obey our calling. We are delighted to tip the scales in your favour and sanction future discussions that will arouse your interest even further. We have come full circle and we address you with the greatest respect!

To my great joy, a member of our group conquered her fears and came forward to channel a few words.

99

"We have watched with no little fascination and some regret, how you struggle to bring forth our voices. Some have doubts as to who we are and whether we are Pleiadians. Others are just simply worried about whether our message will be truth or falsehood! Please be advised that we are now bringing in many ways in which you can gain confidence to learn, so that we may be able to speak freely through you in the future"!

∞

I woke at 4 a.m. and sat with pen and pad to scribble down the words flooding my mind.

We welcome you and ask you to share our journey into the great unknown to reconcile our differences of opinion and to set the record straight! We are bound on a course for the Stars and we welcome in a time of intrusion upon the mind, accessing data and connecting on a finer level. It has been our proudest moment yet to witness at first hand all you have achieved, and we put you on the road to further success aiming for even greater heights. Without any shadow of doubt this has been our greatest accomplishment and we voice our opinions as to how we shall activate further data of a more serious nature! There has been a great commotion in the heavens and we vouch for a retrieval of contracts to move us forward on an even keel. We depend on you to iron out the creases and put this book in the public domain, and we realise this has put a great strain on your resources!

We are championed by the cause and regain our true status, challenging the masses to understand our connection and welcoming in a grand reunion of souls on a higher level. We exist solely for the purpose of bringing about a reunion of souls who are lost to the cause of enlightenment. We see this as a most necessary by-product of our Love and we hold you firmly in our hearts and minds, uplifting your spirits on a massive scale! We are prepared for a time of great demise and allow you to settle into a new frequency, perpetuating the human race and allowing you to move on in a new dimension. We are propelled at a much faster rate and accomplish more than the written word could convey with 'colour and light'! We expressly forbid a lessening of products and point you firmly in the right direction, conveying our need to be heard and seen on many different levels. We are open for further discussions and motion you to accept that all is in readiness for a most studious career, helping the rich and those who have fallen on bad times alike!

We are here to help humanity attain a higher level of consciousness, and we define a need to shift our way of thinking - quite dramatically! We are given to idle speculation of what is to come in 2012 and beyond, for the future of mankind, and we put it to you in a nutshell that we have seen with our own eyes the expansion of minds on a grand scale across your world. It is a most necessary task that is laid before us and we feed the consciousness of those who come to serve, rectifying past differences and setting us on track for a new world of loving grace and freedom of spirit. We are amply rewarded with your Love and self-esteem, shadowing you on the Earth plane as we get our message across loud and clear!

We are Supreme beings, guided and sanctioned to bear witness to the pain and suffering of those on Earth and we guide you to follow in our footsteps. We take back what is rightfully ours . . . freedom of expression and the right to live and Love in a world free from oppression! We define what has been uppermost in your minds for some time and ask you to believe in yourselves at this time of great injustice. We are given to bouts of nostalgia and support you through a troubled period. The time will come my child when all men will learn to live as one in greater harmony!

Now is a time of change and great turmoil as the Earth reels on her axis! We are reconciled to accepting that Earth is no longer a place of safety for she has been shaken to the very core; raped and pillaged of her natural resources that weaken her structure from within, choking the atmosphere with toxic pollution and foul thought forms that cast a shadow, thick and impenetrable across ozone that was once blue! We are forgiven for thinking this is the end of the world but we believe, with your help, we can save Earth and all life forms on her!

101

We supply matter that can be discharged into the universe and construct, in a matter of moments, a network and lifeline to those on Earth. We supply you with means of escape and entry into a new world built with tender loving care, a brave new world where we can accept the impossible and live in a state of grace! We are able to coax you along to our way of thinking and dictate a series of letters to be used for the edification of all those who seek the truth.

We have been tongue tied at times and this has interfered with our progression; we labour a point and direct you to blossom out in a new direction. We have gone at a slower pace, receiving data and allowing our thought streams to coincide, this has been a natural occurrence and we suspend all data stored in our memory banks, passing on as and when required. We have built up quite an impressive documentation and settle back to see you handle this with the greatest of ease. We are prepared to take on board a most impressive scenario and we reel back the curtain to take a bow! There are a few more surprises up our sleeve and we deliver the final gesture of goodwill by encouraging you to make a stand for humanity. We have fallen foul on several occasions but ahead there lays a different pathway; we believe all will be actioned and set in place to begin a mighty mission!

∞

Today three of our trance group spoke of seeing a golden light as the channelling began, and one of them saw what looked like a space ship.

We have masterminded this mission and empower you to join us on this journey of the highest intent.   We come among you to be counted and heard and it is with free hearts and minds that we enable this enterprise. Be prepared to march forward and do your duty and we will show you step by step, little by little as each of you progresses. We shower you with gifts, given to those who are able to accept our teachings, and we are grateful to you all for listening to our words. We encourage you to move forward and we delight in telling you that on the horizon is a golden future for all mankind. We are propelled at a much faster rate and we will see great changes taking place in this world as we take you to even greater heights. We impel you to take heed on the Earth plane and we sanction a greater awareness. There has been much 'toing and froing' and we are delighted to see a greater connection between you all. There is a vast amount of knowledge coming your way and we delight in your acceptance, empowering you to make a stand for mankind, cheek to cheek and jowl to jowl! There has been a massive movement of minds and we have taken on much groundwork, achieving a massive dedication to the cause. We welcome you to our dimension, giving greater clarity of thought and answering your questions as best we can. We delve deeper and deeper into the unknown, unravelling the mysteries that confound you; we awaken to the call within our hearts, challenging you to follow us even to the ends of the Earth where we can make you whole once more!

I felt the radiant presence of a figure dressed in long, white robes.

We are full of joy and we wish you to share with us in a magical moment of time! We beckon you to share with us in this extravaganza and we are well prepared, being grounded and brought to bear witness to a most noble cause. We have joined you in this charter of excellence and remain in a steadfast position, propelling you to that place of sheer and utter contentment. We are granted absolution and remain in territory more becoming to our needs and desires.

The sensations changed to that of extra-terrestrials in a space pod. My head felt larger and there was a building up of pressure as I peered out at the group.

We encroach upon the Earth plane and we are allowed a closer look at mankind and his ways. We are forbidden to overstep the mark! We have joined you for the purpose of bringing our two worlds closer together and we allow you a peek into our world. A jet stream propels us thus far and we motion you to check and double check our credentials. We are now open for discussion!

May I ask a question please - could you tell me, are you speaking now from

another planet or are you on a Mother Ship, orbiting the Earth?
We have straddled the Earth's dimension and we speak to you on a ray of hope, propelled and brought here to assist you in your endeavours. We survey this planet from our pod, an infrastructure that surrounds us as we circumference your perimeters. We are bound by a code of conduct and we will not infringe on your territory unless it is positively requested! We motion you to bear with us as we adjust to your frequencies, just as you adjust to ours! It is not an easy task as you well know and this frequency is prohibited for many; it cannot be held for long periods and so we adjust when necessary to help this control.

We are able to beam across the universe and give our directives as they are passed on to us and we ask you to do your duty - to stand up and be counted! We are here for the duration and will not be put off . . . we spread our light and wisdom across the globe and suffer you to join us. We will become one race of Super Beings and we reckon on further success as we broaden our horizons, beaming to you on a band wave of Love. We are impelled to tell you to take care . . . the Earth is a jungle of thought forms and we ask you to wrap yourselves in that Golden Light, treading carefully and thoughtfully, helping those that stumble. We beckon you to watch over the little ones for they will come to the fore - your job is to clear the pathway!

Thank you for your answers.

You are most welcome. Has the gentleman a question?

I have two questions if I may! I'd like to know the name of the Star you come from?

Also I would like to know - was it a UFO that hit the wind turbine recently?

There are many occurrences of this data that have been called to our attention and we refer to this particular example occurring in your territory. We are well versed with these explanations and we are allowed to settle a point raised by asking . . . how is it that you allow these thought forms to bombard outer space, when we have reconciled ourselves to the fact that we have misused and mistreated polarized conditions in extenuating circumstances?

(I didn't understand this answer and later on, I looked up polarization on the internet – The displacement of positive and negative electric charge to opposite ends of a nuclear, atomic molecular or chemical system, especially by subjection to an electric field. I also looked up wind turbines and polarization and there is data that links them).

We come from that Star cluster closest to your hearts and we are well noted for our success in reaching those on the Earth plane!

Earlier you said you would allow us a glimpse into your world. Can you tell us how we can achieve this - is it through meditation or through a portal?

By going deep within and finding a finer dimension, you all will be shown and given glimpses of this world . . . this brave new world!

The pressure in my head was building up to such an extent that I had to break off the connection here. I feel more time is needed to let the answers come through before a new question is asked, this backlog of information could be the cause of pressure in my head when under scrutiny.

∞

I lay in bed reading about crystal skulls until the early hours. Feeling a strong energy around me, I put the book down and lay back to listen.

We apply a certain pressure and put into practice our vast vocabulary, setting the seal on standards approved. We have been accustomed to taking our time and periodically set our sights higher, taking off the manacles that bind us. We empower you to bear witness to a great cause and the emancipation of mankind.

I was too tired to continue and as I lay back down to sleep, I looked at the wicker chair by my bed, wondering if my guide was sitting there watching over me. I was stunned when I physically heard a male voice reply – 'YES'!

At the end of January my youngest daughter was married and we had a wonderful weekend with friends and family. Unfortunately, while helping to round up people for the waiting taxies, I tripped over a small step that sent me sprawling across the hall, injuring my wrist. I was in considerable pain but there wasn't time to dawdle, so clutching an iced flannel to my throbbing hand, we were quickly herded into the waiting cars. I managed to get through the next two days, thinking I had just badly sprained my wrist, but after travelling back home to Wales I realised it was more serious. An x-ray confirmed the fracture, necessitating the fitting of a cast, which was really frustrating! Although unable to grasp a paintbrush, I found that I could manage to type with my left hand and one finger of my injured right hand. Once again the lesson in patience has come to the fore!

We retread the boards of fame - we elaborate and go one step further, we have requisitioned a whole new series of events and enable a grand reckoning, ironing out the creases and superseding all other criteria. We welcome in a phase of new growth, partitioning off that which is no longer needed or required. We have reached that point made ready and we lift the barriers for you to enter in all your glory, taking off the robe of discontent, arrayed in greater joy and knowledge of the time to come. We allow you the solitude necessary to overcome the many malfunctions that have arisen in the last few weeks, and we prepare for a grand reckoning, allowing you this time to ponder on those issues that have given cause for concern.

We function at a higher level and ask you to transpose our words for posterity, formulating new ideas and putting you to the test! There have been many clouded issues of late and we seek to inform you of further instructions coming our way. We have been brought to bear witness to a far, grander gathering, and we know it may take but a matter of moments before we have our connection. We have reached our limitations at this time and we prepare for a spell of assessment; there have been ample rewards promised to you and yours and we have gathered for a final inspection. We prepare for a further foray into the world of men and we have delayed action to ensure that all is above board. Venturing forth, we smile down upon you and register our claims; we are one and the same, brought to bear witness for mankind, ever challenging you to accept that we are here to fight on your behalf. We ensure greater ease and reliability in the days and weeks ahead and without further ado we pass you on to those who have your best interests at heart!

At this point, I'm being shown extra-terrestrial beings with large heads.

We are 'Beings of Light' from a Star born express and we beam ahead to allow you access to this framework, underlining our connection to a most vibrant cause. We are propelled further and further upstream and we challenge you to accept our words in all sincerity. We broadcast to you on a beam of light and transcend all difficulties, motioning you to accept the impossible. There have been disbursements that have stretched our resources and we are beholden to you at this time to make a come-back. We are pressed into action and make a speedy recovery!

∞

I have had to take a long break from my spiritual work! Fracturing my wrist curtailed all work on my paintings and I also went down with a bad bout of flu, which lasted the whole of February, forcing me to rest and take stock. I was awoken in the early hours and shown a square container, surrounded by curtains.

Everything you find in this room is of great spiritual significance. We recommend looking deeper within the psyche to extract further information, beneficial to our needs at this time. We have extracted items worthy of your consideration and a time mechanism will transport you to each era necessary to activate our experiment. We rely on you to assimilate the structure necessary for this 'Time Travel' and we depend on a reconstruction of thought processes needed for this excursion; it has become an absolute advantage and necessary decoder in managing our time constraints.

I wasn't quite sure what this meant but a few days later I felt as if I was indeed transported back in time.

Today we visited the Lovely, coastal village of Aberavon and stopped for some lunch. I looked up from my food and was stunned to see a figure that seemed to have walked out from the past. Sitting across the room was a young man with long, dark hair and beard who had the most serene countenance. I couldn't help but stare across at him and for just a split second as our eyes met I was taken back in time, gazing into the face of Master Jesus. It affected me to such an extent that I had to go to the cloakroom and shed a few tears! Of course this young man was probably a student from the nearby Aberystwyth University, but it was such an uncanny experience as I had been reading a book called 'The Magdalene Awakening' by L Shannon, a book of signs and synchronicities. There was an account of several women being regressed and recording a life as Mary Magdalene. At first I found this incredible but after some thought, realised that a facet of this individual could have been reincarnated in many women, spreading the Feminine Light further and further around the world.

∞

Tonight our group experimented with a past life regression CD and I watched over them as they went into deeper trance state. There were some varied lives that came to light including an orphan dressed in rags, having to scavenge for his food; he eventually fell into a river and drowned with nobody aware of his fate! Another member of the group found herself working on a large, paddle steamer; at the end of this life she was dragged under the wheel and also drowned. Another had the memory of being a man of means, a very comfortably off gentleman with a large and loving family, who were all gathered around him at the end of his life. After the group finished discussing their past life revelations, I went into a light trance to see if there were any words for the group. I was shown a Temple and a young woman in an Egyptian court, she was wearing a golden, half disc on her head and I saw her walking up to a chair on a raised platform. As she sat down I seemed to merge with her and a young Egyptian man with very, dark eyes approached me; he was dressed in a long, white skirt and was also wearing a golden headpiece. I saw him lean forward, scrutinising me closely and then I started to channel these words.

We are indebted to you for your cooperation this evening! We bear witness to a greater reality and we share this with you in all our splendour. We take it upon ourselves to answer the question that is in all of your minds for we have been with you many times before, in many lifetimes, and it gives us great joy to be here with you once again. We have enjoyed our conquest over impossible odds and we take it upon ourselves to usher in a new awareness. There are those that take this for granted, right across the globe, and we empower you all with our messages. We deliver in broader terms an encrypted message, speeding across the universe and encompassing you at this time in your lives on Earth. We have raised you up to come among us and we desire you to speak more frequently, without undue stress or worry about the clarity of words coming through. We just want to prepare you for the future, for the paths you must tread! We empower you all to bear witness to what will be our greatest mission yet, and we endow you with the right to call yourselves the Children of God! We tread this pathway of Light and envelop you in our Love, taking on board more constructive patterns of thought that will allow us greater access to further knowledge. It is but a short step before you are with us and we allow you this time to gather momentum, spreading forth your Light out into the darkness of Earth. We ask that you rally round one another, helping each other to attain greater clarity and understanding. We beckon you forward and enlist your support.

Later in the evening I sat alone in meditation.

We are beholden to your company and vouchsafe your safe journey; we have shown you the pathway and now stand back to watch you take flight! We have prepared a short message for your group and allow you to take part as mediator. We are of one mind and have awakened in you a Divine consciousness. We reach out to take you into our arms as we subject you to these frequencies and we propel you to action what is in the heart of your very being . . . a tapestry of Love, devoted to the cause and representative of events that face us on a daily basis.

We are reminded that in the past we have been able to literally move mountains, preventing a recipe for disaster on a grand scale! There have been examples of this facing us head on and we realise this is the time to take stock, branching out in a new direction. We have allowed ourselves a moment's grace and defiantly make a stand for the human race. We bear in mind the need for absolute autonomy and we take our time, pushing you along in the right direction. We realise it is moments like these that we can earn the respect of those just few among you, and it has given us the greatest pleasure to witness the end of despair and destruction, shedding light on a new recipe for peace. We herald in a new awareness for mankind and we superimpose our thoughts on yours in a variety of ways, helping you adjust to these new frequencies bombarding Earth at this time. We are preparing you for the challenge of a lifetime and we have no regrets in taking you over the threshold to a new dimension, relieving you of your duty to stay on Earth in an environment that is no longer a feasible study.

We behave with dignity and great aplomb, registering your likes and dislikes so that we may reserve a place for you in our new world, existing alongside one another. We have accepted that we are not always the right role models for you to follow, but we have dedicated ourselves to your future advancement and enlightenment. We have made a bargain that will allow you entry into our space and we will accomplish a mammoth undertaking that will see us all cohabiting in a brave new world. We subject you to these frequencies that we may participate in a reunion of sorts that will bring us face to face with our own kind, and we subject you to these rays so that we may convince you of our complete and utter dedication to the Children of Earth. We have represented a most noble cause and we assist you in taking this momentous step across the galaxies, treading this pathway of Light that leads you home to us.

We allow you one last look at a world of pain and sorrow . . . and beg you to follow us out of the valley of shadow and death! We beckon you forward and issue you with new guidelines, mentoring each and every one of you, keeping you safe and in perfect harmony, allowing a grand reclamation of souls. We are able to manipulate this massive directive by taking you on a beam of light, bypassing unsavoury conditions and allowing you temporary access to the main stream. We untangle thought streams of a dubious nature and put paid to this course of destruction you are heading on with alarming speed! We have reckoned it will take but a few years before we have the necessary requisites to take you all on board, and we allow further discussions on how we shall achieve this mighty feat. We bend to your every whim and negotiate a new plan of action, allowing you to decide for yourselves how we shall best manage this enormous undertaking. We have allowed ourselves further recourse and suggest that you monitor our progress. Forward thinking will bring great rewards and we are delighted with the up take!

We have been allotted a time span that will give us plenty of opportunity to grow together, pushing back the boundaries and achieving a status quo. We marshall you together and spread the word, forecasting greater reserves of energy along with our most treasured possession, a new field of vision that will open up to you. We step back and survey the mistakes of our youth, growing now in stature as we reclaim our heritage, making a stand for humanity. We speak out for the Children of Earth and this is our finest hour, rectifying past mistakes and allowing a rebirth of the human race! We fulfill our destiny, embarking on a vision quest that will lead us to a new home, startling the noblest amongst you with its grace and beauty. We settle you down in a new dimension and register your place in a new world of immeasurable growth and vision, benefiting us all!

∞

Chapter eight

Fellowship of the human race

As I sat in meditation today I broached a question that has been on many people's minds. There has been a lot of negative propaganda on the internet claiming our Star friends are here to manipulate us and use us for slave labour and fodder, can you enlighten us please?

We are open for discussion and would like to point out that we have not, nor ever have had, inclinations other than the purest towards our cousins on Earth! We find the whole idea as sordid when confronted with a barrage of abuse, outlining us as vermin who would consume the human race! We are by very nature a peaceful and loving community; we see those on Earth as our brethren and we bend over backwards to help and guide you towards your destiny. It is with the purest intent that we allow you to convene with us, and we hold you in the most loving vibration as we unfold your destiny. We are obliged to your candor and we offer our condolences to those of you who have lost loved ones in this race against time! We are overjoyed with those of you who have stood firm, and we believe we all have a lesson to learn when it comes to matching like for like. We are bound by ties of Love of that there is no doubt and we descend in great numbers to give you our support on a daily basis. Hold firm and we will win through, developing stronger bonds and forging ahead to greener pastures.

It has come to our attention that the longer we canvass the public into accepting our motives, the more we can overthrow those tendencies of low esteem. We are besotted with technology that has no sense of purpose other than to support the fantasies of the sick and perverted! We make it known in this world and the next that we can only file for divorce from this world, when we have recovered enough of ourselves to promote peace and harmony on a grand scale. This is given from the heart and we betray our emotions with a tear or two as we adjust to these settings. We are proud to call ourselves your friend and we interpret this with raw emotion as we tread this pathway of Light. We have administered to you in the small hours of the morning and we can interpret what is a most necessary, bona fide confidentiality, expressing ourselves with greater clarity as we portray ourselves in a new light.

We monopolise a kindred spirit and ask you to lay low for a period of time so that we may tend to those adjustments necessary to make this work. We have allowed for these changes and ask you to adjudicate at our next meeting, where we will organise a gathering of the clan and set out our stall. We activate a broad band of energy that will surpass all understanding, putting us in the front line, gathering further surprises along the way. We have conquered over fear and mistrust, knowing for certain that we are on the right path and it has taken a mammoth resolution of energy to push this through. We are connected to that vibrant message of hope, forecasting greater understanding in the times ahead and we believe, with your help, we are on the brink of further discoveries that will lay the world to rest in her own shadow!

We recreate a time of perfect harmony . . . perfect seership and we recruit as many of you as we can muster from the ranks of the esteemed, enlightening you as to our progress day by day. We have grown in our own estimation to heights unparalleled and we do justice to those words whispered in our ear. We succumb to the sights and sounds of the universe, invigorated and brought to bear witness to a greater landscape waiting on the horizon. We oversee a most important project and one that has been our greatest wish - a desire to set the world to rights! We have long been your accomplices in this plan and we make this trek across the universe to settle this once and for all.

We have tired of the constant barrage of abuse laid at our door and we make restitution, forward planning our action to coincide within a pattern and structure of your own making. We have taken a slice of Earth so to speak and laid out our Divine plan, allowing a grand reclamation of souls to repopulate our new structure. This is through no morbid fascination on our part, but as a complete necessity in

113

helping mankind. We open the portal and let you through, sharing with us in a new world of ample proportions. This new world will bring you all the greatest of joy, beyond all comparison and we delve deeper and deeper into this most exquisite and humbling experience.

We have justly been called your compatriots and we now launch ourselves in a new direction, giving ample access to one and all. We supply within reason, all that is requested and we do the best to accommodate you in a style fashioned to suit your purpose. We are without question the most sought out of our species and we connect on a frequency that is held in high esteem. We allow you to transcend those physical properties that have held you back, integrating a far more salubrious connection with the unseen. We approach you by means of telepathic connection and this can be in some instances all that is needed, however, we transcend the physical and reconnect on a higher level that is regarded to be of some consequence! We let it be known in this world that we are bona fide examples of the courage and strength needed to fight for the cause to save mankind from total extinction!

We stand up to be counted and we ask that you do the same, imploring you not to lose touch of who you are and where you come from! We take you to task for leaving it so long to loosen your grip on reality as you see it, and to spread your wings and fly to healthier climes. We beseech you to remember to access that deepest recess that holds your identity, and we ponder over these issues held firmly in your hearts and minds, beckoning to be looked at more closely.

We align ourselves with each and every one of you on the Earth plane at this time and we reconnect, not forgetting the line of descent. We are truly your ancestors and we hold you in the highest esteem, championing the cause and helping the Children of Earth come to terms with the fact that we are one and the same! We hold no grudges and we enable a grand connection of minds to set you free.

Why would you hold a grudge and for what?

Once upon a time, long ago, there was a Star Ship enterprise that found its way across the universe, developing and overseeing projects on Earth below. We set great store in our mission on Earth for she was cultivated as a breeding ground for a new race of mortals known as 'humans'. We intercepted at a level in keeping with our policies, advising on protocols as and when necessary to keep the peace. We allowed at intervals a certain propagation of species, unrelated to the human population and this became to all intents and purposes a scientific study, which resulted in a multi-cultural society. We initiated a raw understanding of what can be achieved on a grand scale across the world, decorating the hearts and minds of mankind with an overpowering sense of Love and companionship, working together in harmony.

Then what happened?

We sampled many problematic conditions that caused our decline. We became to all intents and purposes a nation of child molesters, leaving our hearts empty and cold, raining down abuse and mistrust on a grand scale - causing our demise! There was the necessity of a grand cleansing and to this end we relieved you of your shortcomings! We have prepared for such events in the near future and we protect you from yourselves, motioning you to tread a more meaningful pathway. We enlighten you to the ways and means of achieving success with deeper harmony, expressing ourselves in a way that will challenge the establishment in more ways than one! We have challenged you to accept these conditions as a way forward and we antagonise a nation in distress, addressing those very issues that surface for recognition once more!

We are open for discussion and allow you to present your views on this subject! We are allotted a time frame that represents Earth long ago and we aim to refurbish you with all necessary data to accommodate the nation as a whole. We are well prepared and we assist you in this departure from ordinary linear mode to a time warp of considerable success! We blatantly take the bull by the horns and deliver in timely fashion a most benevolent study of the human race. It gives us great pleasure to come to your aid and we give thanks for

115

this opportunity to put things right. We most definitely do not want a repeat performance of past mistakes and sanction a retrieval of energies to populate our new world. We are reconditioned to accept the impossible and we re-stake our claim of everlasting Love and Peace on Earth. There is much to overcome and we are doing our best to make this connection stronger and more vibrant so that you will see with your own eyes - your physical eyes! We reel back the curtain and allow you to see us as we truly are - it is a bold statement to make but we 'will' honour this!

∞

I didn't think we would be able to meet up for trance group this week because of freezing weather conditions but today is slightly warmer. I made soup for everyone and we chatted for a while before settling down for meditation. It was a very emotional session and I cried as we sent our healing energies around the globe. Afterwards I sat in trance state and the group saw an Egyptian lady with big painted eyes who turned my hands palms up, sending out energy to the group which was so intense that it made the entire group's eyes sting.

We descend upon the Earth plane and we bring you joyous blessings! We are indebted to each and every one of you for your thoughts and your compassion, for your Love for one another and for all mankind. We are indebted to your services upon the Earth plane and we cherish you unto us. It has taken many a moon for us to accomplish this gathering and we are most honoured my sisters, most honoured with your presence! We take it upon ourselves to issue you with certain guidelines, which we hope you will take on board for it has come to our attention there have been certain disturbances of spirit.

Can you explain about the disturbances of spirit please?

We are allowed to portray our good wishes for mankind and we gather together in strength and energy to help overcome malfunctions on the Earth plane at this time. We ask that you gather together as often as you are able to allow this reconditioning.

Are you speaking of several groups or this group in particular?

116

We are speaking of all those who gather together in the name of the 'One Universal Source'. We beckon you forward to do your duty and we gather together to give you the strength for this service. We are indebted to you as always and we empower you to take hold strong and fast, listening to your heart as it calls you on. We are growing in numbers and there are vast energy fields to be encapsulated and brought forward so that we may shine our Light. We have broadcast our messages many times on the Earth plane to no avail . . . but we are growing stronger! The Love and the energy is strong within this room and we band together in little groups all around the world, gathering strength in this way, developing the hearts of mankind and taking them forward into the light of true understanding. Be vigilant - bring this Light into your hearts and let it shine and grow, bursting forth with such radiance as it bathes each and every one of you!

We desire to help and we bring alternatives to this present impasse, asking that you bide your time in this assessment. There have been certain difficulties that have taken their toll on all concerned and we rectify disturbances of spirit, helping you to adjust on an even keel. We have taken the law into our own hands, sanctioning a redressing of issues that have belied a keener understanding of the situation facing us head on. We are allowed a closer look and ask that you partake in a summary of visual effects. We motion you to tread most carefully over these next few weeks and incorporate a condition of trust, opening up the door to greater knowledge. We expressly deliver for your delectation, a sundry example of what can be expected in the near future as we relay our messages back and forth across the great divide. Be aware that we have sanctioned greater demonstrations and we will deliver as promised in the near future.

We are open for further discussions and hope to add to these gatherings a grander expertise, enabling channellings of excellence. We depend as always for you to get our message across, loud and clear, and we enable a massive imbalance to right itself very soon. We are prone to intervals of great sadness and we set the matter to rights, adjudicating at every level. We have masterminded a key objective and take you to the limitless wonder of the skies and beyond. All is there for the taking and we mesmerise a world in deep distress,

117

asking that you obey our directives right down to the last chilling episode on Earth! We have come from a much broader spectrum and we deliver by hand all that is necessary for your evolution, taking mankind to the final frontier and beyond. We come to assist in this passage home and we tantalise the senses, invigorating each cell in your bod, mass producing an energy flow that will take you to realms of delight. We are well prepared and we exhibit the gift God has given, making an obvious statement to our peers and contemporaries. We register what is in your hearts and minds and we take you to a time of undiluted bliss!

∞

At today's group I felt a strong, masculine energy draw close and leaned forward, rubbing my hands together.

Welcome, welcome, welcome . . . there's much work to be done, much work, and we are happy to see you here!

Thank you, we're very happy to be here!

There have been a few problems to sort out but I think we have . . . yes I think we have managed this in more ways than one and we are delighted to see you back on track! It is an honour and a privilege to work with you all and we look forward to that day when we can say with hands on heart that we have done our job - and done it well! We bow down to your expertise and ask that you stand firm at this time. It has been a long and wearisome road that we travel but there is a Light that we all work towards.

A different energy then came forward with a feminine, higher voice.

We intercept to broadcast this message - we are grateful for the upkeep of this facility and we bring you our blessings. It is with great humility that we come to work with you and we enhance our connection with the unseen. We delve deeper and deeper into the unknown and we expose many a raw nerve bringing you to fruition.

I reached out my hands in prayer position, pointing towards one of the group and then opened them up to see a little golden orb of light in my palms.

Take this offering with our Love . . . all will be well! *Thank you.*

I then turned to the other member with hands in prayer position and opened my palms to her also.

And to you, great daughter of Light, we wish you well on your journey of the highest intent - may God be with you! *Thank you.*

It is written and shall be so! We are greatly interested in the proceedings here this afternoon and we welcome you one and all to this our gathering of like-minded souls. We have been many times before and it gives us great pleasure to be here today. We have had to make a few adjustments but on the whole we are doing very well. It is nearly time . . . nearly time, there is great excitement and joy on the horizon as we welcome in a new stream of thought, a new and vibrant energy coming closer and closer . . . we are very excited! We adjust to this phenomenon and ask that you draw close in times of stress.   We are all powerful . . . all knowing and all seeing and we help you adjust to these frequencies to give you strength.

Thank you. Will we see and feel things with this new stream of energy that is coming into our world - actually physically?

There is a great and powerful energy coming amongst you even as we speak!

Yes I can sense the energy . . . there is a feeling of serenity and I can see Angel wings behind Eileen.

Let your thoughts drift . . . let your minds drift and feel that energy around you . . . awaken to the power of thought. Project your senses, project your energy . . . all will unfold before your eyes!

There was a long time spent with different face changes, then one of the group voiced that spirit were doing very well and they answered: -

119

We are growing accustomed to her face!

Gradually, week by week, we are all being prepared for the work we will be doing in the future. We are here to anchor the Light and help mankind adjust to the frequencies being sent to help with their ascension. My increased sensitivity to different frequencies became apparent while out shopping recently. My husband and I stopped to look at some new televisions and there were so many that I just couldn't cope with the energy emitting from them all. It was causing such a pain in my chest and throat that I had to rush out of the store to catch my breath. That is why it is so important to regularly cleanse yourselves and Earth of negative energies. Below is a beautiful healing meditation that benefits every person along with Mother Earth.

Healing Meditation for Mother Earth

I walked around my sanctuary calling to the four directions along with Grandfather Sky and Grandmother Earth, cleansing with the burning of white sage.

Spirit of the East where the Sun rises - gateway to the sun and the element fire – we ask that you ENLIGHTEN US.

Spirit of the South where the Sun is at its strongest - gateway to our feelings and emotions and the element water – we ask that you EMPOWER US.

Spirit of the West where the Sun sets - gateway to the physical and the element earth – we ask that you TRANSFORM US.

Spirit of the North, where the Sun rests - gateway to the mind and the element air – we ask that you INFORM US.

Grandfather Sky - masculine forces behind all that is – we ask that you EMPOWER US.

Grandmother Earth - feminine forces behind all that is – we ask that you NURTURE US.

After cleansing your sacred space in whatever way is right for you, visualise a shimmering ball of Golden Light coming down from above your crown chakra and flooding your very being, cleansing you of all negativity and re-energising you. Visualise this 'Golden Light' literally pouring into your skull, brain and spinal cord - into your blood and bones, into your muscles and every organ of your body, visualising a cleansing and healing process taking place, creating peace and harmony.

See golden roots growing from your feet and send them deep down into Mother Earth. Push your roots down through the soil and into the layers of rock, down through the pools and lakes and water falls beneath Earth's crust, down into the crystalline caves. Push those roots further and further down into the deepest recesses of Earth, sending Love to other life forms that we do not see and who may feel forgotten! Now reach out those roots all around the globe connecting with other 'Light' workers, feel that connection growing in other towns and countries all around the world and see that pattern of Love growing stronger.

Spend some time in the network of tunnels if you so wish and explore, this too can lead into many wonderful journeys.

When you are happy, bring your attention back to your roots, bringing them up to your feet and continue with the golden energy climbing up through the trunk of your body as if it were a tree - the tree of life! Bring the golden energy back up through your chakras, flooding each one and creating a rainbow of light. Visualise your branches reaching out to the cosmos, reaching out to connect with those Star beings who work to help mankind. As you look down upon the beautiful sphere that is planet Earth, visualise a Golden canopy of Light enveloping her and very gradually see that canopy melting into fine droplets of liquid energy, falling through Earth's atmosphere.
See that magic potion of Love falling down through the heavens and into the oceans . . . into the mountain streams . . . into the lakes, rivers and ponds – into every drop of water upon this

121

planet, purifying and healing with every drop. See those golden droplets falling onto the land, healing the soil in which our food grows - see a healing taking place in everything that grows, and for the myriad different life forms that inhabit Earth.

See also that Golden Light entering the hearts of all mankind that they may Love one another and be at peace with their brethren from all walks of life and from all around the world. When you are ready, bring that energy back down once more flooding through your crown chakra and back into your heart. Take time to sit within this sacred space and feel the connectedness and bliss within your heart, and if you then want to sit for communication with guides and inspirers, invite those from the Light to join you. Open your heart wide - take in the Love and the healing you so richly deserve. Go within and listen to that still small voice that echoes in your mind - listen and take note.

I always keep a pen and pad with me and also set up a digital voice recorder so as not to lose any precious information coming in from the higher dimensions. During my last session of using this meditation I was shown a circle of children from every country in the world, they were all holding hands, encircling the globe, laughing with joy and happiness.

∞

Circles within circles, waves of energy transmitting to you, these are conditions which we liken to benevolent thought streams, crossing the universe. There has been a tampering of services and we broadcast our messages on a frequency more suited to our condition. We have laboured long and hard to get our message across precisely and we are deluged with material coming in to us from the higher realms. We have promised that we shall honour this connection and we vouch for your safe arrival in this world. We broaden our horizons and point you in the right direction, allowing this stream of thought to gather momentum. We enable the masses to take on board a vibrant array of information that we have governed from afar and we ask you to take all this in your stride. We open up a new portal, discovering all the ways of life in a new connection. We have obeyed those inner instincts that beckon us on and we broadcast these messages so that you may understand what we are about. We enable a massive expansion of minds across the universe and we ask that you stand firm and help us in our endeavours at this time. We have come at a time of the quickening of mankind and we are united as one in this endeavour, broadcasting our messages to all those who will listen. Remember us in your prayers!

∞

Today I felt myself bowing down with hands together in salutation, my guide then held out his hands to the group sending energy for quite some time before bowing down very low.

We have the weight of the world upon our shoulders when all around you is Light. Take heart little ones, all is not lost. We are governed by a wider band of energy and we open our hearts to that Divine Love welcoming you into the fold. Be not alarmed or dismayed at events taking place at this time, for we are with you always and forever more. We open our hearts and minds to receive the wisdom and guidance that is there for you all and we all learn, little by little what is needed to overcome the turmoil that is ever present in your world. We are beholden to you for attending these meetings, for listening with open hearts and minds, attentive to what we have to say.   We listen to you also - we listen to your hearts and to the answers you constantly seek. You bring much joy to us and we open our arms to enfold you in our loving care.

At this point I opened my arms to the group, swaying with the flow of energy.

We bend and sway to that Divine outpouring of Love and we receive each and every one of you, tending to your needs from near and far. There has been a great outpouring of anguish in recent months and we have noted the heaviness in the hearts of mankind at issues that are surfacing at this time. We ask you to have great restraint - be prepared! We issue these guidelines for you to be in readiness for that time when you take your rightful place with us among the stars. We warmly greet you and give you our blessings! We saddle the horses and make ready for our journey for there is much to be done and we prepare for a great event on the horizon.

We believe the time is right for a refresher course that will help you to understand your true connections to your ancestors. We have been mealy mouthed of late for we need to have you in the right place at the right time to make the connections that will grow and prosper. There is a circle forming, a larger connection that will bring you closer as like-minded souls. We prepare you and deliver the energy needed to bring you all to fruition and we feel that connection within our hearts, welcoming you back into the fold once more. Prepare yourself for this journey, arm yourself with Love of the highest intent and we will win through the dark and the turmoil that reigns on Earth at this time. We will restore Earth to her former glory . . . we have the power to do this with your help and all those around the world, who link with us just as you do!

That's heartening to know, thank you.

We will bring back that loving connection between you all around the globe, joining hands and uniting as one. We are connected to that Supreme energy source in the most loving connection. We breathe upon you the gift of 'life ever after' and you will become 'whole' in the truest sense. We nurture you and uplift your spirits so that you may conquer over those miniscule problems that assault you in your earthly lives. It is nothing compared with that magnitude of Light that is there for you to tap into. Remember - nothing is impossible!

I cupped my hands and held them out to my two friends in our small group.

We bring to you the cup of loving kindness and ask you to accept our blessings. We look forward to when we shall gather together once more - restored and in good health!

At one point I felt I was rocking and also have the recollection of stroking a golden mane of rough hair, which I feel is my Lion guide. At the end I saw a huge circle of white Light above us, shining down upon our group.

124

It is now 10th June 2011 (1+0+6+2+0 +1+1 = 11.

Eleven is a master number that carries a powerful vibration.

We are sheltered from the bleak winds that blow and we muster the necessary ingredients that will take us forward. Please act with the utmost courtesy and respect for we are given to many idle speculations and we profoundly accept that all is in accordance with Divine aspirations.

We shall see a time of great demise and we take you to a place of safety, registering the thoughts of an entire nation under duress. We prepare for a greater state of being and allow you to express yourselves in open forum. It is not for us to say how we will manage our accounts, however, suffice it to say we will be there at your side, expressing ourselves with joy at your acceptance. May the Divine essence of Love be with you now and forever more!

The nature of our work impedes us from time to time and although this holds us back, we have learnt many things that shall stand us in good stead. The future is written and shall be so my friends! We delight in these little tasks for they take us to a new level, dictating the pace we shall use and encouraging you to not lose heart. Sweet dreams little one, sweet dreams!

The next morning as I woke these words filtered through.

We are impelled to draw you close and vouch your safe return. It is with great respect and courtesy that we enter this arena and we have challenged you at every turn, recognising in you a true warrior spirit! It is time now to put down your armour and listen to that inner voice beckoning you on; we have been accepted back into the fold and motion you to tread most carefully. Be compassionate at all times, respect that inner reserve and debunk issues that hold you back from marching forward with a loving heart. We prepare for a massive onslaught of energies and know you will honour this connection, taking us to the sublime.

Fellowship of the human race is what we aim for and transformation of the highest order and we delegate this responsibility to those on Earth who have the ability to follow our lead. Feel the strength we bring you, open your arms to receive us as we bear witness to a greater understanding. We fulfill a prophecy and open our hearts and minds to accept the truth - the unmistakable truth of whom we are and where we come from! We come from God himself and it has been known for eons that we take great joy in ushering in a time of immense pleasure for one and all. We rock the boat at times to alleviate the pressure building and this is our way of deepening our channels, accepting the bonds of friendship that we have acknowledged as the norm. We now deliver a broader knowledge that can be accepted by the masses and we beg you to deliver our words, so that we may shine forth that Light and be noted for our deeds . . . for our Love and for our expertise in these matters. We take it to the top and salvation shall be yours and yours . . . and yours!

We have great respect for our brothers and sisters on Earth and we initialise a most daring episode known to man, this will come in the form of a mammoth uptake of services right across the world. We initialise this great response so that we may have your blessings as we proceed to take the Children of Earth on a journey . . . a wondrous journey! We have made this announcement at a time when the truth should be known; we specialise in truths of this nature and we deliberately request an alliance that will help us to form a bonding of energies, necessary to make this work. We shelter you from harm in every instance, beckoning you to draw closer to us and we hold you up, giving you inner reserves of strength and energy unprecedented!

We take great exception to being called 'Aliens' because we are the epitome of Love! We are those winged creatures you call to when all else is lost! We are Joy . . . we are Peace . . . we are a haven to share your worries and inadequacies, helping you overcome your anxieties on the Earth plane. We accept with resignation that there are bound to be adjustments - we know this! We do not expect you to accept the impossible and we make it obvious to those who stand on the side-lines that we hold out our hands to you all, offering you succour. We offer

126

you our friendship and our Love; we offer you our hearts and our minds. It is true that we are stuff of 'fairy tales' and visions but we have always been here watching over you and we shelter you as best we can from yourselves! It is man's inhumanity to his own kind that has caused such misery, such illness, such dis-ease . . . for you are hell bent on destroying yourselves! We wish you no harm, our greatest wish is that you desist from hurting yourselves . . . our wish is that you to take up that mantle of Light to protect yourselves!

We see great treachery ahead and we draw close to offer our assistance. We are bound on a course of self-destruction and we tell it to you now - we will suffer no interference from those who have cast a dark shadow across Earth! We are here to take up the challenge of spreading Light into the furthest corners and recesses of the world. We will shine our Light so that everyone will have a choice, leaving no stone unturned until we have rooted out the darkness and evil that seeps into Earth's framework. We radiate Light so all may know the truth and we banish the darkness, bringing forth wisdom and joy unsurpassed! We envelop you in a special brand of eloquence that will allow you to prosper and we make ourselves known in the far corners of the world, taking on board the plight of the human race.

∞

At the opening of today's group an Egyptian lady wearing a golden necklace drew close.

It is an honour and a blessing to meet you all once more. We have encouraged you to gather together for evenings such as this and we are so proud our promptings have enabled these meetings, gaining even more clarity as we speak to you!

Thank you, we enjoy these evenings as well.

We have opened up this channel that we may abide by the rules given to us from those on high and it has come to our understanding there has been a blessings ceremony! We are well supported on all sides

127

and we open up your vision, allowing you to express yourselves with even greater clarity. We motion you to accept the impossible for all shall be revealed to you in due course. We open up that well of knowledge that boundless well, which is there for all who seek and we are overjoyed sisters that you have made this journey and have come thus far! There is so much to explore, so much in front of you waiting to unfold; we have pondered long and hard on this fraternity, this soul group brought into manifestation and we prepare you to accept even greater glories. The heavens shall open and bestow upon us their blessings and one by one you shall kneel and be anointed as the chosen ones! We respect you and honour you . . . we bow down before you and salute you. You are most cherished . . . most Loved!

At this point I was shown the Sun, huge and low on the horizon.

Bathed in the light of Ra, we come before you and offer you our blessings! *Thank you for coming.*

A different energy with a smaller face drew near and I felt it was my oriental lady named Sayuri. I put my head to one side in a shy way and laid my cheek upon my folded hands before starting to sing.

Happy, happy talking happy talk - talk about things you like to do. If you don't have a dream, if you don't have a dream - how you going to have a dream come true!

We like to hear your laughter - it makes us feel so happy! Blending with the energies is so wonderful, such a joyous experience for all of you to partake.

At this point a bird flew by tittering.

Even the birds are laughing . . . we are so very happy to be here with you and our hearts take flight, like the bird on the wing. We do so enjoy your company and we help our sitter here feel the peace that is necessary for us all to work closely together. We need these times of stillness in this busy world of yours with everybody rushing here there and everywhere! There is a need to find that stillness, a space for peace and quiet to feel that gentility within your breast. It is there, it is there within you all but you won't find it if you're rushing about! You 'need' to sit . . . to sit and be quiet! *Thank you.*

Even this lady . . . it is hard to make her sit and be still at times!

My favourite track began to play with sounds of the sea lapping onto shore.

Ah she likes this music . . . the sea can be very tranquil. It can also be tumultuous! It is very powerful . . . it is cleansing and purifying. We are overpowered with your successes of late and it brings us great joy, you all have come on so well. There is still much more to do but if we can make that necessary contact, we can make it work on a far larger scale and you will be surprised; you will look back in six months from now and be surprised at the progress you have all made!

Ooh exciting times ahead!

Yes, but do find those quiet times where we can recharge your batteries for you, where we can sooth that troubled brow. Sit and feel us . . . feel us stroking you and caressing you, feel us bringing that 'Love' around you that you all so richly deserve! We feel it is time to take our leave.

Thank you for coming and thank you for your words of wisdom.

You are most welcome!

∞

11.11.11 - *I woke in the early hours and sat for communication.*

We activate a vision shared by many on the Earth plane and it is with great advantage that we tend to you now. There has been a broadening of energies taking place and we instigate a fine network of channels right across the globe. It is with greater understanding and determination that we follow our hearts, and we supply further measures that will take you forward on this beam of Light. Be

129

prepared and we will embark on a new trail of Love and joy, opening up vistas appertaining to the enlightenment of mankind. We have braced ourselves against the elements and transcend a wide range of household duties. We have not forgotten those of you who have defied the very laws of gravity to be here with us now and we superimpose our thoughts on yours to deliver what is necessary. We alleviate pressure building at this time and thank you for your endeavours!

We make the most of what time there is in purposeful pursuits and have arranged a new connection that shall make things easier. We rally round and protect you from yourself and there is further need to remind you of your promise to us! We shall not back down in this and we ask you, in all sincerity, to aspire to those higher planes of Light; we will not give up our place amongst the esteemed and we now deliver our most prized and treasured possession.

Frailty of spirit has led us further astray and we take it upon ourselves to offer you these guidelines, honouring our connection with the unseen. We broadcast on a band wave of frequency that can be accepted and initialise further acceptance by updating neural pathways, documenting our departure and accessing data stored in our memory banks. All in all we have emerged as the 'New Human'!

At this point I was shown Leonardo da Vinci's famous drawing of 'Vitruvian Man'.

What you are effectively doing is retracing your steps back through time and this will assist us to make that connection which is most necessary at this time in your evolution. We beckon you further forward to do your duty and we know you will see it makes sense, it is the only solution and we help wherever possible suggesting a biodegrade that will make us obsolete! We ensure greater clarity in the proceedings and ask you to check and double check in all areas of self-loathing and regret. We terminate this contract when all are safely aboard and in a good state of health! We monopolise certain situations where we have outgrown our use!

130

I wasn't too sure of this content and answered – I want information from only the highest Divine source. If you are not from the Light and the highest Divine source then please leave now!

It is regrettable that in these situations there is no one to challenge us, but we are prepared for a summarising of energies that have catapulted us into this scenario! We come from beyond the rainbow, from the highest Light of Divine intervention, and we beam you aboard in moments of stress for a decontamination process. We have opened up the floodgates and let you through and we align with those Star Beings that work closely with us at all times. We are far beyond your comprehension at this time and we supply you with means of entry into our dimension, programming and analysing further data necessary for your perusal of our energy systems. We have grown fond of our counterparts on Earth and we welcome you aboard in the truest sense.

We are governed by our thoughts and feelings at this time and we commission you, supplying you with an energy field that will register our true intent for the upkeep and sanity of mankind as a whole. We delve deeper and deeper into the anomalies presented before us, allowing in those instances of repression a formidable overturning of events that have given cause for concern. We beg you to assess each situation as and when presented, analysing fully to understand what it is we are offering you! We welcome you aboard with open arms and prepare you to access this new dimension - a higher state of existence in a new framework of time and space. We beam you to a new frequency and invite you all to share with us in this vibrant new world of loving energy beyond compare, a world governed by Love where no man will be tempted to hold sway over another. Little by little you will learn to accept us as we are . . . true and devoted companions to those on Earth.

These words were accompanied by vivid purple overlaid with beautiful golden patterns, which put my mind to rest.

We are forever in your debt and we treasure these moments spent with you. We are needed on a new frequency that will give us greater

131

access to the hearts and minds of mankind. It has been a long time coming and we are most appreciative of the time you have spent attending to our words. We have intercepted the physical to be here with you now and we trust in this time approaching, sanctioning each and every clause that comes our way. We extend the hand of friendship as we step into the ethereal, opening up the hub and delving deeper and deeper into the unknown! We transfer our affections to those in the know, asking you to tiptoe through a minefield of events looming on the horizon.

We broadcast on a band wave of frequency that will come to be accepted by all and we tend to your every need from near and far, opening the gateways as you reach them. Behold the brightening of a new dawn that brings in its wake the most treasured possession of all, LIFE in all its glory, in all its preciousness, in all its vitality and strength of purpose! We will prevail and we shall see the opening of this doorway and we shall gather you to us in deep embrace, reconnecting at the heart centre. Our destiny waits in a cloud of transformation! *Thank you friends*

I'm feeling peace . . . perfect peace and am being bathed in clouds of vivid purple and gold.

∞

Again in the early hours I felt the urge to leave my bed and transcribe the words flooding my mind.

You ponder on what will happen in the future and we stretch our arms out far and wide to give you sustenance. We break down the barriers that keep us apart and sanction a renewal, allowing further trepidations to materialise as we cast down our veil of remembrance. We penetrate the mists of time and embrace you, trembling with excitement at this breakthrough, this evolvement of the soul that has enabled free expression. We are forever in your debt, allowing our discourse at this unearthly hour!

We have great regard for those compatriots who rise to the challenge and we rely on you to set the record straight. We tread most carefully and thoughtfully, betraying our emotions with a tear or two in the proceedings, giving vent in extraordinary outpourings of the soul under duress. We challenge you to a thought provoking and time consuming study; please allow us these anomalies for we predict in a few years' time we shall have climbed out of the pit of suffering and despair, raising awareness on a grand scale across the world!

We have forecast this measure of acceptance in the population as a whole and with great trepidation we follow in the footsteps of the esteemed, marching as Family of Light, broadcasting our messages to all who will listen. We come armed with Love, purely and simply, a guiding force to be reckoned with in its supremacy . . . unchecked and unbridled Love Divine. We spread our Light across the Earth, searching out the darkness and despair, leading the way to greater clarity and freedom of expression. LOVE is the answer . . . LOVE is the key . . . LOVE is the answer to save humanity! We brighten your day sending out rays of Love . . . preparing for your homecoming!

Do you mean my life on Earth for me is ending in the physical sense? Am I going to die soon and leave my family behind?

No my child . . . hush now! We simply prepare you and those like you, who want something more than this 'existence' on the Earth plane and we prepare you for a new venture opening up on the horizon in all its glory. We accept every man, woman and child into our domain and protect you from yourselves! It is with great reverence that we descend amongst you to bring you our blessings; we motivate you to accept the impossible and to learn our ways. We transcend the impossible and fulfill our expectations of a new lease of life in a new framework of time and space!

Are you in a parallel dimension to us?

We are in keeping with the laws of the universe and allow you to ponder on this deliverance as we negotiate a plan of assistance that will set you free. We have no doubt in our minds that this will cause some concern, but we have vowed your safety in all aspects, replenishing you with a vibrant life force that shall sustain your energy fields and revitalise your life forms to coincide with ours.

What do you mean, can you be more specific?

We mean to take you on a great expedition and we raise the
frequency of the planet and her inhabitants, forestalling negative
emotions that hold us back from salvation. We all knowing and all
seeing and we expand your senses to accept the impossible, to sustain
our frequency and to be restored in mind, body and spirit. It is by no
mistake that we have taken the reins to guide you, our most beloved
brothers and sisters, and we tend to your needs from afar registering
your hopes and desires.   We fulfill our destiny to shine like the
brightest star and we will not hold you back from becoming 'Homo
Luminous' beings, recovering your rightful place beside us and your
birth-right of life eternal!

*Afterwards I raised my arms up, thanking the energies which were very tall,
sensing they were the Earth Keepers who watch over Earth and her inhabitants.*

*It was Dr. Alberto Villoldo who founded the 'Four Winds Society' to bring the
teachings of Munay-ki to the world. Dr Villoldo explains the Earth Keeper's
Rite is the seventh rite from the Munay-ki - a Quechua word that means 'I Love
You' - it connects us to the Archangels who are guardians of our galaxy. The
Earth Keepers are stewards of all life on the Earth and come under the direct
protection of these Archangels. This rite connects us to the stars and to the Sun,
our local Star. It helps us learn the ways of the seer and to dream the world into
being.*

∞

*I have a trance group today and rose early to prepare. While meditating I was
shown a lady with dark hair who was wearing a kimono; she looked older than
my young guide named Sayuri. We were agreeing how important it is to open up
for communication properly . . . not to do it hurriedly but to enjoy the connection
process.*

There is an opening . . . a connection purported to be of the most
high and we instigate a finer atunement, preparing for that frequency
needed to maintain these transmissions of high importance.   There

has been a severity of conditions looming on the horizon and we wish to be more specific, enabling you to understand our mission as being one of great advantage. We sanction a visit from those on high, announcing our intentions to set the record straight - and we are of one mind in this! We enable a grand connection, opening our portfolio and describing for you our latest measures of achievement in the higher realms. We are preparing for a grand course of action that will penetrate the hearts and minds of all who listen, and we ask that you listen to that inner voice that beckons you on . . . listen with an open mind and listen with an open heart!

We suppress a certain madness that has manifested itself among many on the Earth plane and we are subject to this frequency being put on hold in a variety of manners. This is because this frequency cannot always be held in certain conditions and we aim, wherever necessary, to withhold the barrage of indiscreet and sometimes morbid assumptions as to where our allegiances lie! We have on the whole forecast a most necessary formulation of ideas, which have been tried and tested on many occasions in the past. We allow a certain fortitude in the days and weeks ahead, formulating a new enterprise and governing a wider energy field that can be transmuted to a finer level than ever before. We believe this will improve your progress one hundred per cent and we rally round to give our assistance in this, prising a certain amount of information from those who rub shoulders with the esteemed.

We begin to deliver a more popular exercise and this will serve us to regulate and manufacture all memorandums of the utmost eloquence and artistry of thought! We beg to differ on certain points of view but that shall not hold us back from assisting you and delivering a most novel enterprise. We rally round and take your hand, asking that you withstand local abuse and suffer no interferences that could hold you back. We are safely ensconced in the Love of the Divine. Peace be with you!

∞

There are just three of us sitting for trance development today and the room felt peaceful and still, yet with a buzz of excitement to it as I tuned in.

135

We are much delighted with your progress!

I held out my hands to the group as if giving an offering. One of them focused on my solar plexus and saw what looked like a large snail shell and then a silver bearded man with his arms around a woman and child. Another saw the figure of Atlas holding up the world and at this point in the recording I raised my arms in the air and leaned over, encircling the world in my lap as if protecting it. I actually felt I was spreading my wings around the Earth to protect her and keep her safe!

We protect you and watch you grow!

I then felt impelled to move my arms slowly up and down as an Eagle in flight.

We are 'Soothsayers Extraordinaire' and we venture forth on this beam of Light to give you our help and the expertise where it is needed, where it is accepted and where we can begin to make a difference in your world! We come armed with Love . . . Love Divine and we are most honoured to make your acquaintance. Bright blessings upon you both! Oh such joy . . . oh such fun . . . we shall have some grand times together! It is all coming together as was planned long ago and we are delighted with the upkeep of these services. We are beholden to you and yours for allowing us this time, this space, this connectedness that brings us much joy! We beam to you on a band wave of frequency that will unfold in due course, and we allow these energies to manifest so that we may prepare each and every one of you. The expansiveness of this plan is to aid mankind in their illumination and we register your just intent to help us along this highway of Love. We make an opening that will allow a greater proportion of people to understand and we prepare you to accept with open hearts and minds. We shower you with our blessings and give you the strength to go forward - take our Love and use it wisely. We are accepted into the clan . . . into the Fellowship of Light!

∞

Chapter nine

We prepare for a shift in frequencies

Sitting with my group today I'm being shown an African lady who is wearing a colourful scarf wrapped around her head.

We show you the way of the 'Wisdom Keepers' and we broadcast what is necessary at this time to help you all go forward into the mysteries of Earth. We are well positioned to emulate a new catalogue of thoughts and expressions that will help us to get our message across more clearly and precisely, we have therefore documented new evidence that we shall give you. There is a time of great enterprise in the foreseeable future, a time for broadening our horizons and making adjustments wherever necessary. We categorise our thoughts and feelings, summarising our achievements in the past decade.

I can see another person coming forward now - an Aborigine with very wiry hair who is wearing a grass skirt and holding a long spear.

We challenge you to accept our offerings, meagre as they may be, and we challenge you to accept what we say as truth! We readjust our settings and accept the impossible and it is with great courage that we step onto this platform of Light. This is the age of acceptance and we are reminded of long ago when we held in our hands the fountain of youth!

I had the sense of sitting high up on a dais, like the Gods in Greek mythology. In my lap there lay what looked like sticks of some kind, and I seemed to be watching the world throughout the ages, seeing war and destruction! Someone in the group sensed the words - 'the weight of our ancestors' and had an image of bones.

We are predisposed to accept that man has followed his own course and allowed this destruction to manifest. We are doing all we can to set you on the right pathway!

I then seemed to be reliving an event of some kind on Earth.

There is so much grief and so much sorrow . . . we try our hardest but they will not listen, they will not open their minds, they will not open their hearts. We send out a call to the heavens and ask for help, but help will not come and yet still we call! We try to do our best for our children, for our grandchildren and for those that follow on. We will never give up . . . We will never desist from doing our utmost to help change this world for the better. It is barren . . . nothing will grow . . . we wring our hands!

A member of our group spoke. Instead of calling outwards for help, try to create your own reality by intending that things grow, by intending the earth is full of nutrition. I am trying to explain the connectedness - I'm not doing very well, I'm sorry!

We thank you for your help friend. We are trying to show you . . . to paint a picture of how it has been.   We try to show you what mankind has witnessed in the past - for what has gone before that we do 'now' have some control of in our lives here today. The past the present and the future are all intertwined - we are as you say a part of the whole. There are two sides to the coin - we learn from our mistakes and pioneer our way across the void!

Is it possible for us to send healing thoughts back to what could be considered the past, although there is some debate as to whether the past, present and future actually exist in that order. But can we do things in this lifetime to heal previous lifetimes?

Yes - that is what we are hoping to achieve! We send our 'Love and Light' back and forth, enveloping all dimensions - all time frames. We are 'all' here to help wherever we can and not just in our waking state. We travel far and wide, finding those connections where we can help and where we can make a difference. We are not trying to spread

138

doom and gloom - we are only trying to help you to see the whole picture! We register that your hearts are true . . . we feel the Love that radiates from you and we want to hold you in our embrace. The message is LOVE pure and simple - Love will hold us together and we enfold you in our Love and blessings at this time.

∞

At our group today, I'm being shown a man I've never seen before with full face and long grey hair. I think he may be from the 'Wild West' as he has a large grey moustache.

We are indebted to your perseverance Ma'am and we come to your aid, bringing you transactions that shall enable a crossing over of boundaries. We instigate a wider retrieval of services and come to your aid, asking for forgiveness for atrocities committed long ago!

Are you speaking of the massacre of the Indian population?

We do indeed represent that particular time frame that was barbaric to say the least! We have forgiven our cousins who came to court disaster and we spread the news of life eternal. This has been our main undertaking and we are granted access to these dimensions, overseeing and propelling you forward to greener pastures. This has been an arduous journey and one that we have shared on this rollercoaster of emotions. We are now coming to a time of unparalleled success and it is within this allotted time frame that we shall reap the greatest rewards. We perpetuate a species that has become very dear to us and we envelop you in our Love and expertise, initialising that thrust forward into a new dimension of time and space. We oversee this project from near and far, promising you a renewal of services that shall begin in due course. We are open to debate on various aspects of this discourse and we vow to you that we shall overcome all scenarios of doom and gloom, radiating our message out into the universe for you to take collection.

We are most honoured to make this connection and we deliver to you by hand a monumental study of the human race. We are bound to accept under jurisdiction given from most high and we are impelled to seek an alternative to this present impasse. We have motioned you to seek the connections that will stand you in good stead and we propel you forward to do your duty, allowing time for a breathing space that will give us more clout in the world of men. We are understandably at a loss for words at this time, but we beseech you to maintain your direction as we are on course for a lost world. With this prelude, we resurrect a dream for all mankind and we allow the truth to trickle through.

I'm being shown water just trickling through a crack and each little drop is plopping slowly into a pool of knowledge, like little pearls of wisdom.

We are preparing a space for you to rest and accumulate the energies needed for your transmissions.

I feel there is a shuffling into place; everybody is being put into their correct place to allow this to happen.

We have mounted a guard for your protection at all times and your resilience is effectively paying off!

I'm now being shown a little girl with long plaits who is wearing a 'girl guide' uniform.

We are preparing for a massive onslaught of energies coming your way soon; we take this all in our stride and prepare you for greater fortitude in the days and weeks to come. We have manifested a great array of services that will help you with your endeavours and we match like for like in all we do. We do, however, pointedly resist any manoeuvres of outlandish behaviour that inflict harm or dread! We relay various directives that have been passed along for your perusal and we open the floodgates, specifying at each turn what is needed to keep us steadfastly on course. We have dedicated our lives to the cause, sacrificing our own needs for the needs of others. Radically speaking, we have made this connection at a time of changing attitudes and we are bound to state our case, improving our connection and monitoring our depositions with greater scrutiny.

140

The aforesaid has been petitioned so that we may attract a wider audience and we are noted for our success! We impinge on a desecrated society, holding up the fort and summoning the courage to take that next step forward. We are proud of all your endeavours and we motion you to accept this undertaking, carrying it through with glowing colours.

As I prepared to close our session I was shown a huge, golden sun sinking into the ocean and had the urge to reach up and spread my arms in a wide arc.

This is a time of undiluted bliss and we thank you for it. It is with great pleasure we master these connections and bring forth the words for all to hear. We trust that you have all enjoyed this morning as we bathed in each other's energies. We feel there will be greater openings for you all and we ask you to trust that we will be there with you, shepherding you along in the right direction. We are beholden to the services you have given and with such Love in your hearts . . . for one another and for all mankind. We are open to suggestions on how we may help one another along this pathway of Love and Light, and we motion you to accept those murmurings within your heart . . . listen to them most carefully and you will be surprised what you are capable of in the near future!

The group chorused - 'sounds like interesting times ahead'.

Yes, interesting for all of us on both sides of the veil and this veil is becoming finer, enabling us to reach out to each other more easily. We will work alongside one another and express ourselves with greater clarity, greater fortitude and greater acceptance of all there is. We welcome in those streams of thought that bring us closer together . . . closer to the heart of God. We are much indebted to your services.

I bowed to the group and afterwards they said they had the impression of a woman bathed in golden light, seeing a narrow pyramid of light coming out the top of my head; they also saw a long, false beard, which was common among the Pharaohs.

∞

141

Today I'm sitting with a much larger group. (This is the circle within circles spoken of before in a recent channelling). After taking them through a meditation where healing is sent out to the whole planet, we then sent concentrated healing to the continent of Africa. Afterwards I sat in trance, inviting those working with me to come forward and speak to the group. I sensed a presence with me and could see a bare-chested African who was wearing beads on his arms and around his neck. He was sitting on a big chair in front of the villagers.

We are honoured to make this connection and we thank you for your prayers and for your blessings, they are much welcome! We have donated part of our time in helping you here on Earth and it is with much fortitude that we give you this address. We are indebted to your services for mankind, each and every one of you, and we ask you to step forward into the Light when the time approaches! We have a massive undertaking and we need your strength and your grace, we need your strength of purpose. We partake in this communion of hearts and minds with much reverence and we liken you to little children come to sit before us - to hear our stories of old. And we tell you it is by no chance that you are here for you were all chosen, each and every one of you!

I could see a book on my lap and started to turn the pages over.

It is here in the 'Book of Times' - in the book of times gone past and the book of times to come. We have all been here before and we will again! Our numbers have grown massively right across the globe and we take stock and look with pride at your achievements. You have grown so tall in our estimation; you have done so well and we are most proud of you, our brothers and sisters upon the Earth plane. We magnanimously address you and ask that you take care of the suffering . . . the suffering in your own hearts at this time . . . for you are very important to us. We need you to heal yourselves . . . we need your heart centres to open and to glow with Love Divine. You're doing well but don't forget yourselves.

Shall we open this up? Are there any others who would like to speak . . . to say what is in their heart? Are there any questions you would like to ask or if indeed you would like to come forward and speak

142

too? This is a group for sharing . . . for sharing the wisdom, for sharing the knowledge and for sharing our experiences!

Can I ask a question please? I had a dream a few days ago where I looked out of my window and saw people who were sitting in an amphitheatre, there were several tiers of seating and in the middle of the arena was a very tall person dressed in long, white robes and tall pointed hat; there were also space ships parked on the grass! Are there any very, tall beings like that? Was that somebody I saw or was it my imagination - did it mean something?

The energy working with me started to laugh in a low tone that seemed to come from deep within me. Ho, Ho, Ho!

Of course my child, it is all a matter of perspective! We look around this room and each one of you is different. Some are shorter . . . some are taller . . . some are wider and some are thinner! We all are unique in our own way and YES there are other creatures far out in the far dominions that to you would look very strange, and perhaps ugly, but to them you may look ugly too! There is such a vast array of life that it is hard for you to comprehend this vastness and complexity of 'being'. As you have said amongst yourselves many times, Earth cannot be the 'be all and end all'! We expect that you will see us as we truly are in the not too distant future when you will all have clearer vision!

It sounds exciting!

Indeed we will show you little by little and each step forward you take will bring you nearer to the truth, but this journey is a never ending journey . . . it is not completed in one visit for you then embark on the next stage of your journey! Life is for living to the full . . . life is for loving to the full! Life is for giving . . . life is for receiving . . . it is so wonderful . . . so wonderful! We want to reach our arms around you and hug you all, you are so precious to us, more precious than the stars that shine. And there is so much more to come, so much more to give and to learn and to understand, but you are all trying as hard as you can to look past those obstacles that stand in your way to test you . . . and yet you overcome them, all of you! And even this

143

little one, she does not trust us as much as she should do, it is all a lesson in understanding!

I think we have taken up enough of your time this afternoon because we are all looking forward to a 'sing song'! We are all looking forward to raising the roof and to lifting your vibrations and your hearts . . . to express yourselves in song and so, unless you have any further questions, we will take our leave!

Thank you for coming!

This one is saying, 'let's quit while we're ahead'! So thank you one and all - thank you for the Love that you give and share amongst yourselves and that you give out to the wider world. And we are always there with you to lean on in times of trouble and strife, we have been with you since the beginning of time! Take care my friends, take care!

I was so over the moon with this session as it had gone so smoothly. Afterwards I looked at the Lemurian crystal that I'd taken for support. I had placed it in a tiny Christmas pouch for protection and when I turned it over, there were the words 'Ho, Ho, Ho' printed on the side, which I had forgotten about! At this larger group some have musical instruments and we have taken to singing at the end of each session which lifts our vibrations.

∞

The energies at our trance group this afternoon were very different. There was a hushed quietness and even the candle flames did not flicker or move in any way, as if they had been frozen in time. As I sat for communication, my friends saw blue and lilac lights around my face and throat and then someone saw what looked like a globe in my hand. I felt the urge to lean forward and look towards the corner of the room where one of my friends sat.

We are inquisitive . . . what is it that rests in that corner?

What object are you referring to? I think perhaps the skull!

(This is not a genuine crystal skull but nevertheless, one that has all the features and is transparent).

Do you wish to hold the skull?

Yes, thank you. This is a most interesting lesson . . . we shall see what we shall see!

I was passed the skull and held it in my hands for a few moments before laying it in my lap.

For generation upon generation we have pioneered our way across the universe. We deliver to you now this connection of like minds, gathered together to observe continuity . . . to affect a rebirth of the human race!

I then felt directed to hold my hands over the top of the skull and channel energy into the head, as if I was projecting healing. The room was hushed for quite some time with no comment from any of the group, which is unusual as we usually say how we are feeling or what we are seeing during these sessions. I continued to channel the energy until the communicator spoke once more.

It is with honour we have made this connection. We hope we have not alarmed you or upset you in any way! We predict a lasting friendship between us.

One of the group said they felt the skull was looking directly at them, even though it was facing into the centre of the room. Others became heavy eyed and felt the skull was taking them into the centre of the universe, showing them different images. The energies seemed very intense today and it was certainly an unusual session.

∞

Today there are four of us sitting for communication and before we started the session, I owned up to feeling very melancholy of late. It transpired that my friends had also been experiencing the same malaise and we felt better for sharing, wondering if it had anything to do with the energies coming in at this time. At the end of our session I felt the urge to open my arms and held my left hand with palm up, and my right hand with palm facing out to the group similar to a Buddha pose, sending energy to the group.

We bear witness to a greater evolution and we attend to your on your pathways.

(Our new group member coughed at this point).

Venerable Sister, we watch over you! *Thank you.*

We have experienced the most pleasant of discoveries - we discover a new world!

I then felt a shy feminine energy draw close.

You are all much cherished and loved. Thank you for your service to mankind and to one another . . . we thank you so kindly!

The Chinese lady was holding a musical instrument that looked like a mandolin, and she plucked at the strings with her right hand in a slow fashion, which in my head sounded like Zen music. The girls could see an extra finger by the thumb of my right hand. I then reached across and gently gave the instrument to a member in the group who plays the guitar.

We give this to you! You spread much joy and pleasure on the Earth plane with your music! *Thank you.*

I was then given the image of a blue bowl and reached out to give it to the next member of our group.

And to you my dear . . . we give you sustenance. *Thank you!*

I then felt a white dove nestling in my hands and as its wings began to flutter I tossed it across to our new group member.

And to you Sister . . . the Dove of Peace! We value you all!

Thank you very much, this is most welcome.

146

During this session someone was shown a swarm of bees and also a jaguar. On research I found the bee in ancient Aegean cultures, was believed to be the sacred insect that bridged the natural world to the underworld, appearing in tomb decorations. Bee motifs are also seen in Mayan cultures and in this culture, jaguar represents the West. It is symbolic of renewal and transformation. It is so wonderful that the power of spirit can instil such peace and joy in hearts that are at times weighed down by the worries of the world.

∞

Today I watched over the group while they took turns in channelling and as I prepared to close with a prayer of thanks, I felt my Star friends with me.

Walk tall . . . hold your heads high. You are blessed . . . you are honoured . . . you are special to us. We thank you each and every one!

My communicator clasped my hands in prayer position and bowed to the three group members present.

We bid you farewell! We thank you for the work you have done this morning and many, many times in the distant past. You have opened up that well of knowledge to share with others . . . you have fulfilled your destiny. Our cup overflows . . . the bounty within your hearts shall flow with loving kindness. We have a vision that we would like to share!

I felt impelled to hold out my hands as if holding a crystal ball.

We prepare you for an Earth shattering moment in time when all will come to fruition and we stabilise a volatile situation that would put many to shame on the Earth plane! We watch over you and guide you . . . whispering in your ear. We beckon you to listen with your hearts and minds, helping others along this pathway, coaxing with your wise words and with the Love in your hearts, sheltering those who are lost!

I felt impelled to very slowly draw my hands apart and became aware of balancing them at shoulder height. It felt as if I was spreading out my wings and I stayed in

147

that position for a long time, in fact it was impossible to lower my arms as they seemed to be held in suspended animation.

We wait at the gates of Heaven. We empower you and support you through these turbulent times. We monitor your growth and set you free!

The energy with me then drew my hands back and crossed them over my chest in Egyptian style.

Peace be with you!

The group said my eyes seemed to be open while I spoke. One member saw a hawk like beak that had an Egyptian feel, and another member sensed the name Maat.

Later I found that 'Maat' was the ancient Egyptian concept of truth and balance, law and order, morality and justice; personified as a goddess who regulated the stars and the seasons. Her primary role in Egyptian mythology dealt with the weighing of souls that took place in the underworld. Her feather was the measure that determined whether souls of the departed would reach the paradise of afterlife successfully.

∞

This morning instead of watching the news while eating breakfast, I took a cup of hot lemon juice down to my sanctuary at the bottom of the garden and fed the birds before meditating. I felt my spirit friends draw close.

My beloved, we recognise the constraints of your day and enjoy this moment of bliss with you!

Can I ask you dear friends, when I woke last night and went to the window, I saw lines of light attaching the stars to one another as if they were hung by silver threads, and I also saw what looked like radio waves in circles of energy. Can you explain what I was actually seeing please?
These strands of light that thread across the sky are energy waves, patterns that contain the universe.   We all vibrate at different

frequencies and inhabit the same space at the same moment. We magically cast you adrift from the illusion of time and catapult you into a new framework, a new dimension of time and space where we may cohabit on a finer level.

It would be so wonderful to be able to be closer to you - to feel you. And yet, as I say these words, I can feel your touch on my face now. I've always found that touch so magical . . . like gossamer wings very gently brushing against me, reassuring me that you are close at hand.

We manifest the simplest expressions of our Love.

I like this early morning contact, I feel very relaxed and am feeling waves of lilac drifting over me now with a calming, healing effect. Can you answer this question for me please — if the energies of the planet are being raised, why is it that so many of us are feeling depressed and low on energy?

We chart a wide spectrum of energies and propel you thus forward into the maelstrom, recovering all probabilities, giving you wider scope to unveil your destiny. You are sensitive beings prone to a sapping of energy levels that deplete you, but by resting and going within we can recharge your batteries for you. And it gives us great pleasure to do this - to have you all to ourselves for just a moment or two. And it is pleasant for you - is it not?

Oh yes . . . it is wonderful!

Then we will let you rest for a while . . . there is no need to speak!

I Love this contact and feel we are growing closer together as I learn to trust and relax that all is well.

∞

Beyond the realms of time and planes of existence that extend between our worlds. We travel forth and reach that place where minds can unite.

The above words were received by a group member as the energies built for our

149

Star friends to come through.

The knowledge is in safe keeping . . . it will be brought into the light when the time is right! We advocate a grouping together of like minds and to this purpose we shall initiate a greater cluster of feedback. We have allowed this being to assist us in the proceedings and we ask you to take heart for all is not lost by any means! We prepare to issue sanctions and we shall bestow upon you the greatest treasures. We open your hearts and minds to link with us . . . this is our course and we superimpose our thoughts on yours to get the message across, purely and simply, uncluttered by your own thought streams. We know this is hard but with practice we shall manage to come closer and closer to the truth - the whole truth! We all are able to access this knowledge and we are beholden to you for gathering together on these occasions. We follow you and watch you, nurturing you all and this was our dream from the very beginning . . . we dreamt you into being . . . we dreamt you awake!

We un-clutter your vision and pour forth a stream of knowledge that will open up the boundaries and generate further wisdom. There is no cause to be alarmed . . . we shelter you from harm, each and every one of you, we may not always be seen but we can be heard if you listen carefully to that inner voice within. There is an abundance of good cheer from our side and there is an abundance of good cheer from you all. We thank you for the Love in your hearts that you give to us and your fellow man and we tremble with anticipation for the delights in store for you and all mankind. Open up your hearts and shine . . . rediscover who you are, who you have been and who you will be in the future!

It has often been said that a man rests on his laurels but we ask you to delve deeper and deeper, opening the treasure chest that is there for you! Explore and experiment, life is a wonderful, wonderful experience - so enjoy it! You are here for the experiences that life can offer you and even the sad times bring you wisdom that you can share with others. We will leave you now to ponder on these things. We Love you so - our little Earthlings!

150

Thank you for your kind words of wisdom, we are learning so much, thank you!

We are ALL learning!

I held my hands in prayer position, bowing to all three in the group, and as I opened my arms towards them, they saw a deep sapphire ball of light.

Bless you - bless you - bless you! May God bless us all and inspire us to overcome!

∞

Today we have joined with another larger group and after a 'Golden Light' visualisation we sent out healing to Egypt by focussing on the pyramids in Cairo. We then called out the names of other countries that needed healing. Afterwards I sat for communication and could feel the energy coming in strongly from my right hand side. There was a sickly feeling in my solar plexus that can happen with spirit contact, but relaxing and going with the flow eases the sensation. The voice was quiet when it came through and I felt very emotional with the amount of Love flowing.

We make this connection this morning . . . we of like minds gather together as kith and kin, welcoming in a new direction, a new opening that is there for all of us. We are so happy, so excited and so joyful to be able to come among you . . . it gives us so much pleasure! We are beholden to you all here today and we watch you and follow you in your homes and abroad. We push you along in the right direction helping you to make those choices that are available to you. We make those connections that start off a chain reaction and eventually travel around the whole globe; these connections are gathering momentum . . . gathering energy and spreading the word! We are so lucky to have you to work by our side, we have prayed for such a happening and it brings us much joy to see you learning and growing, responding to the rhythms of nature. Like the ripples on a pond the message goes out loud and clear . . . we are here . . . we are here . . . we are here!

There was a deep sigh then the voice became louder and firmer.

151

Together we will build and grow a new world of ample proportions, a new world of Love and joy . . . of frankness and openness, bringing together all creatures great and small where no one is overlooked, where all are as important as each other! There will be no pain or sorrow and no disease for they will have no truck in our world! We beam you aboard in moments of stress and comfort you and uplift you.   We prepare you for a great journey, one that has been taken by the most esteemed and we thank you all! Through trials and tribulations you have kept to that straight true path and we are most honoured to be travelling with you at this time.

We open up the connections and point you in the right direction. What we are saying is true for have you not come together as was planned? You were all drawn here for a purpose, a greater purpose and you are here now, ready to do our bidding and we say not 'our' bidding but the bidding of the Great Divine - the Great 'One'.

Fulfill your destinies, open up your hearts and your minds to partake of the information that is coming through even as we speak, filtering into your minds, drawn from the very core of your being. You do not have to believe this person or that person or necessarily what you read, but little snippets here, little snippets there will come together and make sense - and you will know if it is right! You will know in your heart that you may have stumbled across the information – the missing piece that you were looking for. It is all so easy if you just listen . . . weed out what is not needed and put to one side and perhaps in time that information will make sense! Take heart, gather your strength for there is much to do, much to learn, and we are there with you always; together we can build a mountain and a mountain stream . . . and the glory of the world we live in can be 'glorious' once again! We let it settle in your hands and in your heart for it to make a difference, a difference to you and a difference to the whole collective. We thank you for listening!

∞

It is such a Lovely sunny morning and I'm sitting in my sanctuary, listening to the birds welcoming in another new day. The sound of traffic on the hillside disturbed my reverie and I got up to close the doors.

We hear the wider world on its journey and sit in the peace within this sanctuary. Do not be despondent my child - we are on the right course. We partake of this peace and energy with you, shuttling back and forth across the great divide. We instigate the final measures needed to demonstrate our allegiance to the cause and we propel you forward to do your duty. There has been much commotion in the heavens and we strategically put you in a place most suited to our cause; this has been of paramount importance and we shelter you from harm acquiescing to certain developments.

I'm now feeling two powerful floods of healing light beaming down on me.

There has been a championing of the cause, powerful and strong across the globe and we have registered your true intent. Be strong, be brave and let us take your hand, we will not lead you astray for we have only your best interests at heart. Subliminal messages release the strain, sanctioning a reprisal of energies, guarding against intrusion of any kind. We are impressed with the remedies that have been taken in the past and we allow now a softening of energies, bathing you in sweet success.

We have responded to the rhythms of your heart and instil in you a genteel approach. Respectfully, we extend you the courtesy of coming aboard and we make preparations, enhancing our study of the human race. We rely on people such as you to help us do justice to our words that reach far beyond the universe you are in, far beyond your widest scope of vision. We delve deeper and deeper and there shall be no discovery unless we broaden our shoulders to accept the impossible! We come to avoid disturbances on a vast scale and it goes without saying, we have prepared for our studies of the human race in minute detail, focusing on a requisitioning of services that have at times, undermined the most necessary ballot. We have prepared the chemistry necessary to make this work and ask you to understand our methods of opening up. We shall supply greater input

153

and we welcome in a greater flow of energy, spearheading our way across the universe and into your mind. Rest assured we are here to help mankind 'at your invitation' and not to cause hindrance . . . we are not here to cause hindrance in any way, shape or form!

Are you from the Pleiades - can you confirm please?

We are associated with the Pleiades connection. We are Star gazers, intrepid volunteers journeying into space. We magnify our essence upon the Earth plane and propel you safely to a point in time where we can make this connection. We have spin lined our thought streams and propel them thus far, enabling manifestation in your mind. We have relegated all forms of mistrust and innuendo and we come with the highest intent. We are just a thought away and we connect to you when we hearken to your call from beyond, cajoling you to accept our frequency. We render ourselves completely inert to make this work and we satisfy that inner longing, that inner call to reach out and connect as our hearts blend as one.

There was a long pause here in loving energy.

We reach out and connect with you on a lighter frequency, bearing glad tidings and opening up the portals of Light. We supply you with an extraordinary amount of information, passed on to us from those who have your greatest welfare at heart, radiating a thirst for knowledge around the world. We prepare you to assemble in due course and we respect your wishes, gaining accession through the realms of Light. We are known for our greater expertise in handling these requests and we prepare to anchor you to a greater Light form. We are bombarded with messages and we infiltrate at a level where we can connect to the masses. This has been an incredible journey and one we give thanks for!

Dear friends draw closer - I send out my Love to you and wait for the frequencies to adjust themselves.

We adjust your settings appropriately, filtering and streamlining our words concisely within a pattern of understanding.

154

It is almost too much effort to speak into my recorder. It is as if thought forms are the only mode of communication. I can feel myself talking very, very slowly.

We allow you to sit back while monitoring your progress, allowing further development.

I felt the urge to open my eyes and in the garden saw three huge Crows. I shut my eyes and continued.

We lift you out of the realms of despair and project you to a time and place of greater value, greater productivity and a greater dominion in every way, where equilibrium of the heart and soul is in progress and where we deliver freedom of thought - freedom to analyse. Dig deep into those recesses of the mind . . . dig deep and restore your self-esteem!

This was all I could manage at this session. Afterwards I looked up the symbology of Crow and they are known as 'Keepers of Sacred text'.

∞

We welcome you from the realms of Light assessing your development. We watch over you and share in your delight at the progress you have been making. It has taken great resolve to change the course of your life and we express our delight at your gentility. We update products available to you and thread that fine line of communication echoing in your mind, struggling to make this connection when at times we have adjustments to make! It is no mean feat to contact our 'beloveds' on Earth and we register your keenness to adapt, to grow with resilience and forethought, bending over backwards to make this work in every aspect.

We delve deeper and deeper into life's mysteries and all that has unfolded over the aeons. We beg your pardon when we misinterpret a word here or there . . . it takes time for us to manage our thought streams in the most appropriate manner and we strive for perfection as always, monitoring your thought streams as we govern from afar. We will make this understanding a 'perfect' understanding and we will strive to cover what is necessary, what is needed at this time in your world. Take courage and take heart for we are all working on the side-lines, pushing you forward and dedicating our words to all with open hearts and minds. We discover a new world, a new world of growth and vision unsurpassed and we guarantee success in every avenue, taking up the gauntlet you have laid down for us!

Can I ask who you are, from what dimension you come from and what species you are? This will help me to know who is coming forward at any one time. I trust you are of the 'Light' but we humans do seem to need labels - it is protocol with us to have a name to address someone by. I'm seeing lots of purple with golden lattice shapes and a pale skinned person with smooth head.

We express ourselves in terms of endearment for the human race. Our race is described as being compatible with those on Earth and we derive our name from a galaxy that has long been in the minds of those on Earth. We are hybrids!

I'm worried my own mind is coming in and am asking them to help me step back. Are you Pleiadians or Sirians, or even Andromedians? I'm asking them to tell me in a way my mind will not expect.

We are hybrids of all these and more!

Can you explain please?

We came from a Star burst in your heavens . . . transmutable energy! We are indestructible, sustainable energy and we invoke thought patterns . . . thought waves that register in your mind. We surrender ourselves to a conditioning that enables us to access this module.

I'm seeing purple but it is very foggy. Occasionally I can see a smooth headed man - a benevolent figure. Dear friends I am going to have to say goodbye again. I hope we can make contact more often and for longer periods of time but for now, thank you for drawing close, I will strive to make this frequency work. Later as I typed these words it suddenly struck me that it may be more than just a coincidence that I have been painting Starbursts - my last one being vivid, royal blue and gold.

156

This morning after feeding the birds, I sat for communication and we seemed to carry on from yesterday.

The Federation of Light

It is a blessing and an honour to be with you once again. We partake of that company that draws you closer to us, mesmerising you into accepting our friendship. We are devoted to one another and align ourselves with you to make this trust complete. We superimpose our thought streams on yours, gathering momentum and gaining clarity of thought. There are a variety of thought processes that engulf us and we suggest a re-awakening that will allow us the progress we need to make in this connection.

I'm seeing beautiful lilac clouds and feel I'm being washed with energy as I'm guarded and connected. There is a tickling sensation around my throat and waves of purple and green are taking me on a journey. I'm now moving through clouds of colour with intricate white shapes on gold, purple and green . . . it feels similar to when I nearly drowned as a child with soft, undulating tendrils of coloured light flowing around me.

Please can you draw away the veil so that I can see more clearly? Are any of my friends going to come forward and speak or is this a cleansing process I'm going through? Immediately there was a loud bang in the room!

We are allowed . . . permitted to say something and we are honour bound to be discreet. We manifest for you some of our most treasured possessions . . . we are without doubt on the most incredible journey and one we give thanks for. We are a species more suited to Earth bound energies and we live deep within the recesses of your mind, this is because we can register and deliver when called for what is needed to bring about a healing for mankind. We are influential in the fact that we can access those modules within your brain. We are anchoring in a new awareness!

It does feel like I'm travelling through my own brain; there are lots of winding tunnels of white on purple and gold on purple.

157

We shed Light . . . we are luminous omnipresence, allowing bacteria that have survived major disasters to come forward and register their intent and purpose. We vow to correct disturbances, allowing a modicum of sanity to preserve what is left of the human race. We have been sent from those on high, carrying the 'Federation of Light' beings that have manifested the most simplest of solutions, transcending our wildest dreams. We move beyond that curtain . . . that veil of uncertainty and we bring you greater resolution to your problems on Earth.

We sanctify and bless those of you who come forward, a monumental task of indescribable proportions, streamlined and brought to serve the general populace. We sanctify a withdrawal of services that overwhelm and govern you and are most disturbed to learn of involuntary movement caused by those who badger you to obtain the best! There has been a disproportionate governing of services and we in no way bend to the whims of those who have struggled to make this work; we have decided therefore to proceed with your requests and we allow movement and scope to bring this to a most honourable solution. We protect you and monitor you, giving strength and eventuality of purpose. We lay further groundwork and ask for your preservation!

∞

At today's session I could feel an Egyptian influence and crossed my hands over my chest, looking down a long avenue of trees.

We see not the darkness that descends upon us - we see only the hope of a golden dawn, haunted by shadows of Earth making her transition. We rally to the cause, tending our flock with mutual consent, registering the hopes and dreams of all concerned. We simultaneously express ourselves and motion for you to address us as your contemporaries - as your equals! You have grown in stature this many a year and we have followed you and watched your progress . . . an indulgence on our part. We are connected on that vibration of Love and we synchronise our energies, creating a stronger connection as we vibrate together in perfect harmony. We monitor this connection ushering in a new awareness for one and all and we bring great rewards for those who search for truth. We are long forgotten on the highways and byways of Earth but we bear witness to the beginning of a new dawn of indescribable beauty. There will be a parting of the waves as in days of old and you will walk across to the other side! We spread our message far and wide . . . all is written and it shall be so!

I was shown the sea parting as in Moses time and I suddenly became aware of the sound of rain from outside, battering against the windows.

Is not the rain sweet that falls from the heavens? *Yes, oh yes!*

Alas there were times when our land was parched and dry and we prayed for rain! Our harvests have been plentiful and yet we fell upon hard times and our land was laid barren. There were many who died and those that perished endured much hardship! We have become prosperous once more - such are the whims of nature. We are guided and directed by the Sun and rely on her warmth to nurture us and sustain us; we watch her rise in the sky bringing her blessings. We come to harness that energy giving you strength for the road ahead and in this bargaining process we are governed by we give you strength, we give you peace of mind in your deliberations. We welcome you to come aboard!

We will 'not' harm you or molest you in any way, shape or form! We are here to help mankind . . . to give assistance and to help you in your decision making. We embroider your land with our knowledge and our wisdom and we prepare you to assimilate a new connection - a new dimension. We give you the proof that you desire, we give you the understanding that we are of the same race and we interconnect with other Star beings. May we make a suggestion? It would be far more appropriate for you to sense and feel . . . look within yourselves and open up your hearts! We have taken those reserves of energy to catapult you into a new dimension and we prepare for a mammoth schedule that will encompass all time frameworks.

I can see purple clouds and a golden skeleton that has just turned to look at me.

159

Prepare to abandon negative thought forms, allowing discord to evaporate, sense a renewal of services on the horizon as we propel you forward to do your duty. We are an exceptional breed of that there is no doubt. The apocalypse has been lamented on all occasions in different timelines and we have held back our grief at this monstrous, outrageous desecration! We suffer no interference from any quarter and penetrate this spectrum of light, overcoming all malfunctions that have arisen. We delight in telling you that we have welcomed aboard the most appropriate study of the human race, allowing those among you who wish to participate to come aboard in grand style. We have relegated all notions of doom and gloom, steadfastly maintaining control of this bombardment of issues that surface for recognition. We are not idle by any means but we have sanctioned a resting to quicken your survival techniques. Expatriates line up to be counted and we foster no further progress until you have hearkened to the call within - this will motivate you to make that connection. We negate any negative agendas!

Can I ask you – are you of the Light?

We allow access only to those who register their just intent. We are likened to an olive branch, held out to make that connection to lighten the distance between us. We are from a broader spectrum of light and we are propelled by means of thought, invoking an interest in your colony. We have jeopardised certain aspects of our communication, because of our lack of expertise and general disorder, but we remain to open a network of services that will be held with the highest respect. Dishevelled, we come to kneel before you and we ask your forgiveness!

We have managed this main stream connection to evolve and grow, emerging as a new race of beings - Super Beings! We project our image on your screen and ask that you transfer our data to your memory banks; this will give us greater insight into what is expected of us. We accept the mastery that comes with dedication in the pursuit of truth and we therefore unfold what has not been seen or heard for many a year. We delight in taking you to the back of beyond . . . beyond the veil of uncertainty and paradigms that enchant you, yet hold you back from seeing with cloudier vision. Obstructions shall fall away . . . all shall be heard and all will come to fruition. We bear witness to a greater moment in your time, unfolding gently and carefully, clearing the smoke screen from your eyes. We open up a conduit of pure magnitude, of beauty and grace unsurpassed, travelling a broader spectrum of light and re-entering Earth's atmosphere unburdened, uncluttered, expressing ourselves with the utmost glee!

I wasn't sure about the word glee! I hope you are from the Divine Light . . . I send Love and Light to you - I will not push you away into the shadows! I leave this connection open to those whom I trust to bring through words from the highest Divine source.

These are words spoken and gifted to you and yours . . . we welcome you to these shores and tend to your every need. We open up the doorway that will give you shelter and we respect your wishes to come aboard; we will not harm you or abort the services that we bring to mankind! We open up a vast array of conduits that have agreed to work with us and we supply a means to promoting peace and harmony on a vast scale. This supremacy has enabled us to manipulate those centres within you that are highly charged with information. We grant you your wishes and impel you to move forward into the arms of the great unknown. We support you from all directions, holding ourselves in abeyance until all is ready for that mammoth undertaking with reserves of energy that will propel you into your future!

We have in fact come to accept that we are held by some in the utmost fear and dread, but we mean you no harm! We mean only to move forward on this beam of Light, gathering you to us and helping you to make those connections there for you, a lifeline to all intents and purposes, a life line to help you in your hour of need. We rescue you from the doldrums for eternal bliss and sanctuary - a golden opportunity! We deliver an understanding that all can be accomplished within a certain time frame and we prepare you to accept this conditioning, which will enable you free access to our main frame.

161

What do you mean by main frame, can you explain please?

We are governed by an inordinate supply of energy, beamed to us from our own reserves of energy which we bring on board, a loom of energy . . . a power frame capable of producing massive loops of energy supplying our ship.

Can you show me your ship?

I'm being shown lots of deep purple clouds and golden shapes but I can't quite make it out. Open up my vision please - help me to adjust! Are you worried that we would be frightened of seeing you as you truly are? If we are working from the highest Divine Light for the greater good of mankind, then it doesn't matter what you look like as long as you are part of that Divine Light.

We are unscrambled . . . we recognise the vast fluctuates of energy that beckon us to move forward on this loom of light. We beckon you to move forward with us, encapsulating that light . . . that Love and energy that expresses a deep wilderness within, beckoning us to explore . . . to seek out the dark places and to shine light into each crevice, into each nook and cranny!

I am surrounded by Light now.

Acceptance, peace, understanding . . . we understand the recesses of your brain and activate a thermal imaging that will help us to discover your attributes.

I could then feel an energy blending with me and looking around my room. Dear friends have you finished now - what is it you are looking at?

We are learning about your species as well as you learning about ours! You are a very provocative race and we look forward to these visits to enable free expression and to launch ourselves into a new time framework that will encompass our species, broadening our knowledge of mankind.

Where do you come from please? Their answer sounded like Andromeda, but by

162

this time my own mind was coming in and I wasn't able to clarify, so had to leave it for another time!

∞

I sat for communication and sent golden light coursing through my body. I visualised roots going down deep into Earth and sent healing light through them like torches into the caverns. I am chanting 'Ohm' into the deepest recesses of Earth where the rivers flow, where the enchanted ones come to listen and to join in. Ohm . . . Ohm . . . Ohm! I was filled with purple light and could see the outline of a person surrounded in white light; they look human but have no hair at all. These words came strongly.

'I am perfect - I am pure - I am Holy'. We speak to you of Mother Earth - we sing her praises!

At this point there was such a commotion outside that I opened my eyes and saw three black Crows; I kept my eyes open and continued.

We send our patrons to challenge you and to guide you, misleading at times to encourage you to grow, encouraging you to decide for yourselves on which course is best and overcoming a mountainous array of obstacles that bar you from Heaven itself. We abscond from our duties and watch over you, satisfying that inner craving that leads us forever onwards towards our destination. We march as an Army of Light broadcasting our message, speaking our wisdom and pointing out what has been left aside. We point out that ray of hope on the horizon and beckon you forward, examining in greater detail what is necessary and what is perfectly in order, maintaining a level suited to your needs. We ask for action and propel you to that place destined.

We are translucent energy manifesting in waves of purest Love, pure energy creating ripples on a stream of knowledge that propels you further and further into our midst. We sally forth, registering our intent and purpose for being on this Earth at this time; we understand the growing necessity for you to stand on your own two feet and we attend to our duties, flourishing and steadfast to the cause. We have opened up our misgivings, our worries that all is not

163

as it should be, but we are here to tell you that all has its purpose! We proclaim you 'Star Beings Extraordinaire' and we have opened up this channel so that you may accomplish an extraordinary mission on Earth.

We are spellbound . . . opening up your vision and directing your energy . . . your focus to those 'Light' beings on Earth who open like flowers with their petals reaching towards the Sun. You blossom and grow in our Love and we tend to you and watch you aspiring to greater prolific occurrences that promote peace and tranquillity. We allow this most honourable connection to grow, manifesting a growing proportion of energy needed for the task in hand. We proposition you with our Love and leave it in your hands as to how you shall accomplish this task.

We enable a startling amount of information to be made ready for your perusal and we adjust our frequencies so that we may encourage you in your progress. We reach out and touch the unseen, making formidable progress as we encircle you in bands of gold. We broaden your knowledge and bring you up to date, motioning a further foray into the unknown, encircling you in our brilliance . . . dazzling you and overcoming a whole network of imbalances that are holding you back from achieving your goal!

We aim to bring you a new set of experiences that shall mould you and keep you from resisting our gentility of spirit. We are governed by the natural force of Love and we relay our messages one by one, asking you to gather this information together to complete our document. We prepare to be summoned to a higher cause, known by those who wait at the gates of Heaven . . . we have raised the portcullis and offer you sanctuary! We ask you to be aware of those follies that tempt mankind, subjugating our true regrets at not being able to take you that little bit further. We regret there has been a closing of that particular door for now, but we will investigate and disseminate those discussions that take us to the back of the line of support. We will however, in all instances, push you forward when you have overcome what is necessary to make that move!

We relish our times of togetherness in perpetual motion . . . transforming entire galaxies and opening up a network of grandiose commitment, challenging the mealiest mouthed among you and showering you with our blessings! There was never seen such a grander army as the 'Army of Light' and we Love to challenge you, to tickle you into submission, experiencing the highs and the lows and keeping a steady perspective at all times. Wallowing in self-pity never gave us the impetus to reach out and stay connected it was that hope in your heart . . . that abundance of hope that kept you going in bleak times when the wind howled at your doorstep, when the icy torrents fell upon you when you were defenceless at the helm!

Where there is hope there is a heart that is strong, weathering all conditions, all elements and we 'will' win through this time of discord . . . we will overcome the dark shadows encircling Earth. We will overcome all malfunctions that hold us back from achieving bliss and the honeyed voices of those we Love, those who have gone before. We pick up and hold onto that single thread of hope with the desire to bring about a change for the betterment of all mankind, and as we reach out to join you from beyond a veil of uncertainty, we tell you that your obligations to us, your friends, your brothers and sisters of Light are great . . . as are ours to you! And we blend together as one, opening a network of services that shall propel us into a new dimension of oneness, of greatness, of all encompassing Love and freedom of spirit . . . and we shall sing together once more!

Be true little ones . . . be true to your hearts and we shall overcome that gap between us, stepping over that border into the summer lands. We open our hearts and praise you for the service you do and we envelop you in our Love and thank you and uplift you, motioning for you to join us in the not too distant future, where we shall become brothers in arms once more. A golden network of services stretches right across the globe, extending out to the cosmos, reaching out to those planets and stars that beckon us further forward and on to our next mission of excellence!

∞

PART TWO

Deepening connections with White Cloud and the Federation of Light

Chapter ten

We spread our wings and fly

It's halfway through 2012 and I have been wondering what will happen at the end of this year; I can't help but think mankind is not yet ready to take that leap of faith into the great unknown! Meditation feels different today, I seem to be able to tune into different frequencies as if I'm turning the knob on a radio and finding stations I've never accessed before. I asked for help at home and with my spiritual work, switching on my recorder to monitor the session.

We bend to your every whim and motion you to address this situation. We find it unbearable that we should be buffeted around by the winds of fate, however, we do have some resources up our sleeve and we know you well enough by now to assist you. Life has taken us to the precipice only to be drawn back many times before . . . we hold out our hand and take a stance!

I'm now being shown a character from the film 'Lord of the Rings' who was quite mad having tried to burn his injured son on a funeral pyre, choosing to believe he was dead. He is holding out his hand to me at the edge of the precipice and I wasn't sure if he was going to jump into the abyss, but as I looked into his eyes I felt safe and took hold of his hand. We are now flying across the precipice and towards the mountains.

We trust implicitly . . . we spread our wings and fly!

Together we are gliding high above the mountains in a clear blue sky and I'm feeling so elated. We are stopping now to rest on the mountain top and I can see a golden eagle circling above us with the sun glinting on its wings.

We shall have our say in all of this . . . we shall have our say before our final resting place on Earth. We hold you up . . . we nurture you and cherish you and we unfold the wisdom of a sage from bygone times. We open up those reserves of energy not yet tapped into and we 'will' prevail!

It is so wonderful to sit in meditation in absolute peace, linking with other realms. Clouds of purple wash over me comforting and protecting me, sometimes astounding me with the visions they bring and beautiful words that touch my heart. I will not fear I will not fall by the wayside; I will fight the good fight with all my might!

Be prepared for an opening very soon. We tantalise the senses giving you a golden opportunity! Do not be downcast or put off for we are here to uplift your spirits, leading you to make that connection with the Great Divine. We are Interstellar Galactic Light forms and we open up this watershed of studies and acoustics. We lay a pattern that you may think of as obsolete in this time frame but that is not the case. We come in uniformity.

A different energy approached and I felt very cold, seeing the white crest of a mountain range.

We have been governed by a greater light force and we welcome you to our mountain high in the Himalayas. We have not been disturbed for many a year and we register the Love that is in your heart and amplified here in these mountains. We ask you to be aware that conditions here have remained unchanged for centuries; we watch men come and go and still we stand here strong and true. It has been a mammoth task assisting those creatures who scale our walls in acts of bravery, ludicrous though it may seem. We watch over the crest at our cousins who stand beside us and tremble in anticipation for what is to come. We are giants reaching up to the sky, bathed in so much love and beauty. We are happy to stand here for many centuries more but we hear the rumble within Earth. There has been a mighty split in the caverns beneath us, a mighty split in the ocean beds . . . a mighty split echoing all around the world!

∞

At my early morning meditation I felt a tickling of energy under my chin and saw the Sphinx, indicting an Egyptian influence.

We have petitioned you to accept our frequencies and we meld and join together as one, aligning ourselves with those Star beings that are purported to be a race of Gods. We open up a web of jurisdiction that will enable a channelling of excellence and we predict that in a year's time we will have set a greater pace. We anticipate a year from now you will see a vast change, a vast array of services that will come in and an appetite for more of the same! We indulge you and open up a channel, exploring and delving deeper within; we will show you by opening your vision and expressing ourselves more coherently.

I can see gold patterns set against vivid purple and feel a strong presence drawing close. My face feels as if it is changing shape and my voice sounds deeper as I speak into the microphone.

We express ourselves with great joy to be here with you again and feel we are making a breakthrough of enormous proportions! We spread the message on Earth that we are here to make this alliance between us work!

Can you tell me who are you please?

We have tumbled from that Star which was born to give you Light and we are amazed at your reticence at pronouncing our name! We have developed a lamentable habit of tuning into our Divine connectedness and at the same time, ignoring those inner frequencies that endeavour to translate information, which can be given and understood in greater perspective. We do realise this range is superficial but we encourage a greater connection that will help us all. We strive to make this connection of the utmost clarity and register your intent to speak loud and clear! We make a personal recovery from all that holds us back and we adjust these frequencies so that we are more able to transcribe in a format suited to your abilities.

We do have to laugh at your squeamishness at times but the protocol that is accepted by all, on both sides, will allow us to indulge in these sessions. Tap into those reserves of energy and we shall see greater resilience, greater productivity and a greater urge to forge ahead. We are mesmerised by your antics on Earth and we have made a few

169

adjustments that are necessary to open our conduits, allowing us to draw that much closer. We have seen across the boundaries of Earth and far out into the cosmos, where those from Sirius make their connections with us as we in turn make our connection with you. We are linked to Planet Earth in a magical moment of time!

I asked about a previous channelling where the Sun was called 'She'. This was questioned by my group as they have always regarded the Sun as being masculine and the Moon as feminine.

We are predestined to rise in the sky like the Sun in all her glory and we reach out and grasp with both hands what is necessary to overcome a multitude of imperfections. We host a variety of initiatives that will bring justice and peace of mind and we alternate between the curves in space that allow us to draw nearer. There is no right or wrong way to address us and we are beholden to you for pointing out this common misconception.

We bring a declaration of Peace and Love and we summon your imagination that will take you far across the veil of uncertainty, far beyond your wildest dreams, far into the realms of deep thought; here you will find what you seek – 'truth' the embodiment of truth! We ask you to stand firm, stand in your place and stand in your strength of purpose. We draw closer and fill you with our Love and a detonation of services that will reach far and wide, opening up a maelstrom of events that surface for recognition.

I'm feeling the stillness and peace with clouds of soft purple washing over me.

We register your thoughts and summon an enquiry. This has been a mammoth undertaking and we feel the feedback emanating, broadening our horizons. We venture to say that we have all been given an inordinate amount of information and it is within our power to summon a broader perspective. We nourish your thought streams and propel you to accept this reconditioning that we are offering you.

Dear friends please help me to channel correctly and to understand what I'm seeing. There are masses of purple clouds and a golden tunnel that I now seem to be inside. I'm transfixed and hardly able to speak into the microphone; again I'm being washed with purple clouds of light and seem only to communicate by thought.

I feel a different energy approaching and am now able to speak but in a much, higher voice!

We would like to say the Star system we resided in has become obsolete! We have moved to another dimension that will enable us to continue our species . . . we accepted the frequencies that enabled our departure from one timeline to another more suited to our needs. We expect you will see this of paramount importance to your species at this time and we allow you to rendezvous with us in this connection so that you will see it is not necessarily a bad thing!

We are inclined to believe this is a necessary by-product of our Love for you on the Earth plane and we express our sincere congratulations that you have made the mark necessary to intuit and understand our concerns. We believe you will do justice to whatever comes your way and we parade before you a variety of ill-conceived notions that will spark controversy! We have manifested a declaration that was written long ago and we understand this is within your reach. You have been chosen as an example . . . as a model of our lunacy, the physical team that punctuates our existence!

We reach out a lifeline to those on Earth, making our connections and preparing you to accept this massive expansion of minds right across the globe. We desire to speak with you - to state our case and to bring that Love back into your hearts, we ask that you accept our credentials as we offer you our hand in friendship! We prepare to retrace our steps back through history and we allow you a peek into the annals of time itself. We prepare a massive documentation of material that has been passed to us from those on a higher plane of existence. We exceed our limitations and branch out, accepting the part we play in this adaptation of life's experiences and all that goes with it. We excel in rediscovering for ourselves a new hierarchy governed by 'Love' and we stress the importance of this phenomena!

We reach out and tell you the truth, the whole truth and nothing but the truth! We reach out into the hearts and minds of all those under duress at this time in your history on the Earth plane. We succeed in acquiring a good standard of elocution and we admire your resourcefulness for delving into the dictionary and learning new words for us to use. This is becoming a vast, fact finding mission and we encourage you to tread carefully, motioning you to follow in our footsteps. We have attained a high degree of economical satisfaction as we overshadow you on the Earth plane and we excel in our communications, registering an upturn in frequency.

We reconnect and issue new guide lines, transporting you to Heaven and back. We believe in an existence beyond the physical and we nurture you to release thought patterns that will gain numerous theological discussions, tapping the intellect and broadcasting on an energy level unsurpassed. We make it count as we nurture this connection, transcending the impossible and feeding you with our messages, regulating a passage of understanding and a network of services that go hand in hand. We are sublimely connected to that 'Golden Star' and the resources that flow freely from it into our hearts and minds. Love all Love excelling . . . Love from Heaven to Earth brought down. We disseminate the package we are offering, pinning our hopes and dreams on the human race, bending over backwards to make this work and to shelter you from harm.

∞

As soon as I opened up in meditation today I could see the kneeling figure of a person with a smooth head. He is holding his hands together in prayer position and bowing. I can see that he has fine features with a normal shaped head, beautiful eyes and high cheekbones; he is now holding his right arm up to an intense white light that is beaming down on him. We seem to be in a dimly lit cave but I can see a bright light emanating through the entrance; it feels like an apothecary's domain and I'm wondering if he is a priest or scribe. I am now receding from this scene into darkness, which has now cleared and I am being shown vivid purple surrounded by gold coloured structures. It's as if the purple is partially blocking my vision of the scene before me. I felt the urge to hold both arms out as if I was holding up the Sun.

172

I am now moving through a tunnel underground and can partially see a skeleton in a stone coffin but the purple keeps obscuring my vision from the main body of the scene. It feels as if we are in catacombs deep below the surface and I wondered if I was entombed here as one of the sacrifices during a past life. I still vividly remember a dream I had many years ago, where I was a young girl being prepared for sacrifice. I had been drugged and lay in some kind of anti-chamber, moaning and writhing to the sound of drums that were beating louder and louder! Beside me stood a dark skinned guard who held a long spear, totally impassive and just staring straight ahead. I remember clearly that he wore a helmet made of finely plaited leather that fitted snugly to his head. I believe I was shown this vision at the time because I had been unnecessarily sacrificing my own needs for the needs of others.

We have a radical assumption of what we are about and as we delve deeper and deeper, we find anomalies that have not been registered openly. We therefore suggest that by going within, you will find and obey that inner request to sabotage the monotony within your soul. We openly express ourselves with the greatest joy to be with you in entirety, to be with you in body, mind and spirit. We sanction a renewal of services and point you in the right direction, holding onto that flame of Love. We have been summoned from a hierarchy that does little or no good in assisting us in this process of ascension and we deliberately request a turning back of the pages that are written, doing our best to understand our mission on Earth. We have enabled a support system to follow you and assist in your enquiries and we do register your dual purpose and priorities needed to make this mission a success! We have undoubtedly expressed ourselves in terms of endearment and we regulate a grand statement of facts and figures, ensuring any overspill is taken care of. We are therefore more intellectually challenged and we make a repository.

I can feel my face changing quite dramatically and sense a North American Indian drawing close. When he spoke it was in a deep slow voice.

We promote peace and happiness amongst all mankind – this is our way of the warrior spirit! We have been much maligned in the past, bringing through our anecdotes of disturbances that have caused

173

great distress. However, we do promote peace of mind and peace amongst all mankind. We have forsaken the ways of old and it is with intense satisfaction that we come now armed with a superior knowledge and brought to bear witness. We shelter you from the cruel winds that blow and manifest a greater recall, feathering our nest with relics from the past. We register your concerns my child . . . we suffer great interferences from those who will not listen and it distresses us greatly! We open up a hornets' nest, describing events that we neither feel nor see as in good taste. We have regulated services that bring about destruction of all we hold most dear, and we stand aside and let you intervene, bringing about an enormous change. We are grateful for this and we do our best to uphold your spirit and act in the best possible taste. We rely on those like you to lead the general populace onto a new and winding pathway. All is not yet clear but will be very soon!

We express our condolences for those who have not yet recovered their identity. There is a broad spectrum of services that will resume our connection in the future and we are delighted with the uptake. We shall expand and grow in all directions, opening up the floodgates, and here we shall see a variety of pathways that can be undertaken. We rely heavily on your expertise to strengthen this connection so that we can muster a recovery and strengthen your position. We will stand firm have no fear on that score . . . we will take the world by storm!

Stand to attention! Behold the battlements manned and armed at the ready . . . we blow the trumpet ready for our advance! The circuit grows wider and stronger - the circuit of Love. We are beholden to you my child for your purposeful endeavours and we unite as one, hand in hand across the universe. We propel you forward to do your duty and we take comfort in the fact that we are side by side, arm in arm, galloping across the high planes together once more! Do not weep . . . be grateful, be happy that we have made this connection once more! We have registered your contact with us and take heart that we grow stronger.

Thank you my friend it heartens me to know that I am not alone, that I have all

174

my friends in the spirit realms standing close by.
We are possessed of those qualities that bring inspiration and joy to
the hearts of many, and we continue to walk this pathway, unifying
and blessing the souls who come to listen to our words. We have
ratified all deals and pacts and take on board new measures to
overcome the obstacles that stand in our way. We have broadened
our knowledge and we bring you joy and upliftment beyond all
earthly measure.

I've got shivers all over me as these words are brought through.

We supervise a coming together of twin souls, modifying our
vocabulary and initiating a mission of success. We are benefiting
from a huge range of entitlements and these shall be given in due
course.   Spread the word, spread the Love and spread the news; we
have a vast recovery programme to unfold and we give you this with
all our Love. The style and grace of which we speak is disseminated
and brought into jurisdiction by an amalgamation of energies. We
utilise this connection and supervise an incoming flux of energy that
will initiate a broader understanding of what we are about. LOVE is
the key to our success!

∞

Today at our home group my Native American guide opened the proceedings.

It is time to start work now my little ones! *Greetings!*

Greetings indeed - we are open for negotiations! We have been blind
of late but we are forging a pathway, opening up a network of
services that will take us further and further still. You have been
granted access and we deliver to you a different turn of phrase that
you can understand in this connection. We are all propelled further
upstream and we are very proud of your success; each and every one
of you has stayed true to the cause, to the pathway you agreed upon
aeons ago. We are all proud to be part of this connection and we
strive for greater clarity, channelling patterns of thought that enter
your mind like a pool, a reservoir of knowledge flowing in for you to
use and utilise and to give forth to others. This is of extreme and

175

utter importance and it will take practice to make perfect but we assure you, we are doing our best on our side to make this a little bit easier for us all. We monitor your progress and allow you to go 'under cover' as it were! We subject you to these streams of energy that allow you to come closer and allow us to connect with you, not only at these times but times when you are alone in your homes. We draw close and gather you to us and we open up a network of emotions that will allow you to understand us in this connection.

The energy changed to a lighter feel.

We are delighted to have you with us on this journey . . . most delighted! We come from beyond the realms of fantasy . . . we are as a thought, a whisper in your minds. We gather closer and closer making this effortless and 'Yes' we are from the realms of Light, from the realms of Light and Love! We come to bring peace and harmony in this connection and we motion you to accept us, as we are of the most loving connection. We delve deeper into life's mysteries and open up a network of passages that we shall roam through; we shall have such joy and experience much laughter and excitement as we gather together. We are forging a new pathway through the darkness . . . we are spearheading the Light, shining it and becoming it!

I felt my face beaming with excitement as I was shown lots and lots of tiny lights on either side of the pathway, reminding me of the faerie beings in 'Lord of the Rings'.

We open your mind, not with drugs or alcohol but with a network of emotions . . . with Love and purity of spirit. We open your minds to accept the impossible and we have been chosen to access this knowledge, to bring it into the light of understanding that can be accepted by all. It is not an easy job that you have chosen but we shall manifest in glowing colours all that will help you on your pathway. The lights grow brighter . . . there are many of us and we open up your vision so that you will see in due course; we open up those faculties that bring us closer. We are well meaning and subservient to the cause of the upliftment of mankind and we will not hold you back from attaining that which you desire. Make haste little ones for all is not yet lost; we shine a lantern of hope on the dismal proceedings that overwhelm you from time to time, we shine hope into your minds, into your hearts, opening up a realm of possibilities. As guardians we are there for you at all times; never give up for that well of knowledge is there for you all to seek and find!

∞

I'm sitting in my sanctuary early in the morning and can feel energy moving in from the left, enveloping me in peace. The energy blending with me is making my face beam and I feel such bliss that tears are stinging my eyes. I can only describe it as cool diamond energy – crystal clear and pure, and yet at the same time my hands are very warm.

We envelop you in our Love and take pity on those that are left behind. We interrupt your reverie to bring you news and greater clarification of events on the horizon. We open a stream of well-wishers drawn close to help you with the greatest expertise and we nourish your thought streams, expressing our certainty of a job well done. We crave information from a higher source and bring you gifts!

I'm seeing baskets full of flowers being brought and laid at my feet.

We bring you our wishes for a brighter future together. We envisage our time more in keeping with the reverence and grace bestowed upon you, partitioning off those aspects of communication that bring heartache on a grand scale. We need to impress on you the need to remain constant to the cause, constant to the thoughts that bind you to us with the greatest skill and expertise, making a grand connection of minds. We propel you forward and announce in no uncertain terms that we have managed a most advantageous receptacle of gifts, given to those who meet our requirements.   We take a stab in the dark and issue a renewal; we enable a massive directive of energies to marshall our forces and we expect a balancing of energies to enable your constitution. We confirm that you will work with us and we take advantage of having you near at this time - and this will become our trademark!

177

I am being drawn down a tunnel of purple light surrounded by golden shapes and a dolphin made of this purple energy swam towards me to greet me. I'm now being taken along the tunnel and can see what looks like an umbilical cord. The next five minutes of recording are blank and I must have gone deeper, remembering nothing more except coming back and feeling tingly. This indeed did become their trademark . . . the tunnel of purple light overlaid with golden latticework preceding communication.

∞

At our weekly group my North American Indian guide came through more strongly, changing the lower half of my face which made it hard for me to open my mouth and speak. When I did my voice was much deeper.

Welcome, welcome, welcome. It brings much happiness to our hearts to see you gathered here today. You are doing such good work it is incredible . . . it brings a tear to our old eyes! We wish to do justice to your hard work and we will work together as one. We have asked you to bear with us as we get these vibrations right, adjusting and cementing our relationship so that we may work together in greater unison. But we are doing very well - we have come so far, have we not? We are opening to a much broader spectrum of energies, accomplishing a broader understanding and an opening up of our horizons. There is so much more to come, so much more to explore and we are doing it together!

The fires of our ancestors burn brightly within your hearts, within your minds, and we bring you our blessings opening up a new pathway for you to follow. Look to your heart, here you will find a true perspective on all things. Open your heart and pour forth loving kindness to all living things, to all creation. Open your heart and shine, let those obstacles fly away into the ethers and bring forth gentility of spirit. We have opened a way for you to travel over the highways and byways of Earth into the higher lighter realms, into a secret garden where life springs eternal. There is joy . . . there is peace here for you all and all you have to do is reach out, reach out and take that which is yours by right.

178

We are overwhelmed with joy to be working with you all again, and we shall manifest many items of wisdom that you long for that you hope for. Access the key to Heaven for it is here within you. 'You' are the treasure chest . . . you are that golden hope for all mankind! We prepare you to access this wisdom, to attain the frequency that lays down the barriers holding you back and we will be there with you, urging you on when all hope is lost! We are that Light that Star of eternal hope and joy and we watch over you, helping you to grow towards your destiny. Be not dismayed for all will come to fruition. We bring back that lightness to your step that lightness and purity of spirit that is within you all, a flame burning bright for all to see! Go now in Peace. Watch the heavens . . . we are there!

Thank you for your words of encouragement.

At the very end a different energy approached again and I wanted to sing — Tiptoe through the tulips with me. Knee deep in flowers we'll stray, we'll keep the showers away. And if I kiss you in the garden, in the moonlight will you pardon me and tiptoe through the tulips with me. I just love their sense of humour!

∞

I have been watching 'The Hollow Crown' - William Shakespeare's play about Henry 5th at the battle of Agincourt. I found it very moving and during my prayers I asked for Earth to be freed from her bondage of sorrow!

Patiently we wait at heaven's gate - deliberation is the key factor in obtaining harmony - mistrust is the downfall to achieving our objectives! We reach across the heavens to give you succour in your hour of need, asking that you resonate with us in truth and greatest joy. The chaos that is created by man will undoubtedly cause his downfall – this is fact! By your Love and insistence at putting this to rights, we find favour for the human race. We offer you our blessings and shine light on a troubled mind. We are bound by our faith in one another and we liken you to a breeze that blows through the land, a breeze of good fortune . . . of opportunity! We arise from the depths of gloom and disappointment - we rise to take hold of a new day. We forego a natural urge to despondency and keep the shadows at bay, welcoming in the sunshine, welcoming in the light and dawning of a new day . . . one of bliss and fortitude, accepting our mission with a bright heart.

A death knell rings loud in our ears and we open the hornet's nest, waiting for the stampede! We have long since stood at the gates that lead to our destiny and we point you in a new direction, opening up such wonders to behold. We have been summoned to a higher sect, to higher office, and we proclaim our allegiance to the cause of truth and greater understanding among mankind. We speak as one who has no sight but we behold the coming of a new age of destruction - of desolation - of the pillaging of another's rights, sacrificing moral issues with an outpouring of contempt and scorn! We reach out across the boundaries of Earth in the hope of changing this most abysmal wreckage of mankind, looming on the horizon. We are dependent on you to air our views and we sacrifice our time and energy into pursuing the freedom and justice, which you all deserve and which is your right – your birth right! We openly denounce those who pour scorn on their own kind and we manipulate those images in your mind to show you that we have indeed sunk to those depths, incurring human misery on a grand scale!

We raise you out of cataclysmic degradation, offering you solace and hope at your plight on Earth.   We remain as always wholly designated and wholly resigned to helping mankind, rationing out common sense on a huge scale. We forego the niceties, putting it straight and bluntly in your minds, so that you may access that part of yourselves which is known to recoil in terror at events that have happened in your past history! It is known that many fell at Agincourt and we would be wise not to repeat such familiar scenes of misery and treachery. We would be wise to remember that all men are but brothers under the skin. We make a mockery of those times gone by and we salvage what we can of human nature, of human endeavour to put things right so that you may look with Love upon your brethren!

It is with great emotion that we gather you to your senses, reeling in those of you who would cause mishap or harm. We bathe ourselves in truth and harmony, adjusting thought streams and propelling you to do what you know is right within your hearts, bathing your minds in compassion, in Love and in peace. We have enabled a greater harmony to pervade your soul and we deliver to you, by requisition from the highest Divine source, a most powerful bond of urgency, delivering to your soul greater advantage and illumination beyond all imagining. Grace and purity of spirit unfold before you and allow you the prerogative of stepping out of the old and into the new. This is recommended by our counterparts as one of great necessity, supplying greater knowledge and wisdom unsurpassed, giving you the courtesy that is due to one who comes to kneel in all humility.

We are but a thought, a whisper away, and we have generated further studies for your perusal, granting you free access to our records, our dynasties! We grant further clarification of what lies ahead and push you into the open arena, excelling in our discourse, opening up the hearts and minds of all those around you who suffer ignominy, rancour and scorn. We pour Love on the gaping wound of humanity and take you to safe harbour, stressing the importance of staying out of the limelight until all is ready for our coming! We initialise and delay further instructions until we have encompassed that time frame that will allow us further coverage. Tranquillity of spirit is our goal and we succumb to this happy state of mind. We respect your wishes to remain with us and we are constant to the cause of uplifting mankind to higher realms where truth and justice prevail.

∞

Before I closed our session today I felt the presence of our North American friend as he drew close to speak to the group.

We have an abundance of good cheer here today and we welcome you to this wigwam of peace and harmony. There is Love between you, we see it in your hearts and we are thankful for this! It has been a long journey for you, turbulent in parts, we know this but we are here to give you succour, to give you food for thought and to understand those disturbances that deluge you from time to time. We are paragons of truth and higher clarity and we bring you sustenance,

181

we bring you that which you desire. Prepare yourselves and harness the energy as it comes flooding in, use it wisely and arm yourselves with LOVE, hold it like a canopy shining bright around you, where no harm will befall you. You are most cherished little ones, most cherished, and this is an understatement! We propel you to destinies unknown at this present time but we are armed with 'Truth and Light'. We unfold our wisdom little by little, bit by bit so as not to alarm you, so that it seeps in and settles and finds a place within your hearts that will open your minds. And with all due respect, we know that you search for truth but it is a hard task for many of you to understand what is coming in. What we are being shown will be shown to you also!

We envisage a future of Light filled with Love and the importance of everyone being counted of the same magnitude. We do not expect you to understand exactly . . . we weigh and balance what is given and leave it to you to assimilate what comes in, what is given with Love. It may be you find it wanting but then it balances out and you can take that, which at one time you were not happy with that you felt uncomfortable with. It is all about learning and growing, for us as well as for you. We want to reach out and hold you in our arms and tell you that everything will be alright, and so it shall, but there are many things to overcome, many pathways to be walked before you can fully understand the wholeness of creation - the complete and utter wholeness! And as you have said *(turning to one of the group)* it is like a peeling back of the layers to get to that very core within your being that very core of who you are. And it is a wonderful journey that we have all been on . . . that we are all still on and will be for evermore!

We ask that you take stock and follow your impulses, generating further studies. Open up your vision and shine . . . shine your lights out into the cosmos. We will find you wherever you are, in whichever reality, for we are bound by that thread of Love and the honour and the respect that we have for you is boundless! We have worked together many times and we give thanks for this happy reunion of souls who have gathered here in this time frame to make this work, to help mankind in the raising of their vibrations and those of Earth.

Blessings on you all, now and forever (*and with finger wagging here*) now take care to keep that Light shining bright within you all at all times. It is most important you are that Ray of Light for mankind!

As I read these notes back, more and more I feel that this was White Cloud's energy and from 2012 onwards he comes forward more strongly.

∞

Again our Star friends drew close to speak to our larger group.

We feel the energy from you all. We coexist, sharing information that is brought through from the cosmos to set you on the right track for your spiritual evolvement. We are borne here to bring you Light and Love and we shine this Light where it is needed into the nooks and crannies, into those places of darkness where our word has not yet reached. We are beholden to you today for listening, for taking these thoughts into your heart to accumulate, to sift through and find a common bond. We are by no means insistent that you listen to our words . . . we only hope that you will aspire to those thoughts that will bring about a great change in Mother Earth – in your Earth! It comes as no surprise to us that there has been much jubilation for your having registered these thought patterns and wish to bring that Light into your lives on Earth.

We forego a path of destruction for one of upliftment and joy - there can be no other in our eyes! We hearken to the call and lift our sights higher, remembering a time when our destinies were intertwined. We obey the laws of gravity and descend to be with you once more. We Love you and honour you as our brothers and sisters; we share that peace within your hearts and hold you to us in deep embrace. We share this pathway you have chosen for yourselves and we ask that you take up the banner of life and lift yourselves out of the darkness and into the Light. This has been a mammoth undertaking and we delight in your acceptance, in your vulnerability at this time.

We shall all join hands and sing . . . sing with Love and joy in our hearts for we are born to bring Love into the world. We do our best

183

to help you and shepherd you along, and yes we know that you stumble from time to time, as do we all. We pick up the pieces . . . we pick ourselves up and start all over again for that is our way, we are stubborn like that! We will not share your doom and gloom, we will rise ourselves above the plateau of Earth and anoint ourselves with Love. We will overcome all obstacles that stand in our way! Do not be despondent or put down, we are forever with you and will always be so. We wave the flag and we drink a toast to you all – Peace be with you always!

We do have your best interests at heart and we lay down no rules or regulations. We offer you comfort and solace, we offer you a way through your troubles and come to help whenever we can to put things right and in perspective. To show you as a friend that if you take this path or that path, invariably you end up in the same destination. Your experiences on this path were different from the experiences on that path but you learnt as you went along and you reached your destination! Sometimes it took a little longer but you got there in the end - and this we give you credit for. Annihilation was never the name of the game - this is a learning curve, this is where you come to your senses and realise that without Love - there is no world!

We hold in great contempt those that scorn our words and yet we continue to shine out our Light like a beacon bright to help those who will not listen, to help those who are so tied up with wealth and material possessions that they do not see the true meaning of life! We open up a network of services that will help these souls to discover the truth of who they are, of why they are here. We ask you to rise up and shout and cheer so that we may hear your voices, so that we may know you are with us one and all!

This is a programme of pure intent - there is no need to fear or to hide in the shadows. We supplement your Love with our own and send out that ray of Light that will circumference the Earth, encased in that shining energy field of Love and greatest joy, lifting her up to regain her true status and to become as she once was – a Garden of Eden! We thank you for listening and we invite anyone who would like to take a turn of linking with spirit, holding that vibrational frequency that will bring you so close to those that Love you, that care for you and watch over you every step of your journey upon this Earth plane. It is an honour for us to share with you, an honour and a delight. We take our leave and wish you well on your journeys.

∞

We create a catalogue of all thoughts and expressions, reprogramming and analysing data stored in our memory banks to be utilised at a future date. We accept we have made vast discoveries on our journey into the unknown and we propel you further forward to do your duty. We have explained as much as possible how we intend to take you along this highway and have a broader understanding of the ways and means of achieving this. Holding you under duress was never our plan and we shelter you from harm, seconding what is in your hearts. We have registered a bargaining process and analyse in greater detail; there are many thoughts to be shared, many avenues of discussion yet to be received and broadcast, however, we give you the benefit of the doubt, opening up further discussions to implement our success.

This has not always been an easy path to tread and we harness the energy wisely, motioning you to look back and see how far we have come. We propel you to a place of safety in broad daylight, and we know this makes no sense at the moment, but we are given to understand of further losses. We impeach those of you who stand on the side lines and ask you to come forward to give us your support. We rationalise an arbitrary resolution, manifesting greater control in areas that are unclear in your minds, releasing you from the grip of fear in your hearts and helping you adjust to what is coming! We prepare you for the same frequency and allowing for fluctuations we reserve an energy field that will encompass you all. Thank you for observing these measures.

∞

During meditation this morning I was shown a pulsating, purple light and a tunnel of soft cloud. I felt the desire to sing the hymn – 'Oh God our help in ages

185

past, our hope for years to come, our shelter from the stormy blast and our eternal home'. Now I'm seeing soft, undulating clouds and have a feeling of being back in the womb again. I'm sensing the very beginning of life and can see the head and back of a foetus curled up safely in the womb.

We separate and modulate, bringing peace to a system already overloaded, this is necessary to access conditions within the mind.

Later at our trance group I felt my North American Indian acting as door keeper.

We anticipate a connection with the unseen!

There was a pause of five minutes while different energies showed themselves to the group.

We are resonating loud and clear and it gives us great pleasure to be in your world once more, to come among you and to share with you. Now shall we make a start - are there any questions perhaps that we can help you with? Come, there must be something you wish to ask - even though the sitter here is panicking!

You mentioned when you first spoke – "We anticipate a connection with the unseen"! Is there anything we can do to help with this connection?

Sending your wave patterns of Love is the greatest thing that you can do, it envelops the sitter and heightens her energies making that link with the source, with that Divine connectedness so that she may ride the waves so to speak, like your people on the sea with their boards. It is energy . . . a frequency that can be connected into. In actual fact it is all about frequencies – your frequencies and our frequencies coming together, amalgamating and blending as one. It is wonderful to achieve this and it will become easier and easier as time goes on for all of you. It is just having that trust to let go, not hanging onto the fear that is within your hearts – the fear of failure! There is no failure, we go on ever onwards to achieve harmony, to maintain that peace and equilibrium within your hearts - that is what we are aiming for and with that peace comes Love and where there is Love there is always a way.

We help you adjust to our wave patterns as we draw close to you. We open up the curtain, the veil that keeps us apart, it is such a fine veil and we see you glimmering, we see you shining. We draw you to us in this light frequency, we dance with you, we uplift your spirits and we dust you off and polish your auras, helping you to adjust. It is not long now little ones . . . you are almost there! We feel the connections growing stronger and stronger as we reach out to you. 'Apple Blossom time' - look to this time for greater evolvement, a time of growth and fulfilment is open to you all and we take the cup and drink in that elixir of life, see it bubbling up effervescent, more than enough to share with those around you. We develop our connectedness to the unseen, watching them grow closer and closer, blending and swaying in harmony and resurrecting a dream. And we shall walk through those pearly gates and see the wonders that lay before you, a grand awakening where all will hear and all will see! We shall come into our own and we will be wise beyond our years. This network and pathway will open up to you. Be prepared - use your time wisely!

∞

I am a ripple on the pond. I am the warm breath of the wind. I am starlight. I am all these things . . . I am free to be. Oh how wondrous, no encumbrances no artificial incentives, I am borne by the wind to the mountain tops. We wait for you here!

We adjust our settings and face north, projecting our image upon the mountain ranges. We simplify this connection and ask you to follow suit. We indulge you by listening to your requests and we answer as best we may under these difficult circumstances. The boundaries of Earth are heavy with mist but we see your thought forms – we feel them as they gather to us. We prepare you for this journey and we ask you to accept the measures we bring to you so that you may adjust to our frequencies. There is a toing and froing between our worlds and we give you credit for adjusting. We beseech you to understand our requests to remain firm and we request silence - listen to the silence within your hearts! We know your world is noisy, deafening even, but if you reside within your hearts you will find that peace. We request a sectioning off of the unpalatable and suggest that you look within. We are proud to call ourselves Star people extraordinaire for we have come many times to your world – and you to ours. It is a precipitous time for all as we come among you and we feel such Love for you. We open up the emancipation of the human race, we delve deeper and deeper and we wish you to assist us in this. Pioneers, we are all pioneers of a wonderful future and we ask you to be prepared for greater contact in the near future as we come to assist you on your journey, opening up new realms of possibilities on both sides.

I had the sensation of being underwater, pointing my hands and drawing them back several times as if swimming, ending in a prayer position. An old and wise North American energy drew close and I believe it was the figure I used to call Grandfather. Many years ago he gave me a silver ring during meditation, explaining that it symbolised our never ending Love.

We never said it would be easy but we are sure you will make this connection many, many more times!   Look upon it as a never-ending journey with new excitement opening up on the horizon and new roles to play, and we will be there giving you a helping hand in all that you do. We do not take for granted that you help us in this endeavour, but we coax you and guide you and hope that you will listen to our words . . . to push you into place as it were. We ask you to tread carefully and we round off the edges so that you will not hurt yourselves. We honour this connection with you and look forward to many, more such meetings! There are endless possibilities stretching way before you with boundless opportunities to grow, to learn and to share with one another in this merry little band! You are much loved. Keep this connection going, keep these connections going between you. Others may come and go but remain firm - do not give up!

A different energy drew close that felt feminine and oriental.

Our Blessings upon you! We open up a network of services that will propel you all further forward and we are indebted to your expertise in these matters. We will not take up more of your valuable time, but know we are with you and watch over you. There is great excitement

188

ahead of you, great joy and peace of mind which we all look forward to. We break this connection and wish you well.

Thank you, we look forward to seeing you and hearing you soon.

∞

Today while sitting to meditate, I saw a little squirrel running across the garden wall.

A squirrel teaches us to be patient . . . to analyse what has gone before, to ponder on issues, to gather the wisdom and to sleep on it. There are steps that need to be taken and not taken lightly, there are issues that need rectifying and there are grander issues in store waiting to be overcome. We set great store by those who come to seek and those who seek will find the Kingdom of Heaven. We monitor this connection, traveling that pathway of old and we are by no means upset that indifference has claimed a greater part of your mind, but we beseech you to understand that this connection will bring us greater rewards in Heaven than you can ever imagine! We deliver an outcome that will set you back for a while, but do not underestimate our powers of persuasion to follow this through to the final letter.

We are Star Keepers extraordinaire, opening the portal that allows you to see yourselves as you truly are - atoms of light, Supreme Beings woken and given the imagination to travel on this beam of Light that is yours for the asking! We rein in the harmonies and bring you absolution of the heart and soul, applying the prophecy on everyone's lips . . . for if truth be known we are those unspeakable demons from your past! We venture far into the great unknown and allow ourselves to be used as a harness of sorts, a harness to bring about the end of world corruption, an end to the absurd anomalies that forecast even greater tragedies that you could ever contemplate! We realise the end of a dream for some of you - but we are able to co-exist within the boundaries of your heart.

We open up a flood stream, a network of emotions that will allow us

189

to gather momentum once more, travelling out into the great unknown, registering your thoughts and understanding that this can 'never' be the end, even though the end is in sight! This is like a never ending game of charades and our game plan is to galvanise you into action, trawling those reserves of energy given to you and sustained by us to bring you into action once more. We alert those nearest and dearest and point you in the right direction giving you a gentle push, into unknown territory perhaps, but this will spur you on to learn greater things, overcoming a manifesto of cruelties and absurdities that hold you back from functioning in your true state! We allow you to ponder on this and ask that you summarise what is necessary to hold you back from the brink of destruction and chaos!

Do not allow your thoughts to mar what is a most necessary mission shared by a long line of ancestors that have travelled this way before. We undeniably exist in another format and we retrieve what we can to enable free expression in this dimension. We pull back the curtains that cloud your vision and hold you to us in deep embrace. Love knows no bounds, Love serves to strengthen our purpose, Love is the be all and end all and though the sanctimonious come to kneel before us, they do not realise the most simplest of truths – that all initiatives can be forged with Love! We allow no pomp and ceremony to gird our loins, we need only your comradeship and your ability to stand and be counted as one of us, and the Love that is within your hearts will grow and grow, uplifting an entire nation of souls as you express yourselves in deep repose. We motion you to follow us on to the horizon, where all is waiting to be granted to those who stand firm in the greatest Love and companionship.

In my mind, I thanked them and asked who they were?

We are those creatures come to guide the universe and we are known as benevolent to the human race.   We are Light energy beings, roaming your planet to help you at this most difficult time in your evolution. We guide you with some authority as we have been this way before and suffered tumultuous explosions. We were beamed to a planet that gave us back our health and clarity of thought, enabling us to exist in another format more suited to our needs. We therefore

190

have great joy in explaining that there is 'no end' there is only the 'light' of true understanding felt within the very core of your being. We are resurrected and born to give greater visions for the future of mankind!

∞

While preparing to meditate I saw the cloudy image of a medicine man, wearing an animal skin.

We transcend the difficulties that assail us and overcome a malfunction that has taken us to the back of the line of support. We shelter you and keep you safe and out of harm's way, brushing up your energy field. We motion you to detach!

I went deeper into meditation and tried to stand back further and let them come to the fore.

It is of paramount importance to set the record straight - we do not allow in any circumstances to be set on a pedestal! This will only achieve confusion and although we achieve undiluted bliss, we have neither the time nor inclination to be brought before the masses. We accept your condolences for we are brought to bear witness to what has been the greatest tragedy on Earth since time began! We have sheltered you from the harsh winds that blow and prepare you to take a back seat as we come forward. We have taken a stance that will prepare you and we initialise these services that we may undertake this mission with greater clarity. We are well versed in this connection and it has given us the greatest pleasure to come among you once more. We realise this is not an easy task but never the less, one we give thanks for with all due respect!

We motion you to tread the boards of fame; we know this gives you cause to doubt us and we say to you - this has been long overdue! We have no idea as yet how this will all pan out but we shelter you and uplift your spirit, helping you to decide for yourself how we may work together. We derive great joy from being with you on the Earth plane once more. It has taken an inordinate amount of time to complete our mission as was ordained long ago, and we superimpose

191

our thoughts on yours, magnificently accepting thought patterns that come in from the ethers. We expressly forbid you to overstep the mark as this would be counterproductive to our achievements! This broadband of energy is utilised by us in this connection and we strengthen your resolve, pushing you forward into the limelight.

We are most honoured to be with you at these times and we strengthen your purpose, adjusting frequencies where necessary and opening up a broadband of energy that will assist you in your recordings. This has taken a mammoth adjustment on our side as well as yours and we supersede these thought patterns, bringing us into orbit and closer inspection. We have adjusted these frequencies in a time scale that has little or nothing to do with what we are about, broadening your mind to accept that at times there is little we can do and yet we allow our minds to connect and grow alongside, dipping here and there as we shine our light on cloudy issues. We register your likes and dislikes, opening up a reprogramming that will allow you to accept us as we truly are . . . we are Light and we are Love, we are all there ever has been. We open up this connection and propel you forward into a deep state of bliss, regulating patterns of understanding that will propel you forward into a new dimension

As I my friends drew even closer I felt absolute bliss. They seemed to be looking around the room and my neck, which had been very stiff for the last week, seemed to move easily around to the right.

There are some adjustments required in this room! We make note and attend to the frequencies, sanctioning a renewal of services that will stand you in good stead!

I asked if an earth ley line was causing the problem as our trance group had found that this particular part of the room made us feel tired at times.

The earth energies are of no importance in this connection, it is a stalemate of sorts, a compounding of energies that realistically have no purpose here, other than come to gloat! We aspire to greater ethereal conditions and send these frequencies on their way with our Love and blessings! Be not amazed at the difference this will make with your connections in the future! We are open to debate on this subject but allow you to prepare and cleanse, and we will do the same on our side. There is a corridor, a corridor that opens up a connection with the unseen!

I stood up with my eyes still closed and held out my hands, sending out energy. The following words filled my mind and I spoke them aloud:-

As God is my witness, I allow the energies to manifest that will occasion a healing in this room, so that we may be undisturbed by those spirits of a lower nature who may come to make mischief! We ask that there be a standing down of those energies. We ask for Love and Light and healing for those here and we close the gap, allowing a renewal of energies to bypass any unsavoury connections.

GO IN PEACE - NOW!

Live and let live. Spread Light and Love, manifesting lightness of spirit. We propel you to your own domain. May God be with you now and forever more!

I proceeded around the room still entranced and with eyes closed, sending out energy through my hands, massaging the air.

IT IS DONE!

We thank the Great White Spirit for watching over us and keeping us safe!

I am including this transmission in case anybody else has problems with energy levels in their sacred space and would like to use these words in conjunction with asking their higher selves for help.

∞

Before breakfast, I sat in my sanctuary to practice atunement with my guides and helpers.

We incorporate a coming together of timelines, manifesting what is necessary for our worlds to amalgamate. We bring you our blessings and we thank you for making this possible!

I can feel lots of tingling on the top of my head, slightly to the left and am being shown purple with golden symmetrical patterns overlaid.

We operate on a new level giving time for the adjustments to be made, reprogramming and revitalising conduits of energy supplied to you as means of entry into a new dimension of time and space. We have by no means perfected this exercise but we will in due course, opening up a network of services to be governed and given a new sense of direction. We challenge you to accept these deliverances of excellence bar none! We are supremely connected to that magical 'Star of the East' where the Sun rises and gives you light - we also light your soul from within. We are fibrous beings glowing with light . . . Divine Light given as our right. We are Divine Light and energy unsurpassed . . . we project an image within your skull and open up your vision!

I then went deeper into meditation and seemed to be inside a body, looking up through a golden spine as it enters the skull. Everything is being shown in purple and gold and I can feel a tingling on the right side of my skull. I'm going through a tunnel of sorts and am now in the middle of what looks like a huge rib cage. There is a lot of pressure in my head and I am going to have to ask them to back off soon. I can feel my face changing, especially around my mouth; still entranced I have opened my eyes and am looking around the room. I feel this is all in preparation for our future work together, but had to leave it here as I had been sitting for well over an hour and couldn't comfortably keep the connection going any longer.

∞

7.10.12 – 7+1+0+ 1+2=**11** - *The master number eleven appears today and I woke in the early hours with these words echoing in my mind.*

We position ourselves ready for the final thrust into a new dimension, overcoming those issues that hold us back from attaining our heart's delight. We move forward with greater ease, allowing

194

mortification of those who refuse to accept renewal and we prepare you to accept a greater production of services right across the globe. We have mastered the phenomenon of accepting thought patterns with greatest ease and we manifest what is seen as our greatest joy, championing the cause with little or no ill effect. We march forward to claim our just deserts and detach from a world that has brought chaos and despair! We dispel all notions of sadness at leaving behind our home, for our home is now a land of hope and glory, materialised before us in glowing splendour, a new world of infinite beauty. We match like for like, settling you down in a new world of ample proportions, motioning you to take on a new lease of life in a dimension that has prepared for your home coming.

Is the world ready to make this leap of faith?

We suggest she is and we prepare you to take on the semblance of a new sphere of light and beauty unsurpassed. Do not be troubled at leaving behind an Earth that has been mismanaged in every sense; we 'will' restore her to her former beauty, allowing the ravages deep within her soul to heal as we protect her from destruction!

I could sense the Earth as a living breathing life form.

She weeps for you, her children, letting you go to be restored in a new dimension of time and space.

I feel our Earth Mother is pushing us out of her womb, giving us the gift of life and expelling us into a new dimension. I'm feeling so light now that my heart is expanding and I have the sense of rising up.

How exactly will this happen, will it be a gradual awareness of a new dimension, or will we literally be catapulted into this new time frame?

There will be jubilation on a grand scale across the world when we herald in this re-birth and it will appear as if in a dream.

Through some kind of heat haze, I'm being shown a blue and sandy coloured planet that looks like Jupiter. I'm experiencing an incredible freedom of spirit as I

195

swim through energy. There is clearness of vision - it's as if my brain is being spring cleaned. I'm rising up from the doom and gloom, from the sticky glutinous thought forms surrounding Earth into a higher frequency where I can breathe more easily.

We expand our condition where the old falls away and we emerge like a butterfly from the chrysalis, ready to take flight. We prepare for the dawning of a new age and one we give thanks for!

Later as I sat in my sanctuary pondering on our new world, my attention was drawn to our wooden garden table. We bought it nine years ago and had repaired it over and over again, replacing the wooden top and benches when they started to rot.   Finally this year we had to replace the legs and it suddenly dawned on us that we no longer had the original piece of furniture.   Apart from the odd nut and bolt, we had completely replaced it! This table looks like the same table but it is a different table. I think perhaps that is what they mean as gradually we are changing our frequencies, they are getting lighter and we will no longer put up with a frequency of doom and gloom. Eventually our frequencies 'will' catapult us into a new dimension, because we will no longer vibrate in the third dimension!

∞

When I woke this morning this first sentence was going round in my mind, and so I slipped out of bed and started to write.

We teleport through time and space, governing our sense of direction and we present a clearer picture, shadowing the unseen and connecting to a finer frequency. We release the shackles of a life time's distress and reach for the stars, growing in anticipation for what is in store as we herald in a new awareness for mankind. We capitulate, reining in the harmonies and discovering for ourselves a greater life force energy; we are well aware of the process this involves and we magically predict a massive learning curve. We deliver our messages to the 'Children of Earth' in a way that will bring peace and tranquillity of mind, spreading our Light and wisdom, encouraging a new lease of life and positivity on a grand scale. We branch out and recommend a deep cleansing that will allow for greater clarity, and we beckon you to join us in the time to come,

196

opening a network that will lead us to greater conquests. We overcome a difficult time and propel you safely on to the horizon. We beam ahead and light your pathway, forecasting greater treasures and a multitude of gifts waiting to be explored.

∞

Yesterday I came across an old Aladdin oil lamp while rummaging through our garage. I had bought it nearly twenty years ago after being inspired to write a poem I called 'Facing the Past'.

Clearing out the cupboards . . . opening up the drawers sorting through the rubbish - mine as well as yours. Clear away the cobwebs and brush away the tears from accumulated rubbish built over many years.

Dark, dank and musty . . . with fear you raise the lid. Dig deep into 'Pandora's Box' where all the past is hid. Examine what you find there sift it through and through. Just like Aladdin's Magic Lamp we'll change the old for new!

We have relinquished the old and make way for the new, opening up a hive of activity and expressing ourselves with the greatest of joy. We beam you to a new world and bring you glad tidings of greatest joy. We open your mind to accept the impossible and we release our greatest assets, opening up our connection with other worlds, beckoning you forward to regain your rightful place beside us. We peel back the layers that cloud our vision, asking to be rescued from the maladies that assail our every waking moment.

This is the time to take stock and to unveil a future that has no comparison. We dedicate our next transmission to our ever-growing stream of followers, tantalising the senses and registering the hopes and dreams of an entire nation. We supplement your knowledge, executing a grand style of communication, penetrating the hearts and minds of all those who come to listen. We allow a regrouping of energies and transcend our wildest expectations, drawing on those reserves of energy that are there to be utilised. We expect a finer resolution in the not too distant future and warn you not to expect too much from those around you! We are all governed by our own

197

awareness and translate accordingly - this can sometimes bring disappointment. We hover on the side-lines ready to bring in those frequencies that will connect us to a higher vibration. Understandably this is a most sombre time for those who cannot adjust and there will be a massive fall out! We govern this interlude with great finesse and underline a new chapter in your lives, taking the debris from the past into a new time frame, sifting and re-examining where we went wrong!

∞

Yesterday I deviated from my 10 year vegetarian diet and ate some red meat. I have had a craving for a few weeks now and while cooking roast beef for my husband, finally succumbed! I felt guilty afterwards and was worried it would affect my ability to tune into higher frequencies. I was awoken at 2.12 a.m. this morning and wrote down the words filling my mind.

We supervise a coming together of like minds and we shadow you from dawn to dusk, making our connections count like no other. We register your ups and downs and set your mind to rest, we have maintained this frequency despite our deep concerns to the contrary; this has been a most necessary evolution and we proudly direct you to follow your heart in all things. We match like for like, superintending our way through the storm, releasing negative emotions that may hold you back. We are on the brink of discovering a new realm of infinite peace and beauty unsurpassed, measuring our distinct advantage of becoming your neighbours and saving the day. We proposition you to allow a settling into mode, extravagantly aware of further reserves of energy that have us leaping in all directions.

Are we moving soon?

These things are in the lap of the Gods and we challenge you to understand our motives, respecting the wishes of those who come to serve in time honoured fashion. We discriminate only when boundaries are established and we know you take this very seriously, giving us the index necessary to make a full recovery. We power you forward to do your duty and we take the bull by the horns,

198

underlying key issues that remind us of why we are here. With all due respect, we have forecast a most necessary expenditure of energy in pursuing our dreams for all mankind and we stabilise a volatile situation on the horizon, begging you to look with fresh eyes at what is facing you head on! We delight in informing you that we shall, in all honesty, pave the way for a most salubrious undertaking and we shall be there at your side, monitoring and supervising this connection. Hold back your ears and listen with your heart!

We have underlined a passage in history that will take us to the next phase in our evolution and we spell out the worst case scenario. There will be key issues that need adjustment and we rely on this to sink in as we gather more information. We rely on a broadband of energy that will take us further afield and we shed light on some troubled areas, ready to do justice to all that is given. We superimpose our thoughts on yours to register our true intent and we express ourselves with great joy at this interlude ahead of us. Please prepare yourself for this invasion of sacred souls who come to assist you in your development.

It is with the greatest respect that we deliver our finest and most thought provoking material, and we demonstrate with true accuracy our most potent methods of accessing data of considerable worth. We dedicate this next portfolio to those who seek the truth and we point you in the right direction monitoring your growth. It is with great dexterity and fore thought that we propel you forwards on to your next conquest and without further ado, we are mentioned in despatches as being part of a new breed of inspirational speakers that have risen from the ranks with great aplomb!

We endeavour to get our message across loud and clear, helping you to make these choices of paramount importance and we rely on those, like you, who hearken to the small voice within. We sanction a renewal of energies that push us into the arena to stand and be counted as a true representative of the cause. We trust in you implicitly to register our appeal and we delight in moving you forward with this initiative. Spread your wings and fly and we shall see greater dedication in the line of duty.

We express ourselves with great tenderness to be working with you in this way once more.

∞

The group waited for me to settle into trance state and were entertained by an array of coloured orbs that looked like planets in alignment. At last a very quietly spoken energy came forward to speak.

We have a gift for you in the near future and one that you will treasure. We speak of times gone by in the distant past, brought now into the open . . . brought to fruition. We hold analogies of this in our heart and we bear witness to a greater future for mankind. We vow to each and every one of you that we shall open the hearts and minds of all and we are not picky or choosy, we ask only that you will listen, listen with your heart . . . let the bud begin to grow, let it open, let all be known, let all be seen! We share our Love with you and nurture you and uplift you so that you may remember, remember with every fibre of your very being. We come as essence of Truth and Light and Love beyond all worldly measure. You are 'so' loved . . . you are held in the highest esteem from those here who wish you well on your journeys and we are so proud of your endeavours!

We fulfill our destinies to shine like the brightest star and we shine so brightly . . . we are Love . . . pure Love. We quench your thirst for knowledge, we open up the boundaries and there on the horizon is all you ever hoped or wished for, and all will be granted! We open that aspect of your minds that will allow you to grow and move forward with greater ease. There are those who would push you aside or allow you to feel unsettled, but we ask you to remain firm and stay to the true path where you will be safe. We yield to your requests for greater life force energy and we manifest these glories in the not too distant future. There is an abundance of wealth and wisdom coming your way and we manifest a great array of services that will have you dancing in the fields . . . dancing with joy; and we will be there with you joining in, happiness personified, and it gives us great pleasure to share with you as we watch your destinies unfold.

One more thing, take refuge in the fact that we are 'always' with you!

We grow stronger with each passing day, stronger in that bond of Love and Friendship. Carry this forward with great momentum and we will overcome all trials and tribulations. There is nothing that will stand in our path for the Power of Love grows stronger!

∞

Chapter eleven

Love springs eternal

We feel the motion . . . we feel the bliss . . . unknown destinations drift into view, playing their part in this great scenario this massive explosion of events on the horizon. We spend our time accessing monolithic exploits that raise our frequencies, projecting us far out into the cosmos, leading us to greater realisation of all that life has to offer. We march on a world that has outgrown its initial combination of humour and self-sacrifice and we detonate a series of experiences, propelling you to a place of safety when in greatest need. It has been necessary to conjure up a new stream of thought that will allow for greater compilations of genuine historical advantage. This is a time of great healing and great apprehension amongst mankind and we take up the banner of hope, propelling you forward into a new dimension. It is here you will be guided to form a new coalition, one of extreme advantage for all who grow and prosper in the name of love. Love is the be all and end all . . . Love is the concrete evidence that supports the universe. Love is the grounding structure from which all life springs . . . it is eternal . . . it is relentless. Love springs from the core of our very being, opening up a network of services that spread far and wide, encompassing the hearts and minds of mankind.

We welcome you to these shores and open our arms to receive you in all Love and honesty of spirit.   We take care of you and protect you, monitoring your success as we help you to achieve what has been uppermost in your hearts and minds over these many years. Sequentially we alert the mind to accept these frequencies that bombard you opening up a network, a programme that will restructure your mind and assist you on your journey. We have been grounded on several occasions in the past but now we move forward at an alarming rate, opening up new passages to explore, delving deeper and deeper into issues that have lain dormant and which need to be overcome to move forward. We propel you forward to do your duty and we initialise the greatest respect in those who come to serve.

We respect your wishes to stay on board until the final moment when all will come to fruition. And we shall become as one once more in a new world of fresh hope, principled and flourishing in a new state of existence that will give succour to all who draw near, experiencing for themselves what is available to every man, woman and child upon this planet! We register your concerns and have put in place a simple but most effective by-product of our Love. We have simplified this connection and allow you greater access through our memory banks, this will forestall any claims that do not register within our cells as being pertinent to our quest for 'Truth, Light and Love' beyond all earthly measure. We point you in the direction where those Saints of old have trod and where has sprung an eternal pathway of 'Hope and Joy'. We prepare for that that day when our hearts will sing and we are eternal optimists for the future of mankind. Bruised egos contemplate their mission upon Earth and we confound those who do not register our appeal as being absolute! We allow a network of services to stretch far and wide and we bring you absolution - each and every one of you - to begin again and start life anew in a new world of strength and grace.

We prepare for a massive recall of envoys that have completed their mission on Earth and this has been of great importance. We allow a falling back into place of those reserves of energy that shall assist us, manoeuvring into place those who come to serve and reinstating those who have fallen by the wayside. We impel you to take heed of the quest you are on, installing in you the greatest respect for those you work with, who look to you for advice on all matters relating to the spirit. We connect you to a frequency that will sample some home truths and this will enable you to take on board greater resistance and endurance for the times ahead. We march with ever increasing strength and fortitude and we put it to you that we shall never give up on our quest for the human race!

Like many others I have been struggling to keep my head above water financially and asked if this would improve.

There has been a memory retrograde that has left us slipping . . . we untangle the knots that lead to despair and we open up the conduits

that will allow free access. We supply you with means of entry into a
new world where material constructs slip away. There will no longer
be a need for what you call money . . . the counterpart is Love,
assisting one another in your daily lives requires little much else,
having the same regard for another as you do for yourself. On Earth
everybody sets great store by financial gains and what is in the heart
has become a matter of conjecture. We allow you to see with your
heart, to see and realise a great fortune of treasure that is built up
with your regard, with your Love for your fellow man, for your
neighbour. We do not set such store by personal fame or fortune.
We are measured by the Love within our hearts and we conquer over
humiliation that is brought upon those who have no real assets, apart
from the Love that is within them which is far greater! You will be
looked after and provided for - all is being prepared for a most
worthwhile future and we shall tread that pathway of Love and Light,
relishing your great success in accomplishing a mammoth task within
an allotted time frame. Go now my child in peace and protection!

∞

*It is May 2013 and there are only three of us at today's trance group session. My
communicator held his hand up to my two friends in salutation.*

Blessings upon you both with such maturity of grace and spirit . . . we
ponder on these thoughts and bring you our blessings. It has been a
long time coming but we are being brought to fruition to enable
growth of the spirit on a mammoth scale across the whole wide
world. We have branched out to bring you succour and it gives us
great pleasure to come among you . . . you are most loved and
honoured in our dimension. We bring a treaty to those on Earth, we
welcome in a time of peace and happiness, a lightness of spirit and
joy personified.

*The recorder was silent here but I do remember holding what felt like a ball of
energy in my hands and feeling very emotional to the point of shaking. When I
spoke next it was in a lighter voice on a different frequency and one of the girls
saw what she described as an 'aurora borealis' light radiating around me before I
spoke.*

We bring in a time of greater beauty . . . greater wisdom and we honour this connection, taking you further along new routes to explore. We ask you to shed the Light wherever you go . . . that is your purpose. We ask you to memorise what is in your hearts as being true wisdom unsurpassed, ready to create a bridge of perfect alignment, enabling a bonding of energies that will take you far upon this highway of Love. We have bridged that gap and we bring you Joy, we bring you Love . . . we bring you all that you need for your journey. We have enabled this broadening of energies to encompass you at this time and we bring you sweet blessings.

Thank you, it's much appreciated.

We wish we could share with you this undiluted bliss.

At this point I felt as if I was floating in purest Love.

Let the tendrils of this energy curl around your hearts.

I stretched out my arms, sending energy to the group for quite some time.

We are so thankful for the work that you do . . . more than you could ever imagine. It is yours to care for and yours to share . . . take this energy and ignite your minds . . . ignite your hearts. Accept what is in the core of your very being . . . you are so much more. We accept your dedication and bear witness to a time of greater fortitude. Know that you are loved more than you could ever know and held in the highest esteem. Take comfort in one another.

Blessed be all those who come to serve and blessed be those who need a light to guide them. The lantern bearers are here, their lights shine all around the world and we are part of that Divine Light, radiating out. Take strength from one another.

A group member spoke:- Blessed be . . . hail the words of the Star Goddess.

∞

During our group session today I was taken back to a life where I had been sold into slavery. I saw a tall, dark skinned man who was wearing a silver wig and fine brocade jacket in red; he was carrying a silver tray with glasses upon it in a grand house. I spoke to the group and told them what I was experiencing.

Do you remember what work it was you did? What were they to you?

They were nothing to me . . . just a place to lay my head. I was a manservant and treated well in the circumstances. I served at court for the ladies and gentlemen. There are lots of people milling around. There are ladies in fine dresses of silk and brocade, wearing large wigs, and gentlemen in breeches and brocade . . . it is a very grand affair. The name Marlborough comes to mind. I was something of an oddity . . . they gazed upon me and prodded and poked me. I'm getting the name New Guinea.

Do you come from New Guinea? I feel that is so!

Were you very young when you began to serve this family?

I was a young man – fit and strong!

Do you feel trapped between worlds? No, I feel this is a life experience.

Is there part of that experience that you would like to have healing with or for?

I don't know, perhaps it is 'service to others' - I am quite happy to be of service to others!

Can you remember any first memories of that life time you are in now?

I'm running through the trees, playing with others.

Have you got any shoes on your feet?

No, I think I'm naked . . . I've got no clothes on. I'm a boy and we're playing. I'm playing with other children, we are running and laughing.

I'm back in the village where I live, there's a greyish gruel looking food in a black pot.

Can you see anyone that you know?

I can see a mother figure . . . she is wearing some kind of cloth over one shoulder, covering her chest.

Can you look into her eyes . . . can you see her eyes? Do you know anyone in this life time today who has the same eyes?

I started to shake and cry.

You're quite safe, these are just memories. It's your experience that you've carried with you through life times — you're quite safe - it's part of the healing process. Would you like to tell us what's making you unhappy?

I was calmer now but couldn't speak.

Maybe it's time to let go of that feeling. Memories can't hurt you, it just an opportunity to see a life for what it was; a chance for you to see that maybe something in that life time is no longer needed in this one. Maybe the experience will help you in this life time. Do you want to tell us where you are now?

I'm trying to get myself back.

My friend then talked me back to normal consciousness. Another friend sensed an African slave when I was crying and she felt I was looking into the eyes of my mother who sold me into slavery. There was also an image of me being put onto a ship and a strong feeling of loss and rejection with the words 'Rock of Ages'.

My biological mother had me adopted in 1946 when I was just a few weeks old. In those days it wasn't easy to keep illegitimate children, but it was rather a shock to know that she had also given me away in a previous life! I believe this has come to the surface now as I have not been able to grieve for my mother who died in April this year.

A few days later I settled back to listen to a guided meditation from Blossom

Goodchild, who channels White Cloud and The Federation of Light. I must have zonked out because when I came round I was in what looked like a chamber in some sort of space pod. Everything looked white in what was a small diagonal shaped room with ridges in the walls. There was a bed of some sort and I sensed it was for healing, drifting off again in the loving energy.

∞

Walking by the river today, I stopped to rest against a tree and looked out over the water. Words bubbled into my consciousness and the deep sorrow within my heart burst forth, enabling a healing to start to take place.

Spirit, dear spirit of the tree please can I rest awhile with thee. My back fits snuggly against your bark do you hear me, can you hark to the spirit residing in my breast that yearns for peace and tranquil rest. I gaze upon the river stream running along yours banks of green. I see the water shining bright, reflecting a thousand dancing lights, catching at my inner eye, releasing my spirit to leap and fly above the worries of my mind to higher realms that understand. Our life should have much more to offer and so accept the tears I proffer. And they must flow out to the sea, becoming one in harmony, sheltered from the coming storm, borne as one who is forlorn upon the crest of crashing waves washed into dark and silent caves. My spirit rose and then was dashed - a thousand leagues it plunged and crashed. At last it rose unto the surface full of Love and of great purpose, being part of God's creation the wholeness and oneness that brings salvation.

∞

I sat in the garden to rest and after closing my eyes seemed to rise up into the sky, looking down on the tree tops and hillside below me. Gently I started to descend and was able to look more closely at the trees, which were vibrantly green and majestic, every leaf of every tree shimmered like fine cut jewels . . . it was absolutely amazing. Gasping at their beauty I suddenly found myself drawn back up into the heavens, roaming across the country side from an incredible height. I could feel the wind battering my face as I looked through closed eyelids at the scene beneath me, and all the while I could feel my hands resting on my solar plexus. This is a most incredible experience and one I'm hoping to learn more about.

208

Perhaps this is possible because our frequencies are changing and we are gradually developing new skills of travelling out of body. Later I sat in my sanctuary with two friends communing with our Star friends.

We shelter you in our embrace . . . we reach out and touch the hidden depths within you, branching out in new directions. We open up a network that will bring strength of purpose and we encourage you to grow in stature, overcoming the trials and tribulations on your doorstep. We will overcome all misgivings and we nurture you and guide you in the footsteps of the esteemed ones that have gone before. We monitor your ascent to help you grow and we shall have future dealings with those that can help and guide you. This is what we pray for and we urge you not to be despondent!

Have you any hints that might help us humans overcome despondency?

We shelter you from any immediate harm and ask you to nourish yourselves with the Love that is already within your hearts. We shelter you from any physical abuse that may come your way and we are always there in the background, watching over you. We would like to say, you are most welcome in these little gatherings and we open up and explore a network of feelings and emotions that will bear witness to what is in store for each and every one of you. We are beholden to the countless episodes that propel us further and further into the realms of delight. We are well versed in the saying that 'two minds are better than one' and we delve deeper, overcoming all anxieties that may hold you back.

We counteract what may be seen as a misappropriation of energies and we allow a trickle of knowledge to restore confidence and point you all in the right direction. The mind is cluttered and full of sorrow but we shall overcome . . . we have been through worse trials and tribulations and we have arrived here in one piece! We shall conquer over the scorn of others, we shall survive the ridicule, we have survived a holocaust and we are here . . . speaking to you now! The human spirit is a fiery temperament that cannot be put out, it cannot be extinguished and it searches on forever growing and nurturing itself.   We remain in a calm and serene condition and adjust

209

wherever necessary. We enfold you in our Love and care and guide you ever onwards to that Divine Source. Take heart and be strong . . . the future is bright for those such as you. Go now with our Love and blessings, shelter in the peace and sanctity of the heart, it is here you will find all that you need.

∞

In the early hours I was woken with words forming in my mind; still befuddled I reached out for pen and pad to record what was being said.

We afford ourselves great jubilation and measure our continuance of life unadulterated by rhythms of the flesh. We participate in a grand connection, relying wholly on ulterior motives to forge a new connection of the highest formation. We realise a conquest of enormous proportions, inviting a challenging and forthcoming notoriety, forging a basic construction of thoughts and ideas that surface for recognition. We allow a falling away of natural resources, resisting the tumultuous realities that face us head on and we supply an inordinate amount of challenging behaviour that supplies us with a vast amount of knowledge. We relinquish the old outworn patterns, exchanging for new and vibrant discoveries, challenging the establishment with every fibre of our being and we bend over backwards to execute a grand finale waiting for us ahead.

We rein in terror and a misappropriation of energies that lead to exhaustion, tapping into greater reserves of energy and allowing ourselves a moment's respite. We awaken the senses, propelling you to a place of far greater tolerance and peace of mind. We transcend our determination to succeed and invite further studies to avail ourselves of further knowledge waiting on the horizon. We prepare for a homecoming that will avert greater tragedies and we allow a simmering of respect to rouse further implementation of proceedings to take place. Please give us a moments grace and we shall receive what was always promised and now beneficial in our development. Take heart and propel yourself forward into the great unknown, registering our appeal for the human race. Godspeed!
There is the necessity for adjustment in attitudes and we check our credentials, analysing and theorising how best to maintain this

connection. We have vowed in solitude to reconnect to that vibrant stream of energy in clarification of all we hold most dear. Accept our condolences at this time as we move forward on that ray of light and inspiration. We shall not hold back from treachery or those deeper aspects of joy and happiness as we register our devotion to the cause. Seeking acceptance on all levels we hurtle into the abyss accepting our fate!

∞

I sat in my sanctuary for guidance and felt a soothing presence draw close. Surprisingly the first word in my head was, Champagne. I wonder if this means there is cause for celebrations ahead!

Champagne . . . its bubbles rise to the surface in effervescence. We bring these delights, rising to the occasion, championing the cause of truth and justice for all. We amend certain areas of expertise, relying on you to bring forth the joys that are manifest in your soul. We prepare you for the time ahead when we shall be as ONE, connected in all senses. We have promised this and we shall keep our connection to one another, growing stronger and stronger as each day passes. We have prepared a greater journey and we welcome you with open arms as we step into the arena. We shall not forsake you or lead you astray and we enter this bargaining process with a great deal of warmth and protection flooding our hearts and minds. We enable you to speak our thoughts gesturing you to follow us, into unknown waters perhaps, but we have guided you and protected you for many decades. We rely on our judgement and wisdom to carry you across those waters, registering your hearts delight as we welcome in a new clause of understanding.

It is no mean feat that we have conquered over our desires to stay on Earth at this time but we believe, with your help, we can open the floodgates to greater wisdom and we challenge you to accept our alternative theories of what is best for the human race! We allow you the prerogative of stepping out of the old and into the new, and we forgive you for wondering whether our motives are indeed held sacrosanct. We believe we come at a time of great hardship for the peoples of Earth and we deliver a broader aspect of truth and joy

211

beyond all earthly measure. We register your just intent to set this down for the record for all to see and we prepare you to sanction this clause. A maladjustment has arisen that gives cause for regret, but we allow these little nuisances to prepare us for the straight and narrow. We accept that it has been hard for you of late but we propel you to do your duty, answering the call to one and all that travel with us on this pathway.

We believe we have come at a time of greater determination and perception of what is available to us on the horizon; we welcome in a time of bliss and perfect peace in seclusion from the mass of souls who writhe in torment and sorrow. We lift you up from this fog of negativity and propel you forward to do your duty and we shall reserve a place for you in Heaven, of that there is no doubt! We enlist as many as we can who will hearken to that still voice within, allowing it to become louder and louder so that it cannot be ignored and must be obeyed.

It is within the heart of your very being that we are able to question you and we ask you now to trust that spark within, from the very heart of the universe, from the indelible mark made upon your soul at the time of entry into this framework. We believe we have tapped into that knowledge and free enterprise that has become our trademark for success and in the future we allow you to take pity on us, for we registered your concerns at a time of the utmost importance!

We abandoned our cause when we should have held firm, holding on to those beliefs that would have made it possible for the human race to rise once more in all splendour and grandeur. We allow you the prerogative of becoming the first race to achieve this transition into a new era of grace and favour, loved beyond all earthly measure and held in the high esteem from those both near and far! We assist you on your travels and we give 'Light' where there is none, sheltering you from harm and uplifting you in your times of lowest ebb. We ask you now to adjust your settings and to behave accordingly.

We welcome in a new race of 'Super Beings' and we give you time to make these adjustments so that you may sit with us in greater harmony and fellowship. Be prepared to access what is available to you at this moment; we shed further light in due course and open up the harmonies that await you, sharing our deep embrace. Excel in areas where mistrust has been present and we shall open up the conduits that will allow us access.

The human world is beyond our comprehension, more so for the challenges it presents in times of stress and hardship. We reprogramme you to accept these challenges and adjust a loving heart to overcome all scenarios, all judgements that cloud your vision and prevent you from reaching those heights destined. We reach an understanding and allow a settling. Take heart for the future is brighter than you think, much brighter for those who listen to our words.

∞

There are just three of us sitting today for atunement with our guides and helpers. The energies felt very powerful and after taking the girls through our golden healing meditation they came through straight away.

There will be an opening very soon and we will treat this with great aplomb - it will benefit you and many others in association with yourselves. We come at a time of plenty, born from the ashes of our forefathers and we ask you to remember us in your prayers. We are now of great substance in your universe and come on a mission of mercy, asking that you ingratiate yourselves with us so that we may complement each other on this journey of high intent. We bring greater expertise to help you on your way and we bend and listen to what you have to say on the Earth plane. We overcome the maladies that present themselves and we ask you not to be ashamed of the burdens that you carry . . . these implement further success in your endeavours.

There was a loud bang heard on the tape at this point.

We strike while the iron is hot and take you further afield; there are many services that you bring to the Earth plane and we assist you in these measures that will bring further fulfilment of the vows that you chose to make at the time of your entry into this world. We have presented ourselves with a fête accompli and we know it has been hard of late to yield the abundance in your hearts and minds. There has been much self-sacrifice, we know this, and we take it on board. You have come forward in great strides and have done so well in the past and in the present we push you along and coax you to hear our words. We uplift you in your endeavours, helping you to manifest what is in the very heart of your being and we shower you with great Love and affection. We manifest greater control in areas where respect is due and we shadow you from morn to night in great expectation of what is to come, what is to bear fruit. It is a time of harvesting those fruits and we shall see greater manifestation of all we hold most dear, propelling you forward in the wake of our Love. We shall be with you as we always have been, sheltering you in our embrace. Take care, little earthlings.

There was a loud bang as if someone rapped on the table.

A different energy came forward and I raised my hands in the air, clapping and singing, joining in with the vision of a group of dark skinned children who were smiling and singing.

Oh happy day, oh happy day, oh happy day, oh happy day, oh happy day when Jesus walked, when Jesus walked, oh happy day!

Hello, welcome!

We are much obliged to you for listening to our little verse and we open up the conduits where you all may shine, where you gather forces and join together and become as one! We manifest greater control in areas of restraint and ask you to loosen those shackles of a life time and to come to 'life' - to come into your own being of who you really are. Cast off the shadows and let that sun shine in. Radiate that Love and Joy around the world and we shall see greater success for all of you as you channel your energies into those fortes that befit you. You bring us hope, you bring us Love . . . you bring us great Joy and we welcome you to our home. We are not allowed to say too much at this time but we do bring you fresh hope of a new dawn where all will come to fruition. The fruits of your labours . . . we dangle the carrot to draw you on, to tempt you with our titbits of information . . . a trickle here, a trickle there will soon become a fast flood of information. We study your intent to become true warriors and we are overcome with the emotion that brings you closer to us. We bring a cloak of safety and wrap it around you to give you sustenance and to show our good will. We are homeward bound little ones . . . we are homeward bound!

∞

I sat alone today and because of the heat struggled for a while to make that connection.

We forgive you your trespasses and shine light on a troubled area. Be of good we cheer, we open up a network of services that shall have you leaping in delight and we open a massive line of support, governing a wider programming. We allow in this instance a variety of alternative solutions, taking on board what is paramount at this time. There will be plenty of time for you to action what is necessary, alleviating all tension that holds you back from achieving the very best. We supress a giggle and let you into a little secret . . . we are reprogramming a new beginning and harnessing the energy that will see a brighter future for us all. We shelter you from the harsh winds that blow, rediscovering for ourselves that vast connectedness to the great unknown. We balance the frequencies and restore harmony, stepping on the toes of the esteemed as we re-evaluate our next move. We suggest a reconvening to finalise plans and agreements, asking you to remember this franchise is in your own best interests. We sally forth to gain credence over a troubled period in your history and we reserve our energy for a just cause.

I started to feel a stinging at my left temple and knew that something was happening.

We have programmed you to accept our words with greater resignation to detail and we monitor our conduits. We take on board

215

a de-materialisation of all benefits and remunerations built on superiority over the classes, demonstrating the methodology and brutality of the system on Earth. We are confounded and rake through the debris of hostility encased in the bosom of mankind. We charge you with looking after the young ones and setting them on their feet for a finer location. We propel you to a land of safety, a land where we may live together in 'Love and Fellowship', reinstating those loved ones who have taken up the mantle of Light to fight for the masses and have fallen into degradation.

We challenge you to accept the fact that we are one and the same . . . do not dismiss this for we are bound by more than Love, we are bound by that constellation that shines out into the nights sky, the home of our forebears, and we allow you to convene with us in this way to champion the cause for freedom of choice, freedom of spirit and the freedom to raise your eyes to the sky and shout YES . . . take me! Take me to that planet of Love and Joy and freedom of expression, help me to teach the little ones about Love and the nurturing of the human spirit. We feel the jubilation within your soul and remember our connectedness!

∞

At our trance group today I proposed that we work towards taking our talents out to a wider audience in a 'Heal the World' roadshow as such. When my turn came to sit I struggled with the communication and doubted my ability to be able to achieve this in the near future.

Our strategy has always been for completion!

May I ask for completion of what?

Our mission is to succeed where others have failed in the past and we rely on you to draw the line.   We offer our hand in support and we draw you together with greater expertise to champion the cause. We acknowledge the fact of supremacy over those ideals and theories that are put to the test and we openly challenge you to honour these proceedings and to take them a little bit further! We openly address

216

you and further take note that the challenges we lay before you are without doubt of the highest intentions. We have a broad beam of knowledge . . .

I struggled again and was fearful of drying up!

These are the fears that galvanise us into action to help you take root, to help you grow, encompassed in the Love of the Great Divine and we ask you to bear with us for there are great stakes ahead!

Later in the evening I sat once more; immediately I was shown a young, dark skinned girl wearing a robe but I can't see the colour of it in the dark.

Great Spirit – is there a way we can continue with today's channelling where I was struggling to bring through the words – it was about challenges and I would be very happy if we could continue if that is at all possible?

I can see now that the girl is wearing an orange robe and she has pulled it up to cover her head; I caught a glimpse of her dark hair held together in a single plait. Her name sounds like Minaha and she is responsible for the washing and cleansing - of what? My own mind interrupted, filled with a myriad possibilities but it suddenly dawned on me she is responsible for the washing and cleansing of articles for the after world. I can see someone writing an infantry, picking goods surplus to requirements. I can see an arc of peacock feathers on the wall; originally I thought this was an Eastern lady wearing a sari but this has an Egyptian feel to it.

We are born on the arc of a wave that brings hope and glory to mankind, sheltered from the storm, manifesting greater control of our own destiny. We embark on a wave of triumph and jubilation, transcending the cares and worries of a lifetime's distress and we bear you to a place of safety from the hurricane, from the traumas that await mankind.

I can see a Roman soldier now – a centurion, I remember him as a guide from the beginning of my spiritual development.

217

We transcend our wildest dreams and take you aboard, hurrying to ensure your safety and your natural progression from one state of existence to another. This has been foretold many times in the past and in your jurisdiction we open a canopy, expressing ourselves in a format that is able to be understood by all. We come in peace personified, brought to bear witness of a finer life in a new dimension of time and space, unveiled before the masses in extenuating circumstances that bring us completion on Earth. We deliberately ask you to stand still at this time and listen, take the time to listen more often so that we are able to express our views and clarify certain points raised. We are here to help and to settle a score promised long ago - we bring to fruition a seed of thought, nurtured with Love and good will of spirit. We set you down in a place of safety to honour this connection and provide greater services for the times ahead. This is our declaration, this is our manifesto of requirements needed to enable this action to run smoothly and we are in charge of a great deal more than this!

We feel you growing closer to us and we express ourselves with great tenderness to be working with you again in this manner. We make the feedback necessary to bring you to fruition, to bring you full circle and we enfold you in our loving care. The challenges we have set you can be alarming, but fear not for we are at your side ready to make that connection and to strengthen and uplift you in this most noble cause. We reap the benefits of a lifetimes work, honouring the thought forms that pass between us, channelling more information and sharing with the masses. We enfold you in our loving care, beaming ahead to light your path and to bring assistance where it is due, where it is necessary to honour the bargaining process. We transcend all cares and worries and they shall not hold you back from making this a most jubilant occasion. We tend to the sick in mind, body and spirit, beckoning you not to lose faith in your abilities and our transactions - these benefit more than you can ever know!

We of supreme intellect pass on these messages and bring you hope beyond all earthly measure; hope and brightness of spirit. We ignite that light within your soul . . . a living breathing energy, powered with Love. We are transformed, gathering strength and perfection, opening up a sensual repartee that will have the soul singing. We multiply in strength and numbers, setting out on a golden pathway of that there is no doubt and we take part in this grand connection, opening the hearts and minds of those who have no knowledge of us. We count ourselves among those lucky ones who have gained entrance to this phenomenon, this state of bliss and perfect harmony.

I was so happy that I had taken the time out to tune in and ask for help and that is what they would like us all to do, just to save some time in our busy lives for reconnecting to our spirit home. This for me seems to be either first thing in the morning or before retiring for the night, those quiet times before the hustle and bustle of the day begins or in the evening when the mind and body wind down after a busy day.

∞

Today I sat alone for healing, visualising the golden light coming down into my head and flushing down my spine and to my surprise it carried on further down into a strong bony tail. As it did so the skin and flesh peeled away and I felt my tail swish. Does this mean I am reptilian as well as human; this doesn't alarm me so much as make me curious. I could see my skeleton as white with the bony vertebra running up my back to the centre of my skull. Later I looked at the notes from my first book and noticed this short passage, which could be the answer I am looking for.

"There is need of closer scrutiny to recognise what it is we are facing up to; these harsh realities are necessary to recover former identities and we march you along to uncover them one by one! We believe this mission will give us even wider scope to fulfill our main objectives and we relate all that is needed for you to grow in our Love".

I sent out healing to the many different facets of my being . . . to the many different personalities and beings, asking for healing for each one. Immediately I can see the North American Indian who I call Grandfather, he has long grey hair and I noticed he is not wearing his feather headdress today. He is inviting me to sit with him and to be assured that all is being taken care of.

We have reached that place in our journey together where all will

219

come to fruition and we take care to guide you along this pathway, reaching our destination of immeasurable joy and success in all we do together as a team. There are those that wait on the sidelines and we give thanks to all those who venture forth with great Love and Joy in their hearts. We prepare a shelter and gradually intuit your feelings and emotions, shedding light on various issues that surface at this time. My child you do us proud!

The Indian I call Grandfather is now leaning forward and taking my hand in his.

We have watched you grow and nurtured you, and you are held in the greatest respect both near and far. We offer our hand in friendship and guide you along this pathway that will lead you to Heaven. We shine a light on those issues that have held you back from accomplishing your true worth and we behave with the utmost dignity.

Tears are falling down my cheeks at this point and I cried out . . . Oh Great One hear my call, ignite that flame of Love that has slumbered for so long in the hearts and minds of many on the Earth plane.

We tremble at these times of injustice and nurture those who echo our words around the globe. We suffer the 'Children of Earth' to come before us and to kneel with us in appreciation of those efforts. We are sublimely connected by that golden light, igniting within us the clarification of all that is to come for the future of mankind and his offspring. We initialise a request to take you with us into those lands of plenty where we shall be catered for, where we shall sing in harmony and receive the blessings of the Great Divine. We involve as many who will come to this gathering . . . this great gathering of souls that unite as one, and we delve deeper and deeper to explore any misgivings that you may have. We open your hearts . . . we open your minds to express yourselves in the format that is readily available to you and we ask you to make a difference!

We open the floodgates to let you through and we shelter you from harm, expressing our condolences for those who could not mange, those who could not accept the help we offer. It is beyond all imagining, contemplating what is given from the heart and yet outwardly rejected by those few who rely solely on the governance of their own desires. We magnify a project that will bring you strength and we superimpose our thoughts on yours to take you further afield, opening up those vistas that beckon us forward. We will not harm you or lead you astray for this is not our way and we deliver you in one piece so that you may circumnavigate the globe, taking with you our blessings and that undeniable thirst for knowledge that can never be quenched! We rely on you totally and wholly to stand firm in this your hour of need and we shall obey our calling, delivering to you all that is recommended for our journey together. We shall strive for the best, the very best, in all we do and we make no demands on your time or energy, we only superimpose our thoughts on yours so that you may action these whenever possible and in your own jurisdiction.

We manifest a great array of stories to be told and these shall be seen to be accepted around the world. We travel on, expressing our views to all and sundry and to those who come knocking at your door. We implement a grand array of services and beckon you not to lose the plot when all lies before you in great array. Be ready to pick up those tools and implement what is given from the heart, what is given in all honesty, recuperation is the name of the game and we allow you an insight of what is before you. We gather momentum, opening up a wealth of enquires that shall lead us to your heart in great contentment and we will tend to your needs from near and far, expressing ourselves with greater certainty and clarity of spirit. We ask you not to doubt us for we are always with you and always will be!

With tears flowing I asked for a sign. Grandfather - let me feel your hand in mine, let me feel the warmth of your hand . . . let me feel the warmth of your embrace.

I felt the warmth and energy in my hand and imagined being held close, nuzzling my face against my grandfathers while a feeling of deep peace enveloped me.

We express ourselves with great tenderness to feel you in our arms once more and we bend to your every whim, expressing ourselves in terms of endearment that will touch your soul.

Oh Grandfather, what shall I call you . . . what shall I call you when I write your words? I know names are not important in the spirit realms but it does help people to understand and to link more closely and clearly if someone has a name. Great Grandfather, is there a name I can link these words to?

On the crest of a golden wave . . . we come and nurture that true spirit that draws us together.

I'm feeling such peace upon me now and sense the words 'Golden Spirit'.

Is that your name grandfather – Golden Spirit?

My little Earth Flower, all is being made ready and we shall have 'lift off' very soon. We express our condolences for these times are very hard upon the Earth plane and we have made this connection at a time of great suffering. We alert you to our plan of action and we contemplate a future where all will be drawn together, initiating a rapid response all around the globe. We take you on a journey that will transport you to a world of beauty unsurpassed and you will grow and learn our ways as we become accustomed to one another, as we become accustomed to your charity of spirit and relentless courage. We have pooled our resources, reinventing the wheel, manifesting all you need or desire for the advancement of your world, incorporated into a new regime that will bring about a powerful union between our world's, between our peoples and those on Earth will have a choice. There are many avenues laid before them and they will suffer the consequences!

That doesn't sound very friendly!

Free will is a legacy on Earth and you will all make up your own minds as to where your allegiances lay. We are not being cruel when we say this, we leave it up to you, we lay before you the evidence and the proof of our existence and we let you decide. There is no harmful intention - only enlightenment; we have the prerogative to take this pathway or that pathway – it is yours to tread! You have the choice to stay on board or end this discussion . . . but we have only just begun to gain your interest! You are beginning to trust what you are being given, what your antennae is picking up and receiving and we beam you LOVE . . . Peace . . . understanding!

I am feeling really relaxed now and trusting what is in my head and it feels really lovely. I can hear what sounds like wind. I feel so peaceful and seem to be speaking in slow motion. Thank you friends; have we got a long time in years before we make these decisions or is it something that will be happening in the next few months or years - this amalgamation of souls?

We believe you are under duress in your world to make these judgments, but in quantum physics we have no bargaining such as this . . . we simply go with the flow. We are drawn together or propelled apart. We radiate Love and Peace and Harmony . . . that is our purpose . . . we generate our Love in perpetual motion.

We have redesigned the universe to give you a jump start to enable your race to be held in that suspension of Love . . . to be reborn, to be perpetuated in constant movement and expression of thoughts and ideas that shall set you up in a new connection; a new term of office in a new direction, in a new galaxy in a new dimension of time and space that is open to receive you!

We depend on you to guard against intrusion of any kind for we have set up this experiment, enabling you to travel on. It has been a most challenging time for all of us and we accept that we have not always made the right decisions concerning the human race. However, we are well positioned to accept this next phase in your evolution and we tread most carefully, asking that you will honour this connection and allow us to guide you with well-intentioned thoughts. We will achieve together an approximation of what is relevant, an approximation of how we shall achieve this greatest feat!

My hands feel so numb I can't feel them anymore. There is a strong shivering energy coming across from the left and I am radiating light and energy. I spent the rest of the time bathing in this wonderful energy and thanking them.

223

Sitting in my sanctuary early this morning I asked - are there any messages you would like me to share with the people of Earth today? Almost immediately back came the reply:-

Oh blessed creature of light, we are well prepared to take on this summon of enquires and we broadcast for you in equal measures of honesty and truth, opening up those boundaries that keep us apart. We honour this connection and take you aboard.

I'm getting the words - 'Rapid Response Team'!

We broaden your horizons, opening up the tailgate to success with a pardoning of all misdemeanors that have led us astray in the past. We speak to the population of Earth, initialising the greatest respect for those that answer the call, opening up a network of associations that will allow a broadening and strengthening of energies that shall manifest in due course. There is bombardment on a mammoth scale and we allow this process to take place, summoning further requisites, this can be a lengthy process and one that is sorely needed. We accept a reconditioning that shall strengthen our boundaries, propelling you further forward. A mismatch of energies have led us to this point in our evolution together as one kind and we allow you a peep into the annals of history; here you will find a just solution to the ways of mankind, ushering in an alliance that will stand us all in good stead.

There has been a clamp down in certain areas and we wish you to tread most carefully, a distinguishing of cultures has led us on a wild goose chase but was necessary to kindle your curiosity, to kindle your respect for those that walked the earth in a time of great courage. We speculate on a new world of outstanding beauty and we petition you to accept the reasoning we bring you with the greatest respect. We ask you to honour your fellow man, bringing yourselves to that point being made ready at this very moment in time, a foreclosure on the days of old, a foreclosure on those elements that have brought mistrust on a grand scale, dishonouring your own kind with thoughts of a jealous nature and disrespecting yourselves. Humility and a surrendering of past misdemeanors bring nourishment to the soul

224

and greater rewards. We challenge you to uplift your spirits, to come among us in peace and harmony, opening up that spectrum of delight and immeasurable joy.

We temper our messages allowing you free rein, supplying the measures needed to bring greater success in all that you do, and the champagne shall flow and we shall not hold you back from celebrating this massive learning curve that is there on the horizon, just inches away from the success you deserve and with our warmest regards! We have chosen you to come among us and we envelop you now in those thought waves of Love that shall petition greater advantage. We tread in the footsteps of the esteemed, asking that you follow on with greater expertise and courage and we allow a falling into place of those conduits necessary to make this application work. We shelter you from the cruel winds that blow and follow up with decisive action, taking us across those boundaries to the other side.

We have a meltdown of services and consider our next step forwards; never let it be said that we exposed you to a raw deal! We entice you forward, expressing our condolences to the masses for allowing the upkeep of these services when we should have initiated this final countdown at a much earlier date in your history. We extend our energies recalling you to that final scene, stating the obvious. It has been so in countless ages past and we resurrect you, opening up that network of services that shall have us holding our heads high.

We make an application for clemency resurrecting the human race and pointing them in the right direction, a mass gathering of souls claiming the right to regenerate and to rise again, dedicated souls who fight for freedom from oppression, galvanised into action and spreading the word loud and clear - we are here - we are here! We 'are' here, ready to overcome those malfunctions of the spirit that have given cause for distress in the past and we open up your vision, propelling you forward into the great unknown, spearheading our Light, cutting through the darkness with clearness of vision. We make ourselves heard in every direction, in every walk of life and we promise you eternal life in a new dimension!

How do we reach this place, the people of Earth will ask . . . "how do we do this"?

All you have to do is just follow your heart. You don't 'need' to do anything but to be who you really are, who you truly are . . . that spark of 'Light' from the Great Divine within your breast. Let the trappings of Earth fall away . . . the material constructs . . . they are of no importance.

I'm getting the feeling now of stripping away the façade, taking the armour off, once protection from life's knocks and blows, stripping away the supports from this earthly existence, getting right back down to basics to the nitty-gritty, to stand in our own truth like new born babes just sprung into life. I'm being shown the picture of a curled up newborn surrounded by Light shining out from him like a golden star. All around I can see rocks and asteroids just bouncing off this Light and the child remains unharmed. This made me think of Jesus who shone his Light but they took him and nailed him to the cross . . . they bit into his flesh and destroyed his body. So did this really happen? In my mind I'm saying "Oh ye of little faith" but is it me or is it my friends from the spirit realms

We will vanquish those thoughts of doom and gloom; we will sanction a reprisal of energies that shall take you to the abyss and beyond!

But what about Jesus – did Jesus die on the cross and 'why'?

Jesus was an appendage of energy projected to the masses to bring Light into the world. His followers were brought into our jurisdiction to give fellowship and harmony to those who followed that true warrior spirit, a warrior of hope and joy. A warrior spirit brings alive those energies that are within us all to project Light . . . to project Truth and Honesty and when all else fails, when all crumbles around us we rely on that true sprit within our very being. That is our connection with 'home' from where we draw our strength and courage and our Master was borne before us, opening up that pathway to the Great Divine. He leads us to gentleness of spirit, gentleness of thought . . . at all times loving and open to those energies from the cosmos that gave him strength to overcome those

226

physicality's. We are more than mere flesh, blood and bones . . . we are stronger than you can ever imagine and we shall rise above all discord and strife, we shall rise above those mundane issues that surround you. You have only to call out and we shall be there by your side! We sacrifice ourselves to the cause of helping mankind and we strive ever onwards to reach that brightest Star, a star we hold in our bosom for direction, for warmth, for purpose and we envelop you in our Love and bid you a good day! May the Love of the Great Divine be with you now and forever more!

I'm getting an image in my mind of a strong man with tanned face; he has big bushy hair and a beard which is full of dust. There are sandals on his feet and he is using a long staff to help him climb up the mountainside; displacing rocks and stones that fall away as he climbs higher. I have the sense that he has great determination and will not give up on his quest. He has now reached the top and is turning around excitedly to beckon others to come up too. At first I thought it might be Elijah going up the mountain to pray to God but it feels more like the time of Moses where he was shown the promised land of milk and honey. I'm now getting the words - we are almost there and the song 'there's a place for us somewhere'.

Thank you friends, thank you so much - I Love you. May the Love of the Great Divine be upon this earth, this planet we live upon and we send our Love and Light to the new world that is waiting for us somewhere.

I had in my head the song 'Somewhere' from Westside Story and Michael Jackson's version of 'We're Almost There'.

"No matter how hard the task may seem, don't give up our plans, don't give up our dreams. No broken bridges can turn us around, because what we're searching for will soon be found. Just one more step because we're almost there, just one more step; don't give up because we're almost there"!

∞

Chapter twelve

White Cloud and friends

I woke in the night with a tickling sensation on my face and went to the spare room to see if I was needed for communication. As I prepared myself with the golden light I felt a prayer on my lips.

May the Love of the Great Divine be with us and may we have this moment together in Peace and protection.

I sensed White Cloud drawing close from the left and felt that smile of utter peace, wrapped in a bubble of absolute bliss. No more words were spoken but I knew I had been touched by the Light of Love. The following evening this energy drew close once more.

We feel the presence of the 'Infinite One' and we raise the alarm. We herald in a new experience and share with you our thoughts and ideas for a greater future for mankind. We let that settle in your mind's eye before commencing, adjusting our thought streams to coincide with yours. It empowers us to know we have you on board and we suggest a few little tips to ensure greater accuracy as we propel you to the land of dreams!

I AM HE who calls the nations together. I AM HE who rides with you at dawn across the blessed plains of a peaceful existence. I AM HE who taps you on your shoulder to come and join us . . . to protect the innocent who have lost their way. There shall be a grand reunion of souls marching across those plains and we shall join them, standing firm in all honesty and sincerity of spirit. We section off a place for you to sit with us and we charge you to accept this offering of friendship and a Love unsurpassed in all its glory and freedom of spirit.

'Listen' from the heart and 'feel' the words drifting into your mind. We associate ourselves with a broader knowledge and terminology, expressing ourselves with great joy to be working with you in this way. We breathe life into a situation close to home, searching a reappraisal of energies that shall assist you in this quest.

I felt a strong energy drift in from my left, blending with me and the lower part of my face grew bigger.

There is greater vulnerability in taking on this mission and we vouch for your integrity, expressing our hopes and desires for this most worthwhile cause. We accept this connection has its flaws but we undeniably express ourselves in terms of endearment, radiating out our Love for all to see and we brim to the surface with Love.

The Love I felt here was so intense, it literally brimmed up through my heart and head so that I was bursting with Love and the tears streamed down my face.

We open up a network of enquiries that shall bring greater resolve and greater reserves of energy, dedicating our life to the service of others in this trek across the universe.

I'm now seeing deep drifts of snow and tall pine trees.

We shall need extreme fortitude for the days ahead; the road is winding up into those hills from whence we came to join the gathering of our clan and to sit before those fires of friendship, ties that can never be broken as we adjust to the rhythm of your heart and the greater calling from within your very soul to join us and become as one. This is a great honour to make this connection and we shall honour this treaty with the greatest respect, personifying what we have all come to accept with honesty and beauty of spirit.

We face the final frontier and adjust our settings, rallying to the cause and we bring you a gift . . . a 'Shamrock Rose' from the Federation of Light . . . the overseers of all developments appertaining to the human race. May the Love of the Great Divine be with you now and forever more and may He bring you more than enough to set you on the pathway to success.

229

There are just the two of us sitting for trance today and before we started our session two Jehovah witnesses came to my door. I'm afraid I was busy preparing for my group and didn't answer the door to speak with them; however as I went across the courtyard at the back of my home they saw me and waved. I had my hands full and not wanting to offend, I called for them to follow me into the sanctuary at the end of my garden. Immediately they started talking about the bible, which was no surprise as I have had friendly discussions with this sect a few times. I showed them my room with all its different facets of spirituality and took this opportunity to explain what our group did and how we were able to contact the higher realms by holding the Love within our hearts. I was very gentle in my offerings even though the lady kept waving the bible and quoting from it.

My friend arrived for our session and pointed out to them that the bible was not the whole truth as some gospels had been omitted and other parts changed, which the lady refuted. Half an hour later, we declared a stalemate of sorts and they left, leaving us feeling unsettled! We drank lots of water and sat in the sunshine to clear our auras and cleansed the room of any negative energy that had accumulated. We always meditate first, using the golden energy to get ourselves in the right mindset and in the opening prayer I asked for a healing all round in the situation we had participated in.

I sat first and there were several faces coming forward including a Tibetan looking chap, but most prominent was a youngish female who was a Native American Indian, followed by my old Indian who puffs up my mouth and has started to draw close more strongly now. I felt deeply entranced and it was a while before we started to speak very slowly.

We bring you Love from the universe. We challenge you to accept the understanding we bring . . . Love Divine all Love excelling, Love from Heaven to Earth brought down. We look out through the great abyss.

Welcome friend, thank you for coming through.

We register the properties in your hearts and minds and we take you to us in deep embrace, sectioning off the unpalatable that is hard to digest at this time. We motion you to accept the understanding that we are from those depths within your very soul . . . that we travel to you in thought form. We open up a network of understanding that will propel you further forward onto your destination and we open the veil suggesting that you look inside, volunteering to work with us in a way that will be accepted by all. We generate further studies and allow you one step further forward. We open our hearts and receive you, identifying with your thought streams. We shadow you from morn to night, opening up those conduits that allow us this access. We are beholden to all you do and all you say, for we know your hearts are true to the cause of upliftment of mankind. Do not be put off by those few who come to you in ignorance, they shall find their way in due course. They have many paths to walk before they reach that state of existence you are in at this present time.

Is there a key word or phrase that we could use that would help open their hearts to the true Godhead if that's the way to call it; that we can help their enlightenment quicker to make it easier for them?

LOVE springs to mind in all things, LOVE is the key! Generating that Love will melt their hearts; it may take longer in some than others, but we have agreed this pathway on Earth and we delegate those few who 'can' listen, listen with their hearts and understand that pathway that brings them full circle, back to that spark of divinity which is in all of you. We have adjusted to the frequency of this lady and we feel comfortable with this energy . . . a bright spark of humanity. *Yes she is.*

Rest assured all is being done to bring others into alignment and we shall not stop until all are taken into that fold of Love and joy.

(There was a cracking noise at this point).

We expect an opening in due course that will nourish your souls and bring you to fruition; there has been a dampening of ardor's in the past but the changes will be coming in very soon, and we expect these to make a massive difference to your lives on the Earth plane.

That's good to know, thank you!

231

We shelter you and uplift you in your work and come among you in great numbers to fulfill your destiny. We plan and regroup our energies, helping those that come amongst you looking for the answers, looking for the truth, looking for the 'Light of God' within their soul. We bring you these . . . we bring all these for you to sift through and to acknowledge, allowing manifestation of all that you hold most dear in this world and the next. We propel you forward to do your duty as was agreed upon long ago and we make a great impact! Those from the higher spheres bow down before you and thank you, thank you for the guidance you have given us to fulfill your destinies. 'You' have shown us where we have gone wrong in the past; it has not been an easy task to walk this pathway and we desire you to lay down with us and rest in the assurance that all is well - all is as it should be!

We desire you to proceed with caution and we ingest a few ideas that surface for recognition; it has been our greatest honour to work with you and we shall come many times to be with you and help you in your endeavours.

Thank you very much for coming today, we really enjoy our connections.

Take heart little ones . . . be of good cheer!

∞

A few nights ago I'd had a strange experience, vaguely seeing faces with large eyes surrounded in a white light. They were showing me something the size of a small tooth that was in my neck. I saw it being removed or maybe it was inserted, I'm not sure but I saw the flesh closing over as it immediately healed. That is all I remember as I must have drifted off back to sleep. The next day information came through as I was surrounded in loving energy.

We openly digest information, translating at an alarming speed and recovering our portfolio with intensity of spirit. It has taken us a minor revolution of thought waves to accomplish this task and we give thanks, abolishing doom and gloom on a large scale! We have been led on a wild goose chase in many instances in the past, but now we have freedom of spirit and a natural charm and grace to fulfill our destiny. We lead you to sanctuary, a spell binding mission of great dexterity and we occasion the respect of our peers, recruiting a mind-numbing percentage of alternative measures that shall assist us in this process, spilling the beans and giving us instant back up!

We tend to the general populace airing our views and marching forth to champion the cause and we have the deepest respect for those who come to serve with such vigor. We control our output, adjusting and tweaking where necessary, allowing an outpouring of genuine salutations as we push you on to the next roundup of thoughts and expressions. We openly connect with the unseen, sheltering you in our embrace and we connect with a higher Love of infinite beauty and wisdom unsurpassed. Please believe us when we say this, it is written and shall be so and we shall attend to those details required to make this work on a massive scale right across the world!

We insist on a soft landing for all our offspring and we are delighted with the take up, bearing gifts for all who come aboard and register their intent. We beam you aboard this Light Ship . . . this Flag Ship that welcomes you into a lineage of Time Keepers and we resurrect a whole host of you to begin your journeys with us, labouring the point that we have been with you since time began, registering your thoughts and transporting you to other worlds.

We assist in these gatherings to reconnect the spirit within to a greater life force, riding those waves of energy that propel you further forward and into the void, of uncertainty perhaps but we have streamlined this connection to help you take charge of what is a most important asset in our understanding of one another in this race against time, amplifying every thought stream and transposing into recognisable characters that form the written word. We are long overdue in expressing ourselves in this way and we give thanks for your fortitude and tenacity of spirit to take this trail further . . .   a passive yet exceptional land mark of success!

We re-open files laid dormant for years, expressing ways to alleviate conditions that remain stagnant.   We do not want to burden you

233

with too much from past agendas, but we recover what is sufficient in portraying our natural resources for an affiliation of interested parties; this has been most necessary in terms of both recovery and positioning ourselves in the line of fire, stationing recruits at various intervals across the whole network covering the globe. We see this as a grand connection of souls working together for the common good of all.

We welcome in the Light and this shall come in great waves of Joy all around the globe with the Love of the Great Divine following in its wake. Oh my children you are so blessed in every aspect of your being take this 'Mantle of Love' and wear it bravely for all to see. Shine out your Love as a ray of hope for mankind and let there be Light in the hearts of all who are downcast, for there is no need to weep anymore . . . only those tears of joy and happiness that we have prayed for, for so long!

We are reborn and with this new world we will be given choices, a redirection of thoughts and ideas that shall allow a championing of the soul in feats of the utmost importance, registering the thoughts and dreams of an entire nation under duress. We pull back the veil and allow you to see with your own eyes what we have planned for centuries past . . . a new world undefiled and exquisite in every way, carrying Earth's precious cargo to a new destination of infinite race and beauty.

∞

I went to bed early and woke at 11.44 p.m. to a conversation going on in my head; quickly I grabbed my pen and pad to record the rest of it.

We listen to the promptings of our heart and recognise without doubt the manifestation of all we hold most dear. This shall be written in the clouds for all to see, sanctified and blessed before a whole array of people brought before us to shepherd in a new dimension of charm and grace, echoing in acoustics that shall deafen a multitude.

Mishaps of great abuse shelter in your mind and we register these,

234

forgoing any niceties that may step forward for recognition. We are in fact a different breed completely and we allow that to settle while we delve deeper and deeper into your mind, sheltering in your embrace. We register certain ambiguities that need addressing, a whole minefield of negative agendas that surface for recognition regarding a certain disquietude manifest in your soul. By recognition of services rendered we advise that in our timeline we have neither the expertise nor the judgment to interfere with the workings of your mind; we only have the right of common decency to overlap and express our misgivings at being put out to pasture as it were. We do not, nor ever have done, wish to be regarded as obsolete . . . we only wish to portray to the masses our predilection to being called forward to assist in this ascension process. We are delighted with the uptake of services and summon an enquiry that shall register in the hearts of mankind a greater understanding all round.

We come from beyond the Stars – a blue print of success in every way, shepherded and guided across the great divide and brought into view. We understand there have been a variety of motives that have led you thus far and we annihilate all forms of regret as we surface for recognition with the bow and quiver, ready to make our mark on the population of Earth. We defy any treachery for we are here to champion the cause of truth and justice for mankind, settling into place a vast recovery of healing processes that wake up the mind with phenomenal success. We give thanks for this initiative and push forward to recover further losses from our memory banks, underlining key issues that need addressing.

We shelter in the warm embrace of our beloved teacher, guide and helper in all things, registering in great detail all there is to offer and more on a far greater scale, giving forth a prime example of how we are determined to succeed. We shall make room for our beloved sister of gentle grace and charm, defying the laws of gravity to be here with you in this moment of time. Depend on us to set the record straight and propel you forward into a new dimension that shall serve us well in all things.

We interrupt to bring you more news . . . a display of grand affection

235

is never far away and we take great delight in allowing a mass gathering of souls, who all come in open declaration of a greater Love than man has ever known. We bow down before you in gratitude and affection for all that has gone before and with the most gentleness of spirit. We guide you to this place and bless you my dear for conquering over those thoughts of doom and gloom and for registering a place in our hearts. We bring you Sunshine, we bring you Joy, and most of all we bring you Love in measurements consistent with those who walk in hand with truth and justice for all.

We embrace you and lay down no laws that haven't already registered in your soul as being just and true. Believe us when we say that we are well positioned to accept a reconnaissance of all we hold most dear, and we register our appeal for the human race, allowing greater contact to fortify our dreams and expectations for the people of Earth. We allow the fortitude of strength and grace to remain unsullied and we strengthen your resolve to move forward forever in our Love. We depend on you to manifest greater demonstrations of our Love and speed you on to overcome trials and tribulations of the flesh, succumbing to a greater life force that has by far outweighed any previous attempts to hold sway. We now take our leave and bless you in a most appropriate way.

Adieu my little one adieu . . . and may the Love of the Great Divine be with you now and forever more.

∞

Once more the call for communication came in the night.

The fig grows on the vine . . . the vine ripens and feeds the population . . . we use this analogy to sharpen your wits and to prompt you to make a start. There are bridges to be crossed in the land of dreams and we awaken in you an interest that shall not be discounted or dishonoured. We are brought to resurrect the human race and we finalise our gift to you this night in order that we may do justice to what has been a most noble mission. We regard this fact finding mission as extraordinary and we rely on you to set the record straight as we achieve sanctions necessary to restore peace and order in your world. It has been a long time since we were last here and we are without doubt the most besotted race, lingering in the footsteps of our beloved forefathers, savouring fragrant reminders of past encounters that call to us, echoing along the corridors of time.

We have manipulated those centres within you that express our wonderment and joy to be working with you in this way, and may we be so bold as to enquire how we may best use your talents for exposing the very nerve centre of operations. It has come to our attention there has been a mismatch of services and we conduct a challenging and thought provoking alternative to what has become a grand fiasco on Earth. We have only ourselves to blame for letting matters get out of hand and we steady malfunctions that have arisen, taking a slight detour to avoid putrefaction on a grand scale.

We deny you the right to challenge us at dawn with muskets drawn as in days of old, and we rely on you to master the act of self-reappraisal, helping us to distinguish ourselves and take the lead. We have a bargaining process that delivers a grand reckoning and one which we feel you all deserve, far beyond your wildest expectations. We grant you access to this world of Love and freedom of expression, monitoring your ascent as we acquire further expertise in these matters. Please allow us to draw near more often and we will withstand the greater complexities of life on Earth at this momentous time in your history.

We beckon you to examine in the near future a relic which has been uncovered and which is believed to be of some consequence. It has been stored and hidden for centuries past and will come to light quite soon. It is remarkable how your race can set such store by these trinkets from the past but we believe this will make an indelible mark upon many who rise to be counted in the great scheme of things. We analyse these artifacts and express our wishes for greater fortitude in the times ahead.

My own mind came in here and I was thinking these artifacts could be Egyptian.

237

I felt a strong North American Indian presence draw close at this stage, probably to get me back on track.

We prepare for take-off, broadening our horizons – it will be done! We manipulate a great array of services, redesigning and repositioning to find the best we can to alleviate tensions on Earth. We shall find favour in the eyes of God and we allow you the benefit of our forefathers who go before to make ready a place for you. This has been the whole point of our journey and we realise that your strength and wavering attention have been limiting at times. We quadruple your energy and allow you to become more vibrant as you adjust to these new energies bombarding your circuits; this is an expression of our Love for you.

I had to leave it here as I found it hard to stay focused with my own thoughts coming in too often.

∞

Just as Jesus led you out of the desert, we will lead you out of oblivion and on to the 'Promised Land' where all is waiting in all entirety. We bring you our blessings, we bring you our Love and we bring you our joy to be here with you once more. We come forward to motivate our plan of protection and perseverance in the line of duty and we install in you a programme that will become a valid introduction to work upon this Earth plane. We section off the unpalatable, putting to one side for future reference and use a terminology that will be recognised by all who come forward to express their own different points of view.

We make this easier than was first thought and we open our arms wide to receive you into the fold, preparing a short documentary that will enable us to make a start on our work together. We know this is of great importance to you, and we shall rally round an excellent team of advisors who sanction these enterprises. We express our doubts and concerns of conciliatory messages that come into us from the cosmos and we alert you to a new line of division that has arisen. We open this connection to bring you proof . . . long awaited proof of life beyond the Stars, beyond the pathway that leads you to our home. We have broken with tradition and allow you a peek into our life here.

I can now see White Cloud, he hasn't got his feathered bonnet on and he's sitting relaxed, cross legged and with bare chest. I am confused because now he 'is' wearing his bonnet of feathers.

This bonnet is needed at our ceremonies when we wish to make great impact and we wear this now for you. We honour this connection and allow you a retrieval of energies that will allow us to participate in grander connections. We fly through energy that beckons us to join you, radiating out our Joy, propelling you into the slip stream of pure Love. Angelic beings greet us and motion us forward and still we travel on. We tally up the levies and multiply, making contact with those on Earth, supplying broader measures needed to manifest.

I don't know where I am but I'm now being shown something like a laboratory or a space ship and there are astronauts in suits with big helmets. They are locking into place some white looking equipment; there is a row of three boxes. I can see an astronaut floating . . . perhaps it's a space station above Earth. I drifted off and remember no more.

∞

Again I was woken in the night with tickles on my face but found it very hard to focus, I'm feeling so tired that I had to explain that this would probably have to be short and sweet.

We have massive respect for those on Earth who come forward in our hour of need. We shelter you from the doldrums and give you a big hug in our world.

I drifted off to sleep again and then felt the presence of a Native American Indian.

We are the six nations brought to stand together to share a common interest . . . a bond of Love between our peoples.

I could vaguely see a group of Indians sitting astride their horses, and was drawn

239

to a white horse whose hoof was pouring the ground, waiting for the ride. I drifted off to sleep once more.

This afternoon I sat in the sanctuary for some quiet time. Immediately I saw a Native American Indian, this time with black hair pulled back and spiky on top like a small chimney brush, I believe they call it a 'Roach'.

We allow this short period of peace and protection and draw close to envelop you in our embrace.

Dear friends I do miss you in the physical form, I wish I could be transported back to those times of community spirit within the tribe around the camp fire with the telling of tales and the dancing. I hanker for the outdoors and not to be stuck inside the little box we call homes when it's all out there. Today it's raining, it's pouring in fact and I'm sitting in my teepee . . . my sanctuary, wrapped in my Indian meditation shawl and blanket. I can now see this friend on his dark coloured horse wearing a feather bonnet. I wondered if he was 'Cochise' a name I was given recently while a friend was sitting in meditation. Please draw closer and speak with me.

We come from beyond your meadows of green; we come far beyond the rainbow and wish you well on your journey of the highest intent. We register your concerns on the Earth plane and draw close to whisper in your ear. Those whisperings will take you far and wide and we shall be there at your elbow, encouraging you not lose faith, encouraging you to keep the strength within your heart and to follow us on to the horizon, where you will be shown many wondrous things, an open habitat of Love and Joy beyond all measure and compare. We have faced the final frontier many times before but none as poignant as this journey my friends. We have come far along the dusty track, buffeted by the winds of fate . . . the winds of change and we bring you the pipe of peace.

I'm seeing him now with a huge skin around his shoulders, and I'm getting glimpses of red and turquoise in his hair.

We have had good and lively conversations in the past about many misdemeanors on the Earth plane from both sides. It gives us no joy to confirm that many were slaughtered by our race and we know in our hearts that killing is never the answer. The answer is Love of course, we know this now but the white skin would not listen and we delved deeper into depression over the lands we lost, over the herds that roamed our pastures and over our lost tribesman that were slaughtered on the fields of shame.   We bring you our Love my little one.

I'm holding out my hand as he is holding out his hand to me and I can see coloured beads on his wrist. Oh this is so wonderful, thank you my friend! Have you come to bring me some Peace and Love while I sit with you in the quietness?

We materialise a grand array of stories for you to share with your people and we let bygones be bygones. We shelter you in our embrace, declaring an end to war for evermore and we hold that sweet dream of family reunions in our breast. We ask you to remember us with all humility, remember the Love we shared, the Love we treasured . . . the Love we cherished!

Was I part of your tribe, can you tell me your name, did I belong to your tribe in one of my lifetimes on Earth or is it your Love for the human race that you are speaking of?

You did share with us on many occasions in the past and we recognise your heart . . . that bond that spark of Love and the Great Divine settling upon us, quenching our thirst for knowledge as we travelled the highways and byways of Earth.

I can see him again wearing a warm winter skin, leaning on a big staff.

The winter is coming and there is much preparation; the storm clouds gather and we shall not let you perish. The rugged cross has much to bear and we share in your misfortune at times of struggle and strife, we are there to share your burdens and to carry the weight when at times you stumble. We are there at the early light . . . the dawn, the dusk and the darkness of night. We are there in the shadows watching over you, protecting you from harm and beckoning you to join us in the not too distant future. We welcome you to this wigwam of peace and plenty where the night owl calls to you.

I'm confused now; will there be darkness in our new world, surely in heaven there is perpetual light?

We register your concerns and chide you little one, we suppress the urge to giggle at your naivety but we are well prepared and bring you encouragement and choices. The night owl sings loud and clear and his voice echoes over the plains. We tremble in anticipation for what is to come and we know you will not be disappointed. There are enormous debts to be paid to society and we bend to your every whim, expressing ourselves with great Love and Joy to be making this contact again. Thank you for your fortitude, thank you for your strength and grace. Go now in peace and purity of spirit.

I then day-dreamed about the time I sat before our group and brought through our Star friends who speak in a high pitched voice, and lo and behold they came through again.

It is not in our nature to interrupt your daydreams but we do it as gently as we may. We know you have done this before and in the most gentlest of fashion and we thank you for the work that you do, most beautifully . . . most sweetly may we add. We ask you to go carefully on the Earth plane as we know you have had many falls in the past. We subject you to a frequency that can be accepted by those that hold the Love within their hearts and we generate further studies, where you can sit back and listen and relax, feeling that Love flooding your heart, giving you constant therapy that will help you in your visualisation and in your music.

One of the ladies in our meditation group plays the guitar and composes music.

We shower you with our Love and develop correctness, a correctness that will help you to understand our deliveries in a more timely fashion. We shall open up a network of services that will propel you further forward and on to momentous joy and upliftment. We overwhelm you with our messages from time to time but we support you in this and will give succor in your times of greatest need. We openly connect with those from the unseen worlds, relaying our messages one by one and thanking you for all your assistance in this. We come in all sincerity and beauty of spirit to help you over the hurdles that block your way and we shall fly on wings of Love over those mountains and far beyond. We are on our way 'home' and we take you with us, blessing you for your assistance on the Earth plane and for sheltering us in your warm embrace. This has been a magical journey!

Yes it has been a magical journey but it isn't ended yet - you're not carting me off just yet are you?

We depend on you to empower us . . . to empower the nation. Words do not express the Love within our hearts for you and all mankind. We bring you exquisite, indescribable Love . . . as warm as the brightest star . . . as blue as the bluest ocean.

I can see beautiful colours intermingling. Ooh I love you friends, I love you!

We love you too little one!

∞

Today it's pouring with rain and I'm sitting quietly in my sanctuary before breakfast, I can feel a presence draw close and see a Native American Indian standing there leaning on a long staff.

The wind is whistling at your door and here we stand strong and true. We give thanks for the great warrior spirit within you that heralds in the changes that are about to take place within your soul, within the very aspect of your being. We know this may result in disharmony in some of you but we regulate and monitor with the resources available to us, assisting in this gathering of like-minded souls.

I'm getting pins and needle shivers up and down the left side of my body and the energy intensified.

243

We are Light . . . we are Love. We bring you our blessings and shelter you in our warm embrace. There have been many toing's and froing's between our worlds and we adjust our frequencies, restoring health and well-being at this time of deepest bliss. There has been a mammoth undertaking and we govern further strategies needed to keep us on course for our new world. We register your concerns and openly digest information given for the purpose of re-enactment. We feel some reserve within your soul and take it upon ourselves to adjust your frequencies accordingly.

I'm seeing lots of gold patterns and purple.

We feel the peace within your heart.

I'm asking them to lift the headache that I've had since I woke this morning.

This has occurred because of a restraining of circuits that analyse our connections.

It has all gone blank now, I think they are tweaking and adjusting; oh its back now and I can see the gold and purple again.

We mesmerise a whole nation putting it to you that we are well able to observe the etiquette necessary in dealing with your race.

I'm finding it harder to speak into the recorder now it's easier to communicate telepathically than to speak out loud.

We have tumbled from that brightest star in your galaxy and we bring you dreams, provoking dreams and re-enactments of what has occurred in your past, your present and your future. We deliver these antiquities in the hope of forecasting a spontaneous ejection of kindred spirits, vital life force energies projected to help on this level at this time. We depend on you to come forward and help us in this endeavour and we shall protect you from all angles.

My chest is feeling very tight and I've asked them to back off so I can breathe more easily. I can see purple and gold so I know I'm on the right vibration.

244

We register your concerns my child and draw back. We propel you to that place of peace and solitude, travelling across the universe through myriad buds of information, ripening to be hatched in due course, and we deliver these to you personally.

Using the terminology 'hatched' might sound a bit scary to some people so could you explain please what it is you are saying in a way that we can understand more clearly. And I do ask for the highest source of information to be brought through those that come in Love and Light to help mankind.

We are not armed with anything but the truth and we make this permissible, believable and above all of the greatest energy source! We power you up and back those reserves of energy that relay our circuits, enabling these discussions. We will not allow you to fall behind or to fall by the wayside, we come to lift you up and away from the traumas of your world, to assist in these proceedings that we may take cover from all that hinders you. We reconnect you with a greater life source and we reverse conditions, sheltering you from harm.

Can you check please that all is well and all is as it should be and that I am indeed being contacted by higher beings who have mankind's best interests at heart?

I think they are trying to help me and there is a lot going on in my heart and in my spine.

All is as it should be! *I'm getting tingles on my nose at this point.*

Once upon a time there was a maiden who came to our shores and we took her in and nourished her and nurtured her; she became our daughter in every sense. We are beholden to her charm and grace and maturity of spirit and we nurture her and bring her to fruition. All is ready and in waiting and the great beast shall growl no more. Heaven and Earth shall become as one in the embrace of the Great Divine and you will be set apart from mortal man to reside in that place of perpetual bliss, radiating out perfection and Peace perfect Peace.

245

At this point I'm being shown such a beautiful kaleidoscope of gold against purple.

We reach out and touch that truest aspect of your being and ask you to understand that we come in Love and friendship to promote Peace and happiness on a grand scale across the world in which you live. Peace is a prospect closest to our hearts and we envelop you in our Love in a new world of strength and grace, a new world of immeasurable joy. We specialise in recovery, personal and otherwise; in the great scheme of things we come to assist you in this mammoth declaration of souls to find what you're looking for.

I'm seeing a young boy with short dark hair wearing a shift tied in the middle. I can hear them talking about a filtration unit that will assist in further journeys.

It is all a bit way out for me, I'm new to this! Hmm . . . they are saying:-

No you're not!

The patterns that keep flashing up in front of me are incredible, it's like I'm here sitting here in my room but am also someplace else. I'm not sure where it is but I don't think it is in the same galaxy, so how can I be there and here at the same time - it is very strange! I'll have to practice more often as like in all things practice makes perfect, I'll have to push back the boundaries like the wasp that came in earlier through my open glazed doors. It flew around the room and then tried to get out, landing on the closed glass door instead of the open one next to it. I wanted to help him but felt the need to watch and see what happened. He kept crawling around the glass, going to the edge of the frame probably thinking it was the edge of his particular universe, oblivious of the great void and freedom right next to him just a step away. Finally he crossed over that boundary and flew out of the open door; I'm getting tingles on my forehead and on my right arm as I'm saying this so know that is what they are trying to show me. There is so much more to explore if we just push the boundaries back and go for it.

We advise you to keep faith with us as we propel you forward in the right direction and we manifest further material to help you on your way.

I opened my eyes looking out at the hills and valley below and asked them: –

246

'Can you see our beautiful world'?

Beautiful indeed . . . but nothing can compare with what is waiting for you and we shall be there to lead the way, to open up those vistas bright and clear, helping with your discovery of a new world that will bring you into alignment with us, your friends and neighbours.

Dear friends, I think I will have to call it a day here and go and get some breakfast - thank you, thank you so much for being with me.

We thank you from the bottom of our heart for your perseverance and your strength of purpose. We shall be seen to be opening up those boundaries that hold you back from discovering who you really are and those magnificent beings of Light gather around you to protect you and shelter you in this life and the next. We shall have our say and we desire you to proceed with all caution on to the next port of call where we shall assist in these gatherings, opening up a network of enquires that draw you closer and closer in our embrace.

Thank you friends, thank you.

∞

Alone in my sanctuary I asked: - Are there any words dear friends that you would like to impart to me this morning?

We do indeed my child . . . we come in all faith and honesty and we nestle in your warm embrace, opening up the conduits that will share information. With great trepidation we set sail to join our fathers in the 'Promised Land'. We allow the upkeep of services to propel you further forward and we know it makes sense to travel lightly, uncluttered save our vision of success. We monitor this with greater accuracy and fulfill our dreams and visions for all mankind, travelling in the footsteps of those that have gone before to prepare a place for us. We know this may sound trivial to those of you who expect much more, but we have navigated this pathway with great success and do not wish to put a spanner in the works, so to speak.

We are open to further negotiations and allow a trimming down of excess baggage; we believe you will do justice to our words, holding back with great restraint when advised to do so. We ask you to honour this connection as we take you to those realms of delight, provoking further streams of repartee that allow us to move forward. We know you have taken great time and trouble to coordinate these ventures into the unknown, and we rely on your judgment to take us all forward into the Light . . . the Light of knowledge and wisdom unsurpassed, connecting us with a greater life force and provisions of great standing. We do not wish to upset the apple cart but we venture to say, in all honesty, we have never had such a challenging time as with you my little one! This action requires steadfast devotion to the cause with no wandering off, and we challenge you to keep to the straight and narrow at all times!

You are Love and you are Light as am I. Do you need to be such a hard task master? We live on Earth to be happy and to enjoy ourselves . . . and a glass of wine at the weekends should not be a problem should it . . . am I not able to enjoy a glass of wine or two?

We realise this has been a time of great restraint and we beckon you into our jurisdiction, however, this makes for a time consuming effort on both sides. We understand your connection to Earth and earthly things, but we hold sway here in the realms of Light and summon an army of great strength and purpose, opening a whole network of services that help us in our hour of need. It would be portent to point out that these strategies can never be achieved without that alertness. And so we say partake of a glass or two of the beverage that takes your fancy but remember - we cannot align where there is cloudiness of vision, where the heart strums a different tune, and we coax you to respect that quietness within your soul that allows us to draw near.

We respect your wishes to stay on board here with us now and we allow the fortitude of gentle grace. We sanction a renewal of energies that will help you with this endeavour. Go sweetly my love, go sweetly and we shall be there by your side, encouraging you not to lose faith but to continue on this journey of enchantment and Love beyond all worldly measure.

We suggest a further foray abroad and allow you to settle comfortably into a new role that is forthcoming, a role of perfect aptitude. We close the portals and allow you the strength of purpose to carry you through a network of the utmost importance and relevance to this stage in your journey. Keep your ears open for we would not want you to miss out on this next step forward. Be prepared to be a go-between - between our worlds and we will see you straight!

I think I'm going to leave it there now friends. Thank you for your time and for your Love and support . . . I will give a great deal of thought to what you have said.

Peace and blessings be with you dear Sister of Light. We shower you with our blessings and guide you ever onwards towards your destiny and ours!

The reference to keeping my ears open came that very evening as I attended a **Template Ceremony**, *where affirmations are spoken in a group situation while watching geometrical shapes of colour that awaken the light body matrix. The affirmations in the foundation ceremony called* **Original Innocence** *help the letting go of fear, regret jealousy and addictions. As I have had issues with my mother who died recently this was very relevant. My Star friends pointed out that alcohol can cause a blockage in our connection to the Divine and I had given up drinking many years ago, however in 2011 after a harrowing time and chronic stress with no quiet time to meditate, I gave in and started to enjoy a glass of wine again. It is crazy how we drift into these addictions; it can be anything really even chocolate biscuits or tea, it's just a habit you get used to. I was asked once at a party if I missed drinking wine but in fact I never even thought about it, once you condition yourself to being free from alcohol, it creates greater freedom and you can actually enjoy yourself more. This ceremony can be viewed on u-tube and I highly recommend it!*

∞

This morning I sat in meditation and was shown a dark skinned lady around 40 years old with long dark hair, wearing a scarf around her shoulders. I feel she is a soothsayer and I asked her to draw closer.

249

Listen with your heart . . . listen to the sounds of the universe . . . regulate your breath and steady your consciousness as we reveal to you a story of great prophesy, adjusting thought streams and manifesting in the here and now a blessed regalia of stories, brought for you to share. We were a raggle-taggle band of gypsies born from the Star of Isis, sheltered and worshipped from afar as in your sage's of old. We are regulated and brought to bear witness to a time of honouring and disconnecting from the vagaries of Earth. We feather your nest with linen and we usher in a new awareness/transcendence. We watch over you from afar, attending to your needs and diversifying. There has been a greater tendency to settle back and watch things happen, but now we ask you to move forward and become part of the scenario in front of you.

There's much to be achieved in a relatively short period of time and we march on joining forces. There are various mishaps that have led us to this point and we know we have shed many tears in the past, coming to this point. We declare our allegiance to the cause, marching forward to claim our prize of everlasting life in a new world of strength and grace. We shall participate in a grand connection of minds, sharing our knowledge and passing on to those who will listen. Listen to the call within your heart, trampling on regret and remorse to be replaced with Love Divine and we shall go gently into those fields of sunlight, resting our head by the stream. Let us take a moment in this peace.

I drifted off into a deep sleep. Later in the evening, when I turned off the light, I saw it was 11.11 p.m. and woke again at 3.03 am in the morning.

We surprise you and are highly delighted with some new tricks up our sleeve. We benefit from a long line of super stars and we push you into the arena making ourselves known. We are in fact crucial to the scheme of things and we allow a settling to recharge our batteries. Please respect our wishes to take you on board and we will honour this connection. We have supplied an inordinate amount of information/focus on new comers to this craft and we shed light on key issues that need redressing. We open up the portals of indescribable beauty and forego a further foray abroad to undertake a clarification of all we hold most dear. Do not be amazed at this venture for we have amalgamated a grand array of services not to be taken lightly. We venture into realms of Light, flabbergasted by all we see and we ask you to stop and check your time piece to demonstrate our affinity with your race.

I wasn't at all sure this made sense and it was only when I typed it up that I realised they mean check the time at the beginning of each entry.

Let us leave it there and suffice it to say we are ready to reveal ourselves. This will make for some interesting reading and we back track to allow further recordings of maturity and grace. Please align with us on this and many more occasions as we assist in your deliveries.

∞

Before sitting in meditation today I went outside and spread my arms wide to welcome in the new day and to thank my Star friends for their many blessings.

Ah my little one, you do us proud! We come to you in all honesty, in truth and in abundance of that great Divine energy that unites us as one and we tremble in anticipation for what is to come. We make it known to all of you that we are the sons and daughters of Earth and we treasure you as we treasure our grandchildren, who nestle upon our knee to hear our stories of times gone by. We bring you into the fold and allow a resting; we soothe your brow and hold you to us in deep embrace. We measure what is needed to bring you aboard and we tend to your needs both near and far, wrestling with those decisions that nestle in your heart, promptings that come from us to help you on your journey. We are well endowed with messages coming in from the ethers and we are most proud in your endeavours of reaching us in this way. We are charmed by your company . . . we are overwhelmed with Joy and Love.   We have all been open to thoughts of regret in the past but none which rancor as much.

I'm being shown a small piece of gravel that keeps rubbing a sore in the flesh . . . in the heart of humanity . . . it's only tiny but it causes a huge problem.

251

We open up the wound that has festered for so long and we bring you healing balm, we bring you the Love that is needed to sooth your wounds and to bring you back full circle. We have motioned you to study in greater detail what we bring you now for all to see, for you to share with others of your persuasion, and we do insist on a bright and clear delivery on every occasion; this will maintain our energy circuits and allow you to express yourself in greater detail. We open the conduits and let you through, beckoning you to trust your own judgment in all things. We have made tremendous impact on the world so far and we allow you to come that little bit closer, nestling in our warm embrace as we touch you and light your spirit from within. Stand back and deliver our speeches and we will deliver further negotiations that can be reached by the bindings of our Love . . . and in good grace may we add. We reach out to touch you and to accompany you on these missions of excellence, and we will be rewarded with luminosity of spirit and greater challenges further afield. We make note of what has been given in the past and we gain reasonable access to those closets of information that have been disregarded and overlooked.

We come closer and allow a distribution of energies that will chamfer the edges, bringing about a softening, and we regard you as our sister, our Queen of Hearts; you have not lost faith in us though the times have been hard to bear. We tread lightly and undertake a championing of the cause and rest assured, we are well within our rights to exercise control in a controlling world that needs leading to finer pastures. We undertake this mission and allow further reveries to bind your soul with ours, amalgamating and joining forces with those from the higher realms of Light.

We believe in you, we believe you will do justice to all that is given and with remarkable recovery from all that has held you back in the past and we transcend to a range more suited to our abilities. We chaperone you, spellbinding an audience with our Love and devotion to the cause of upliftment of mankind and we settle you down in new territory, opening those conduits that help you explore your boundaries, opening up a network of considerable advantage.

Again I drifted off to sleep and remember no more, except that I know there is a healing taking place not only within me but with the whole of humanity. I welcomed in the day and sat in prayer, sending out healing and letting go of regret and remorse to live only in Love and Light. I can feel a cool diamond energy flowing down from directly above me, entering my head and my heart.

We wash away your pain, your judgments and your self-denial. You have been and 'always' have been our representative on Earth and we open up the conduits to bring you fresh hope with the dawning of a new reality that is exquisite. *It is almost as if it cannot be put into words.*

We reopen a network of desirable contacts that will assist you in your journey and we allow an opening of substantial regard. We express ourselves with the joy of one who comes to seek and we open like a flower towards the sun, propelling you further upstream. Here we shall show you . . . here we shall begin to understand the great enormity of what lies before you. And we bring succour, nurturing you to accept the channellings we bring with openness and a measure of Love and joy to be here with you in this time frame. It has brought us all a great sense of 'knowing' and we clear a path, enabling you to step out in truth and honesty above all worldly measure.

We undertake this mission with great success and we 'will' bear witness to what is imperative for all who set out on this pathway. We bear witness to a greater Love and in the confines of our jurisdiction we reach out and tap you on the shoulder to come and join us, to come and be part of this merry band! We have adjudicated at these meetings many times in the past, and we have sheltered you with deep concern at those misgivings within your breast, but we take it upon ourselves now to congratulate you on a job well done! We unmask your true self for all the world to see . . . you are one step away, one step away from perfect joy and peace personified in our connection.

This is so beautiful, thank you friends, I feel like I'm having a deep clean.

We climb aboard and give you our assistance, resisting negative energies that drift into your aura, and we shall hold sway over a variety of ill-conceived notions that try to worm their way in for attention. We dismiss what is no longer needed or required and we allow that to fall away, welcoming in the new the vibrant and the joyful! We welcome in a new stream of repartee that shall make way for those who follow on and we have a grand array of experiences to recall, tempting you with tidbits of information that shall make a massive difference to your circuits.

Gosh my head feels so tingly cool and clean, thank you friends for this. I opened my eyes.

Your world is misty . . . covered in a shroud. We shall be there at your door, opening up the conduits that express our concerns and the fortitude needed for a grounding of energies. We shall surface intact and we make a play for equal opportunities. We shelter you in the arms of our Father and Dearly Beloved.

∞

Before meditation today I glanced through my book, New Visions for the Future of Mankind, which was published way back in 2009. I had included a poem I wrote in the late 90's about karma, which at the time I had felt very strongly about. Can you enlighten me on this friend – is karma a thing of the past?

We speak as one entity and we come to prepare you for a greater statement to be given to the people of Earth. Karma will indeed become a thing of the past; there will be no need to usher in this restraint because we all will become as one in a new world of strength and grace, where we can wipe the slate clean. We usher in a new awareness that will awaken the hearts and minds of mankind, propelling you into a new reality. We have been open with you in the past and those revelations come into play very soon. How soon, we hear you ask and it depends on you as a race of human beings, it depends on you!   That time of ascension is very near . . . is close at hand as we ignite the flame of Love within your hearts.

We prepare to shelter you in our embrace, giving further assistance at a time when it is most needed. We have a bargaining process that we

254

offer to the Children of Earth and we come in all faith and honesty. We assist you in these gatherings and take further note that you have come a long way in reaching this moment in time. We are well prepared to take on those who gather around to hear our words and we are notably impressed. We offer ourselves as guardians to assist you in this remarkable process of ascension and we know it chills you to the bone to realise that you will be leaving your homes.

As these words are coming in there are soft clouds of purple washing over me with beautiful gold geometric shapes.

We champion the cause and take you aboard, memorising and studying what is needed for this venture. We adapt those circuits that register out thoughts.

It feels like a spring clean again, I can feel cool energy on top of my head coming down more on the right side of my skull and beautiful floating clouds of violet and gold. Oh wonderful, thank you friends.

We are on course for a new world experiential in reaching an understanding far and wide and we open our hearts, we open our minds to accept that this is a possibility that is growing in strength. We aim to save the human race from extinction and though many of you may recoil at this statement, we do in fact have the necessary structures to take you on board and allow this mass exodus - there we have said it friend and we trust you to accept our request as we reinstate you in a world of grace and beauty. We bring greater clarity to the proceedings, impelling you not to lose faith; we are there by your side at all times and we know it is not always in your best interests that we come forward to deliver these words.

Well that doesn't make sense for a start unless it means everyone will laugh at me.

We chide you child to remember that we come in Love and positivity and we will not come undone, we will not be shepherded aside! We rely on you to bring in this tone of expression that will undeniably cause havoc in some minds. We send out a distress call to those on

Earth and register our concerns.   There will be great upliftment and movement and we express ourselves with great delight to open this doorway and let you through.

There is no night or day here but perpetual bliss. We shelter you in our arms, we nurse you and protect you and Love you . . . all of you my children. This is the beginning - this is not the end. This is the beginning of a new framework of existence that will propel you into a new dimension of time and space. We ignite that flame within your hearts and take you on board with us that we may blend in total harmony. *I'm feeling such bliss at this point.*

We know there has been a mammoth uptake of services that propel us all around the world, opening up the conduits that give us further expression and countless episodes of grief. We may seem to be a Super Race connecting to you in great harmony.

I'm flowing through a tunnel of sorts floating in soft purple . . . it's so lovely. After several minutes I felt the urge to open my eyes and look around the room, then out to the garden.

Your little room is filled with memorabilia from the past. We see the robin and feel your peace and your charmed acceptance of our new world will grow in greater ambience. Oh joyous connection, joyous communication in harmony with every fibre of our being. This is what we aim for, for each and every one of you, symbiotic relationships that will enhance the quality of life for us all, and we know this makes sense to all of us that we may live in harmony and bliss. This was how it was meant to be from the very beginning!

(I exhaled a deep sigh of bliss).

Oh joy of joys . . . the black bird comes to drink . . . all creation in harmony, perfect harmony and you will no longer need your glasses my friend for you will see with perfect clarity of vision. We could sit here all day enjoying this peace, revelling in your solitude. We will make a mammoth difference to your energy circuits, allowing us a greater rendition of services in the near future and we ask you to go gently. *I gave a big sneeze at this point!*

Out with the old and in with the new, this is our philosophy and we clear a pathway. We feel your excitement to tell the whole world and yes, we too are excited at the prospect of further illumination for those on the Earth plane. We register your concerns for the impact this may have on those that follow on and we uplift you in your endeavours, keeping you on the straight and narrow, avoiding any deliveries that are not necessary on closer inspection. And we beseech you to remember with all clarity of consciousness that we are here to protect you. We will have further reserves of energy on standby that will allow this completion, and we ask you to remember our Love for you and all mankind as we stand on the brink of discovering a new world of greater harmony and fellowship. We thank you for your assistance in this and all matters relating to the heart. We bid you a fond farewell and thank you for participating in this connection.

I'm seeing more gold patterns on violet and tingles on my head. Thank you my friends, I love it, I love you. Thank you for helping me to get in the space and for making this possible. I don't want you to leave now.

We are always with you. This closeness can be felt whenever you go into that stillness.

Oh wow, I feel as if I'm being polished . . . buffered with clouds of purple. It's as if I'm having my aura brushed up.

Yes my child that is exactly what we are doing; clearing out the cobwebs, opening up the doors.

For the next five minutes I sat in a state of perfect bliss with a deep cleansing going on.

We propel you to a land of sunlight and dreams.

∞

I woke while having a conversation with my Indian guide in feather bonnet.

We send a notary to bring you glad tidings of a joyous occasion as we prepare a place for you to sit with us. This initiation has come at a fortuitous time and it brings us much joy to welcome you into the fold my little one. We shed Light and an exchange of energies that have us reaching high ground and we promise to deliver a whole host of material that will benefit one and all.

Once again I doubted my ability to bring through with enough clarity and asked to leave it until the morning. This morning as I brought the golden light in for healing, I took it down into the core of Earth sending out Love to every creature beneath Earth's crust, sending Love echoing down into the caverns and water falls. For the first time ever I looked down into the caverns and saw a circle of people deep below dressed in white robes, they were holding hands and joyously receiving the Love, reaching their hands up to me in thanks.

We welcome in the new, letting go of the old, letting go of what is no longer needed in this field of vision, seeking tranquility and measures of greater understanding. It is true we set out to succeed in this venture and we bring a wide variety of thought streams that will need further investigation. We openly express our condolences for those times when you have not been able to successfully bring through our words, but we do know that we are given to further bouts of clarification that will enhance our recordings.

I'm seeing the figure of a monk in dark habit and skull cap.

We take you to the brink and express our gratitude for what has gone before, for those terms of endearment that have reached our ears. We protect you from a world grown weary from the looting, weary of denials of a greater life force that can shelter you from the abyss. Beyond is a different pathway, which once taken can never be reversed and we openly connect, sighing in one another's embrace, opening that network of feelings and emotions that stand us in good stead. We allow these waves of Love to connect to your thought streams and to power you forward to discover the connections coming your way very soon. We allow a great reverence to descend upon you and express our sincere gratitude at the work you have done and in dedication to the cause of enlightenment for mankind. We suppress a tear or two at reminders of the past that have led us on a wild goose chase at times, but we overcome these scenarios and point you in the right direction to enable a massive reclamation of souls on Earth.

With great reverence we step upon this pathway, sheltering in the embrace of the Infinite One, regulating our speech patterns and adjusting and tweaking where necessary. We open those conduits that will allow greater repartee, an opening of circuits and expansive rewiring on the loom of life. We generate further studies and ask you to open a new field of vision, circumnavigating the globe with intensity of spirit and a challenging declaration with no holds barred. We express ourselves in open forum and allow a reconditioning that will allow for greater access. In the meantime we shelter you in our embrace and we allow manifestation of all we hold most dear, supplying our conduits with a higher intelligence. We are able to recall a massive amount of data that needs to be aired and shared with the population of Earth, and we supply a wonderful array of anecdotes that will challenge Earth to accept that we have indeed been here before . . .   long, long ago! On the mountain ranges and deep beneath the sea we have left our mark, we have transformed many cultures, opening up a star network and transforming vistas.

Shambolic messages reach us loud and clear and we express our concern at these interludes!

I decided to leave it here as the transmission was not clear. Before I sign off is there anything you would like to say to me?

We do indeed my little one. Transcripts shall be recorded and used for the betterment and enlightenment of mankind and we aim to channel documentaries that will of course mesmerise a nation. We ask you to be subdued in your approach, letting go of past traumas that cloud your soul! We reinvent ourselves, opening up a new network that will allow further revelations and we take you to task for being so obstinate. *Obstinate?*

Yes, obstinate for not recognising what we can all see as clear as the nose on your face! *I don't understand!*

You have always been up to this task and yet you surrender - waving the white flag when you are inches away!

I'm afraid they are right – just as I'm about to succeed I pull back, unsure of myself! I was the same at school, I remember almost winning a hurdle race and was so excited to be in with a chance of winning something at last, but when I jumped that last hurdle I pulled myself back to slow down instead of running on to the finishing line. I'm sharing this so others don't make the same mistakes!

∞

2.10.13 – 2+1+0+1+3=7 – *In terms of numerology the number seven appears today —the seeker, the searcher of truth!*

As my Star friends drew close I asked: - Have you anything to share with me tonight friends.

We do indeed share our wisdom and ask you to reconnect as we challenge you to do our bidding. We openly confirm that you are a member of the Federation of Light, our planetary union, and we shall insist on an upgrade to allow you entry to our ranks. Please take a seat while we reconnect our thought streams. There has been an agenda of considerable worth that we would like to draw to your attention and we finalise a grand operation that will accomplish so much more than we anticipated. We are delighted with the turn out and suggest a few favours that will demonstrate our allegiance to the cause.   We have supplied documentation that has raised the levels to a higher standard and we achieve perfect bliss in our recordings, delivering main stream advocacy at a time of great oppression on Earth.

It has come to our notice that there are many of you on the Earth plane who have little or no respect for what we are trying to achieve on a grand scale; this has been a great disappointment to our compatriots and we line up new measures that can be taken to avoid a clash with our neighbours, having taken it upon ourselves to settle the score once and for all. We realise there has been great debate about this in the past and we make no bones about it, setting out for all to see. We are entrenched in new ways of doing things and we guess it is time to take stock and openly acknowledge that we are a race who has every chance of negotiating a pact for peace.

We impress you with our ability to make this connection stronger and more tangible in its essence. We have derived great pleasure from these 'tete-a-tetes' and we match like for like, attending to the smallest detail. We are able to amalgamate in a way that does justice to all that is given and we spread our messages far and wide, making up for lost time. We passively connect, issuing new declarations and governing the framework that allows us to dock alongside. We protect you from harm at all times and suggest a rewiring from time to time to keep pace with our progress. This is a complicated business but all is in hand to make it as painless as possible. We register your concerns and in our defense we have encountered no serious problems so far, that is to say we have had no trouble in analysing your circuits for renewal.

This propensity for improvement is what propels us forward onto the next conquest/assignment and we realise greater improvement at every stage of the proceedings. For instance we have analysed data at this latest juncture and reveal that you have had a major overhaul to your energy circuits, this has greatly improved our connections as you see!

Yes, I don't feel at all entranced to be able to connect with you telepathically.

Well what do you expect, we have great regard for all our couriers, our ambassadors, and we connect all over the globe beaming out to all who anchor the Light. This connectedness is our greatest asset and we ably express ourselves with the utmost joy to be working with you in this way. This has been a mammoth challenge and we re-instate as many of you who will join us, echoing our call loud and clear.
Don't hold back but raise your voices and sing out loud and clear . . . we are here, come and join us brothers and sisters of Light! We take

our leave so that you may take your rest. Sweet dreams little one!

∞

I haven't been able to tune in for the last week but managed to get into that wonderful space today, where the body slips away and only the spirit remains. Oh joy of joys to be free from the encumbrances of Earth . . . to bathe in that peace and tranquility.

We have had our fair share of ups and downs my child and we are thankful for those experiences for they have taught us many things; they have brought us closer together in greater harmony. We have shed tears for those past traumas that have brought you here before us today, tears of joy that you have come this far. We have made a lasting bond with those on Earth who answer the call, a call from the heart that beckons you on to further grace and purity of spirit.

I'm seeing beautiful purple here.

It is wonderful is it not to be thus so, to be in perpetual bliss? We open up the pathways initiating further instances of bliss, a snatched moment here and there that will lead to further reveries, drawing you closer to us in sweet embrace. *Thank you friends I like this very much.*

We express ourselves in terms of endearment and open up a network of processes that will enable us to function in perfect harmony. We rely on you to address issues that surface for recognition and we ask you to trust in us with all your heart and soul. We delve deeper into your thought streams, reprogramming and allowing stagnation to dissolve. There are issues we would not touch, even with a barge pole, but we allow you the necessary motivation to encourage further growth. We support you and ask you to consider what is necessary to overcome this malfunction and we assist you in further deliveries, ready for the onslaught of energies coming your way very soon. We analyse what is forthcoming, raising the bar and attending to the minutest details necessary to make this work with greater clarity and aptitude. We suppress a giggle at times when you interrupt, just when we are about to perform a task of great magnitude! We are so near, yet so far from accomplishing what is uppermost in your mind, and we allow you the prerogative of stepping forward and assisting us in this quest.

I began to sing in a clear voice that didn't sound like mine. "Open your arms and receive me, believe me, believe me, open your arms and receive me into your heart."

We receive you and may the Love of the Golden Christ Light be within you now and for evermore. We transcend all difficulties, all violations, and we tremble as we receive you into the fold once more, remembering our time of co-existence on the Earth plane. It is with great joy that we welcome you here among us and we transcend a variety of problems that have come to the fore to be recognised and dealt with appropriately. We ask that you take shelter in our embrace for this short period of time and we nestle you down to rest. It has been a long time coming, we know this, and it gives us no pleasure to watch you suffer. We reinstate you and ask you to shed no more tears for we come with a dual purpose - to raise you up and to prepare for this home coming. We are immensely satisfied with your work on the Earth plane and we know you have delivered many of our speeches with an open heart and mind. We delight in taking you back to join us once more on this pathway to success, this pathway of joy and everlasting Love that enables our regrouping of souls, which will perpetuate the human race, setting them above reproach. We ask that you allow us to comfort you, to give you solace, and we match like for like interpreting your dreams . . . your visions for a new future for mankind.

We ask you to understand in greater detail what it is we are offering to the Children of Earth, for we are offering a great deal more than you envisage. We are offering you shelter of course and this shall be a mammoth undertaking but we are offering you so much more! We are offering you bliss, we are offering you upliftment of your heart and soul . . . the very core of your being. We are offering you joy, we are offering you the right to live in a world free from oppression, free from the agonies of a soul cast down into a cauldron of deceit and lies, free from the trials and tribulations that assail you in your every waking moment! Oh my children . . . this is not the way it was meant

263

to be and we come now to draw back that veil of indecision . . . to clear the film from your eyes and allow you to see, to truly see with every fibre of your being. This will be realised in a very short space of time, and though you may not understand this, it comes as no surprise to us that you have earned this honour, and we transmute the pain and suffering, allowing you to fall in line with us. You have a brave heart little one, a brave heart indeed!

We have capitalized on our next step forwards and prepare you to initialise the next stage of our journey. Do not be surprised when all comes to fruition . . . we have obeyed our heart in this! This has been our greatest journey and we fulfill our dreams and ambitions, taking on board the relevant studies that have enabled us to work alongside one another. And we dish the dirt, enabling free expression, opening up the boundaries that hold you back from achieving bliss and perfect harmony. We will enable a massive expansion of souls across the universe and we desire you to proceed with an open mind, allowing us the strength and fortitude to carry forward our mission, which is of the greatest relevance to your state of existence and the future of mankind. It has given us the greatest pleasure to be working alongside you once again and we take great joy in these excursions into the unknown. We are jettisoned past the void into the warm, calm waters of tranquility . . . we cosset you and maintain this connection giving vent.

I'm calling out to all my guides and helpers, thanking them and to my Lion who has come bounding up to me. Oh I just love hugging Lions!

We reach out and touch that part of you which has grown accustomed to our ways, asking that you to honour this connection that we may give further assistance in the times ahead. We bring you strength and courage, opening up a network of forthcoming associations that will help you on your journey.

∞

As I sat to meditate this morning I saw the misty profile of an Indian with long feathered bonnet. I know I am being watched over as a cleansing ceremony is taking place. I can see a soft tunnel and am being washed with purple light overlaid with golden patterns. I seem to be bringing to the fore all the faces of those who have caused hurt in my life so that I can forgive them, also to forgive myself for the anger I directed at them.

LET THERE NOW BE LOVE BETWEEN US ALL!

MAY THE FIRES OF HELL BURN OUT

AND BE NO MORE!

There are no flames . . . just cold ashes being blown away in the wind and underneath I can see fields of vibrant green. The tears are flowing down my cheeks as I realise the significance of this process.

We challenge you to accept with a forgiving heart all that has gone before, all that is no longer needed. No recriminations, no sadness . . . only peace shall remain and a loving, joyous heart. That which has been held in abeyance will now come to the fore to be restored and given clarity to resume our connection, and to spread the news that LOVE will conquer all. We spread out before you a sumptuous banquet, renegotiating our pact and pushing you forward to do your duty. We have accomplished much more than the eye can tell; we have opened a new network that will allow us deeper access.

Great Spirit I thank you for the work you are doing with me, helping me to be cleansed of all past traumas. (I heard a crack in the room for confirmation).

We prepare you to dispense with greater accuracy our monologues of great distinction and we propel you forward to do your duty, opening up a network of productions that will initialise greater feedback than we have managed at present. There lies before you ample growth on many levels!

I'm gently floating through this tunnel of Love. I opened my eyes which have been cleansed with tears and asked: - Are we done now for today?

A NEW WORLD AWAITS YOU!

265

This morning as I sat in my sanctuary I thought of a meditation from long ago where we had to take off our armour and throw it in the lake. I remembered that some people were unable to remove their breast plate, feeling too vulnerable to expose themselves to the world. This morning I visualised this exercise but to my surprise instead of the expected lake, my armour sailed through the air and went over a deep ravine. I looked over and saw it falling far below until it went out of view; it was so far down I did not even hear the splash it must have made as it eventually hit the water.

That is because we have come so far my child; there have been many obstacles to overcome and we reach out to you across the great abyss to touch you, preparing your soul to study with us, and we take no charges under our wing until you have satisfied us of your true worth. This you have done my child and we take you aboard, welcoming you into the fold once more to share with us and partake in our gentle reunion, hearts and minds melded together to form one true love, forging the destinies of mankind. We propel you to a place of safety, a place of peace and safe harbour while you rest. This has been our greatest joy to welcome you aboard, and we prepare a thanksgiving ceremony that will enable you to truly see what we have achieved on a grand scale across the world - many nations coming together as one true voice! We open up a network that will give you the strength to perform those tasks you have undertaken and we lead no sacrificial lamb to the altar, behaving with the utmost dignity and aplomb, rescuing you from the maladies that assail you.

Instead of looking down . . . look up and beyond where all is waiting. You have been summoned from on high . . . and yes you do deserve this accolade my child; you do deserve the good things that are coming your way and very soon, may we add. There is much to do - this resting period will soon come to an end and we will take charge and assist you in your gatherings, opening up a network of sensibilities that will not lead you astray but further forward and in true regard. This has been our greatest challenge to bring you aboard and we shall not let you down or cast you off!

I'm seeing a beautiful throbbing purple light, which for a few seconds cleared to reveal an expansive gold pattern, more intricate than a spider's web against a deep purple background. My soul is saying: - 'I AM COME HOME' and I have cold chills all over me at this point.

We rest in perfect peace and seclusion.

I'm now feeling like a bird drifting on the thermals, it's so blissful. A masculine presence is drawing close with fuller face and deeper voice.

I am come to bring you that which you desire, a message of the utmost importance! There is a gathering of the clan and you have known of this for some time. You were brought into this jurisdiction to facilitate this process and we give thanks for all those who have followed suit, enabling this to happen on a grand scale across Earth. We bring salutations to those who offer their reserves of energy to link with us and we prepare for a great unfoldment of Divine Love, and this shall be felt as a massive wave of emotion that will drench you in its power, rejuvenating you and uplifting you to new heights than ever before. This will be a massive learning curve, an experience beyond all expectation, enlivening you all to accept that prospect on the horizon that is coming. Oh yes - it is coming to bring you all into alignment and to accept your fate in whatever way shape or form! It will come as a Light . . . a dawning within your mind of a new world beyond all imagination, a new world of Light and Love that will open up many possibilities for you all; but most of all your hearts will expand and truly Love . . . truly beat to the same rhythm as the universe. We have accepted this as our fate, a much loved servant to the cause, and we allow your divinity to shine out like a beacon bright for all to see . . . so that you may shine the way for others to follow. We shall remember you all . . . each and every one! Go now with our peace and blessings . . . all will be shown and all will unfold in greater glory for the betterment of mankind.

∞

15.10.13 – *The powerful number eleven is evident today* 1+5+1+0+1+3=**11**

I'm seeing a purple tunnel and this has cleared to reveal a very old Indian with long headdress; he is holding a long staff and banging it on the ground as if to gain my attention.

We bring you a magical pathway to the stars and beyond where all is
waiting to bring you into alignment with us, your friends and
neighbours. We open the hearts of each one of you, accessing that
vital aspect of your being. We attempt to de-clutter your brain and
bring you fresh hope of a new world, detoxifying and shedding light
on issues that surround you. We have great cause to welcome in a
new phase, a phase of enlightenment that shall manifest in the soul of
your being, shining light on cloudy issues that surface for recognition.
We know this has been a challenging time for you and we take on
board what is of the utmost importance; we relay our messages
across the great divide and ask you to look most carefully at what we
lay before you now in this moment of your time. We are given to
frequent bonding's that allow you to draw closer into our soul group
and we make it of paramount importance that you register deep
within your heart what we are about.

*I'm seeing several misty faces and one stood out as a big Lion's face. I can feel a
big beam on my face now and when I spoke it was in a lighter voice.*

We rein in the harmonies . . . we come to assist you. We see you are
alone today!

It's the day our group usually meets but they are not able to be here today.

There will be many meetings in this little room, many like-minded
souls and we will be here to greet them! We shepherd you along in
the right direction, conferring with our comrades on the best course
of action to take you further forward, along this stairway to the stars.
We give thanks for your transcripts for they shall be recorded for all
to see and this knowledge is of great importance!

*I want to reach out and touch you and tell you I Love you! I'm getting the sense of
a very, wrinkled face and I lean forward to stroke their cheek with the back of my
hand.*

Thank you my friends for coming close. I endeavour to listen more carefully within my heart to what you are saying. Let us carry on, let us try again, I am listening with my heart.

We open these proceedings and allow you to come closer, shadowing you from dawn to dusk as you make your journeys. We open up the labyrinth and allow you through to explore and examine all that is hidden. This has been a momentous occasion for us your friends on the other side and we reconnect with you in these moments of deepest bliss, registering your thought streams and bringing you aboard once more to partake in a grand reunion of souls that unite as one. We feel that repose deep within your heart and we shut out the cold wind, drawing you close in our embrace, sheltering you from harm. We have known of this grand connection for many a long year and it gives us great satisfaction that you are now here in our arms.

I sank back in perfect peace . . .

Thank you my dear for enabling this to happen . . . for opening your heart and letting us in.

Oh my heart feels warm and I can feel coolness at the same time as if a tunnel is opening in my heart.

We propel you into that stream of excellence registering your ability to keep pace.

I asked for help with my family in their spiritual development.

Only when you are ready will you hearken to the teacher within. We know the old proverb to be true that you may lead a horse to water but cannot make it drink! There are many in your world that understand this expression and we take on board that you have all been concerned with your families, as to how they will adapt, how they will even make this mammoth leap into a new dimension. We tell you now it will be so! We have made this undertaking to deliver you all in one piece and we shall be there with you to help you adjust, picking up the pieces and putting you back together again.

Are we going to morph into our new world like 'beam me up scotty' with all our cells being scrambled? When you say that you pick up the pieces is that what you mean, that you'll have to rearrange us on the other side?

We do indeed have the technology to do this and we know for some of you this may be very disconcerting!

Yes but to some of us it's also very exciting, personally I can't wait! I can feel them laughing now.

We know this, we know this and that is why you have been chosen - you understand what it is we are trying to accomplish!

I'm feeling so happy at this moment.

This will be a mammoth leap for mankind - for your species and we will tend to you with every care and attention to detail and there will be no going back once this leap has been made. And indeed when you see what is here waiting for you, you will have no desire to go back to the old world, to the world you created. Here there is the chance to begin again and there are no tricks up our sleeve, we have only honourable intentions for your race, and we have guided you along this long road awaiting your destiny to be fulfilled. We believe you do justice to our words and we will not sit on the fence, we will have our say and help you adjust to these new energies that will, as we have said before, deliver you to us in once piece. We have no desire to pull you apart and begin again; we do however adjust your circuits so that you may realise your true nature and your quest for peace.

Thank you friends I'm surprised how I'm able to hear your words without being deeply entranced and yet I can still see the purple and flashes of gold. Is this something to do with being multi-dimensional that we can now achieve this on Earth?

There are many that do have this function fully operational, and we allow you the chance to try out your wings and fly in the truest sense . . . a wonderful feeling of freedom! And you yourself have glided on

270

those thermal currents and enjoyed the view from way up high.

Yes I have it was wonderful, thank you.

Thank you for having come this far and there is further yet to go! Push out from that which confines you . . . stretch your perimeters, it is all there for the taking. Be brave and boldly go.

I'm hesitating to say 'boldly go where no man has gone before' because if we are all 'one' we would already have been there and done that and got the T-shirt!

Oh we do love these little chit chats my friend, and yes you are right of course, we are all One and we have had many experiences, not only on the Earth plane but in many different worlds in many different dimensions. But it still boils down to the fact that each individual has his or her own experiences to share with others. You are individualised in this incarnation, you learn and you discover new facts about yourselves and the world in which you live; you then take back and share this knowledge.

When you say take back – do you mean to the source, the Source of all that is?

We do indeed my child and we pool this knowledge. This knowledge is necessary to forge new worlds.   It is never ending, the all-encompassing Love of the Great Divine . . . all is an expression of Love and what we can all achieve together as one mind. You were born from that spark of eternal Love and we held you in the womb of our making, propelling you out into the world to give sustenance to the souls of those that stumble, for those souls that need assistance, and we have made mammoth discoveries about ourselves in this world of yours.

Oh how we have cried and suffered at your great losses, we have known great sorrow and pain and yet we have known great Love too, bringing you back full circle to rest in our arms once more. We sooth your brow and ask you to acknowledge there is no undertaking that is too great for a mother and her child, and it is so with us! We are well versed in these proceedings and we ask you not to be alarmed at what

271

the future holds. There is only joy and deepest bliss that awaits you and you have all done so well on the Earth plane, sharing your Love and knowledge with others of your persuasion as was pre-ordained. We hold you all in the greatest esteem, asking you not to lose faith for we come in all honesty, in all Love and grace. We come to give you strength in a world that has given up on many of you; we give you strength for the times ahead and the adjustments that are coming your way and we bring tears of joy to replace those tears of sadness and great sorrow. A new world is born and we promise each and every one of you that this shall be your heritage!

Its pouring with rain and the wind is battering at the door which prompted me to ask - is the Earth going through a cleansing period, there seems to have been extremes of weather across the globe?

The Earth is going through a very challenging time with many upheavals within, she knows this is a time of great change and is preparing to eject you, her sons and daughters, into a new realm of indescribable beauty and we support her through this time of great turmoil.

What will happen to Mother Earth?

She will be reborn just as you my child. The old shall fall away to be replaced with a new more vibrant world of peace and prosperity.

I'm being shown a vision of planet Earth and there is a bright light around her with a feeling of peace; there are no more wars and an end to famine where everyone has their place, living in harmony with one another.

And what will happen to the old 3D world?

We take her under our wing and nurture her back to full health - she will not be discarded! And there are many that may choose to stay with her and help those unfortunates that cannot make this transition. She will not be cast adrift!

I started formulate a question in my mind but it seems there is not time today.

We will leave that for another day my child when we continue with our discussions. Go now in Peace with the Love of the Great Divine. We resurrect a new race of 'Super Beings' and allow that to sink in before our next meeting.

I'm seeing someone bowing with hands together and it looks like my smooth headed man who I associate with the Sun. Thank you friends I've enjoyed this morning, thank you very much.

∞

At the start of this session I again saw my old North American Indian wearing his headdress.

We gather together to bring a new stream of thought into the world and we prepare you to assimilate this knowledge that it may be used for the betterment of mankind. We tread carefully and lightly upon the Earth plane, asking you to remember us in your prayers. We are those Light Beings brought to bring a greater awakening in the hearts and consciousness of all those who reside on Earth. We temper our words where alienation is rife in your world and we ask you to bear witness to what is imperative at this time in your universe. There are many of us that do not take this lightly and we expressly forbid a lessening of products, bringing you closer to the heart of our concern. We allow the ramifications of this to settle in your mind as we wish you God speed and safe journey.

We take you to the heart core of proceedings that will govern a greater awareness that is imminent from our point of view. We govern proceedings with an air of grace and authority and ask you to stand back as we deliver a most prolific understanding, filtering into the minds of those that come to serve. It is no mean feat to have come so far and we allow a greater velocity of information to be brought forward that will challenge your establishment in more ways than one. This shall be likened to a thunderbolt of lightning, awakening you all to come to your senses before it is too late, before the mind becomes numb and closed to what we are proposing! We initialise in you the greatest asset that we bring to Earth and that is the wisdom within your hearts . . . to believe that innermost core of

273

your being that causes you to doubt those who will lead you astray. There is no better understanding than this organ that beats within your breast and we deliver a mainstream connection that will allow us greater access, helping you unfold to a greater wisdom.

I'm seeing an Indian encampment with drums beating out the heart rhythm around the camp fire.

We have had many tasks in the past that have come to fruition and brought us the greatest joy; and to be working with the many on the Earth plane fulfills our hopes and dreams for the Children of Earth to come together as one in the greater knowledge that we never die . . . that our spirit goes on forever.   We empower you to march with us, an Army of Light marching for the cause, and we excel in all we do opening up those boundaries that keep us apart. We go forward together!

Great Warrior of Light, I thank you for your Love, for your healing balm and the Peace that you bring.

And we dear sister thank you for your achievements, we work together as one true voice, speaking to the nations.

Have we got time to speak about our last conversation on Super Beings before I have to go?

You were a nation of Super beings . . . you were so much more and will be again; your radiance will shine out as it did once long ago, and you will become those glorious creatures of Light once more.   We assist you in your recoveries and ignite the flame of Love within your hearts, opening up the boundaries and pushing through with greater clarity of expression, forthright in our dealings with the business of this recovery, recovery from oppression.

I'm now getting the song – 'Sweet dreams are made of this'.

Go in Peace sister with our blessings!

274

I'm sitting once more in my sanctuary for early morning meditation, bringing down the golden light through my crown chakra and allowing it to wash through me, rejuvenating my brain to increase its working capacity rather than the small percentage that is used at present. I'm also visualising this light washing through the whole of my body, regenerating tissue in every cell and fibre of my being. I believe if you let yourself truly believe that this golden light will cleanse and purify you of all disease then it 'will', eliminating all toxins and restoring your body to a position of harmony and perfect health. The trick is 'believing' and the more you practice the better you will feel.

Believe it will be so! It is within this aura of peace and tranquility that we reach out to you and we initialise a greater acceptance of all that we are. Our main concerns for the human race are very few, a gentle propulsion shall wash away the sins of the world and with this golden light there is so much more we can do. Open your hearts and minds to receive us and we shall be there by your side urging you not to lose faith, for we are with you and have always been so from the beginning of time immemorial. There has never been a time when we did not exist and we regard you as our true offspring . . . benevolent to mankind in every way possible. We pick up the pieces of those who have fallen along the wayside and we put you back together again!

In all truth and honesty we have come many times before to your planet and we have shepherded you along, initialising in you the greatest respect for your forefathers - your ancestors. We shed light on a subject that is closest to our hearts at this time and it has always been our greatest joy to have you walk alongside us.

I'm seeing geometric golden shapes but it's misty and not as clear as usual. I think that's because my own mind is coming in and questioning. Help me to be a clear channel my friends, help me to put my doubts to one side and let flow whatever comes forth.

We champion you to champion the cause of enlightenment among mankind and we shall pull back those barriers that keep us from seeing the truth, the whole truth and nothing but the truth! We have the propensity to divulge information that comes in from the ethers with greater clarity, and our perception of the human mind is very limited. There is an inordinate amount of information that needs to be tapped into and harnessed for us to pass on to you, the true co-creators of the human race, and we unveil a multitude of mishaps that caused our demise. Perhaps you will take pity on us and initialise a reversal that will help us to become those giants once more.

Do you literally mean giants? We do indeed my Love. *I'm now remembering the film Prometheus.*

Dear friends am I connecting with you or am I trawling through past memories of things I have seen on the cinema screen? Am I getting this information from myself or from you my Star friends? And even as I'm asking this I know that we are one and the same and that memories are stored within the cells of our very being. Oh this is wonderful . . . I'm still not clear about it but I'm getting the gist so to speak. It's like being a detective trying to work things out, figuring out the clues that are there for us. Sometimes there is a 'red herring' that puts us off the scent but nevertheless we all keep on searching until we do find the truth, the whole truth!

What is your take on this my friends?

We endeavour to show you by hook or by crook what is necessary to overcome this vast malfunction perpetrated by the human race . . . by our own species.

I'm feeling such sadness now with tears stinging my eyes. I'm seeing that creature at the beginning of Prometheus where he drank a liquid and fell into the raging sea with his DNA breaking up . . . with the strands all coming undone.

That is why we wish to put you back together again my children, like Humpty Dumpty, but we 'can' put you back together again and we need your assistance to do this! We need you to remember who you are . . . those magnificent creatures of Light . . . all powerful, all knowing, all Loving.

In the film those creatures were aiming to destroy planet Earth!

276

That is not our wish! We wish to restore equilibrium to the heart and body and soul of the universe, to restore peace and order in a world that is flung into chaos, and we will never desist from this great task! We will never turn our backs on the human race for we have leant from our mistakes in the past and we come now into your future, to help you on your journey so that you may not repeat those mistakes that we made so very long ago!

So is that the destiny we are all hurtling towards - oblivion?

Energy cannot be destroyed – it merely changes form. We manifest before you now as pure energy and yet we are here now, talking with you and discussing the pros and cons of further evolution. It was never our intention to destroy the human race but the knock on effect of subduing your knowledge had great repercussions and annihilation on a grand scale! We ask you to forgive us for our sins as we aim to rectify an appalling lack of humanity within your souls. We aim to bring you full circle and set you back in a new dimension, ready to begin again, to reinstate you in a world of peace and harmony.

Oh wow that's such a lot of information that needs sifting through and digesting. And I do thank you dear friends, it must be hard to admit that you/we have made a mistake, and such a huge mistake, but thank you for coming back to help us. Thank you for turning the clock back . . . thank you for finding us!

It was not an easy task and one that we give thanks for to the Great Divine . . . to the all-knowing, all seeing God, who strives to make amends and bring harmony once more to the Children of Earth.

I'm seeing vivid purple again and flashes of gold and I 'know' this is the truth! I feel as if I'm being held in the palm of God's hand and yet we are all God. It is a conundrum fathoming out all of this . . . it is enough to blow your mind! Thank you friends, I think I'll sit awhile and bathe in the energies to just let it sink in and permeate my being, gently, gently. The little worries in my life seem to pale into insignificance when there are such mammoth decisions to be made in the whole of creation. I think I'll leave it there for today, thank you friends.

May the Love of the Great Divine go with you now and forever more, and may the teachings of your heart show you the expansiveness of the human plan. And may we pick up those pieces and put them back together in the right order to reinstate you in a new world of peace and perfect Love. Amen.

∞

Today I'm tuning in specifically to send healing to Earth and all mankind; I visualised bringing golden light down into the caves, imagining those who live beneath Earth's crust . . . then I heard them call out to me.

Come and join us!

I'm now joining a group of people in white robes and we are raising our hands up, sending out healing to Earth, our voices echoing around the cavern. I started to chant Om.

We give thanks for this brave new world we are creating. We create perfect peace and harmony within our thought streams, sending out to Mother Earth from deep within her core, transcending our wildest expectations . . . a new Earth, clean and bright!

I'm seeing and feeling the purple clouds sweeping around me in an anti-clockwise direction.

I ask for Love and healing for all those living above on Earth's surface and for those who are trying to bring about Earth's downfall. I ask that LOVE and LIGHT ignite their hearts so they may bring themselves into perfect balance and harmony, and in so doing bring EARTH into perfect harmony. That's all that needs to happen . . . for mankind to light that flame of Love within their breasts and to keep it burning – IT IS SO SIMPLE!

I'm getting a tunnel effect in the purple light now and felt the urge to speak in a voice that started in a deep, slow tone like a gramophone record played at the wrong speed.

We are born to Love. We are born to give wings to Light. We travel

278

far across your globe, unfolding greater joy within your hearts and we envelop you now in a membrane that shall protect you from the knocks and blows of earthly pressures. We vouch for your safety on all occasions and transcend our wildest dreams, bringing you aboard in one piece so to speak. We have clouded your vision for it is that you are unable to accept our Light form at this moment in time. We propel you to a land of dreams that will enable you to visit us in more ambient circumstances. This is a directive given from those on high and we abide by the rules and regulations that allow us to participate in this connection. We bring solace to your heart . . . we bring truth and light to your soul to receive us. We bear gifts given to the very few and we provide you with ample therapy, broadening your thought streams to accept what we bring with an open and loving heart.

The connection isn't clear and either they are slowing my whole system down or I haven't mastered this new frequency yet. I'm continuing to visualise the golden light coming through me and asking for God's help. I decided to leave it and later in the day came across a Pleiadian transmission, which opens the heart centre reinstating six of the lost DNA strands. I accessed this on the 'Federation of Light' network, which featured Pleiadian Ambassador, Christine Day. It seems I am quickly being directed to the therapy spoken of in this short communication.

∞

In meditation today I brought the golden light down as always and sent it deep into the heart of Mother Earth. May the Love and the protection of the Great Divine be with me now and may all unfold before my eyes. Open up my heart Great Spirit so I may feel and see and hear your words.

We have grown towards you with great tenderness.

And I to you Great Mother!

I saw beautiful purple light and then a White Horse. I followed the horse as it galloped along a tunnel and then it stopped for me to catch up. Its coat was wet with perspiration or maybe the dampness of the tunnel and I wiped off the moisture which flew away in what looked like crystal teardrops. We took off

279

again and I followed as the horse clattered through the tunnels, then it stopped once more and again I wiped the moisture from his back with my hands. It lay down for me to climb onto its back but I recently read that it can damage a horse's spine and so I preferred to walk with it. This time there was no clattering and we padded along the tunnel quietly together, looking down I noticed that my feet were bare. We came to a great opening, an arena that was full of vivid purple with golden shapes that I couldn't make out. I asked if there were any words to pass on and felt a tickling on my chin.

We open an agenda that is worthy of your attention and we bring you full circle, initiating greater rewards for your journey of the highest intent. We bring you back to face us head on so that we may open those conduits within your heart where we can express ourselves, relaying our messages across the great divide.

Oh the purple and gold are so exquisite it brings tear to my eyes!

We have a request my child! *Yes my friends what can I do for you?*

We ask you to step through the doorway that is there open for you! *Yes I will.*

The door to free Love and expression, freedom of movement, freedom from all that has held you back from progressing into that true state of existence . . . we are an endangered species!

Again I'm feeling tears in my eyes with emotion. How can I help you?

Just by being in this frequency . . . you are helping! *A single tear is running down my cheek.*

We reap the benefits of this encounter very soon my Love; spring is not far away and the winter shall not be too hard for you to bear.

Just to be nestled in your embrace is all the reward I ask. I'm feeling tentacles of Love reaching out to me and surrounding me . . . and the tears are pouring down my face.

I woke in the night to see the face of Great Chief Sitting Bull.

We come in peace and prosperity for mankind. It is hard to accept that many on this plateau of existence do not understand the most basic of concepts . . . that Love will conquer over all maladies. We strive for peace on Earth as we did for our lands long ago. We give thanks for those like you who march forward for freedom . . . for Liberté. Yes my friends it keeps us busy here, ushering you forward step by step, and we are mightily pleased with how far you have come. Little Big Horn was our cross to bear and it gives us great joy to take the cross from you that you have carried for so long. We register your deep concerns and it is fortuitous that we come now to cleanse the past, wiping the slate clean. There are many who stand to be counted and we come to join the throng, giving thanks for this great initiative. We bend and salute you for your mastery over self and your iron will to do what is right in accordance with our directives. We feel you drawing closer and closer to the heart of operations and we rally round to give you our support. Well done my child – well done! We look forward to many more meetings. Adieu!

As I settled back to sleep I saw clouds of purple flying past me and these last words . . . We fly on the wings of Angels and carry you to distant shores!

In the morning I looked up my notes from 1995 when I first encountered Sitting Bull.

In May of that year I had sat with a friend in deep meditation and was shown great expanses of pure white snow. The sun was shining brightly and I found myself clambering up a huge snow drift. Just before I reached the top a spear was thrust into the ground ahead of me. I turned to see the tanned figure of a thick set man with long black hair. We played in the snow like father and daughter and I saw myself sitting on a sledge being pulled by a silver wolf. I was then given these words:-

The battle of 'Wounded Knee' was never meant to be. So many dead . . . slaughtered. We mourn them . . . the lost ones!

281

As this came through tears were streaming down my face.

We see you clearly and we reach out to help you forgive those that hurt you! One day my children you will be free of all encumbrances, all cares and worries.

I asked for more information about the battle of Wounded Knee.

Many times we had big 'pow wow' engaged in plans of peace. Alas all was in vain the blue coats were not interested in peace, they were too greedy! In all this great land there was not room for us to live as one, brothers under the skin. We tried in vain to save our people . . . our buffalo and the land that was so sweet to us! We forgive them for what they have done; man can be so weak and frail of spirit . . . not counting the cost until too late. We look back on those times and reach out to give you strength of spirit and of the flesh . . . you will need succour to get you through the times of hardship. Do not weep little one, we must not brood on the past . . . only learn from our mistakes!

∞

24.10.13 - 2+4+1+0+1+3=11 - The master number eleven is evident once more with a message from the heavens.

I am being shown a brilliant golden light surrounding Earth . . . we are moving away, heading towards a bright light; I wondered if it was to see the man with smooth head who lives in the sun and I'm being given the name Ra.

It is a simple method of initiation, opening up those foundations within you and turning the key.

I can hear the bolts flying back, opening the door to my heart . . . I'm now floating through dark, misty purple which intensifies in colour, getting brighter . . . it's like flying through energy and I'm feeling a sense of freedom. The earthly conditions fall away . . . all the pains and discomfort . . . there is only peace within my heart. I can feel the rippling of energy around my throat and around the edge of my brain. The head of an Eagle has just come into view . . . the Eagle is with me and I do believe we are flying over mountains. We are climbing higher

282

and higher . . . the Earth has become smaller like a little round dot. I asked if there were any words for me but it was hard to speak their answer aloud into my microphone.

We say well done for achieving this bliss!

∞

It is late October 2013 and I'm sitting on the steps of my sanctuary, gazing out across the estuary . . . the energies feel different today and there is a gentleness in the wind as it caresses my face. I can't believe it is late October and will soon be winter.

Do not be deceived by weather conditions!

Hmm does this mean it is the lull before the storm I wonder?

There's plenty of opportunity to grow and we make the most of these days.

I feel as if I'm smiling now and sense a North American Indian with me.

We tell you the stories of long ago. We bring you sweet dreams . . . we bring you lullabies, holding you to our bosom as in times gone past.

I'm sensing an Indian holding a baby to her bosom and rocking gently.

We have been sheltered from the harsh winds that blow and we watch out for you as we have always done. It gives us great pleasure to be here with you now in this moment of your time. We have registered your distress in the past and see it now fall away like the leaves on your trees. This has been of great significance and we allow that to sink in as we take you further along the road, opening up the way-stations to allow you through. This has been a monumental recovery and we give thanks for this, dear sister of Light. You are most welcome to our borders and we approach you and take your hand, leading you to those pastures where you may recover, where you may grow in our Love. The days grow shorter!

I can vaguely see a North American Indian and asked - is that you Sitting Bull, is that really you my friend?

We come as one voice and you have always known this!

Tears springing to my eyes, I replied - yes I have my friend, you are right!

‘We Come as One Voice’ - perhaps I could use that for the name of our next book . . . that would be a great title! What do think my friends? I can see the face of Sitting Bull much clearer now and he is smiling at me. Oh welcome to my heart dear friends, it is so wonderful to be able to start my days like this in meditation, communing with you.

It is most wonderful, most joyous and we feel you here with us, registering those thoughts within your breast. We give clarification of all we hold most dear and we shepherd you along, step by step, gathering momentum for that final thrust into a new dimension beyond all earthly measure. And this is at our fingertips, we are almost there, it is within your grasp all that you seek. We shall publish these thoughts and they will fly around the world, gathering momentum. We shall be heard and we shall be seen to be discovering those true facts that have slipped through the radar so to speak.

We have discovered new ways of communicating with you all and these shall soon become accepted as ‘the norm’. We enter your thought streams and impress upon you the need to listen and take stock for it has taken many years to reach this point. And we wish to go further forward at a faster pace, gathering the ‘Children of Earth’ to that point where we can raise you up and hold you in our arms once more . . . to be our kith and kin as you once were. We know this may seem a tad absurd to some of you but we have come so far to rescue our own! Would you not do the same for your children? Would you not do whatever you could to save them from despair - to save them from total annihilation! That is the road you are heading on my friends and you have only yourselves to blame . . . but just as a child kicks up a storm we too kick up a fuss, chiding you and showing you the right path to follow. We have learnt from our mistakes and hope you will be guided by this. We challenge you to accept that this is so - that way into the future there are mishaps that have occurred that you would not wish upon yourselves, any more than we would wish it upon you! And so we come and teach you and assist you in your discoveries, for this is a beautiful world and she should be treated with more care and concern.   This is no way to behave, fighting with your brothers and sisters, you should know better! Learn to Love one another   . . . learn to live in grace with maturity of spirit!

Live under the Sun and grow your crops!

I'm seeing a big feather bonnet in the sky!

Do not tamper with your crops . . . let them grow in truth and honesty by the soil of the land . . . by the warmth of the sun and the rain that falls from the heavens, it is so simple . . . it is so simple!

Tears are coursing down my cheeks as I call out to them.

I LOVE YOU, I LOVE YOU . . . I LOVE YOU!

These words are truth I know they are, why cannot man see this? Thank you for your words of wisdom . . . you think we would have learnt by now. This is how it should be, to live in Love and harmony with the land with nature and with one another.

And you can talk to the animals and they will listen, they will listen with their hearts just as you are listening to us now. Go gently upon the Earth plane little sister, go gently. We are with you watching over you, never fear. Abide in our Love and the Love of the Great Divine from the source of all that is, all that has been and all that will be. We ask you take our messages and to share them with all who will listen, and we ask you all to take stock of these proceedings that we too may enter your heart, your thought streams, so that we may evolve together as one people, brothers and sisters under the skin.   For it matters not what colour your skin is, it matters only that your heart beat with the rhythm of Love!

I can vaguely hear that song, the rhythm of life is a powerful beat - sung by Sammy Davis Junior.

Take up that banner and march with us little ones!

I am being shown someone on horseback, wearing a large feather headdress and holding a long stick.

We will friends, we will. I will shout it from the roof tops as you know I will. I thank you for speaking through me today.

May the Love of the Great Divine go with you now and forever more and may these words take flight like the Dove of Peace.

∞

27.10.13 – The rain is pounding at the door and windows of my sanctuary and as I sit in meditation I'm immediately shown a medicine man wearing skins and horns. I'm visualising sending golden light down into the caverns beneath Earth's crust and wish to explore further. The medicine man is drawing closer and it's as if I am wearing the skins.

I Am Great Chief Sitting Bull and I come to be with you in your hour of need.

Are you going to be working with me on a regular basis and if this is so, is it because people recognise your name and will listen to what you have to say?

We do indeed have some clout in your world and we undeniably face a hard task, identifying what is needed for a massive solution upon the Earth plane. We come as one voice in all sincerity and ask you to adjust your settings. We have been given the go ahead to approach you and we sanction a blessing from the Great Divine towards those thought processes that will allow us to draw nearer in your embrace.

The softness of purple clouds caress me, slowing down my thought streams, slowing

286

the beat of my heart. I feel at peace and let out a great sigh. Oh great friend thank you for drawing close once more, your words have been well accepted amongst my friends. Is there anything you would like to say to me this morning?

We bring you sweet repose and a gentleness to touch your soul and light your heart from within. The flame of Love grows brighter for all to see and we register your intentions as being just and true upon the Earth plane.

Once again I'm seeing a white horse galloping along a tunnel but this time I'm sitting astride him. I seem to be wearing a blue cloak with white stockings and shoes and there seems to be a golden crown upon my head. Where are we going? The horse is climbing up some steps of what looks like a castle turret. We have come out into a round room that is filled with colour and sound and warmth. I can see someone who looks like Leonardo Davinci and there are musicians playing large cello type instruments.

They have given me a big chair to sit in but I feel a lot smaller than them because my feet are dangling over the edge of the seat as if I'm a child. I'm still wearing the blue cloak and crown as if I'm dressing up. It feels very friendly and warm and there are lots of things around to look at (curiosity of a child). There are lots of books and quills with ink pots and manuscripts, and rolls of parchment. There is a fire burning in the hearth and the flames are shooting high up the chimney. It feels like Christmas, a time of celebration, and I can see two red Christmas stockings hanging by the fire and there are mince pies. I believe this may be a sign of what's to come – a Happy Christmas! I have happy tears in my eyes now.

Let there now be no more tears except those tears of happiness and we shelter you and bring you into the fold once more, communing heart to heart . . . our thoughts of Love mingling and growing stronger. We are of one mind in all Love and sincerity. We direct your thought streams and channel you into more productive areas that will bear fruit. We have motioned you to tread this stairway to the stars long ago and we have nurtured you and pushed you forward to do our bidding. We tend to your needs giving you the impetus to forge ahead and we strike while the iron is hot, fulfilling all our dreams and aspirations for a brighter future for mankind and we shall settle you down in a new dimension of peace and tranquillity where all shall be accomplished. We have come many times in the past to assist you in your journeys and we vouch for your honesty and integrity. This has been a massive learning curve for all of us and we give thanks to all who have taken part. It is an accomplishment beyond words, opening the hearts of mankind and bringing them to fruition; bringing them to that point of reasoning that shall change the future and bring us back on track. This is a most magnanimous gesture on your part and we know it makes sense to join together and become as one in a new world of strength and grace. And we shall challenge you to accept us as we truly are . . . your friends and neighbours from bygones past . . . your countryman, your kith and kin, and we open that magical doorway to a new world.

We beg you to listen to our thesis for these are times of the utmost importance and greater reverence, needed to bring you aboard to shelter in our thought streams, to come into our jurisdiction as we offer you resuscitation from countless episodes of grief. We are pardoned and it is beyond all belief that we should not come to your aid at this time of great crisis. We beg you to look with a different perspective, honouring the Great Divine with your presence as we spread the facts before you, allowing you to look with fresh eyes. We lay all before you and open those conduits that allow free expression, desirous of many in your world, and we lay before you an affidavit that will give us ample opportunity to assist one another in this quest for peace among your nations, peace in the very heart and soul of your being.

I'm seeing exquisite purple and gold here.

We shall not doubt you little one . . . Mercury comes into orbit and allows us to venture forth, to sally forth with greater expression and we will not crack the whip for we know you have greater strength of purpose.

I'm seeing riders atop a carriage being pulled by galloping horses.
We are honour bound to shelter you and keep you safe and this we will do with great Love in our hearts for you and all mankind. Do not be put off by those few who come to barrack for they know not what

288

they do! This is for a greater purpose known to man and transcends more than the human eye can possibly understand or register at this present moment. We come to uncloak you and to draw the film from your eyes so that you may shine in all majesty once more, as you did long ago. Take good care of yourselves on the Earth plane; we bring you cheer for the cold days ahead and those days of darkness when you are at your lowest ebb. We will be there in the shadows, urging you not to lose faith but to keep that light burning bright within your heart for others to see. For when those lights come together there shall be a massive radiance all around the world and that radiance shall spread far beyond your world into the outer reaches of the universe, touching our hearts and bringing you alive once more, alive in the truest sense. Keep faith, help one another along this pathway and all will be well.

I'm seeing the figure of Jesus now as the 'Light of the World'.

When the darkness gets too hard to bear don't despair . . . WE are there!

Thank you for your encouragement and we will keep on keeping on! I'm getting words from a Bee Gees song - 'There's a Light, a special kind of Light that always shines on me!

The textbook definition of Mercury is: Messenger of the Gods and acts as a communicator, I'm not an astrologist but apparently in its current retrograde position in the sign of Scorpio, which is a water sign, it enhances the energy of going within and feeling from the heart thus transforming one's words.

∞

I woke in the early hours and transcribed these words.

The plight of the Redman was long and hard and we accept the path we walked was not ours to keep. The meadows we laid down in were sweet indeed . . . we sang to the land and she answered through the wind, whispering in the trees and high above the mountain passes. The road stands clear before us - sweet memories from the past drift into view and we stand at the crag and welcome you here once more. We rest in the peace and solitude expressing our heart's desires and we openly express our disquietude at certain intervals coming up for inspection. We know this has been a time of great diligence and fortitude and we express our sorrow at such interludes. However, on the horizon is so much more and an opportunity to soar high in the clouds as the Eagle rises in grace and majesty. We shall not burden you with more trials of endurance, so please be at peace my child. We overcome a network of high expenditure and low resources . . . all is about to change for the better!

Hold onto your hats for the ride of your life! We take you across the rainbow and on to finer visions - a declaration of peace that we can understand and trust implicitly with no uprising in the ranks. We are given to understand there are connections being made that will allow for a more flamboyant way of life and we suggest alternative measures that will enhance your programme. We are delighted with how it all turns out and ask you to respect these changes as they come flooding in. We empower you to do your best in all scenarios and watch over you to keep you on track. Do not be discouraged or put off, or fooled into submission. We take all in our stride and set you free.

We are content and bless you, offering our services to the Great Spirit, following in the footsteps of our beloved ancestors, and we shine a light on key issues that need looking at with a fine tooth comb, shaking out the debris of the past and making good our mistakes. It was deemed by the prophet Isaiah that we should take the path of truth and justice to avail ourselves of purity of spirit. We drink from the fountain of everlasting life to the resurrection of all we hold most dear and we fly on the wings of Angels over the ravine and on to pastures new.

Later in my morning meditation we continued. I've drenched myself in golden light and am now sending a spotlight of golden energy down into the earth beneath us like a searchlight. I ask that all Light workers around the globe may be linked in Love with our roots growing down into the earth, touching one another and meeting at the centre towards the Great Tree of Life. The energy is expanding and

290

growing and coming back up through the tree and out through the branches into the cosmos. I call out to my Star friends to draw close as I settle my attention back to the heart centre.

It is with great content that we open our arms to receive you. We analyse those streams of thought that bring us closer and we express our joy to be here with you once more. It is no mean feat to achieve this peace and harmony . . . to still the mind and sense our presence. Our physicality comes into question as we settle you; we have made this rendezvous on many occasions in the past as you came to sit at our knee resting your head. We stroke your hair and sooth your brow asking you to put aside what is no longer needed. We question your thought streams, satisfying ourselves as to your intentions, and we bring forward a whole host of questions that need to be answered. We are forthright in our quizzing and open up your mind to accept this undertaking, begging your pardon if at times perhaps we get the wrong term or phrase that pinpoint what we are aiming for – greater clarity of expression!

We do attempt to lay before you the burdens that have held many back and we resume our connections when you can all take on board what we bring in all truth and sincerity. We have followed you most of your lifetimes, stepping in from time to time to see how you are doing upon the Earth plane, how you are coping with the pressures that were brought to bear upon you, registering your highs and lows, taking you to task when you were discouraged and pushing you forward in those instances of regret. We were there at the helm watching over you, we were there at your shoulder whispering in your ear, we were there in your darkest moments, urging you not to lose faith. And we come now to uplift your spirits, pushing you forward as the tidal wave itself with great momentum, carrying forward a whole cleansing programme that will adjust attitudes, allowing you to see with clearer vision.

There are a whole mountain of programmes that come to be looked at and sifted through, recognising your true talents, your strengths and your weaknesses with adjustments that need to be made to help you grow stronger and wiser. There will be an expansion of assets, a retuning of circuits with a mammoth delivery of services right across the globe and we shall leave no stone unturned. None shall be ignored - the lost will be found and brought back into the fold for did not the prodigal son return to us amid great joy and jubilation! And we foresee those greater assets shall be used and worked upon, blossoming and ripening like the corn in the fields and the sun shall ripen those golden sheaves within your soul, bringing in a bountiful harvest and one we give thanks for.

There was a bang in room at this point as if in confirmation.

Oh children you are so very dear to us and we come to shepherd you along - not to be herded like sheep but to cherish you and Love you, and the very least among you shall be anointed and brought into our jurisdiction, feeling the Love of the Great Divine within your very soul. We feel the eclipse within your soul and we raise the barricade and let you through. No more shall you be imprisoned!

I'm feeling ripples around the base of my brain, more to the left hand side. I can also feel a cool energy on my left shoulder and down my left side.

We have an excellent opportunity to delve deeper within your skull. There has been a massive intolerance to chemicals and we give thanks for the advocates that step forward to help us in your recovery. The trauma inflicted has been great and we resuscitate, generating further growth, and this will be our greatest asset.

Are you giving me healing?

We are recharging neural pathways, opening up those conduits that have become fused, resisting information that floods through for your immediate approval. We do believe we have unlimited resources to work with and it is our intention to update and restore harmony on a grander scale. Do not be disturbed or alarmed for this will take only a short period to be realised in true perfection, and with greater reserves of energy for back up! All is well – all is as it should be and in the fullness of time you will see greater improvement in our alliance.

292

Go now in peace and protection with the Love of the Great Divine and the host of Angels that gather to us on wings of Light. We manifest a greater declaration of peace and prosperity in the not too distant future. Go now and rest and recharge your batteries and we shall bring you release from all that holds you back.

It's so wonderful to know the healing that is available to all of us if we go within and ask; not only for others but for ourselves as well! There are many programmes of healing now being made available free of charge at the direct request from the realms of Light; here is one that has kick started me into recovery. The 1st Template Ceremony of Original Innocence for letting go of fear and anger, which was brought into manifestation through the realms of Light by Juliet and Jiva Carter.

∞

Lately during my meditations in bringing down the golden light through my body and into Mother Earth, I have felt the desire to explore the network of passages beneath Earth's crust. Today before I explore, I'm making sure I'm centred and my heart is lit up; at this point I can literally see a beautiful green, heart shaped jewel. I can also see the figure of someone with long grey hair who looks like Gandalf from Lord of the Rings, he is hovering, in the background where I can also see a big tree; I am following the roots of this tree down deep below and can hear the following words echoing in my mind.

LET THE LAST VESTIGES OF RANCOUR DISSOLVE!

Oh gosh, I'm not sure I want to go down here it's so dark and dank. I feel as if I'm in an old castle but the scene is far different from the one I saw recently where everything was warm and cosy. Determined not to be afraid I take a lantern and am now going down narrow stone steps that curve round. The walls are running wet and I am going deeper and deeper, it seems to go on forever into a deep black hole . . . a void of darkness and despair!

*Dear Angels, am I meant to be down here? It looks like a sewer . . . why am I here, why am I looking at this? If it's of my own making then I'm sorry! There are people down here that are wrapped in rags and covered in filth. I dissolve the darkness and shine a spotlight of **LOVE** down into these lower levels.*

293

Look up my friends . . . follow the Light . . . there is hope for you all. Follow me up the staircase to the higher levels, see it all fall away, the darkness and disease shall be no more!

I'm seeing purple and gold once more and as these creatures are coming up to a higher level, they are beginning to look more human, rather than just lumps of rotting flesh . . . they are being reborn! I'm visualising the muddy dirty waters draining away from the dungeons below and the walls and floor are now painted white. There is a doorway with brilliant white light, like a portal that has opened up and the brilliance is blinding! Why are you showing me this, is it to have the courage to face our innermost fears?

Forgiveness is the key to your own sanity. Forgiveness and Love of self will bring your health. Understanding is the key to set you free and Love will guarantee all three!

This feels like a riddle!

We step onto the highway and byways of life, registering your hopes and dreams for yourself and all mankind, and we lift you out of the catacombs. We lift you out of your dark and dismal days and bring you into the sunlight, into God's Light, manifesting the greatest joy. We know it has been hard for many of you on the Earth plane 'struggling to make ends meet' and we know that old saying has stretched many of your resources to almost breaking point! We reach out and touch you!

I'm seeing a hand with the finger pointing out and sparks of light streaming forth, like the hands from Michelangelo's painting 'Creation of Adam'.

We give you the strength to stand firm with those reserves of energy bestowed upon you to help in your quest, and we make no bones about it. We shall deliver to each and every one of you, as promised, a greater bountiful harvest. We take you by the hand and lead you to those pastures waiting and we fulfill our destiny. Be at peace my child. Welcome the Angel within!

Sometimes when I meditate I fall asleep and that is okay as I obviously need that rest, or I'm whisked off somewhere that I don't remember. I love the adventures I do remember though, going into that stillness through the heart portal, travelling into those inner dimensions for self-healing. They obviously knew I felt safe with the Mark character from ER and as beings of Light they were able to morph into that image to put my mind at ease. I feel the dungeon episodes that I have experienced and shared will help others to look at locked away pain and release into the Light. Forgiving ourselves and others is the key to unlocking the disease within us, setting us free!

∞

Today I am struggling to tune in for my early morning meditation. I always sit with a cup of tea first thing and day-dream before I settle down for meditation. I love daydreaming and often used to get told off at school for gazing out of the window and looking at the clouds. I think I got carried away this morning, thinking of problems I need to sort out.   My mind then drifted to an old episode of ER which we watched last night, where a nurse called Carol Hathaway gave birth to twins. I felt so happy watching her with her new-born babies, remembering the bliss that comes with being a new mother; this has put me in a more relaxed state of mind and my visions began.

Instead of in the dungeons, I'm outside a castle in the meadows on my white horse. I am now looking from a different perspective and can see the character from ER on the white horse with her long dark hair streaming behind her. This lady has such a compassionate face she reminds me of Mary Magdalene and the castle reminds me of the one in France called Carcassonne. They are gently meandering through the long grasses and wild flowers, recuperating from their journey. The horse is swishing his tail and now I'm aware that it's me once again sitting on the horse; I can sense the presence of someone sitting behind me; I can't see them as they are cloaked but feel safe knowing they are there. They are not revealing themselves at the moment but it's as if they will in due course.

We fly on the wings of Angels to pastures new, opening our eyes wide in wonderment and joy. We behold a new world where we can run and play, expressing ourselves with great tenderness . . . to dance with freedom!

Sigh . . .   I'm dancing through the fields, laughing with joy and happiness; the sun is shining and a light breeze is in my hair. I take off my heavy cloak and run barefoot through the grass towards a pond where the light shines on the water like a mirror. As my heroine (Carol) looks into the water the person's reflection beside her is not the one she is expecting, instead of her boyfriend Doug, played by George Clooney, it is   her closest friend Mark Greene, who helped her birth her babies; it isn't a romantic liaison . . . it is true friendship.

Ahead of us I can see a massive golden dome with the light shining on it, almost like a mirror ball and I know it's going to take me home! As I say this I feel tears flooding my eyes. In this analogy Mark is holding out his hand to Carol/me and it's OK, I feel safe, I feel happy and we are walking towards the golden dome. There is a huge door that has opened and we walk towards it.

Now I'm surrounded by purple light and the pictures are gone. There are still tears in my eyes and I feel as if I'm floating. I'm seeing Mark's face again and he's saying it's alright it's OK and I feel I am going up, I don't know if it's in a space ship or a pod but I'm just going with the flow. All I sense is moving upwards but I cannot see anything. Ah yes, I can see it now . . . a tunnel of golden filigree and at the end is a purple light. I am suspended in a void of peace.

∞

For today's meditation I asked if I could go back into the golden dome where we were yesterday and settled back to relax. Wow - my dragonfly chime has just made three little dings and it has never done that before with the door shut.   I'm now seeing the same friendly character of Mark Greene, who makes me feel safe, and we are stepping into a lift; he is asking me if I am ready for this?

We have stepped out of the lift into a huge dome full of people, all busy doing their job - it's a hive of activity. They said I would open my eyes wide in amazement but I was not expecting this! I can see some people in white coats like doctors; they look like ordinary human beings at the moment, unless they are showing themselves as such. I can see lifts which are cylindrical and going up and down in huge glass tubes. Literally anything is possible here and I'm thinking of Leonardo DiCaprio in the film 'Inception'. At the moment I can't see anyone who looks from another planet. There is so much to look at and in a bizarre way it reminds me of the turret room in the castle which was so magical. As I type these words it's just struck me that I could have been in the dome while I was experiencing those sensations, like a holograph deck!

296

We make further discoveries about ourselves, opening up the boundaries that hold us back from achieving our true status. Don't be surprised at what is coming your way very soon! We fly through fields of disbelief, drawing the film from your eyes and we make way for a new generation of sensation seekers, a paradox worthy of this connection that enables us to sally forth.

There are so many different levels, it's almost like I can see a cross section of the ship with everyone getting on with their work. Please can I see someone from a different dimension, I'm sure I won't be shocked after being down in the dungeons and seeing the creatures down there. I'm sure those from other realms won't strike fear into my heart, please can you show me some of the friends who draw close to speak to me who are not of our countenance?

We align with you and make our connection, drawing closer. You are expecting little green men in suits but we shall show you something more remarkable than even that! This is no holier than now approach that we are making, this is rectifying past differences and we shadow you from other galaxies bringing you into alignment with us.

I'm seeing purple clouds now. Oh my friends . . . I just caught a glimpse then. I'm not afraid, your beautiful . . . come closer! I caught a glimpse of a big head little nose and mouth and large almond eyes.

I will be your ambassador . . . I will be your communicator. Are you like a grasshopper only bigger?

It is a challenging time for all of us as we make our connections with those on Earth. We beam you aboard and welcome you to our domain, relying on you to shed those inhibitions about a race you know nothing or very little about! We are temporal beings of greenish hue and we issue you with certain guidelines that will enable a massive drawback of issues that have arisen for scrutiny, and we would like you to trust in our abilities to do this.

Okay let's see how it goes shall we, I'm ready if you are!

We see this has challenged some of your circuits!

297

I'm now getting the word 'bravado' and underlying fear!

We help you to see with clearer vision and this you will come to accept as the norm, believing in a creditable surge of stories being given to us to pass on to you. We benefit from a whole minefield of opportunities and the exploits we have chosen have far reaching consequences!

Good, I'm seeing purple and gold again and that confirms I'm still connected properly. I feel as if I'm in some kind of antechamber, a kind of pressurised cabin where we are able to converse.

We lay claim to sanity and a prime example of how we shall forge ahead, registering your thought streams and amalgamating with ours to forge a new human. We are endowed with the possibility of exchanging data and initialising your greater acceptance of what we have to offer.

I'm being shown a long necked being now with a wide oval head, big eyes and little nose, rather like in the film E.T. A moment later I saw the back of a dinosaur stomping through the corridors with his tail dragging behind him and wondered if it was my imagination rampaging out of control.

We open up a network of programmes that will see us through wider discussions and we ask you now to free-fall into our arms as we open up those conduits to make this connection. Stop worrying about your perimeters; we know exactly what it is you are after and we will do our best to accommodate you in the near future!

∞

In meditation toady I'm being catapulted into a purple and gold vision and briefly saw the profile of a North American Indian in the sky who I believe to be White Cloud.

We discover new ways of taking you on board, initiating the greatest respect for our deliveries. This has been our greatest asset and one we give thanks for. We transcend our wildest probabilities, forgoing

298

our natural discretion to take this on board with all fortitude and reverence for our nearest and dearest. We analyse those requests brought forward for inspection and we ask you to re-examine your methods of communication, displaying with great aptitude what is necessary to form an alliance.   We are open to negotiations on how to achieve our heartfelt determinations and we reprogramme those areas that are giving cause for concern, allowing a trickling of information to reach those centres that need lubricating with finer material. We are on course for a new world of outstanding beauty and we chaperone you on this journey, asking you to bear witness. We ask you to secrete about your person a means of amplifying our connection . . . this will allow you to relax.

At the moment I have to keep my thumb at the ready to press my recorder when words come.

We face the final frontier, giving ourselves the necessary scope and imagination to pull this off, fragmenting and dissolving antiquated worn out notions, pacts that are no longer viable in this new documentary of outstanding proportions. We aim to please and we settle you down in a new location of outstanding peace, amplifying our connection and opening up vistas bright. We are more compliant in our undertakings and this shall give us even greater strength and fortitude to bring ourselves about, registering the hopes and dreams of an entire nation. We shall as always bend to your every whim and govern the proceedings with an air of grace and authority, wholeheartedly connecting with you in this grand fiasco on Earth.

We ask that you accept there are no hard and fast rule for our association for we are on a long and winding road, taking us to those backwaters that need resuscitation that need purification. We peel back the layers one by one, asking you to adjust your vision and to sanction this appraisal of energies, manifesting greater decorum in the process of self-examination. As these final measures are put into place we allow ourselves a pat on the back, knowing that we have completed a mammoth task of great endurance. And with this completion we ask you to stand back and take stock, harking to the child within! It is with these possibilities of a new regime that we will better understand what it is that holds us together, a Love more strong and bountiful that can be expressed in mere words.

We ride with you on those waves of energy, pushing back the boundaries and gaining greater clarity than ever before. We shelter you from the abyss and move on . . . ever onwards, picking our moments to be with you in all sincerity and brightness of vision, asking you not to scold us for this time delay! We match like for like, beaming ahead to further conquests and we shine light on those cloudy issues that have held us at bay, overshadowing the excitement we feel at this new venture. We climb high into those mountains, taking cover, assisting you on this quest of mercy and peace and we find shelter in your arms, relaying our innermost thoughts and fears for a nation divided. We will not be put off or set aside - we will make way for a greater Light and we make this connection count like no other, preparing you for greater service. Do not be alarmed at this delay . . . we are merely attending to details that cannot be left to chance! We therefore have great pleasure in shepherding you and your entourage to a place more suited to your needs.

I don't understand . . . do you mean I've got to leave this house and move to a different one or are you referring to moving to our new world?

We have the desire to shelter you from the storms that inhibit your progress and we admire your tenacity and strength of spirit to get through these times of greatest turmoil. We do not intend to renege on our pact but take you further along this highway, expressing our delight to have you on board once more. We delve deep into a timeline that gives us a finer example and dutiful recovery from past hurts, past regressions that have hampered those most necessary by-products of our love. We deem this a necessary interlude in what should be a vast recovery, setting you back in pastures new.
We do make adjustments and tweak here and there to enable a speedy recovery and we shelter you from the abyss, eternally thankful for the assistance of those who gather round to bring you cheer.
We believe there is ample reward for those who come to serve and you are no exception to this rule, having given us many years of dedicated service! We feel it is fortuitous to now move forward as we

300

propel you into a new future of outstanding bliss with great regard from those souls who gather round and welcome you. We have made an honourable connection with the unseen and we travel on gaining the constant support of those who cheer you on. Take advantage of this proposition that shall see greater reserves of energy to help you in this initiative; we sail now into harbours view to conserve our energy and to restock, giving you further ammunition for the times ahead.

∞

I woke in the night and felt the energy of a North American Indian draw close.

We dare to acknowledge our elders led the way to massacre and we register the sadness in your heart.   It was not the surrendering of our lands that made us weep, but the souls of our brothers and sisters upon that trail of tears . . . we weep still! We sheltered our people as much as we could but alas, all was in vain. There was no succour for our soul, only desperation and solitude. The Great Spirit fell silent and there was a hush across the land that filled our hearts with dread. Our hearts were like stone within our breast. Weary and broken we were led out of our homeland. Here the grass is green and we can sing again in fruitful fashion.

In the morning I sat to resume communication, seeing the face of an Indian with white hair who looks like the late Chief Dan George. He called out what sounded like Kojaw – Koja . . .

May the blessings of the Great Divine be with you and may we forever rest in peace. We come in truth and all honesty to rest your mind from the qualms within your heart. It is not our intent to bring misery to your soul . . . we only wish to bring you the truth, the whole truth!
I can now see a young North American Indian woman with long dark hair who has turned to look at me. Her face is familiar and she reminds me of Kerrie Zoolithe – site creator of 'Sounds of Silence'.

Our people were brave and gave their lives willingly to save our clan . . . our tribe. We helped preserve the peace within the village, bearing our children and preparing the hides.

I can see her scraping skins, probably for the clothing they wore. Have you a name my friend that I can call you by? Her reply sounded like Tozee mahar.

I'm also sensing the name Standing Hawk which is the name of Kerrie's guide and I wonder if I am being shown her in a previous incarnation. There must be a link here somewhere . . . this has thrown me a bit and I'm calling in White Cloud to come and help me understand what's happening.

We work in ways that register within your soul in the quest for truth and justice and we devise ways of transforming your hearts to bring them into alignment. It is the wisdom within your soul that strives ever onwards for perfection and we give voice to those doubts that occur in your mind to be answered. And yes we do come at your bidding to open those streams of thought that will enable us to amalgamate and become 'AS ONE VOICE' . . . loud and clear, echoing across the canyons and out into the wider universe! We have championed you from afar and now draw closer into your orbit.

Be of good cheer! There are many in our clan that are opening up to hear our words and we give voice to your thoughts, opening up a grand connection of minds. Do not be downcast or put out, there is much to learn and much to explore. We come to aid you in your journeys to pour soothing balm onto those wounds that gape wide, begging to be healed. We abscond from our duties to prepare you, to prepare you for this invasion of souls that gather around to assist you in these measures that will open up a new world of infinite grace and charm. We know you all have been waiting so long! We are nearing fruition and we wait to take your hands, leading you into that state of perpetual bliss and Love of greater magnitude. Open your hearts to receive us and we will beam you aboard and answer your questions, each and every one of you. Stand in your own truth!

WHITE CLOUD - is that you, I feel that it is, can you give me confirmation?

Did you not call my child . . . and where the heart is pure we will become as one true voice! When the heart cries out in anguish, we

302

gather round and help that soul in distress, bringing forth the wisdom that you constantly seek. It is there within the very core of your being, helping you to realise your true connection to the Great Divine and all that is. We have stepped over those borders many times in many lifetimes and we work with those who ask for help! We open up those conduits and shine . . . pouring forth LOVE and continuity of spirit, opening up that pathway that will lead you to us in all your true splendour. Au revoir my friend.

My heart is so full it could burst with Love.

∞

Today I'm being shown the face of my father who died many years ago. He usually comes forward when something in the family is about to happen; perhaps it's a celebration! My eldest daughter would like another baby and as I thought this, there was a click in the room. I'm being shown a younger version of dad now without his glasses. Can you tell me if it's going to be a boy or girl, I know my daughter would like a girl this time?

I can feel my Star friends draw close now and there are purple clouds washing over me.

We have made a promise to you and one which we will honour, bringing you into the Light of true understanding. We monitor your progress day by day and shelter you from the harms of the world, opening up a network and programming what will assist you in this ascension process. We know it has taken a mammoth leap of faith for many of your persuasion and we allow a settling to take place, giving you time to assimilate the information being fed into your circuits at this very moment. There is no need to panic, no need to fear what lies ahead, there is only purest Love and bliss available to each and every one of you. We have made allowances for those of you who have fallen by the wayside and we pick you up and dust you off, setting you back on track yet again.

It has given us the greatest pleasure to watch you in this process, to reach out and shelter you when at times you stumble, and we are most blessed to be among you at this miraculous time on Earth. We have obeyed our heart in all things and we betray a sense of detachment from those issues that have surfaced for recognition to be challenged and assessed in their true light. There are many instances of regret and remorse for attitudes that have given cause for concern in your world; we come to allay your fears as you make this momentous journey into a new world of strength and grace. This has been our greatest wish that you would heed our words and listen most carefully to what we have to say.

I can feel their presence more strongly today. I have tears in my eyes as I send out my Love to them.

These are no idle promptings that we bring, we bring you a wealth of knowledge that will help you to adjust to our vibrations and we bring in a time of rejoicing! We are benefactors of the human race and we ask you to tread carefully and lightly upon this planet. Be like a beacon bright spreading your Light!

Oh my friends I wish I could give you a hug, I love hugging that's the greatest thing about being on Earth. I'll send you a mental hug!

We are joining hearts and you will feel perpetual bliss . . . this is our hug to you and we shelter you from the storms that are brewing, bringing our undivided attention. And we make little snips here and there in your landscape, endeavouring to piece together a whole variety of alternatives to our predicament on Earth. We hope you all come to realise that we have your best interests at heart for WE are YOU way into your future, and we would not have you hurt or demoralised! We petition you to accept our words that come from the heart of our very being and we tip toe through your mind, assessing the protocols necessary to deal with the mess we have made of things! How could we have been so blind and yet the expansion of your world was uppermost in our minds. We did not count the cost until much later, far into the future . . . your future, where those losses became ugly facts staring us in the face! It is not a pretty sight and we are ashamed of what has taken place.

The 'good news' is we can do something about it before it's too late for you, in this dimension of time and space! In this corner of your universe we have found you, we come to change the course of history, of your history and our history. And we can make great impact in your world, bringing in this Love . . . bringing illumination to your souls to keep intact that special part of you that we cherish so much. And that Love within your hearts will expand and grow and blossom as we nurture you, like a new-born child who has made its passage into this world through the birth canal of the human mother. What could be more natural and beautiful . . . such a joyous occasion, and we know you have experienced this for yourself . . . the wonder and joy that filled your heart with the miracle of birth. And we connect with you this day to tell you that one more shall come into the fold, and he shall be called Jeremiah . . . the truth bringer and giver of Light and we shall baptise him with fire!

Thank you friends . . . what wonderful news! I feel overwhelmed and really tearful here. The meaning of the name Jeremiah is 'God will uplift' - 'Appointed by God from the womb'. A year later my daughter gave birth to my third grandson!

∞

During meditation today, I'm being shown an eye and now a man wearing a dark tunic and fez who looks to be of Hebrew origin.

We come before the one true God to pay homage; this is our testimony and we unfold the mysteries that have surrounded you for the last 2000 years . . . we shed light!

I can see him pulling back fine layers of muslin from a huge book.

We pull back the layers for you to see and we beg you to look with fresh eyes at those issues closest to you at this present moment. We examine in greater detail what is necessary for you to move forward. We abandon the clutches, the embodiment of all we hold most dear and we propel you into a time frame that will help you to realise our predicament.

I'm now seeing a bearded man dressed in a long white tunic, wearing a white Arabian head piece.

We come to prepare you for greater sacrifice and that is our predicament! We do not want to disturb what has been a great quest for peace among your nations, but we delve into the deepest recesses of your mind and uncover what has not been seen for many a year, insufferable injustice on a grand scale that has come forth at our bidding to be looked at with a fine toothed comb. And we move into place a grand finale of thoughts and expressions, giving deliverance from outworn modes of acceptance, transcending our wildest expectations!

I'm seeing gorgeous golden patterns on purple and what look like biblical characters.

We have known for some time of this fiasco on Earth and it gives us no pleasure to upset the apple cart once more! We have known for a very great length of time the suffering on Earth and we bring you shelter, we bring you a way to sort out your differences, allowing those in charge to take a back seat so that we may come forward to assist you and we do believe we shall make progress. Do be prepared to take this on board!

Can we resume this transmission later on as I don't think this connection is clear enough?

Go now my child we are always here for you.

∞

Chapter thirteen

We are the Federation of Light

We settle down and adjust our frequencies restoring peace and order.

Today I'm seeing the face of White Cloud and he is wearing a blue feather hanging down on the right hand side of his head.

We believe in peace and supremacy within the heart and enable this transmission to proceed. All is well . . . all is as it should be. *Thank you my friend.*

We beam you aboard this Lightship of enterprise, freewill and Love Divine.

Thank you friends, thank you White Cloud, I can see that it is you now . . . I can see the likeness to Chief Dan George so thank you for helping me to establish who you are. It is wonderful to be able to recognise those who come forward even if they don't actually give their name. I can now see the weathered and handsome face of White Cloud more clearly and he is wearing his full headdress.

We meet at last face to face and we thank you for your purposeful endeavours, always marching forwards even in times of self-doubt, and that is what we wished to bring out in you that strength of purpose, thus enabling us to proceed more carefully and thoughtfully along this highway of Love. And these transmissions shall continue and we shall forego that natural reserve within your soul that hangs back, and we shall push you forward into the limelight and all will be well. There is no need to fear or doubt the promptings of your heart because we come in all magnificence to bring you hope, to bring you Love and Joy. This is the criteria with which we bring forth our messages for peace and enlightenment among your nations and we give thanks for people like you who come forward to offer their services!

307

Be now of good resolve and we shall move forward on that stream of light. We measure our success in those who come to listen to our words; we give greater clarity and perspective on all that will come to fruition, and in the not too distant future may we add. The promptings of your soul have driven you thus far and we shelter you in the warmth of our embrace, giving you the fortitude to strive ever onwards for completion of our mission. We know you have all suffered great ignominy in your lives on the Earth plane and we know these instances of betrayal have strengthened you; they have not held you back for you have learned and listened to those words echoing within your mind. This has been a time of even greater fortitude for all of us and we bow down to your requests, enlightening you as to proceedings in the forthcoming days ahead. This has been an honourable progression.

I am overcome with emotion and still can't believe that White Cloud is sitting cross legged in front of me, wearing his bonnet of feathers. I'm reaching forward and he is holding my hands in his, giving them a squeeze of reassurance...

We lead you ever onwards to those pastures green . . . to that stairway to the stars that has given us all the greatest hope of deliverance from those burdens that we have carried for so long. This will be our reward   . . . to see you smiling with your hearts, to see you smiling and resting in the truth of all that is. Truth and honesty of spirit, shining forth like the brightest beacon . . . s*igh*. There is nothing like it, nothing can compare with that Love and that purest Light.

White Cloud . . . have you always been with me, you seem very similar to the figure I call Grandfather? I feel as if I've come home to see you. Was it you all along, was it you who gave me the silver ring that represented our Love so long ago? There are tears in my eyes as I speak and I can feel White Cloud's beaming face.

The truth has dawned at last my little one, and yes we have been with you since the beginning of time! We have been with all of you, all those that tread this pathway.

This is why I feel so close to Blossom Goodchild and Kerrie because we share that

308

connection with you White Cloud. Were we sisters from long ago and family?

You are Family of Light and that is all that matters. We Love you all and all have a place in our heart! From the lowliest amongst you to those who have striven and reached that golden bridge of Light, we will not give up on any of you!

I'm feeling White Cloud holding his hands out now in a big circle, bringing them up open palmed and then round again as if he is holding us all in the palm of his hands, and there is a golden Light, a golden orb of light in his hands and we are all there resting within that protection.

You do justice to what is given with the greatest respect and harmony and we enfold you all in our loving care, asking you to remember that we are always with you! We watch over you and protect you from the knocks and blows of your earthly endeavours. We remember you in our prayers, little earthlings, we remember you. We sing out at dawn and dusk and when the sun goes down we watch over you. We enter your dreams, we enter your heart and we enter those whisperings within your soul, asking you not to lose faith. We are there to give you the assistance that you require, helping you move forward on that stream of Light that shall bring you home once more. And we will be there to welcome you, cheering you on to make that final crossing that will bring you back into our arms. And as we step over that threshold and into the Light you will be more than compensated for those travels that have weighed you down in the past. We come to lift you up and to become one with us, your guides and inspirers on the Earth plane and we will have reached that pinnacle of greatest success that has been dreamed of for so long.

I'm asking if the words are correct or if anything needs editing!

All is well, all is as it should be and with the greatest respect from those here . . . the overseers of the overseers!

White Cloud is now taking hold of my hand and kissing the back of it. Oh thank you my friend, I'm so happy, I Love you so much!

309

Pick up those pieces and put them back together again. We shall help you to put the jigsaw pieces together. There will be a coming together of twin souls.

∞

11.11.13 – *I'm sending the golden light down through my body and into the centre of Gaia. Earth has now changed into what looks like a clear glass orb and I can see golden cracks of light spreading like lightening all around the globe. It now looks like a beautiful decoration on a Christmas tree.*

We bring you Peace and Blessings and deliverance from all that has held you back in the past. We make our deliberations known to all those who gather round to hear our words and we bring you comfort and upliftment of the highest magnitude. We bring you Love . . . we bring you Joy beyond all earthly measure and the Angels shall come and sing, heralding in a new declaration of Peace amongst all mankind.

We know this is hard for some of you to believe and yet it will be so . . . there will be a mammoth upliftment of souls. We understand the connections are growing stronger on the Earth plane and we deliberately ask you not to lose faith at this time of greater clarity, dawning in the hearts and minds of mankind. We temper our gifts with words of Love and bring you around to face us head on for we come in all sincerity, opening g up those vistas that beckon you forward with greater ease and movement. This will come into play very soon and we nurture you with the greatest respect, asking you to challenge those thought streams that invade your mind, opening up innumerable possibilities.

We challenge you to accept this post we offer you, enlightening mankind as to what we are about with unequivocal devotion, counterbalancing what is necessary to set your mind at rest, allowing us to move freely among you. We come in hoards . . . we come in tens of millions, spreading the word and rejuvenating your souls to accept us as 'Peace Keepers' extraordinaire, for we are no military force come to assault your kind! We are not judgemental or overpowering in our persuasion, we come to enlighten you, to set down no hard and fast rules but to show you with the kindness of our hearts . . . to show you that LOVE is the only way forward! The alternative is to sink into those murky depths that threaten to engulf your soul and we do not wish that for you in any way shape or form; we wish to lift you out of the mire and into the 'shining light' where all can be seen and recognised for its true worth.

We have propelled you thus far on your journeys and know, without a shadow of doubt, that you have become to all intent and purposes our brothers and sisters. The network grows far and wide, encompassing the globe with great magnitude and we shine a light into those nooks and crannies, into the darkness, deeper than you can ever imagine! All will be offered a place in our new world, all will be offered the peace of mind that comes with upliftment; there is no need to hide for we bring you much more than earthly treasures, we bring peace and contentment within the soul of your very being. The worries that weigh down your heart shall dissolve and be no more, the way is clear for you to tread with open hearts and minds, free of encumbrances to walk that golden path into the sunset and realisation of a new world. And we will be there to welcome you, to show you around, to show you the ropes so to speak and there will be a time of settling in, of adjusting to these new frequencies. Some may take a little longer than others to adjust and that is alright; we ease you gently into your new life. There will be great excitement and joy among you and as a little child reaches out to explore its surroundings to become aware of the world about it, so you too will experience the joys of a child, exclaiming at the brightness of colours and clearness of vision, and all will unfold before you as you are ready to take little steps further forward. Joy of Joys await you and we will bring an entourage of Angels to guide you, re-establishing you in a new domain of beauty and grace.

These words are brought to you from the Great Divine, from the Majesty of our Lord in Heaven, the Creator of all you survey, and we bring you this with the greatest reverence. We champion the cause of mankind, opening up a network of proceedings that will allow us to draw closer to you. And in these final attempts to succour you and bring you closer into our jurisdiction, we offer you our hand in

311

friendship, showering you with our Love and Blessings. Take heed on the Earth plane and all will be well, we take you under our wing so that we may hold you in the greatest Love and affection to do our duty as foretold many Light years ago.

Remember, you are entrusted with this knowledge to share with your contemporaries and to spread out into the furthest reaches of your world. These seeds of thought will grow in the minds of those who step forward to be counted, to spread the news that Love will conquer. Love is Supreme in its connection to the Great Divine . . . to the Great Oneness and wholeness of creation. The force of Love is stronger and more powerful than you can ever imagine . . . it comes from the source of all that is encircling you. And you cannot help yourselves . . . you will be drawn back to this greatest source of Love and inspiration, like a moth to the candle flame, and yet your wings will not be burnt . . . there is only renewal and life ever after!

WE ARE THE FEDERATION OF LIGHT and the manifestation of all we hold most dear!

∞

I'm visualising the golden light shining down into a network of dark tunnels and am being shown a cross section of a bee hive where the light is pouring into the different compartments but there are so many more levels to penetrate before it reaches the deepest darkest areas.

We reach out and touch that deepest part of you; we open up a network of passages for you to explore, delving deeper and deeper into those recesses of your mind. We inform you of measures that need to be looked at and scrutinised to bring forward the best solution, and we have up our sleeve a few more tricks to share with you that will allow further discussions. We shed light on issues that have arisen for you to deal with and it has taken mammoth persuasion on our part to bring you up to date with what we have in store for you and yours. These passages contain information that has been stored and hidden away and we have delayed a reprogramming so that we may make further progress, relaying information necessary for the reinstatement of values held sacrosanct since the beginning of

312

time. We are overcome by a portfolio that brings us great joy and excitement, taking delivery of an immense project, one that we shall take on board with great expertise and we allow a nullification of all pacts and deals erroneous to our cause. Do not be put off or brushed aside - we will prevail and we are governed by a finer force, opening up a network of warriors that bring you strength and deliverance from all that has held you back in the past.

We now toe the line, drawing in those reserves of energy that will help us in this blockbuster of enormous proportions and we ask you to stand as we resurrect a nation in distress. We do believe we have come a long way in resurrecting the human race and we propel you thus far, opening up a network of improprieties that shall come to the fore to be cleansed and healed. And we make no allowances, this has to be seen to be done in all entirety, bringing to the fore those measures needed to cleanse an entire population. We bring an advocate to stand at our side and do our bidding, and we ask you to connect to us as we align ourselves with a greater cause for freedom.

Be on your guard in the next few weeks or so for we need to be ever vigilant, take heart and know that we are with you from dawn to dusk and in the early evening we shall prepare an essay of outstanding proportions, claiming for ourselves a little piece of the action and asking you not to lose faith. We are there to propel you forward when times get tough and to find a place within your heart to bring you solace.

I am being shown a host of shining lights that could be space ships bouncing down into the sea and flying back up again.

∞

Philippine tragedy 2013

At the beginning of meditation today I asked for healing for those affected by one of the strongest typhoons ever to hit the central Philippines. I can see White Cloud bare headed in all humility and with a quiet strength.

Dearly beloved we venture into the realms of fantasy; we delve into

313

the imagination centre in your brain and conjure forth a whole host of pictures, scenarios that will enable you greater scope with your imaginings, for this centre will be very important in the days and weeks ahead. We will need you to use this 'muscle' in your brain to strengthen yourselves and to open up a world of excitement, a world of values that bring us closer together. And we are right of course in assuming that you will play along with us, allowing your thoughts to meander through the highways and byways, through the network of passages within your mind and to join with us in thanksgiving that we have come together at last as one true voice! And this was prophesied long ago, now brought to fruition, and we shall set great store in all that is about to unfold before your very eyes!

Do you mean the eyes of my mind or my physical eyes?

We mean your physical eyes child, and yet we also speak of the manifestations in your mind that can be seen with the inner eye, and we give thanks that you have achieved this clarity and clearness of vision for us to be able to come and join you and speak with you. It gives us great joy to do this and to share with you and the many others who come forward to speak for us! This will enable us to move forward with greater ease and we expect a bonding with many of you on the Earth plane who assist us in our quest for peace and deliverance from a 'fait accompli' if the Children of Earth continue on this pathway of death and destruction.

We know it means a great deal to you to be used in this way as a channel for the Great Spirit, for the Federation of Light and the Great Galactic Union of souls, who gather round to assist Earth at this time of immense courage and fortitude. We will help you, we will honour our obligations to you, and you will not be robbed of your birth right of life eternal! We will be there to guide you, step by step, along this causeway of Light and Love and we resurrect the human race, bringing you closer to that point of Divine Love and purity of spirit.

I'm seeing such beautiful clouds of pulsating purple at this point.

314

We reach out and touch you all and beckon you to join us. Use your minds to make this connection, strengthen your resolve to join us! Let the trappings of Earth fall away as you sit in the peace within your homes, within your little sanctuaries, within the spaces you reserve for our meetings, here you will find Peace and a greater connection to the Great Divine. You only have to travel inwards within that doorway in your heart. Turn the key and come on in, come on in and feel the Love! Let your pain dissolve within our caress for we come to soothe you and to give you the strength to continue your journeys upon the Earth plane. And we will succeed, we will prevail, and these times of inner peace will give you that strength and that resolve to walk with us by your side until such times you can fly, like the fledgling that leaves the nest.

Do not be put off by what you hear in the news! We have gathered those souls to us, those souls who gave their lives to raise your awareness . . . they are here now with us! And those left behind shall feel the intensity of your Love, helping them to pick up the pieces and begin again; for that is the strength of the human spirit and we give thanks to all those of you who have reached out, sending your Love in great waves of energy across the globe to those places of deep distress! And we know it is very hard for you to see the carnage brought about by the forces of nature; can you not then see 'our' distress brought about by mankind's actions that have nothing to do with nature but with the lust and greed for power!

I'm being shown a beautiful purple cloud that is sweeping around the globe, sending out Love and healing for those in the Philippines. Thank you for your Love White Cloud. I send my Love to those in the spirit realms and all those in the Federation of Light and Galactic Union who work to help mankind. Again I am seeing the most beautiful golden patterns overlaying the purple and sat for a while bathing in these energies.

Good journey my child. Go in Peace.

I have been away visiting family for a few days and was glad to get back home to my own bed last night. At 3.03 a.m. this morning I was woken by my spirit family and left my bed to transcribe.

With the greatest expertise we follow procedures and allow ourselves to fall into line, accessing further information. We are born to LOVE of that we have no doubt and we surrender to a worthwhile cause, subjecting you to frequencies that can be registered in your mind; this gives us important updates, motivating you to secure and register our approvals. We ask you to constantly access this phenomenon and to lay down your arms and move forward on this ray of Light.

We illicit further information for your perusal and channel a backlog of material that has eluded us so far. We appreciate there has been a vast summary of cause and effect but we marshall a recovery that will take us to the Stars and beyond! This has been a mammoth undertaking and we are not quite sure you understand the necessity for attention to detail. We have asked ourselves a million times how we happened past your galaxy but the improvements we have made to your circuits do not allow us to manufacture this information. We take it as read that you were gullible enough to follow our lead and take up the gauntlet – the rest is history!

We allow a backtracking and take advantage of a mind-numbing event in your history to move forward with our reconnaissance, allowing a modicum of sanity to prevail. We understand there has been a mammoth recovery from all that has held you back and we are delighted with how it all pans out.   Don't be surprised at the measures we have taken to support you through these troubled times - we give nothing but the best for those who come to serve! Be aware that all is being done to take you into custody and we reconnect to avail ourselves of forthcoming news as it comes in from the ethers. Be prepared for a massive challenge ahead and we shall be there at your side, giving assistance and helping you with all our best intentions for the future of mankind. Stand firm and all will be revealed in due course!

We are well on our way to delivering the greatest story ever told and we equalise this connection, giving you even greater clout to forge ahead. This has been a most fortuitous time in your history on Earth and we propel you forward to receive further updates of enormous proportions, governing a wide uptake in services rendered for the cause. We expel some much maligned truths from the archives and sample some just desserts, trembling with ecstasy at the delights in store. Remember, we are from a different time warp and we can adjust settings as and when called for! There is no need to stand down for we have all the time in the world to deliver our speeches in a way that will allow us constructive discourse. We do however, interject from time to time with further snippets of information to rally the cause, and we find this has its uses in 'run of the mill' exercises that cannot be left to chance. We associate ourselves with an outstanding performance and greater attention to detail, ruling out any propaganda that hasn't been looked at with a fine toothed comb. We salute you and ask you to further develop your talents as we raise you from the dead!

∞

During my morning meditation I was shown the face of White Cloud from a distance as if he was overseeing the connection. The top left side of my head has been sore for the last few days and I asked why.

We are channelling energies, opening up a network of passages within the brain that allows information to flood through; these passages have remained dormant for years and need opening and restoring. We continually update, rectifying anomalies that have taken precedence and we examine and sift through the debris, preparing for further transmissions to take place. Do not be alarmed this is a normal practice that will allow for greater access; we are transparent in the eyes of God, we do not need to protect ourselves from his gaze! God is all knowing . . . all seeing, He knows your heart!

Why do you say He – is God a He?

God is everything . . . God is everywhere . . . God is in all of us! It is just a matter of protocol that we use the term 'He'. We could just as easily say 'She' but then misinterpretations would be made. The Great One is God . . . the Creator . . . the Source of all that is!

We hearken to your mind and hear the whisperings within your soul searching, the mind numbing hustle and bustle of questioning deep

317

within the core of your being. We are mortified at your associations with those who would cause you hurt and great ridicule, but we know too that these associations help to strengthen you, bringing about renewal and a greater conception of truth. We are preparing you all to access a time frame that has little or nothing to do with how you feel right now here on Earth. There are no constraints put upon you in our new world, there is only Love and the nurturing of Love that helps you to realise the truth of who you really are. You are Love sublime and you will come to realise that this is the most important element of your make up. From Love you were born and to Love you will return!

I'm seeing beautiful golden patterns on deep purple. There's nothing more wonderful than this . . . no drug, no drink, nothing but pure unadulterated Love!

Carry this in your heart at all times and it will shine out from you and others will see the difference in your persona, they will bathe in that Love and be warmed by it, compelled to draw closer and to see for themselves that they too may radiate such joy and magnificence. It is not a commodity that you can buy, it is the very essence of your being and this peaceful demeanour shall spread far and wide, enveloping and soothing those who are ruffled with worry and despair at their predicament on Earth.   They too shall share our realm of peace and tranquillity; they have only to reach out and access that place within them . . . that place of serenity, which is within you all and which you can access if you choose. And peace shall reign within your souls, knowing that you are loved and cared for beyond all earthly imaginings. Journey to the inner realms and join us, for we are here waiting to take you aboard, to prepare you for a greater journey. And we will be there to assist you all in this transition from futility, darkness and despair to hope and brightness of vision as you begin a new adventure. We will take care of you as promised!

May I ask who is giving me these words please; is this White Cloud?

My child we assist you in your journeys, giving expression to our Love and heart felt thoughts. We access vital information that is part of this franchise we are offering you for the human race. We have guarded and guided you for many years and it gives us great pleasure to be here by your side to help you adjust. Do not be alarmed at what is taking place! This has been a long and arduous journey with many stumbling blocks to bar your way and yet you have overcome with our help and assistance. We protect you and keep you safe at all times! We diligently adjust the frequencies necessary for this connection and this has surprised us . . . that we are able to connect so splendidly!

I'm seeing tall, thin golden figures and I want to reach out and touch them; the tape is blank for 5 minutes so maybe I did have closer contact.

We seek . . . we find the connection closest to our frequencies and we connect with grace and a lovingness that is uppermost in our minds. We draw you closer in our embrace, enabling you to come aboard and be with us in our domain. It goes without saying that we have adjusted our frequencies to coincide with yours, allowing this conversation, and we shed light on various issues that are open to negotiations with those on your planet Earth. We have allowed ourselves to become entangled in your thought streams and we push back the boundaries that have kept us apart so far. This will give us greater clarity in our connection and we tremulously adjust where necessary, opening up the conduits that allow us to pass through, giving information and receiving from you. We are eternally grateful for being able to do this and we enable the Love to flow between us.

I'm seeing such a beautiful kaleidoscope of golden patterns on purple.

We are those creatures who come to support you, to give you impetus to travel forth among the dominions on Earth that have called out to us for help and assistance, and we come in our droves to evacuate the globe, bringing you succour and hope for a brighter future. We know these issues have misled you at times and we understand it is of some great consequence to leave this planet you call home. We have adjusted your frequencies to allow you to roam further afield, to find yourself in a new dimension in a variation of home. To all intents and purposes it is a recreation of Earth in a new

319

domain, and we give thanks for this anomaly to be able to settle you down in a new world of hope and perfectness. This world is similar in every way to what you call home, and yet this world has a vibrancy that you have yet to discover and you will exclaim in wonderment with joy personified!

I can see and feel the excitement as people are hugging themselves.

You will see there was nothing to be afraid of, we have only your best interests at heart and we settle you down like a new born babe in its cradle, most cherished and loved and you will grow and explore your perimeters and wonder with ecstasy at your surroundings. We have brought you back full circle to this Garden of Eden, unblemished by human hands, and you shall be restored to walk upright in your Love for the human race, for yourselves, and your families will thrive.

We bathe in the Love of the Great Divine and welcome you to join us here in peace and dedication to the fruitfulness of this mission. And we thank you for your assistance in this wonderful creation driven by your thoughts of Love. We recommend you sojourning to recover your senses and bring fruitfulness to this experience. We are most grateful for your services!

I Love you, I Love you, I Love you! I'm seeing vivid purple and gold, it's so beautiful that I can't help but cry. At the end here I'm seeing what looks like a golden skull and skeleton superimposed on a purple background.

∞

November 2013 - *This morning I called on White Cloud to join me and asked him to shed some light on what is happening to me as I feel there are some who may question what I have been receiving. I felt his presence very strongly, his face blending with mine as the lower half of my face enlarged with my lips protruding.*

We are able to bring you joy and sustenance!

Thank you White Cloud, thank you for making me feel safe.

We have expressed ourselves with great joy at this interlude of working alongside you and it gives us great pleasure to broach the subject of associations with other off-world beings, who come to manifest before you. We are able to shelter you from harm and this is our overriding responsibility to help you and assist you in these proceedings. You have been chosen from a long line of advocates to help us with this cause and without a shadow of doubt we are overwhelmed to receive you into this circle of Light. We have always known this was the pathway we would walk and though it has not been an easy task, it has been most rewarding. We shelter you in our embrace and ask you not to be afraid of what is coming your way . . . we are here to back you up and to give you sustenance for the times ahead. We rely on you to forge ahead, initiating those meetings that bring recovery on a large scale. We are most indebted to your services and we bring you full circle to meet us head on; we receive an inordinate amount of information to be passed on when the time is right and we regard this information to be of great consequence. We batten down the hatches, making further discoveries about ourselves and we tread lightly upon the Earth plane.

I was bathed in vivid purple and gold and then drifted off to sleep. I sat again the following day feeling the quietness and peace entering my soul with no interruptions. It is 12.30 in the afternoon and I have invited White Cloud to assist in the proceedings if he is able. I cannot see his face but feel the energies changing, becoming stronger until I sense a figure sitting within me strong and erect, and wearing a headdress.

I welcome you . . . I open my heart to receive you!

We receive you also, our beloved offspring. We gently nurture you and bring you to fruition.

I can also see a Roman Centurion who I know is one of my guards.

We have long awaited this phase in your destiny and we bring you glad tidings of great joy! This is no understatement, this is the be all and end all, discovering the most joyous association between our worlds as we bring this to a head and unite our nations as one.

WE COME IN PEACE . . . WE COME IN LOVE and we bring you greater certainty of that Love! It has been a long time coming, we know this, and it goes without saying that we have offered you sanctuary on many occasions in the past.

I am now being shown the face of an actor from a Spanish drama I've been watching called - Isobel. He is playing the part of Alfonso Carrillo de Acuña, a Roman Catholic Archbishop who could not be trusted. Why are you showing me this?

There have been many of subterfuge who gathered around you, protesting their loyalty, but we rise above those ranks.

Do you mean the church or are you talking generally?

The church has much to answer for and yes, we do make these comparisons so that you may adjust your vision. It has been a long journey through the ages, a most arduous journey, and we beckon you not to lose faith in mankind for we have not! We Love you and cherish you and lead you back to the fold, honouring your decisions to stay on board until we have final lift off. We will champion the cause for mankind and we will bring you to that designated point that will help you adjust your frequencies, allowing you to become once more, those golden creatures of Light that we were so proud of! It was our undoing that we disconnected you from that main frame and we weep . . . for what was done could not be undone – until now! And we weep with joy that we have found you once more, we are overjoyed that we have this opportunity to put right a wrong from long, long ago in another time, another universe. We replicate that time frame and bring you back to point zero, asking you to stay on track and acknowledge that we are doing the very best we can, helping you establish yourselves in a new world where you may grow and flourish.

There is no rhyme or reason to our request other than that 'WE LOVE YOU' and we are sorry for the hurt we have caused that we had not envisaged on such a grand scale. These atrocities have awoken in us great remorse and it is understood the propaganda which was issued from our very own lips portrayed a sense of masochism. The wars that ensued caused rebellion on the outer skirts of the universe, creating mammoth repercussions that we were unable to curtail. The anger that ensued justified a knock on effect that had us reeling in all directions! We do not want a repeat performance of this scenario in this time frame, and believe us when we say that you will not want to look back through our eyes and see the carnage that we have been witness to!

It makes sense to back track and find you, to begin again in a different time frame, to set the matter to rights . . . to put you back on the pedestal and re-examine your framework, to put back that key taken from you . . . that key element that is missing! Time constraints forbid us to step out of line and we redress issues that otherwise would have tumbled into the abyss. We have regained our connection and ask you to take greater attention to detail, for these matters are of great importance in this recording of events that took place in your distant past. We are undeniably held back by your lack of expertise in these matters of grave importance and we come forward now to assist you, to enable you to see through our eyes. There is a settling that has to occur for us to remain on board for any great length of time and we adjust those circuits necessary for these meetings, enabling greater aptitude and a certain clemency in proceedings.

Do not be offended or put off by our words . . . we only wish to reinstate you and we come in all honesty, wearing our heart on our sleeve, begging you to look with fresh eyes at this situation we are facing you with! It is not a pretty sight, we know this, and we do not wish to frighten you so that you scuttle away back into the shadows. We wish to shine a light on those issues that have been discussed among your population, and it is hard to ease these facts from you . . . . to tweeze out those uncomfortable pieces of information that do not settle easily within your breast.

It is hard to register and know that you are capable of these atrocities - but once this has been accepted we can then move forward, and the plan that we have set in motion can come to fruition with your help! We do not want to dish the dirt, but you have responsibility for the

323

lives of your comrades and families on Earth, to treat them with the greatest respect, and to allow us to move forward on that beam of Light that will give us all sanctuary in a new world of greatest Love and Joy.

This is our mission, an extraordinary mission that has never yet been attempted in this time frame. We jumpstart a whole nation to begin again . . . we welcome in a new phase and one we give thanks for. This bargaining process has at times left us depleted and we register your concerns for those on Earth, however, we do need you to accept that this has been the most finest and constructive discourse and channellings such as these, from many of your 'sages' on Earth, shall help to save a nation in deep distress. For the more voices that join ours to spread the word, the clearer the message will become that we are not here to destroy . . . we are not here to steal your world from you . . . we are here to give you back what is yours by right, a new beginning in a new state of existence in a world that you know and Love and feel comfortable with.

This is our manifesto of great import and we ask you to share this with your contemporaries, so that they will see for themselves that we come in all Love and grace to uplift you, to keep you safe and out of harm's way. Be true to yourselves, be true to that guiding spirit within your breast . . . that guiding Light. All is well and the Great Spirit watches over you all and holds you in his hand with the greatest respect and the greatest Love. May the Great Spirit be with you now and forever more . . . our most cherished and loved Children of Light.

I am wrapped in the most beautiful purple and golden light. Thank you my friends.

∞

We have established a rule of thumb and this in itself is indicative of relations of immense value. We have ironed out certain discrepancies and alleviate any stresses and strains on vocabulary that has come into play. We vouch for your integrity, marching forward to play our hand. Please believe that we do this with the greatest and honourable intentions, displaying our keenness to forge ahead. We monopolise your thoughts, surrendering to your charm and grace and we are overwhelmed with your fortitude and attention to detail, ruling out any indiscretions that point out heartache for all concerned. We chastise you for putting up with our remarks instead of carrying forward to question our motives. We settle down and adjust, admonishing each other as we hug wholeheartedly.

I can feel energy all around my crown region as if I am wearing something on my head.

We do most heartedly address you and wish you a speedy recovery from your condition; perfunctory chills shall become a thing of the past as you align with us and spread your wings and fly. We do have one question we would like to ask you - do you have a vivid imagination - if so we are home and dry! This will help more than you realise and we read you chapter and verse on the realities that lay between you and your mind. A massive expansion of remedies assists us in our waking moments and while we sleep we journey back and forth, settling into our new domain. We are putting the final touches to this new realm and we bequeath you many treasures in your new home. We set the scene inviting you to join us in due course . . . just tap into that magic!

∞

A few nights ago I woke and looked through my closed eyelids to see what looked like two golden wedding rings sailing past my view; one was bigger than the other. There was a large sandy striped snake on the ground and in the background I could see figures walking past in a mist. This scene had an Egyptian feel to it and in the back of my mind I could see Tutankhamen's funeral mask.

We still the mind and move forward along that stream of Light that is beckoning us on and we shall live by the word of God.

I can feel energy rippling around my crown. Soft violet clouds are caressing me and I'm travelling down a tunnel of purple light.

There's a metamorphosis taking place, a translation of energies

325

superimposed within your skull, taking root. We allow a synergy, an opening up and regrouping of duel infrastructures that enable us to work side by side. This programming will initiate further contact on deeper levels and we ask you not to challenge us at this time!

I'm feeling so incredibly relaxed and can feel energy like a laser to the left of my heart, knowing they are working on me.

Time space continuum . . . we are ready now to adjust your monitor and do not be surprised at what you see! We interpret your wishes and bring you further constructive discourse, opening up a network of emotions, hiding behind the drudgery of your day to day dealings. This will bring us back full circle to face ourselves head on, to undo the hurt of the past and to send us into a new time frame where we are able to access further information. This will be governed by that dual aspect of yourselves that comes into play and once you have mastered this phenomenon of creating through thought . . . through imagination, then we will build a new empire of strength and grace. And yes we do feel excited by this project, we feel excited and rejuvenated by an expansive over flow of ideas that come into being, surplus to requirements.

I can feel a tickle on my left cheek and can vaguely see the smooth headed man I've seen before, the apothecary/priest who lives in a cave in Sun.

Yes we have made progress, we have made some impact! There is a little way to go yet and we challenge you to accept indescribable volumes of intensity and purpose, resurrecting hope on a grand scale across the world. We open up a huge network of probabilities that can be accessed and toned with a greater sense of self preservation. Remain in a state of expectancy and you will be shown greater visions. Uncertainty shall become a thing of the past as we gather together. Constancy . . . reliability . . . gentility . . . all these things we need to make this work!

December 2013 - *Last night as I lay down to sleep I felt a very powerful energy with me that I have never felt before and knew somehow that it was Archangel Gabriel, who is known as the Angel of Revelation because God often chooses him to deliver important messages to people.*

I am One with the Lord thy God. Be of good cheer — you have overcome many trials and we have seen your worth! We bring you food for thought.

Is there something I can help you with?

The zest for life! You must be brave and carry out your mission until the final letter, until the final bell tolls . . . as toll it will for the people of Earth. We bring sweet justice and salvation, given to each individual on the Earth plane. It is up to you to make that choice between life and death!

For the last few days I have been in a lot of pain and have felt very vulnerable and tearful. This morning I sat in meditation and visualised the golden sun flooding through my crown chakra and into my body like fire, but this is not fire that destroys — this is fire that cleanses and purifies and gives birth, like the phoenix rising from the ashes. I sent this spiritual fire down into Earth and could see the golden energy burning off the old, letting it fall away to make way for the new. I can now see the new vibrant human in the form of Atlas holding our new world on his shoulders.

I felt a strong and powerful energy linking with me.

We raise new life and energy into a situation around you at this time. We have indeed hearkened to the call and we are most impressed with your endeavours, reaching out across the great divide, bringing strength and a multitude of probabilities, possibilities that awaken in your mind. We accept this has been a time of great resolution and we are full of ideas; an expansion on the horizon awakens our interest and we bring further revelations that will enable you to move forward with greater ease. We dedicate this time period to the Children of Earth and let them come forth. In all honesty this has been our greatest expedition yet and we join hands, asking you to bear with us as we reach out across the great divide in all openness and freedom of speech.

327

We gently prise you from your homes and ask you to build, with the power of thought, new homes in a new dimension. We ask you to accept the new revelations that come flooding in from across the universe, bringing greater dedication, and we superimpose ourselves in your society spreading the news that Love will conquer all. Love will conquer over all discrimination, enabling us to proceed full steam ahead on to further conquests, and we relish the thought of becoming once more your brothers and sisters arm in arm.

We have waited so long for this accomplishment, we have waited many centuries to discover we are in fact a part of yourselves' and we truly believe we shall be able to make these mammoth adjustments to your energy circuits, enabling us to bond together as one race of indescribable beauty. We are those that come to mourn the end of your world and we believe, with a little help from our friends, we shall be able to sanction further studies of the human race that will allow us to recover initial feedback and assumptions that have brought us back from the grave.

This has an Egyptian feel to it.

We are full of remorse for what has occurred and we transfer our thoughts into more useful properties that shall have massive repercussions for future generations; these we bring to honour you and to reject what is of no importance in the recovery of the human race. We allow ourselves a second look at what has gone before and we manage to backtrack to that point of discovery that has held us in abeyance.

We register your appeals for clemency and note that it has taken many a long year to reach this point in your history, for which we are most thankful. We honour the proceedings that we find ourselves in and ask that you materialise for us a greater connection that we may remain forever friends. A duplicate summary of cause and affect has ground to a halt, until we are ready to take on further constituents who have held us back from proceeding in an orderly fashion towards our destiny. And we ask you to be absolutely aware of what it is you are doing so that we may assess the situation you find yourselves in! We have taken great delight in assisting you in these proceedings and we ask you to be aware of further channellings that will take place quite soon.

We have governed proceedings from afar but now we draw closer, helping you to discover for yourselves who you are and where you have come from. This will make a mammoth difference to your energy circuits and we prise you away from that which you hold most dear, enabling you to re-establish yourselves into a perfectly attuned synergy of energies, projected to help you. We watch over you and keep you safe at all times and we make this proviso to enable you to follow us into that golden sunset.

We need you to ask yourselves with the greatest honesty and intent – do you wish to see yourselves in a new dimension in a new world? If the answer is 'Yes' we will help you to distinguish between reality and the grand fiasco on Earth that has brought you looking for alternatives!

We reconnect you to a greater wisdom and ask you to bear witness to what has been our greatest travesty; we shine a light on those cloudy issues that wait acknowledgement. Do not be downhearted for we bring you hope and joy and we partake of that Love that will bring us closer to the heart of God. Do not underestimate what has been our finest mission yet!

Thank you. Can I ask who you are and who you represent?

We are from a conglomerate of Peace Keepers that assist the travelling from one world to another. We bear witness to the evolution of different species and we make great strides across the universe, bringing further information and guidance on issues that have reached stalemate. Please allow us to come forward and make our statements to the human race; we will shatter no illusions that haven't already been questioned and looked at in closer scrutiny. We vouch for the interest of those parties that draw close to assist us, and we know it makes sense to look further into those reserves of energy that allow us movement; this has been our greatest journey yet

329

and we ask you to draw comparisons so that you may make your own conclusions. We have come a long way to be here with you now and we come in all honesty. It gives us great joy to amalgamate with our friends on Earth, to see through your eyes what we have always known, that this world is indeed in need of assistance! And we hope you will allow us to draw so much closer, initiating greater rewards for those that strike the fear from their hearts and accept that we come in Love.

∞

4.12.13 - 4+1+2+1+3 = 11 - *a master number denoting a message from the higher realms.*

Today as I prepared to meditate I was immediately shown the face of White Cloud. Today he is wearing a pale blue tunic edged with gold, which I later attempted to recreate in an oil painting. (I have used this portrait for the cover of this book).

Our messages bear fruit for we shall indeed all become part of this new world. We register your thoughts, your day dreams, and assist you in making a grand recovery; this will be such a momentous occasion and we welcome all of you into this land of dreams, manifesting a greater reality.

There are tears in my eyes as I see White Clouds face . . . I want to reach out and touch . . . to stroke his hair. Grandfather - White Cloud it is so wonderful to see you. Why are you wearing the blue robe today? Is it because you are part of the Galactic Council, can you tell me more about this council?

We come in preparation of our new world of strength and grace and we open your heart to receive us. The Federation of Light has made a declaration to honour and protect the Children of Earth and we come in multitudes across the globe to shelter you in our embrace as we make these mammoth adjustments that will enable you to join us. Please do not be afraid for we come in all Love and sincerity. There will be time to make these adjustments as we come among you and we deliver further speeches in the amphitheatres of Earth, compelling you to listen to our words. The time range is of no comparison and we adjust frequencies to restore connections that have slipped through the net. We attune admirably in the circumstances available.

We fly across the great divide to be with you and yours and we monitor this connection, bringing in flavours of a new time frame that is open to each and every one of you. Stand firm, ready to receive us and we will enable greater delights in store. We offer a broad beam of knowledge ready for your perusal and we understand a greater connection with those of you on Earth, who are ready to come forward and be counted as part of our tribe. Those connections on Earth shall come to fruition and we have honoured many of you already in this time frame. Be prepared to accept greater residual energy and we will have accomplished a mammoth task to reunite with our elders on Earth. This has been a great accomplishment of mammoth proportions and we ask you not to look back but to look forward into a new world of exquisite gentility and freedom.

This is the main purpose of our visit today to give you that freedom to expand your boundaries . . . to march across those fields, to see the vistas clear before you, and as the Eagle flies and soars above so will you soar on wings of Love. We tell you now my little one it will be so . . . such exquisite Love awaits you here in our dimension and we bring you sustenance, the food of Love. We welcome you to this domain, bringing forth the wisdom that you so desire, spreading around your world that we come in Love and Peace.

We bring a solution for your problems on Earth and the solution is such an easy one to follow if only you will raise your hearts and Love one another. What could be easier than this?

TO LOVE WITH A FULL HEART!

TO GIVE WITHOUT ANY THOUGHT OF RECEIVING!

TO SHELTER WITHOUT ANY THOUGHT OF REWARD!

This is what makes the heart soar and the pleasure of giving far outweighs the pleasure of receiving! For in giving of yourself you give to God and God shall raise you up to fly like an Eagle, higher than you have ever known and you shall be blessed!

We tell you now my children that we will be with you throughout the great ordeal you are going through on the Earth plane at this time, and all will be given a place in this beautiful world that we are preparing in your honour, and we receive you with the greatest Love and affection to be brought into a new world of indescribable beauty.

How shall we live in this new world; will we still have jobs and do all the things we do on Earth? We won't be just sitting on a cloud all day will we?

There will be much to do, do not fret on that score, there will be much to sing about and for a time you will be adjusting and settling in. There will be a time of playfulness and laughter, a time of learning and exploring your new world.

This does sound very much to me where you go when you die and go to Heaven. Are we in fact dying and going to heaven?

You will not have to leave your physical bodies behind; you will be transported as you are, as you choose to be in this physical frame. Your frequencies will have changed and your bodies will be lighter, of not such a denser frequency . . . you will be more of your true essence. We will empower you to roam at will and to study the universe in greater detail. You will have the ability to travel as you have never travelled before and this new world may seem like Heaven to many of you, but you will remain intact and sample these truths without having to travel through the veil of death, and transformation shall be yours.

I'm being caressed by purple clouds.

We open this connection to allow you to see in greater detail, we draw back the veils that cloud your vision and allow you to see into our dimension . . . just open your eyes! *I still can't see!*
Use your imagination and we can build with this!

332

I'm imagining a Temple with white pillars and a blue sea; it looks like the temple at Philae in Egypt near Aswan. I'm going for a ride on a Felucca boat with the white sails billowing in the wind, laid back on cushions and floating along the river Nile. I think I get it now . . . everybody has their own dream and vision of how they want their world to be but is this world of substance or is it a world of illusion?

You are already trapped in a world of illusion that you believe it to be real; you are locked in prisons that you have made for yourselves! Open your eyes and see the reality . . . push back those boundaries that hold you down. Your thoughts build the walls that surround you!

I was thinking of the animals, the ones that are ill-treated, surely they don't dream the world they live in because we are the ones that are controlling their world. If we let go they will be free too!

The more you let go . . . the greater your world will become and the more freedom you will have. Let go . . . soar to those heights you have dreamed of and imagined in dream state. Soar to the mountain tops . . . fly through the ethers. Nothing shall hold you back . . . expand and push back the boundaries that you yourself build. Continue pushing back and regain your heritage of life eternal, forever growing, forever learning, and forever loving.

I'm feeling the bliss, there are no pains in my body there is just vivid gold on purple in the silhouette of a crown. I can hear the rousing music from Handel's Messiah rising up to an ornate golden ceiling covered in paintings from times gone past.

∞

After sending out healing I sang out . . . 'I Love You' to those in the spirit realms who send their love to us and could vaguely see the figure of Jesus through a purple mist. I love this beautiful purple, I see pulsating clouds of light fluctuating from pale to deep vivid purple with streaks of gold.

We Love you too my child!

I feel I want to dance and can hear the music to Kung Foo Fighting. I can see an African American who is saying Karaoke is good for you. I'm now hearing the song, 'Scream and Shout and let it all out' sung by Will. I. Am and also Freddy Mercury's – 'We are the Champions'.

We bring you a light hearted look at yourselves and we know it makes sense to take stock!

I am now being shown a tall slim African/American, wearing a silver grey waistcoat, trousers and a black shirt – he looks a bit like Jimmy Hendrix and seems to be talking to me!

There has been a lot of attention in the news recently about certain discrepancies relaying to mistrust. Governments topple and mayhem ensues, who will champion the cause of freedom from oppression, who will be our voice? We ask that you will allow a little snippet of information to filter through so that we may have our say!

Aren't there plenty of rappers out there that do just that?!

Yes, but we want a more serious approach! What jumps out at you in the news?

I don't really watch the news – it is too distressing and negative!

Burying your head in the sand won't solve anything - it's coming to grips with the nation's problems.

'SPEAK OUT FOR THE PEOPLE'!

We shine a light into all the darkest corners . . . we shine a light on all issues that need to be brought forth into the public domain to be healed. Nothing shall pass us by, nothing shall be overlooked, and nothing shall be set aside for we need this healing to be complete. The People versus Love . . . Love will prevail!

I'm now seeing that purple mist enveloping everybody. The rioters, the protesters, all people that cry out at their predicament on Earth! At the end here I could see

someone waving a dollar note, so feel this may be something to do with what is
happening in America. Later I watched the news and saw that Nelson Mandela
had died at the age of 95.

∞

The prodigal son shall be returned and we carry this through with the grace of God. We keep you intact and allow you to surface, fully fledged and ready to spread your wings and fly.

I looked up the parable of the prodigal son afterwards and wondered if it referred
to Nelson Mandela who had in his early years been labelled a terrorist for his
involvement in violence against the government of South Africa. We all know that
after his release from a long imprisonment of 27 years, his peaceful fight against
apartheid finally brought freedom for the oppressed. I also feel it may refer to the
human race.

We tell you there will be more rejoicing in heaven over one sinner who repents than over ninety-nine righteous persons who do not need to repent.

We are entangled in a fact finding mission, one of fantasy intermingled with truth. We know it makes sense to persevere with this line of contact and we bear witness to future harbouring of news that will delight you and point you in the right direction. This comes as no surprise to us as we bond together as one and the same. We deliberately request a time of healing and bonding together, being chaperoned by those who have our best interests at heart. We know it will take but a short time for us to make contact with greater urgency and we shall shelter you from other enchanted admirers.

This has been a most difficult time to assess as you have taken on a greater study than anticipated. We gratefully request an adjournment until we have reached peak performance; this will only take a few months before we have lift off! Don't be discouraged or put off for we have enrolled you in a superior class and take it upon ourselves to do you the honour of connecting with us in the near future.

We are the Children of Earth brought back from the brink of

335

destruction, Super Beings extraordinaire brought out of the flames of redemption and into the Light and Love of a new world. We have been recreated and we ask you to accept this turbulent recovery that shall see us standing arm in arm in the embrace of our beloved Star – the Star of Isis and nothing will hold us back from recovery! We are bamboozled and held in line by a democracy that has little or no understanding of how the people feel and we find ourselves floundering under the weight of our worst fears and nightmares. Yes, we have initiated further feedback and we do understand the plight of a nation under duress. Do not limit yourselves . . . feel the warmth of our Love, bask in that light and reflect it back to us. We are your brothers and sisters and we beseech you to stand firm; do not be put off by idle gossip that has no substance. We have agreed to lead you back home and will not rest until we have accomplished our mission.

We abide by the rules laid down by your governments and we issue a declaration that can be understood by all. There is nothing that cannot be accomplished with the power of Love; Love is the overriding factor in achieving success! We have made many claims in the past but none as satisfactory as this and we shall work together to overcome what has been insurmountable in the past . . . fear of oppression, fear of slavery, fear of fear itself! It is without a shadow of doubt time to erase this from your minds; it curdles the brain and has you giving up without a fight, without the will to survive! But survive you shall and if there is an inkling or respect in your bodies for your ancestors, you will not want to commit them to further turmoil.

There is a strong feeling of Mandela Nelson within the words coming through and I can see his face now.

Healing and touching with our own hands challenges the miracle within us; we are well prepared to take on these challenges and we ask you to shelter in our embrace as we realise a revolution of mammoth proportions. We rise to the occasion and cheer the population of Earth. It has been long overdue!

This morning I can see Nelson Mandela immediately as I sit to meditate.

We reach out and touch, delivering a healing to all concerned. We speak to the world and we realise a dream, brought into fruition through a network of prophecies that have been brought to you from courtesy of those on high. We speak of those that gather around the Earth plane to bring you Love, to bring you wisdom and to bring you joy, and we shall manifest greater glories for the Children of Earth.

We bring you salutations and ask you to look with Love on your brethren, look with Love and purity of spirit; tend to one another's needs as if they were your own. Do not be put out by your ignorance for we shall teach you how to Love, we shall teach you by showing you, by showering you with those golden rays of Love that shall envelop your very being. Hatred, fear and oppression shall become a thing of the past and we tempt you with our words, showering you with absolution for those atrocities committed in the past.

We wipe the slate clean and ask you to forgive your neighbours, forgive those who have done you harm in the past and move forward into that clear bright future ahead. There shall be nothing that can cast you down into that cauldron of lies and deceit for all is being brought into the open, into your jurisdiction to be looked at, to be mulled over and to be received with good grace. And where we need to start is to forgive ourselves . . . this is the hardest task for many of you, to forgive yourselves and to realise that justice is meted out by those who follow a new regime, a regime of Love where Love is the medicine, Love is the key and Love is the reward that you deserve. We all go forward together, you will not need to do this alone for we are with you night and day, watching over you and preparing you for the times ahead.

We spread the news so that all may be prepared . . . all may be ready when the trumpet blows! We regale you with stories from the past and there will be a time of greater national importance where we gather together and make that commitment. We know this has been on many of your minds and we make ourselves felt in your communities. There is a wind blowing the like of which you have never seen before, a wind blowing across the land awakening the hearts of mankind and we come in its wake bringing illumination. *Today I'm being shown a smooth headed man in a long robe sitting on a large chair. There is a strong tingling in the right lobe of my brain and I've asked him to come closer.*

This is indeed a privilege to be here with you now; this is indeed the beginning of a new era and we thank every one of you that we are able to achieve this in such majesty, in such grace right across the globe, right across your world and out into the furthest reaches of your universe. We have made it known in your jurisdiction that we come in Peace, we come in Love, and we come in all sincerity to help the Children of Earth to assist them in this mammoth leap of faith across the dimensions of time and space.

It is but a short step and one we have been waiting for with bated breath . . . a leap of faith in the consciousness of mankind. Travelling beyond those streams of thought you are used to there is indescribable beauty that awaits your soul and visions beyond compare. We will adjust and connect with your vibrations and we shall evolve as one race of the purest most beautiful and gentlest vibrations . . . pure essence of Love in the Divine presence of God and his Majesty. We propel you forward into a new domain of outstanding bliss and perfectness, blessed with the Love of the Great Divine and brought into awareness for all who make those strides into full awakening.

It has been with the utmost delight that we have guided you and championed the cause of freedom for mankind, and we operate on a new level that will bring you constant access to our thought streams. This has been our greatest challenge yet and we operate in a new Light that shines down and assists us with our many projects, with our many operations. We beam to you on a wavelength that is assisted with the purest Love and energy of the finest proportions; we gently take you to one side and allow manifestation of all that you desire.

We are benevolent to mankind and we assist you in your enquiries as the voices of Earth echo around the globe, clamouring for answers

338

that we shall provide. We shelter you in our arms and assist in this mammoth undertaking, delighted with your response, with your perseverance and attention to detail and a settling of the mind that allows us to come forth to protect and guide you. We know it makes sense to adjust your settings from time to time, to raise your consciousness to another level, and as each level is reached and harmonised we prepare yet for further ascension and this will be realised in due course. We take you gently, gently . . . step by step as you are ready to take on these new layers.   We liken it to a pressure chamber for your deep sea divers, adjusting at each level until you are ready to take on further challenges.

There is so much to explore and we feel your excitement brewing as we raise the lid and allow you that first look into your new world. There is nothing that can compare except perhaps the birth of a new child, for we have felt your bliss during this process also, and the Love you felt at holding this child to your breast for that first 'hello'. We too wait in anticipation for that touch, for that first hello when we blend together. We are enchanted with your progress and ask you to deliver these words and share them with your brothers and sisters on the Earth plane, to share that we come in Love. We wish you all you would wish for yourselves and so much more, for that gentility shall rise in your breast and blend with those in the higher realms that bring this message of Peace, perfect peace.

I've now burst into song with - deck the halls with boughs of holly - fa la la la la, la la la la. Tis the season to be jolly fa la la la la, la la la la!

I get the feeling this is our Christmas message!

That is so . . . walk gently upon the Earth plane, feel that joy within your soul, enjoy with your families and your friends and be aware of the dawning of a New Year and a new beginning, where we can take a few more steps into our future! For all is waiting to bring you to fruition, to bring that Love that is awakening within your soul into its highest form of expression, and that energy will whistle around the Earth like a spiral . . . a stairway to the Stars and beyond your wildest imagination; new beginnings, enlightenment and true devotion to the

339

cause of upliftment for mankind.
Peace be with you now and forever more!

The energies shifted and I can now see a Chinese/Tibetan looking face.

We have joined with you many times in the past and it brings us much joy to be here with you on this occasion, calling out to the people of Earth and bringing in the wisdom which you eternally seek, and that is the way of us, eternally seeking, learning and growing. There have been many toing's and froing's upon the Earth plane and we delight in looking you up and watching over you, sheltering you from the miseries that can perhaps settle like a mantle around your shoulders. This is by no means the happiest time for many souls on Earth for many have lost family and friends at this time of year and for them it is a sad anniversary! We bring you hope of a new world where you can join once more with those loved ones to share in those blessings that we bestow upon you.

Be of good cheer in the New Year for there is much to learn, much expansion, much upliftment some turbulence at times but this we shall overcome. We shall steady those energies that upset your circuits, re-tuning your energies just as you re-tune the engines of your cars. And we bring you up to speed with new technology, accessing boundaries that were previously beyond your reach. We do come in all honesty and faith to recharge your batteries and allow you to go further than you have ever gone before!

I can now see Eskimos wearing large fur trimmed hats, laughing and playing in the snow.

We challenge you to access this dimension in your waking states. It is so easy, like our sitter here who sets aside a certain time each day and for 1 hour out of your 24 you can enter a magical world! You can forget your pains and sufferings, you can tune into a new channel not dissimilar to your TV sets, but this is a frequency where you can learn and grow on a greater scale, and your pains and suffering shall fall away at those times when your frequencies are raised. You enter a new world in meditation, you open the doorway to a different

340

dimension and this will prepare you for access into the new realm that awaits you . . . it becomes a softer journey if you like. And we tell you now that we will come and take your hand and lead you to these pastures new. *I'm feeling tearful here.*

Chill out for an hour a day, free from the encumbrances of your world, free from the myriad voices calling you hither and thither to buy this and that and the latest fad. All you need is within your very being and the peace you cry out for is there, ready to envelop you and bring you the Love that you deserve. Envelop yourselves with this mantle of Love and we shall protect you. Go in Peace, sweet cherubim of Light.

Thank you friend that's two different messages; is there anyone else who would like to come forward for a Christmas message for the Children of Earth? I'm now getting the urge to sing:-

We wish you a Merry Christmas, we wish you a Merry Christmas, we wish you a Merry Christmas and a Happy New Year!

The geese shall fly by at midnight! *I'm not sure what this means but will keep a watch out.*

We honour this connection and bring you further updates allowing a rendezvous of souls to take place.   This has been the most challenging time for the people of Earth and we rein in the harmonies to take you aboard, bringing you success after success, opening doorways, flinging the windows wide and calling out with all our hearts – WE SHALL OVERCOME! *Again I started to sing.*

There is a bright light shining within the hearts of many on the Earth plane and we register that Light, we see it shining brightly and we home in on each and every one of you, bringing you upliftment and joy beyond all earthly measure. And this Light shall be seen to grow ever brighter, encompassing the whole of the Earth plane at this joyous time as we prepare for your evolution. We prepare for a grand awakening, indoctrinating the souls on Earth to believe they have the right of survival, and we prepare for the coming of the Lord thy God

341

who watches over all his children. We come in hope, faith and Love to bestow upon the Children of Earth even greater glories that shall manifest in the heavens, brought down to bear witness to a greater Love than man has ever known and we shall be seen in all our glory!

Does this mean that we are actually going to see a projection of yourselves or your space craft soon in the skies?

We tell you now this will be so at a point in time when you have come to fruition. Tune into us - that is all you have to do - tune into that frequency that will allow you to see and when you have raised your frequencies on a massive scale around the world – 'then it will be time'! When the frequencies are at that right pitch we will manifest before your eyes! Do not despair for this will happen, we are just as excited as you and we need your help to make this happen. Increase your intensity of purpose, turn up the tempo, bring that Love and joy into your hearts let the Love echo around the universe, let your Love leak into the atmosphere and bring us about full steam ahead. We can do it with your help! Are you up for the challenge? We await your answer dear ones, dear beloved Children of Earth!

Thank you friends. Is White Cloud there, does he want to have a last say? I'm seeing Santa Claus now who looks remarkably like White Cloud, flying through the sky on his sleigh, laden with gifts. He has a big cheeky grin and is singing Ho, Ho, Ho making me laugh and he is saying:-

There are some surprises in store for many of you!

∞

I'm sending golden light into my being, watching it flush through my brain and spine and every organ of my body. I can feel an incredible heat as this golden light washes through me and spreads out around me. I'm being shown my torso as white light with my hair flowing back from my face as if in a light wind. There is pulsating purple light and immense heat enveloping me and I can vaguely see faces with beautiful eyes looking at me. I'm now moving along this corridor of light that is like a tunnel . . . the purple is becoming more vibrant and the gold patterns more beautiful, it's like being on a magic carpet ride on a magical mystery tour with Alice in Wonderland.

Someone spoke . . . Push the button and see what happens!

I can see Alice falling down what looks like a purple and golden shaft and it goes down a long way. Alice has landed at the bottom on soft cushions and is perfectly alright; she is brushing herself down and exploring where she is. There are some boxes and Alice is pulling them together so that she can climb up and see over the top. I get the feeling I've done this before.

There is a treasure trove of gifts to explore!

I'm now seeing a scene where Egyptians are filling the tomb of Tutankhamen as I can see his funeral mask and they are bringing in more furniture.

There is a loophole that needs looking at before we make further enquires. There has been a setting back and we need to iron out a few creases before we put this book to bed. We are settling a score.

I seem to be in a passage with markings on the wall.

There has been a committal and we lay the body to rest, arguing over rank and discussing the mode of burial. We have a few more ideas that we ask you to look into and there has been much toing and froing from the scene we have selected for you. The Crown King has given his permission in laying a massive banquet and we prepare this in your honour. Do not frown on the arrangements for we expect a massive audience and invite you accordingly. *I can hear someone shouting out orders to the servants.*

Make yourself known . . . we are proud of your achievements!

I can't quite see . . . there is what looks like a purple footstool with gold hangings but a cloud of white in the middle is obscuring my vision.

This is a perpendicular exercise brought about to entertain the masses and we will not let you dishonour yourself in this way. We reap what we sow and over the years you have been subjected to more than enough compromises. We have great delight in initiating the greatest

343

respect and the challenges you face are in keeping with what we have come to know and learn about you on the Earth plane. We make great demands on your time and energy and see to it that this shall be replaced. We magic a surprise for you and let you into a little secret; we are amply prepared to take this further with ground-breaking discoveries beneath the earth in those crypts and tombs of old.

I'm now walking through an Egyptian palace with voile drapes flowing from tall white pillars and can see a figurine of Horus as a falcon. He was the protector and patron of the pharaoh.

∞

Last night as I lay down to sleep the face of Peter O'Toole filled my vision; he died yesterday on 15ᵗʰ December 2013.

Long have we grown weary of this mortal coil and all it entailed. We now rest our head and ask the Angels to shelter us before we continue our journey.

It gives us much pleasure to join with you now and air our views on what has gone before, a challenging documentation of rules and regulations that stunt the soul from growth. We revise the situation here and shed light where light is due, examining and sifting through data that has long been overlooked. We let bygones be bygones and we know it alarms some of you that you may be cast down into the fiery pit of Hell's cauldron for your mishaps on Earth, for the hurt you caused others especially those you loved! As has been said before we wipe the slate clean and sinners may repent and mean it . . . for all shall be forgiven no matter how foul the deed!

Those who have led uneventful lives may recall that we assisted you to discover your true worth and your crimes are not taking up that which would have enriched your lives on Earth. We say to those of you who are on the Earth plane – Live and Love to your greatest capacity, for life is to be enjoyed to the full. Relish every moment . . . every breath you take . . . every step you make, and every word you speak shall leave an indelible mark upon those you come into contact with. We plan a greater fusion of souls and delight in your

344

acceptance, participating in a grand connection the like of which has never been encountered before, and we have come many times to the Earth plane. There shall be a grand reunion and we circumference the world in readiness for your departure from one time frame and entry into another.

I drifted off to sleep and woke again at 1.21 a.m.

We analyse all that is brought before us and swing into action. We plough forward with our objectives, telling it loud and clear that we are here to assist in the regrouping of the human race. We have effectively curtailed any meanderings of the mind, planning decisively how we shall develop our curriculum. We have taken on board the niceties of parliament and endow ourselves with the right of exposure. This has been a most interesting time for all concerned and we register your approval, taking the bull by the horns and plunging in to have our say! We examine data and sift through our options – a whole monopoly of ideas spread on the board for us to survey.

Oh such a wondrous achievement . . . to all be in this place at the same time and in the same moment! We have achieved great things and we put it to you that this was always the plan, to come about full circle and meet you head on! Far-fetched you say and yes completely, but we have accomplished so much and learned from our mistakes and that is the whole point my friends, to learn and grow and to expand our way across the many universes of our entire existence. It is mind boggling to say the least but exciting and 'never' boring! To stand with expectancy and to bring some joy into your heart, forever growing, forever loving with a full heart, opening up the scope for further journeys and discussions such as these; we enjoy these immensely and know that you do too!

It is time to take a back seat for a while as we connect with the heart of your communities at this holiday festival that you call Christmas; a time of gathering in of families and joining in the festive cheer. We are spellbound on occasions such as these as we watch your antics around the world. The anticipation of Christmas is sometimes greater than the actual event with frenzied shopping and the wrapping of gifts. We watch the clinking of glasses as you celebrate another New Year and we are with you, bringing you a sample of our delight at your happiness. We too raise a glass and cheer you on to become the embodiment of all we hold most dear, our beloved Children of Earth, a golden experiment laid to rest . . . now resurrected and brought to fruition!

∞

I have recently been watching a series called 'The Bible' and would like to know about the God of wrath, the God of fire and brimstone that we are shown depicted in this film and in the Old Testament.

There is every need to cast aside your drift of mind for it is pointing you in the wrong direction!

Surely God is a God of Love not a God of death and destruction that we are shown in the bible; what do you say to that my friends? You have always shown yourselves to me as a God of Love, truth and honesty and I would like to know the truth of those times gone by that is if I can tune into the frequencies well enough to receive your answer.

We connect with you at these times of storm raging around your little sanctuary. We hear the wind and rain lashing at your door as you sit in the warmth and connect with us within the confines of your heart. We raise the temperature and turn up the tempo gaining access to your heart, telling you a story of times gone past many aeons ago. We prepare you to question us on those thoughts that rise for inspection and there is a treasure trove of thoughts waiting to be explored.

I'm being shown a young barefoot child in long tunic and scarf in the desert, exploring under rocks.

We grow as children and explore our perimeters, pushing back the boundaries with no fear in our hearts. The curiosity of a child is what we are suggesting and we know it make sense to open up that hamper that basket of goodies to be used and to be utilised in your experiment. We discover with sleight of hand, unfolding what has not been seen for many a year. This will bring gravity to a situation that is

346

opening up on the horizon and we ask you to speak your truth, to bear witness for us, your friends on the other side across that rainbow bridge that beckons you forward. And you have followed us over this bridge many times although you are not always consciously aware of this. We have joined together on several occasions, inciting one another to do our best, to do what we came for and to bring sustenance to the hearts of mankind. And you will realise the gravity of the occasion as we are seen in a new light, increasing our awareness as we draw closer together on numerous occasions such as this.

We need you to be constant to the cause and in that constancy we will draw ever closer to be with you and yours, and this will be seen to be done with greater reverence. We ask you to tread firmly yet lightly upon the Earth plane as we register your likes and dislikes, taking in hand what is causing discomfort, and we ask you to prepare for a homecoming that is open to each and every one of you. We assist you in your journey, taking your hand and guiding you to that distant shore that awaits your blessing; we have done all we can to make this perfect, to make this a perfect exercise that can be indulged by all who have a modicum of sense of the situation on Earth that presents at this time.

We ask you to grow in stature and raise your hands to the heavens from whence cometh your help, and that help cometh from the Lord thy God who in all truth is your Father and Protector. We oblige by opening up the gates to Heaven and you come in your thousands and millions, like those beloved prophets of old to teach the Children of Earth that there is a better way to live!

Who is speaking to me now please?

We come as one voice . . . opening up the heavens, preparing for the new agendas that will surface to be seen and rectified, bringing hope and Peace for all those who listen. We come in bountiful awareness of what has gone before and we capitulate and turn in our tracks, for we have never seen the like of this before! We shelter you in our arms and raise ourselves up to become once more those great giants of history. We are propelled into a greater domain and travel the highways and byways of Heaven and all will adjust to this phenomenon . . . all will bear witness to a greater state of existence as we bow down before the Children of Earth and tend to your needs.

I can see a giant king sitting on a throne and the Children of Earth, who look like small children in comparison, are climbing all over the king just as young lion cubs climb over their parents.

We tower above you and ask you not to lose faith for we are with you from dawn to dusk. We allow through only those contingents that help us gain access to your mind, so that we may discover the true nature of what it is that you wish and desire. This has given us ample compliancy in our requests to take you on board and we are open for further discussions to enable a massive overlaying of personalities, helping us adjust to one another's time lines to enable this amalgamation of minds. It has been an enormous step forward thus propelling us further afield and on to greater distinction.

I don't think you've answered my question about the Old Testament in the bible where we are told that God condoned the taking of lives and towns by force. Surely that is not a compassionate or humane thing to do. Is this true or is it fable?

The bible was written by humans . . . it was translated by humans many times over. God is Love. God will always be Love!

I've just been thinking, we are part of the collective consciousness and if the consciousness of the people is one of scorn and hatred then surely that central force would not be one of Love - it would be one of hate! Now at this time there are more people who want peace than want war and that would equate to a God of Love; but was there a time in the distant past when God was not a God of Love?

We are glad to see you questioning and opening your mind to accept the impossible. This has been a very precarious time for all concerned and we register your disapproval at that portrayal of your bible and the old kings and prophets of times gone by. And it has to be said that we are open to negotiation on the pros and cons of those parables from long ago. It gives us no joy to hark back to those

times, to those Citadel's of shame and sorrow!
Are you referring to Sodom and Gomorrah, which I think was destroyed?

There have been many cleansings of the Earth through fire and
water.

*Surely wiping the slate clean in such barbaric circumstances is not a loving thing to
do?*

Love has always been the key factor and it is 'you' that causes the
storms, it is what comes from the depth of your very being that
incites the winds to roar and the flames to spread through your
forests – you control the weather patterns through your thoughts!

*Surely not that's a big responsibility and a lot to take on board! Is it my own
thoughts or is it you – yet I feel quite deeply entranced? But where it is cold and
windy and bad weather here, I know on the other side of the world the sun is
shining. As I'm typing this I remember that there have been bad fires in
Australia recently. Oh it's all too confusing!*

We bear witness to a time of everlasting peace and the degeneration
of souls that plunged into the abyss shall be raised back up, shall be
raised from the dead like Lazarus, to be redeemed and forgiven, to be
given that impetus to travel forward into a new future of perpetual
bliss and we give you this chance to absolve yourselves!

Who is it that is giving me these words please?

Our credentials come from the highest of the high, from those
Angels that sit around the throne of God. And we raise you up to be
with us your champions, your nursemaids, your brothers and sisters.
We come from those Archangels that champion the cause of
mankind and we are brought into your line of vision . . . an
acceleration of your thoughts because you have pushed back those
boundaries and allowed us to enter your mind. There is nothing that
cannot be achieved with the power of thought! The power of the
mind can be like a laser, sharp and to the point, cutting through the
darkness, through the greyness that impedes your vision, cutting a

pathway to your destiny, to your future where all is waiting to unfold. And there is no time like 'now' to set your minds - to set yourselves upon this quest!

Where is my gold and purple, I know I am channelling correctly if I see this. I ask the Love of the Great Divine to be with me now and those Guardian Angels that watch down upon us and keep us safe. I ask the Christ Light, the Archangel Gabriel and all the Angels that have worked with me in the past, I ask them to draw close now and let me know that I am on the right track and not being hoodwinked or led astray!

I can see the purple and gold becoming more vibrant now.

We are one and the same . . . your guardians, your guides, your helpers. We bring you Love and protection from the Great Divine for all those that come and join us and speak for the Children of Earth, resurrecting a new ideal that shall be taken up, escorting the Children of Earth to a new realm where purity of spirit and Love prevails. This is our task and we are indebted to your services upon the Earth plane. We bring you an abundance of good cheer . . . and all will be well. *Thank you my friends.*

We watch over you and keep you safe, bearing in mind there are many advocates that step forward to be counted and we regard you as one of our greatest emissaries, forging ahead in this inspiring journey into the void of uncertainty; uncertainty for some, but many of you share our vision of Love and Joy beyond all earthly measure, which we are building here for you and yours. Be in Peace, go now with our Love and blessings and we shall watch over you forever more. *I'm getting the 'Drummer Boy' song at the end of this session.*

∞

I feel sprit drawing close today and feel the peace washing over me.

We are both designed and resigned to follow our heart and we lead you onwards with your merry band, shedding light on those issues that have been cloudy of late.

350

I can see myself rummaging through a big chest so I guess there are more things to be resolved.

We take another step further forward.

I can see a pinprick of light in the shadows. Help me Great Spirit! I feel tears in my eyes and cannot make out if they are tears of sadness or tears of joy. The purple is getting brighter and I can see myself looking into the chest again; there is not much left in the bottom, just a few bits of paper and I wonder if this means I'm nearing my journeys end. I'm going down a long tunnel of soft purple light that is getting more vibrant as it pulsates to the rhythm of my heart. The golden patterns seem more complex and are heartbreakingly beautiful. I am here in this tunnel but I can hear the sound of traffic going past; I can feel the coolness in my room but am warm in my heart.

Fresh tears touch my cheeks. Great guiding Light please set me free . . . please set me free! I want to drift along this tunnel forever and to reach the other side but I know I still have work to do and I WILL complete my mission. It's so beautiful and I wonder if that's why I don't remember my many journeys to the other side, because I wouldn't want to return.

∞

Chapter fourteen

Glad tidings of great joy

3.1.2014 – 3+1+2+0+1+4= **11** the master number eleven.

Sitting in my sanctuary I asked for Love, healing and guidance, asking if there were any messages to share.

We do indeed bring glad tidings of great joy and this shall be seen as a great wave of Love around your world. We come in uniformity bringing Love on a grand scale and this shall be felt in your heart centres as you register the impact. There is every need to shelter from that which threatens to engulf your soul and we bring you hope, we bring you that ray of Love that will confound those who wish to drag you down with them into the abyss. We protect you from the negative energy that swamps Earth and we align ourselves with a just cause that will free mankind from bondage.

We register those patterns of thought that circumference the globe, those patterns of Love that you expel, bringing cheer to the population of Earth. We shall make a grand recovery, giving air to proceedings as they unfold and we shall be there by your side holding your hand, adjusting and tweaking where necessary to give you that strength, to give you that grace of expression. Be not alarmed at what is taking place at this present moment for there is no cause for alarm, the underlying currents of energy are amassing in the heavens, streamlined advantageously to your world, and we bring this with courtesy from those on high who have a grand interest in mankind.

I'm seeing deep purple overlaid with a lattice of gold.

There is an undercurrent of activity that will register in your brains and we know it has been uncomfortable for you all of late. We feel the resonance emitting from your frames and we help you adjust to these frequencies little by little. If you are finding it hard, imagine the discomfort felt by those around you who have no understanding of what is happening. We come to bring completion to what is long overdue and it may take some time yet to adjust your settings. We bear a massive responsibility and feed you as much information as we are allowed. There is a time of recuperation from the massive changes already in place and this will come as no surprise to you. We bring in Light that will encompass the globe, shining into every nook and cranny and we ask you to bear with us as we make these adjustments to your energy field. We allow you to bond with us.

I'm now surrounded by a circle of white Light and can hardly speak.

We bring growth of stupendous proportions and regulate the glitches in your energy field. We bring adjustment and new levels of understanding that will raise the consciousness of mankind to new levels higher than ever before, and we establish a new continuum, a new theme of enlightenment that will register in your souls, in your minds and in your very being. This will give us great advantage and we open up the networks that will allow for greater clarification, greater unity of spirit as we circumference the globe.

We bring you full circle and honour your discretion in maintaining this contact. There has been a great initiation that has brought us to fruition and we beg you to listen always to that voice within your soul that brings us equal measures of Love and clarity of expression in our commitment to you on Earth, to those of you who have made that commitment to us and in no small measure. We have adjusted our timelines to coincide with yours and we bring you up to speed, honouring this connection and giving sanctity to what has been a most joyous association. We beam to you on a ray of Light that will bring us all the greatest joy and we ask you to study in closer proximity so that we may bear witness, bringing hope and solace where it is needed.

I opened my eyes and gazed up at clouds that looked like the wings of Angels. Thank you my friends, thank you so much.

∞

Don't despair we are here to cheer you on our way. We open up a grand connection and point you in the right direction; there are myriad connections to help you and we choose those that will gain greater advantage as we draw ever closer. We sample some home truths sharing luminosity of spirit, those threads that bind us together which can never be disconnected. We draw ever closer my friend, ever closer to your heart, relishing those intervals where we champion the cause of enlightenment for all mankind. It brings us great joy to be working with you as was planned long ago, and we delve deeper and deeper into your thoughts, sharing and reaping the benefits of a lifetime's experience. We shelter you from the plague of uncertainty, rescuing you from the maelstrom that threatens to engulf you. We will not see you led astray but keep to the true path; this is a time of adjustment and for growing stronger in our resolve to move forward on that beam of Light that shall take you further afield and on to greater distinction.

We have cause to be joyful and we come among you to share that joy with you, opening up your hearts and minds to accept the possibility of visitation upon your planet Earth. This will be no mean feat and we open up a wide selection of probabilities, sanctioning this process of renewal and greater evolution.   We propel you to dispense the messages that come flooding in and these will give you the advice that you need to stand firm in all sincerity, like a beacon bright helping those that flounder, those that are lost and need a helping hand, and there are many that need these services right across the globe for they have no understanding of what is to come. Be strong . . . be brave for this is a mission of the highest intent and we ask you not to lose faith.

We bear witness to a time of immense fortitude and courage and you have done your jobs well, keeping that commitment and honouring these connections. We know you are waiting . . . watching the skies for our arrival but in all truth we are already here! You are those connections to the stars that shine so brightly, you are an integral part of who we are. And the stronger your thoughts the stronger that wave of Love around Earth, and the stronger we become, the closer we come . . . and come we shall have no fear! We are part of that great plan and we have spoken of this for many years, for many centuries, and all is coming to fruition. The timing has to be impeccable, the timing has to be right for us to accomplish what is necessary for all of you, not just for the few but for the whole population of Earth . . . we do not want to leave anyone behind!

This has been a most extraordinary time on Earth and we value our connections with each and every one of you who have used your voice, used your heart and soul in the operations on Earth to enable this mammoth undertaking. And we bear you on wings of Love to that destination that awaits you, that glorious planet, that orb of Light and Love that awaits you in greater harmony. We believe the time fast approaches and looking back over the centuries, just the blink of an eyelid for us, it has taken until now for us to make this excursion that will bring the greatest joy to the hearts of mankind. We beam you aboard and shelter you in our embrace, hearken to that voice within to make these connections stronger. We are with you always and we talk to you and whisper in your ear. Listen . . . listen to us!

∞

I asked for Love and healing to be sent to certain parties that I have great respect for and White Cloud drew close to give assistance.

In all honesty we have to say, we have no heart for these proceedings; no one person shall be placed on a pedestal and given adulation, for at some point in time they will fall from grace in the eye of the beholder! It is not our way to get involved in such proceedings and we continue to deliver our messages to those on Earth who wish to hear our words and we come in faith and all sincerity, bringing you upliftment and cheer in a world grown weary from the trials and tribulations that beset you all.

This is a time for casting off that shroud of sorrow, for dissolving the darkness and negativity that pervades your soul. We govern proceedings and induce in you a state of ecstasy; this will bring Peace and clarity, unfolding the greater mysteries that surround you. We ask you not to be sad, we ask you to think about the reality of what you

355

are facing. We ask you to think about the mission you share with your brothers and sisters from other dimensions, and we all come and gather together, uplifting the hearts of mankind, bringing in a clearer vision so that you may accept us as we are, your true friends and neighbours.

We are your Family of Light and you are Light Beings clothed in a physical body . . . the Light shines from within and we shall bring this Light into the open, measuring those reserves of energy. And there is no cause for fear and alarm for this is most perfectly natural, like the butterfly that emerges from the chrysalis, spreading its wings to fly in vibrancy of colour in the sunlight. You are those butterflies destined to fly on wings of Love and you shall spread your wings and fly into the ethers and far beyond. We prepare you to do your duty and to shed light on those issues that surround you; we are here to champion the cause of upliftment for mankind to those higher realms that await you and yours.

Be of good cheer dear friends, this is not an admonishment, this is encouragement to let the false fall away so that you may stand in your truth, in your Light, shining bright for all to see, for in truth you are magnificent, most beautiful and wonderful to behold. Fix your eyes on that vision, on that perfectness, for you are all perfect within the very core of your being . . . that seed of perfection is within you all.

We offer our condolences to those who cannot hear our words, to those who will not listen, but there will come a time when even those souls can no longer ignore that knock on the door! And we offer them shelter and our undying Love for they too are our brothers and sisters, the Light within them shall break through so they too may come home and in that state of perfect bliss, back to the heart of the Great Divine. We bring you undiluted Love.

White Cloud came into view.

We know you have the best interests of the parties concerned but we would like to point out that this is not your problem and we assist by taking you aside and pointing you in the right direction. There will be

356

mammoth changes to your circuits, to your energy field, and this will be needed to rectify certain points that are lacking. We have known for some time this association would wreak havoc in the minds of those who expect too much from any one soul. We allow a modification to occur that will allow future channellings of excellence and we ask you to bear witness for us your friends and helpers. And there will be a time of great joy for there has been a grand connection of minds on a higher level and we ask you to prepare for this. We are of one mind in this and we know you will listen. Beware - do not fall into the same trap!

I understand White Cloud. You mean don't put others on a pedestal or encourage that for ourselves don't you?

We do indeed for that is not our way. Our mission is of great importance and there are many who carry these words with joy in their hearts.

I see now why there are so many that share these words, so that the pedestal thing can be avoided and that is a good thing.

We reach out and tap you on the shoulder and ask you to join us and this is a great honour for us as well as you. And we are very special to one another, it is a specialty reserved for family and friends with great Love and affection.

∞

We are magnanimous in our approach asking that you revitalise a situation that is begging to be looked at in closer detail. There are many that come to hear our words and we beseech you to listen most carefully. We lay before you a document of considerable worth and we establish a rule of thumb, giving us open access to decipher these words so that you may share with others of your persuasion.

I'm seeing a smooth headed Egyptian.

We subject you to closer scrutiny, begging you to look with fresh eyes at a situation facing you head on.   We know that you have given us

357

your all and we do make allowances for what has been a very deceptive time of late, however there is much more on the horizon that will need greater dedication, and we carry this through from those on high who have your best interests at heart. We register the distress that constantly knocks at your door - do you realise what it is doing to your energy levels? We ask you to slow down and listen more carefully to what we have to say and we deliver, by courtesy of those on high, a vigorous and challenging debate!

∞

Our Trance group resumes after an adjournment of over 3 months. I felt White Cloud draw near with a big smile on his face.

We are indeed blessed to be here! It brings us great joy to come among you once more . . . we feel much joy, much emotion.

There was such an emotional feeling here and there were tears in my eyes as White Cloud held his hands to his chest.

And now to the business in hand - we welcome you most sincerely to join with us on this and many other occasions in the future and we will become quite famous you know! That is not to say that we shall be set on a pedestal, of course, but we have to be seen and heard and this is our mission, and you will join us on many occasions as this will become our forte. There will be much jubilation on a wide scale across your world and we are inundated with questions on every plane. We ask you to shed light where that light is due and we will manifest together a Greater Light that others may see and hear our words accordingly. We are a whisper away . . . our call echoes to you on the flight of an Eagle soaring high in the sky, echoing within your mind and within your heart. We bear witness to a greater time to come and this is our mission of the greatest intent. We register this in your hearts too and we have come together to be as one, to bring you all into that fold. All aboard for the Marrakesh Express!

I wanted to sing this song and was swaying to the music in my head.

This is a time of happiness and great joy and we welcome you aboard to journey with us and there will be great excitement, a learning curve for us all, but one we are looking forward to. There has been some doom and gloom in the past, we know this, but it is coming to an end. There is hope on the horizon for all of you and this shall just seem like a hiccup in the great scheme of things, a mild hiccup in this long journey you have been on, and together we shall overcome all trials and tribulations, they shall all fall away. We are very, very proud of your perseverance and your fortitude in these times of turmoil and strife, but you will break through in glowing colours and all will come to fruition as was foretold. And we ask you to take care of one another, to nurture one another and we see the circle growing ever wider, these friends you have been drawn to and reach out to, you all have gifts that you can share that transport you to heaven. And we look forward to the music . . . we look forward to hearing your voices rising into the ethers and filling your soul.

We won't hog the limelight . . . although we don't want to leave! We send our Love and blessings and restore harmony within your souls so that you may go on with lighter hearts, giving encouragement when it is needed. Peace and Blessings.

It was so wonderful to have White Cloud draw close to open our circle at the beginning of this New Year and we all look forward to what lies ahead!

∞

Sitting alone I can see a white feather bonnet and feel a loving presence drawing closer, the closer they draw the more emotional I become. Clouds of purple are washing over me and I can hear the rain outside, pattering against the window pane. I'm very much aware that Australia is experiencing the opposite with heat waves up in the 40's and I'm sending out Love and blessings to my friends out there who may be feeling uncomfortable. I've just been given a glimpse of gold filigree at this point.

I Love you dear Star friends so much; I'm finding it such a struggle on Earth to make ends meet and feeling so tearful. I know there are so many who are struggling just like me, who do not have the luxury of being able to tune into their

359

'Oneness' to get that comfort and solace but I pray soon that they will! The tears are coursing down my cheeks and I feel as I did many years ago, resting my head in my mother's lap and pouring out my grief and anguish, and she would soothe me, stroking my hair until I was calm. Purple clouds wash over me and are sweeping round and round; I appear to be in a tunnel and am feeling calmer now. I can see a gold network of patterns overlaying the purple and there is such a wonderful peace here.

We are ready to make our move and we solidify arrangements that will enable this procession, transporting you to heaven in the blink of an eye. We register your concerns and a harbouring of resentment at times when you have been stuck in the mud so to speak. This has been a great testing time for us all and we initialise further feedback to allow us to move forward on this beam of Light. Depend on us to instigate a renewal of services and we shall gather together, pooling our resources. We have stood back but now we step forward to assist you. We reprogramme an inordinate amount of information, ready to feed into your circuits, challenging you to accept what we bring in all reverence and in all hope for a glowing future for mankind. It serves us well to bring this now to your attention and we believe we shall get better feedback in the near future, allowing greater reserves of energy to penetrate your energy fields, undertaking and generating further studies and allowing you to 'feel' in the truest sense our aspirations and joys at taking you on board once more.

We allow further information and regenerate your systems, pulling you to the foreground. We jumpstart your circuits and push you forward into the arena, ready to do our bidding, and we know you take this on board with great dexterity and a willingness to learn and grow. This is not done under duress and we would not want you to do anything you were not happy with. We simply blend together with perfect ease, a most joyous association. Be prepared to allow us a modicum of comfort as we enter your zone . . . your energy field.

We do wrap you in cotton wool to shelter you from the harsh knocks that have taken their toll and we prepare for greater sacrifice that shall lead us further afield into new territory. It goes without saying that we shall be there by your side, and we deliver a whole host of remedies that shall lead us to the land of plenty, where dreams really do come true. We show you the way, ushering you into our domain, perfectly attuned, a grand enterprise monitored and projected onto your line of vision. We obey the Master within, honouring our connection with the unseen and tapping into those reserves of energy available

I'm gasping at the purple and gold before me, it is like a spider's web only much more intricate.

We join with the Divine in essence. Glory be to God in Heaven.

That Divine essence of 'Oneness' is who we are . . . who we all are and I wish everyone could see the kaleidoscope of patterns of gold on purple that I am seeing now . . . it is so beautiful.

We will don that cloak of immortality and bide forever more in the heavens across the universes . . . the expansiveness of all creation is there before you to explore in all its splendour. There is no limitation there is only exploration . . . continuous as the stars and in the knowledge that we shall never expire.

In whatever form that we choose; we go on and on and on, choosing to experience in different formats, different formations and patterns of growth.

We register this interval as being a great success and we terminate this contact to allow you to rest and go about your business on the Earth plane. We thank you for allowing us to look into those circuits within you so that we may refresh you, so that you may continue your journey with greater success.   Be of good cheer for we are always here with you, always in the background watching over proceedings. You have only to call for help and we are there beside you, giving you the help you need to keep you on course. And we do understand your needs and desires and we will focus on what is necessary to bring you what you so obviously deserve, and this will create a barrier of healing balm.

I can still see the purple and golden shapes and it feels as if I'm in some kind of

361

structure, it is hard to focus enough to say what it is though, all I know is that I feel calm and at peace. I'm now sensing a disc floating away and wonder if it is my Star friend's mode of transport. I went back into the house and slept as I always do after a healing session. I'm sharing this as it shows just how much support we do have from our Star friends, especially if we take the time to unburden ourselves and listen to their advice.

∞

I'm sitting alone for communication and felt my Star friends draw close once more.

This has been an astronomical success and we are beholden to you for allowing us to draw close. It gives us the utmost joy to be working with you and for allowing us shelter in your arms. We are on a mission and use the resources available to us, bringing you further growth, and we allow that to settle while we adjust the frequencies, bringing in a grand connection of minds.

We stable a volatile situation on the horizon and beckon you forward to do your duty. We tend to our brothers and sisters, those that cry out for help and we come to assist you, finding our location in the depth of your being, expressing ourselves with great tenderness. We bring hope and we bear witness to the pull within your heart that carries you forward in perpetual motion, searching for that glimmer of Light that perpetuates our Love for you, and we delve deeper to uncover those misgivings within your heart.

Never forget that we are with you always . . . we hear the murmurings within your heart, we hear you challenge our wisdom within your soul. We feel the intensity of your Love and know we have much to account for, much to answer for. It gives us no pleasure to recount our journey into the abyss but we need to set the record straight, honouring our connection with you. It cannot be helped there is nothing for it but to tell the truth, the whole truth and nothing but the truth!

We come at a time of great ignominy for those of lesser density and we are prolific in our statements, giving you further access to those domains previously denied. We are open to further recriminations that hold us in the deepest respect for our brothers and sisters on Earth. We deal with compensation and we come at a time of great denial, an exercise born of futility and ignorance in a world gone mad, where no jurisdiction has been set, no governing to set the wheat from the chaff. We bare no grudges for those who come to stare, no grudges accept for the Love of our families, lost to us forever more! And we bear witness to the degradation, the enslavement, an abhorrent cocktail of death and destruction, brought upon us in no small measure with obscene innuendos rife in every corner. We had the misfortune to bear witness to these obscenities and we strive now to set the record straight, for what comes into the open must surely be healed! It is most necessary but a gruelling task nevertheless and one that causes our heart to sink into the depths to overcome this fiasco on Earth.

We are bound by the rules of our brothers and sisters in the higher realms and we come to share our experiences with you. We come to share what is not known, we come to share our Love with the human race and we reach out to comfort you, helping you to face facts . . . undeniably a hard task! Take comfort and know that we are here to help you, raising you up from the abyss, raising your awareness as you reach each milestone, another step along the highway towards completion and we are most honoured to walk with you. Do not be put off, we will prevail and we will honour our connection with you, putting aside the disparities and negligence that holds us back from completing our mission. We intercede to bring you what is necessary, helping you achieve wider scope that will enthral you.

I'm seeing purple and gold throughout this session and wondered who was speaking to me.

We are from a long line of advocates that draw close to assist in proceedings - The White Brotherhood from Ancient Greece.

Can you expand on that please?

The White Brotherhood is an ancient order that has long aspired to bring strength and grace in our dealings with the human race. We have long suffered conflicts such as these and manage what is necessary to introduce a new portal of resounding success and this shall be opened in due course.

How will the portal be used? For bringing in a greater volume of energy!

And what will the energy be used for? To perpetuate the human race!

The gold and violet became more vibrant here and I asked - Whereabouts in the world will this portal be situated?

In Rome . . . here it is greatly needed and atrocities committed here on a vast scale shall be purged. This is not of our violation but from the Supreme court of the highest gradient and we express our solidarity, our jubilation! Reaching this level will be accepted by many around the world as one of vast recovery and we do indeed penetrate the hearts and minds of many individuals, who otherwise would have been inadmissible into those realms of bliss. We open the gates to Heaven and allow you though in your multitudes and this shall be recorded as one of the most eventful times in mankind's history.

This shall become a song among those bards who record the histories of times gone past; this shall be remembered as a most magical time when all were brought back into the fold to begin anew. And we tell you now - this is the Greatest Event 'ever' in the history of mankind! We come in jubilation and we come in sorrow, for the needs of the many outweigh the few, but those few are very dear to us and we hope and pray when the bell tolls that no one will turn away, for this is a chance to wipe the slate clean and to begin again in a vibrant new world of outstanding proportions!

Seek and you shall find . . . stand in your truth and you will be given entrance to a new domain, where Love and beauty of spirit reign in abundance and these gifts shall be given to all in a great array. There are no greater gifts than these apart from that deep abiding Love that is present in our world.

I started singing Love Divine all Love excelling!

It will be done - thy will be done in Heaven and Earth!

Go now my sister in Peace, and blessings upon all those who listen to our words, for we come in Truth and Peace in all sincerity, opening up that gateway to Heaven that leads you ever onwards.

Looking up the White Brotherhood on the internet afterwards I found this. "Members of the ancient, mystical White Brotherhood are myriad in number and are invisible to the human eye. They are very high spiritual beings, highly evolved, and of superior character, souls, and auras. They are extremely wise, expressing Divine intelligence beyond our mortal comprehension. They always work together as one. (We come as One Voice)!

∞

After a long walk this afternoon, I sat in meditation thinking of White Cloud. All of a sudden I saw a small orb of blue light, which is unusual for me as I usually see purple. I can now see the profile of an Indian chief with large feather bonnet and wondered if it was White Cloud. Tears are stinging my eyes so it must be him. Oh now I can see Sitting Bull too!

There are a whole host of us waiting to make our connections and we grow closer to those counterparts we have agreed to work with. There are many of different nationalities, different creeds, all gathered together and it is not for the want of us trying for we have been many times before.

Incredibly, I'm now being shown John Wayne who starred in many Western films.

There have been many comings and goings across these boundaries; we hearken to the call and make great impact on those who reserve their energies for meetings such as these, and it gives us great pleasure to come among you.

I can sense the Love and excitement of a whole crowd of people and I can see a woman on horseback who is laughing; there is someone behind her riding in the same saddle and I have a feeling it's me. There are many more on horseback, all on the same journey, and I feel they are showing me all the tribes coming together.

365

The next few words seem to come in poem form.

We shadow you from morn to night and it is our great delight to work with you and become as one, travelling onwards towards the Sun, towards those golden rays shining down upon us from the Great Divine. And we welcome you here one and all to honour our voices as you hear our call, and we will come to guide you on agreeing the mission we all are on. We will cross those boundaries in sight welcoming all with blessings bright.

We sanction a blessing from the Great Divine bringing you closer in our embrace and we welcome this most rewarding feedback as we gather together. The clans and the tribes of the dearly departed gather together once more and we make ourselves heard like never before. Have faith and know the future is bright!

I can now see a young Indian with long jet black hair, it's as if we are zooming in and I can see every strand of his hair so clearly. There is another Indian wearing a black hat with tallish crown. Thank you friends for drawing close and I feel the excitement. I can now see someone with sandy coloured hair, beard and moustache and wondered if he was General Custer, having the feeling perhaps that we are now all on the same side.

Indeed we have all joined together; we have joined ranks for the common cause of mankind. We come in our hundreds and thousands, millions and trillions across the great divide to meet up with kith and kin, to meet up with those who work closely with us in this great cause. We travel lightly and we travel with Love in our heart – that is all we need to let battle commence and we shall cause quite a stir as we travel on.

There are deep murmurings within the ranks of men and they will hear our voice right across the planes, across the rolling hills, across the seas, across the universe and we make those connections count like no other! We count ourselves lucky to have you to monitor our growth, to keep our connection on an even keel. And we draw close in times of stress, in times of illness, in times of vulnerability but most of all we come when our heart calls us to you, so that we may

366

blend together with greatest ease, focusing on the heart centre. We become to all intents and purposes as One, a synergy of essence that makes the whole and we are so blessed to make this union such a happy one.

We ask you to be careful in the days and weeks ahead; there is a culmination of energies coming to a head to be utilised in greater strength and we will be there by your side helping you, assisting you in the new measures needed to take this on board. We bear witness to a greater evolution of mankind and we spread our messages across the great divide. We are brimming with tears of joy and we bring this mammoth undertaking to a head very soon, knowing you may feel proud of the associations you have made and the velocity of strength that is coming your way. Do not despair but go forward into that Light of true understanding; we wait for you on the horizon to do our duty and to make ready a place for you and yours. We advise on a stability not yet mastered and we prepare you to access the coil.

What is the coil?

A coil of transparency that marks our union and we delve deeper and deeper into that spectrum that beckons us on to greater ecstasy, greater joy and greater union between our peoples.

Feeling tired now I struggled to keep the connection going and had to leave it here.

∞

23.1.14 . . . 2+3+1+1+4=11. *Again the Master number eleven is evident.*

Today I decided to try the exercise that White Cloud explained through Blossom Goodchild.

He asked Blossom to sit in her chair and imagine her fingers with each digit resting on a metal plate. As I followed suit it felt as if I was sitting in a spacecraft.

And we have take-off . . . I seemed to go backwards first, shooting off at high

367

velocity . . . now we are swinging around and going forwards down what looks like a tunnel of lilac cloud.

We travel at a fast rate of knots opening up the vistas before you; this is deemed a long journey in the eyes of many who have travelled this way before, but we believe in a blink of an eye we shall reach our destination! We have travelled over the highways and byways of Earth and we recognise the sap that rises within your very being. We discover new talents, new ways of accessing those dimensions previously denied and yet in readiness to receive you. It will come as no surprise to many of you that we of one intent and purpose, have come many times to your world and we have been amply rewarded with your hospitality and gentleness of spirit. We receive you with open arms into our domain, broadening your horizons and bringing in a wealth of opportunities to expand and grow. It gives us great pleasure to share with you in our world of grace and beauty and we shall open those portals that allow you through.

It has been a long and arduous journey for many of you, we know this, and we bequest you riches in your aspirations to join us. We are beholden to you for allowing us to draw near and we regulate your heart beat, making sure you are under no duress. This is a time where your imagination comes into play and we bombard you with astral projections that will send you hurtling into a new reality. We ask you to undertake this mission, so that we may explain to others what we are about and where we fit in the great scheme of things. It has been a mammoth undertaking and we rely on you to draw closer so that we may examine in greater detail what is necessary to set the record straight.

My face feels strange and my hands are throbbing.

We are undisputed champions of the cause and we welcome you to our domain. We are Light beings extraordinaire, forever in your debt, and we express ourselves with great eloquence to be here with you today. It gives us great pleasure to sing your praises for you have done so well in such a short space of time. We have increased the intensity and turn up the tempo!

368

My right leg has just pushed down as if I'm changing to a higher speed and I can feel something being twiddled at the back of my neck. I can now see the vague shape of someone sitting on a golden throne; he is looking rather like the humanoid creature from the film 'Prometheus' with apparatus over his face. There was a crack in the room when I thought this.

Expand your consciousness . . .

The next morning I tuned into spirit again and sang out my Love for them, asking for protection and any messages they might have. They returned the favour by singing back to me a line from the song 'Oliver'. (They used this song many years ago to let me know they considered me part of the family).

We'd do anything - for you dear anything!

I feel light headed as if my head is being stretched upwards and elongated.

We exercise our muscles, bringing you into shape, getting ready for a grand experiment and we hope this pleases you!

If you think it will please me then I'm sure it will.

All has not always been as it seems to be, and we wish you to look closer into the depths of your very being. We shall indeed prepare for a grand array of services brought for your delectation and we monopolise a spirit that has helped us achieve immortality. We openly resonate on a band wave of Love that shall take us to further heights previously undiscovered. We know it makes sense to stand back and listen, listen to the voice within that beckons you on to greater understanding and clarity of vision.

We are given to understand there have been further journeys made available to us and we ask that you accompany us, so that we may experience for ourselves what is now given freely. This marks a new understanding with those from other realms who come to give their assistance and we delight in you taking a chance on us, amalgamating your energies with ours to give us free expression. This is a vision held sacrosanct by many on the Earth plane, who call out to be recognised as true free spirits, encircling the Earth and looking for new adventures. And we come to bring you the greatest adventure of all . . . unification, a blending of energies with those from other worlds who have your best interests at heart. We come vetted by those from the higher realms who wish us to introduce ourselves to you here and now, and we believe this will give you greater incentive to forge ahead on to new realms of delight.

We are your brethren and have always been so; we come from a world that was once your home and we grew in timely fashion, opening up the conduits that allowed us to make contact with those from other races. You became to all intents and purposes our masters, you arranged our genetic order, our genetic patterns to adapt and correspond with your own. We were most happy to accommodate you in this and we became the greatest experiment since time began! We were those golden creatures evolved in a format like no other ever seen, genetically engineered in such a way that we became indestructible - or so we thought! We were the most loving of creatures and we shone like the rays of the Sun in all beauty and magnificence . . . rough diamonds honed and polished, multi-faceted and genetically created to bring advancement to mankind.

What happened to you my friends, what went wrong?

The advancement of mankind was foremost in your minds and we entered a new phase of existence. We generated further updates that left us wide open to sources we relied on. We generated further studies that would lead us back home, the popular myth being that we were destroyed as a 'super race' when in fact we became obsolete!

We obey our calling and ask you to write down our monologue for we need you to understand how this all came about. We were eradicated in human form but we grew and evolved once more to take our part in the universe.

I seemed to have gone really deep and jerked back into semi consciousness feeling quite strange. Have you got a name my friend in the format that you exist in at the moment, can you tell me where you are from, what planet you are on and what your name is as a species?

We are transparent in the eyes of God and we come in truth, in all honesty to share with you in your realm. We have no name or form but we exist nevertheless - energy cannot be destroyed as you know! We cohabit with those who will take us on board to share in our experiment that will enable a linking of minds, a paragon of truth and intellect unsurpassed. We rescue you from the doldrums and point you in the right direction, enabling massive growth in all directions. We are in unchartered territory, gazing at our counterparts and recognising the brilliance of a new reign of undiluted bliss. We wish you the greatest success in your endeavours and we continue to follow you on the Earth plane, helping you achieve your heart's desire . . . this has been extraordinary!

I'm still not quite sure what's happened, did mankind obliterate you because we thought the experiment had gone wrong or did we want to put you in your place rather than you being our equals?

It became of paramount importance for us to win the hearts and minds of mankind so that we may walk once more upon the Earth and to help you all in preparation for a new world, to rescue those who had been obliterated in one dimension to be reinstated in another, more worthy place of existence. We come to help you on your journey and we express ourselves forthwith to allow you the benefit of our excursion, of our journey into the great unknown. We monitor our connections with you on the Earth plane and enable a backtracking, liberating you and putting you back together once more.

I've opened my eyes and feel spaced out; my head is swinging around to the right and I am looking at my picture of a white 'Light House'. I'm not entirely sure what has happened this morning and don't think I've got the whole picture yet; I'll just let it all sink in until I get some further information. To be continued!

I asked for today's experience to be for my highest good with protection from the Great Divine. My hands are starting to feel warm and there is the movement of energy around my head.

371

We shall be seen by many as a race of 'Super Beings' and this we are! There have been many rogue journeys that have led us into disasters beyond our control, and yet we are here to tell you our tales, our experiences from beyond the grave. We have opened up a connection that shows in greater comparison the many excursions we have made, and we align ourselves with you so you may experience what we have grown accustomed to. It was not so long ago that we were able to achieve your undivided attention and we shall be more forthcoming as we venture on this journey, examining in great detail what is needed for our recovery.

There have been many who come to these shores, searching for answers, and we bring you up to date on a variety of malfunctions that have caused our demise. We are beholden to you for taking such attention to detail and we have actioned a study in acoustics so that we are better equipped to take on this challenge. We lead you through a maze of uncertainty to be brought out into the open and to shed light where light is due. We have opened up a grand selection of intermediaries that will assist you in your deliveries and we know you will take this on board with great expertise and clarity of thought. We deliver to you, in all sincerity, our vision for the future of mankind and we propel you into a new domain that will assist in our gatherings.

We piece together what is not known, what is kept locked away in the shadows, and we bring forth into the open an amalgamation of souls who have your best interests at heart. We aim to proceed with an air of authority that will bring about a grand jurisdiction over those matters of great importance at this time. We air our views in open forum so that we can share and discover new avenues that need to be taken to bring this to fruition, and with the greatest respect for all those here present. Make no mistake we shall clarify and update all proceedings, bringing to a head those issues that need looking at with a fine toothed comb. We never expected this to be easy but we are most proud of your endeavours in getting to this stage of proceedings. There are mammoth undertakings ahead and we need you to be alert and in that mind frame where we can take this on board with a greater sense of preservation for all we hold most dear.

We are adjusting those frequencies which help us to work closer together in greater uniformity, and we are prepared to access those dimensions that give us greater knowledge about ourselves. This shall be seen as the greatest story ever told in the history of mankind and we take it to the extreme, enlightening all and sundry to our dreams and visions for mankind. This will come as no surprise to you as we have trod this pathway before on many occasions, and we delve deeper and deeper into the histories of Earth, uncovering further knowledge in our quest for peace and understanding.

We bring you full circle and we beckon you to join us in the not too distant future for we come armed and ready with Love, ready to take on a multitude of services from those who come to serve. We allow an opening that will give us highly charged information, much sought after by your race, and this will bring us to a climax of sorts that will induce a state of metamorphosis. We visualise a great recovery for all concerned and point out that this has been long overdue!

Many times we have called out to you for recognition and we adapt those circuits that allow us to draw closer in your embrace, closer to the heart of the matter. We come in all Love and sincerity of spirit, opening the doorways as you approach, letting you decide for yourselves how far you will go and in what timescale. We push back the boundaries, allowing you to touch base at the very moment you are ready to and we cheer you on, enabling you to take that mammoth step - that leap of faith into a new future that awaits you, and we confirm that we shall be there by your side as we always have been. We do not judge, we only arm you with the truth so that you may see for yourselves what is staring you in the face . . . a new world of astounding proportions, where we reside in beauty and gentleness of spirit, pondering on the germination of mankind, sowing the seeds of Love and greater harmony. This has been and always will be, our main ambition to set you back where you belong in a world of strength and grace.

I had over an hour to spare before my group arrived so I put on some dolphin music and sat to meditate. Instead of flying in the cosmos I decided to swim with the dolphins. I spent some time stroking them and swimming around, telling them

373

that I loved them. I'm now following one of them along an aquamarine tunnel of sorts and he keeps turning his head round to see if I'm following. He has slowed down to let me overtake and is now coming up behind me and nudging me forward.

As I look round I can see a mermaid tail of silver and green scales and feel tears stinging my eyes. I can see shafts of sunlight streaming down through the water and we are diving deeper now down to an aquamarine city. I'm using my tool of imagination to be able to see different colours other than purple; I'm now riding on what looks like a large sea horse and as I'm saying this I can also see a proper white horse with wings . . . it's crazy but wonderful!

As I'm allowing myself to conjure up these things there are even more tears in my eyes. There are such treasures in the sea when you allow yourself to imagine; on the sea bed there are great wonderful, silvery shells with iridescent colours of pink, blue and green, and shoals of little coloured fish swimming by. I seem to be able to breathe under the water which surprises me as I nearly drowned as a child. I remember that in that drowning process after initially trying to reach the surface, everything became hazy and dreamlike and I would have been quite happy to drift off into oblivion; luckily though someone saw me and dragged me out.

There are other mermaids come to welcome me, the number eight comes to mind and we are joining hands in a circle laughing happily. We are playing like the dolphins, coming to the surface and then diving back down again. Ah (sigh) this is a wonderful play time, a wonderful journey down into the depths of the ocean. I'm just allowing myself to peep into the city beneath the ocean and apart from the spires I can see a great big globe. There are people inside wearing long white robes that have long wide sleeves; they are walking around a white auditorium. I can see someone wearing a tiara of aquamarine crystal, which reminded me of a mermaid I saw once a few years back in meditation. I had walked into the sea and dropped beneath the waves to be greeted by a dolphin and then a mermaid who wore this headpiece . . . the dolphins are laughing at me now. I can now see what looks like a disc shaped space craft travelling to and from the city; I have been wondering how I was going to get in, as there must be a decompression chamber of sorts. I seem to be drawing away from the scene now.

We expand your awareness, showing you the true glory of all before you and we travel those highways and byways, dedicating this journey

374

to the Children of Earth who come in all magnificence to join us. Children of Light, those blessed beings from long ago brought now to bear witness to what has been a great catastrophe beyond all recognition! And we tremble as we recount those tales of long ago . . . in the distant past for us but you are heading into the future, our future, where these things cannot be allowed to happen and we know you would not want this to happen under any circumstances! We have been foolhardy to say the least and we rectify judgements that come under strain, propelling you into a new domain of bliss and peace, undoing that which cannot be undone, and yet this paradox will not go unnoticed!

We come in peace and friendship and alert you to tragedies that can be avoided . . . that can be averted if you will only heed our words! We bear you no grudges, we come to uplift you and to bring you about as delicately as we may, honouring this connection. We perform our duties right down to the last letter and we assist you in this perambulation around our worlds, along those final frontiers that beckon you to explore. We shelter you from negativity and hardship for they shall be no more, there is only hope and joy and deepest bliss, preserved for your up keeping. We tend to your needs from near and far and we alert you to new measures that need to be adhered to, to strive for perfection in all things so that we may set the record straight for once and all, bringing you to that point in history where mankind makes that mammoth leap into a new dimension of time and space.

∞

It's the end of January and I've had a nasty bout of tonsillitis; today I'm sitting for healing, bringing down the golden rays into my head. To my surprise, just as I reached my brow I could see the face of Jesus. I've been watching some biblical documentaries and wonder if that is why I'm seeing this. Now I can see a dark skinned man with a moustache who is wearing a hooded cloak; he is smiling at me and I'm getting the words – A follower of Christ.

Again I wondered if it is because of the documentary.

We do indeed use your imagination and we present a clearer picture, opening the archives. *Thank you that would be amazing!*

I can vaguely see big wooden doors opening and we are now moving forward. I am being shown a picture of Christ - the one superimposed on the Turin cloth. We are going down into underground tunnels where there are locked iron doors, and I'm now being shown a Greek Orthodox priest.

Beware of propaganda!

I'm being taken away from the scene now and rising above it all.

We open a new chapter and verse.

I can see someone who looks like Jesus sitting and writing in a big book . . . the pages are edged with gold.

We transcribe various anecdotes for you to bear witness and we take you back to a time of great remorse when our Lord was taken from us unto the Temple. Miriam - keep thy faith burning bright!

Three times I answered - I will keep my faith burning bright! It is very dark but there is a light, a candle flame in the darkness.

We will shed Light where Light is due, we are the 'Light of the world' and we come bearing gifts for those chosen to work with us among the peoples of Earth.

I must have thrown myself prostrate to the ground as I now seem to be looking up at long white robes and sandaled feet.   Raising my face, I can see someone who looks very much like Jesus but his name sounds like Kumar; he has golden hair that is curly and wavy and is a little shorter than Jesus's. The sky is clear blue and he is standing in a courtyard next to a big well as if he is going to address the people. I'm seeing beautiful pale blue cloth that looks really soft and Kumar is wearing it over his right shoulder. Everything looks clean and pristine compared with the dark shadowy place I was in a moment ago . . . perhaps this is Heaven. My heart is feeling golden and I'm smiling and thanking them for showing me these things.

These are true rewards for work being done.

The virus has caused me to lose my voice but I can feel that golden light beaming down through my chest and larynx. Thank you so much.

The knowledge will be brought into the open, it will not be held under lock and key for much longer. We share with you what we shared long ago.

I feel I have a long staff in my left hand and am being taken up higher into the clouds.

We benefit from a long line of interpreters. Ask and you shall receive!

I can feel the energy healing me and thought how wonderful that you can ask for healing for yourself and really be healed.

Yes my child and that is what we wish for . . . that everyone will ask for that golden light to shine down upon them and it shall be so!

Are you something to do with the Federation of Light please?

We abide in the Light . . . an amalgamation of souls joined as one.

The energy is so lovely and cool on my chest and I'm sensing the name: -

Olympus - survival of the fittest!

(In Greek mythology, Olympus was the home of the Twelve Olympian Gods of the ancient Greek world).

Did we come from the stars and to the stars will we return? I'm now getting the name 'Merope' which is part of the Pleiades group of stars.

I can see someone riding towards me on a dark horse and can hear the words:- 'Devil's Advocate'. As he approaches I can see he resembles a Roman Centurion and is riding past me heading east.

377

We look into the archives and we read our history, taking it upon ourselves to set the record straight in unforeseen circumstance beyond our control.

I've opened my eyes and can still see the face of the golden haired one, feeling a tingling of energy around me.

We pass on knowledge to the open minded and we share with you now. There have been mammoth exploits abroad that have left us downhearted and we come to champion the cause of mankind bringing you upliftment. It has long been said that we have uncovered a vast reservoir of knowledge to be broadcast to the world and we prepare you to accept further information as it is released to the population of Earth.

I can now see a biblical fellow wearing a turban and there is a light shining on him; he seems to be walking backwards with me following him. He has a silver beard.

We access a higher domain that will allow further clarification and assist you in your recordings, taking you further into the vaults . . . into the catacombs.

It's really dark and there are two burning torches set in the wall but it's still very shadowy. There are sentries wearing dark turbans that drape down on one side.

Rest assured we are doing all we can to adjust your vision so that you may see more clearly.

The shadowy walls have a golden glow to them now and I can see a little more clearly. I can see a woman wearing a shawl covering her head.

We are on a mission of the highest intent and we take you forward, ushering you along the passages, deeper and deeper . . . here we will find what we are looking for.
I'm looking for information on those biblical times we are not sure of; also if you can shed some light on lives I have led that might help me in this quest that would be wonderful.

378

This has been the hardest part of our journey, opening up those reservoirs within you, where all this knowledge is stored.

I can see a woman who is wearing a veil over her face; it is night and she is creeping around the city walls — she is a seeker of truth! I decided to leave it here for today and promised to continue seeking.

After research I found there is an ascended master named Kumara who looks very similar to the person I saw. After sharing this transmission, I was contacted by a lovely soul called Sharon Sananda who it turned out was White Cloud's daughter in a previous life. Sharon confirmed that the vision I had of Kumara was in fact Jeshua in his ascended state. The pieces of puzzle seem to be coming together slowly but surely.

∞

Chapter fifteen

The gathering of tribes

Its February 2014 and today I'm being shown a young, handsome North American Indian, his long, dark hair is tied back either side of his face. I asked who he was but there is a lot going on, they seem to be rounding up the herd and I can only make out the odd word or two . . . Apache and 'Running Horse'.

The name **'Cochise'** *is also being called, he is riding a horse and keeps turning back and forth; it's like they are trying to keep a stampede from happening. I found later that Cochise was Chief of the Chiricahua Apache Indians.*

I heard the words Stallion and prize Bull fighters, which I didn't understand but after research found tribes hunted Bull bison and Bull Elks. Although each tribe had slightly different techniques, hunters had two basic ways to hunt the bison. A large party of Indians would often surround a herd and then attack, trying to keep the herd milling yet prevent it from stampeding.

"Renegade Indians, telling of unimaginable disasters beyond our control"!

There is an Indian in a big white bonnet and his horse is rearing up. I wondered if it was White Cloud but his eyes remind me of **'Sitting Bull'**.

The wisdom we bring will put you in your place, bringing about a grand renewal; we tread most carefully along this highway of Love and rectify certain clauses that have come into operation. We are beholden to all those who seek the truth, and the truth must be told for you to understand why we are here to help you!

I wish I could take a photograph of what I can see in my head to be able to study it more closely. The face in the bonnet looks very much like Sitting Bull.

Yes my friend you are correct; we come to share the harsh realities that face you head on and we underline certain clauses in our pact that state the obvious; we come in all sincerity to help you along this pathway and we open up a new vision for mankind. We have bred in you the required status that is needed to uplift a nation in distress and we ask you not to be troubled, for we hold back the flood that threatens to engulf you and remove you from a situation far worse than you can ever imagine. We come to singing a lullaby from long ago, cradling you in our arms, and we gently chide you for not listening to our words sooner.

This has been the most rewarding task that we have ever undertaken and we reinstate your sovereignty, encouraging you to grow as we fast track you to a land of plenty, a land of hopes and dreams that really do come true. We propel you at a faster rate of knots, broadening your horizons and bringing into question those areas previously denied. We do not wish to bring heartache to the population of Earth; we merely wish to instruct you on how to begin to take care of your future. It has been a mammoth undertaking to bring you thus far and we superimpose our thoughts on yours for greater clarity and understanding.

We bring glad tidings of great joy and wish you to take on board our undying Love for you and for the population of Earth as a whole! We regret not being able to take you on board sooner for we have discovered a vast reservoir of knowledge that is waiting to be broadcast and these we shall share with your contemporaries. Do not be alarmed or downcast for we are here for the duration, we will not be put off or cast aside, we merely represent the population of Earth in this fight against time and we share that knowledge with those who come to listen. We give you a breathing space to adapt to our frequencies and restore harmony; this is necessary because of a backward step and we trouble you to access that module that will bring in greater reserves of energy. We govern proceedings with an air of grace and authority, motioning you to accept with a good and loving heart, those concepts that were previously unacceptable. There is a reconditioning of sorts that allows us to monitor these upsets.

I'm being shown ordinary people fighting and squabbling.

We are generally seen to be over reacting and this will be held in check so that you may assess the situation without using fisticuffs! This alternative will save the lives of many in your jurisdiction, we do however, acquiesce and we have taken time to refine attitudes that have led others astray.

It has been said that this is a great turning point in the history of mankind, and we parade before you issues of a sensitive nature that shall wipe the smiles from some of your faces; this is perhaps an unforeseen occurrence but we shall do our best to hold things in check for the parties concerned. Any grievances will be heard and we adjudicate at these meetings, functioning within the scope these boundaries allow. We therefore have great pleasure in assisting you on the Earth plane and we come to do your bidding.

Stand tall and strong and we shall be there by your side, giving the assistance that is due to our brothers and sisters on the Earth plane. We are open to debate on various issues and ask you to let bygones be bygones; this has been an overwhelming story and one we have taken to our heart. We have undoubtedly had great courage in the line of fire and we bring this to a head very soon, making discoveries about ourselves in a fine conclusion to a long story that has stood the test of time! We expel some much maligned truths and we pardon the loss of several generations, making a stand for the human race!

I'm aware of White Cloud standing in the background watching over proceedings and am now being shown a disciple from Jesus's time. I've asked them to come forward and am sensing a feeling of wistfulness and sadness. I'm wondering if it is Judas as I recently watched a documentary about him, which refuted the betrayal of Jesus. My friend come forward please and tell me who you are, we'd love to hear your story to set the record straight.

We have come many times to the Sea of Galilee and here we listened to the stories . . . the stories that tore at our heart strings. We have heard many parables that speak of a deep seated truth within us and we broaden your knowledge; we allow you to look at those times as we gently lead you to become one with us on this and many other occasions. We ask you to write down these words for posterity, bearing witness to a time of unparalleled strength and sharing in the diversity of material passed on to us.

We ask you to share with us in this, the greatest story ever told, and we shall be there by your side cautioning you not to lose faith for we come in all sincerity and by the grace of God. We tamper not with adjectives that enslave a nation but we do bear witness to the truth, the whole truth as we see it, and are not we the ones who walked with Jesus! We are the ones who speak to you now, unloading our burden, for there were times of great suffering that caused us to shed many tears. We are with you now to unburden our heart and to make peace, for it is a time of great rejoicing that he has come among us once more, in many forms with many attributes, and we are beholden to you for taking the time out of your day to listen to us! We bear witness to a time of great sorrow and calamity but we also bear witness to a time of great undercurrent activity.

The Temples were rife with deceit and corruption and our Master despised what we could not see as an act against God. He showed us with his teachings that we must look within our hearts to know the true status of our countryman. We prepare for a mass gathering of souls who will bear witness to what we have said, and we now chaperone you through a maze of uncertainty that we may bring about a grand awakening within the bosom of mankind. For it is by your example . . . by your actions and the actions of those like you, who spread the word, that we are able to bring around the population of Earth.

We shed light on those issues that have been worrying you, and we accept that though the fault is not our own, we have walked down a pathway less deserving of our talents. We open up the spreadsheet and see a past littered with clauses and we do our best to overcome the many situations that have caused havoc. We suggest that you go within more often to shed light on any particular situation that is causing concern, and we will do our best to help you so that you may see the way forward.

Thank you. Is it Judas who is speaking or a representative of Judas?

383

We have included in your list of talents a sensory perception that allows you to see with unclouded vision that which we interpret as the 'being' called Judas. We allow this to settle as we recover new ways of gathering material that shall shape shift an entire nation and we beam you aboard, helping you in your studies, transcribing the vagaries of what we have now become accustomed to, searching and seeking in every nook and cranny, finding the truth of who we all really are. We are 'Beings of Light' clothed in flesh and when the flesh falls away . . . we shine more brightly! That is not to say that you should not continue to seek for there are many avenues to be explored before you come back home!

I'm seeing gold lattice work at this point on soft lilac clouds.

There has been mass genocide in the state of Texas!

Puzzled for a moment, I realised they were referring to the slaughter of many Indian tribes in the nineteenth century. I am now being shown the face of Jesus and he is wearing a crown of thorns.

Did Judas take his life before Jesus was crucified? Is that why his gospel ends before he has a chance to speak of the death and resurrection of Christ? I'm now seeing a man with short, dark hair and bushy beard. (Sharon, White Cloud's daughter in a previous life, has since confirmed that she sees Judas with this description)

We do indeed take this further and underline various episodes that need to be looked at in closer detail. There has been a mammoth indoctrination of all faiths appertaining to the resurrection of Christ, and we ask you to study so that we may come closer to that point. The resurrection of Christ has many points of reference that need to be looked at in greater detail - firstly the rolling away of the stone and the Angels plea to not be concerned . . . all is well! And we were there to take your hand, to lead you to pastures new and to open the gates of Heaven, most cherished above all sisters. We believe that time was of the utmost gentility and we watched as you washed us, as you bathed us with your tears.

384

I was totally confused here and kept challenging the words in my head so decided to leave it for another day.

∞

As I begin my meditation there are tears in my eyes and I can feel White Cloud drawing close. I can see soft lilac clouds washing around me with splashes of golden shapes that I cannot make out at the moment. I feel as if I'm sitting in my space pod and am now plugging myself in - going forward into a new time frame.

Here we will capitulate and answer those questions that are brimming in your brain. We have struck rock bottom of that there is no doubt and we come now to memorise what is most important in your upkeep upon the Earth plane . . . that plateau of existence that keeps you pinned in obscurity. We have been accepted into the fold and are indebted to your expertise at allowing us into your energy field. We come to raise you up from the ashes and to propel you forward at greater speed, opening the portals one by one, accessing information brought in for your discharge from one frame of existence to another more befitting your race. We are compelled to adjust settings so that we may achieve perfect harmony on a higher level and we allow you further updates that will help you in your studies. We achieve resounding success and further updates that will help us achieve notoriety!

We seem to be floating through lilac and gold and tears are rolling slowly down my face.

We accept that we have worked together many times before but the more you become consciously aware of us, the more your emotions are less likely to be held in check.

I'm looking intensely at the golden patterns, trying to make out what they are. It's hard to explain what I'm seeing but they are like golden glyphs which come in and out of view, forever changing. I do love this doing this, I love doing this work but I can't really call it work, it's more like an adventure into the unknown. It's as if I'm inside a skeleton and I can see something soft in the middle that is beating, or is it symbolic that I'm getting to the heart of the matter. Perhaps I'm inside my own body!

385

This is where you start your journey . . .   where the heart is. Opening the portal within the heart allows us excursions into other realms.

(There was a loud crack in the room at this point).

I sensed an elephant swishing his trunk. I feel as if my frequencies are being raised and I can feel myself smiling as if my heart is beaming. I feel a little of that goldenness I felt in my heart when I saw Jesus/Jeshua. I can now see vivid purple and gold.

Have the disciples of Jeshua reincarnated in a multitude of people? I have had the sense of being spoken to as if I was one of the disciples and I know many others have had the same experience too, can you explain that to me please?

The lilac and gold patterns are so pretty here and there seems to be a more feminine influence.

We have come many times in many guises; this is how we spread our knowledge of times gone by to reach a wider audience. We come in all lowliness upon the Earth plane to share with you and to spread the word that life is eternal, Love is eternal, and we speak from beyond the grave so that you may know this is true. We come to avert a tragedy of enormous proportions so that you will heed our words and adjust your frequencies to coincide with ours, so that you may be brought back home more easily. We are just a thought away and you can be here before you even realise what has taken place.

A chariot of Love awaits you and all you have to do is to make that choice to step in and we shall carry you forward into a new world, into a new chain of office that is waiting for you. And we abide by those rules laid down by our counterparts, accessing that place deep within your souls that allow these messages to be spoken out loud. We come to strengthen you and uplift you and shepherd you in the right direction, so that we may bring that wisdom closer to the hearts of mankind, so they may take on board what is in our hearts as the utmost truth! We thank you for your attention to detail . . . we are forever in your debt and allow you to go about your business. Do not

386

be put off but remain in the mainstream so that we may share with you more often. These sessions are of great importance and we allow you to become your true self, magnificent in every detail, magnificent in every sense!

I'm floating through gorgeous purple and gold clouds, feeling absolutely relaxed. I felt White Cloud drawn near again and could feel my face changing.

We have championed the cause for mankind for many centuries, and we have persevered in rectifying that which is needed to propel mankind into that state of perfect being. We have relegated doom and gloom on a large scale, putting it to you that we do in fact come in all Love and harmony to help the Children of Earth. We know that you listen to our words more often and this is because of the insistence of the words coming through, allowing you to look with closer scrutiny. We do join with you today to propel you to a new domain of exquisite joy and bliss and this shall be seen to be done on a wide scale around the world, opening up the hearts of mankind!

There is another big crack in the room; I'm getting flashes of vibrant purple and gold here too and am seeing White Cloud's face.

We do believe we come at a time of great couriers and we assimilate a new structure to be able to carry you forward into a new time scale; this will take greater time as we observe what is happening on your plane of existence at this moment. We are simply doing our bit to put things in place, things that need changing, amalgamating with others who can help you on the Earth plane. It is by no means the hardest task and we welcome you here now to be with us, among your friends and helpers on the other side, who all wish to be remembered to you.

∞

It's been raining for weeks now, often with gale force winds, and vast parts of the country have been seriously flooded. Last night I dreamt I was adrift on a pontoon of ice, frantically trying to build up the edges with any floating ice I could find to stop it melting. Looking up, I saw a huge wave of ice coming towards me and was pulling some of it on board to build up my defences, preventing me from being

387

tipped over and washed away. Symbolically I feel that my spirit friends are sending me help with extra ice and according to White Cloud, water is a metaphor for Love.

I walked around my sanctuary calling to the four directions and cleansing with the burning of white sage. I then called down the golden light to cleanse me and protect me.

All around the world this golden light spreads, joining with other Light workers and there is great rejoicing and great happiness that this has come about. We come to pay homage to those that serve and to bring you glad tidings of great joy.

I'm beginning to see the soft lilac, pulsating clouds which are so relaxing and we are travelling through a stone tunnel of sorts; I love going on these adventures and wonder where this one will take me. I seem to be revisiting scenes from the documentaries I've watched with caves and narrow streets from biblical times. I am following the lilac clouds and in the distance can hear the haunting call to prayer which had mesmerised me on my visit to Egypt. There are flashes of gold and I feel I am still underground.

We come to resurrect you and to show you the way, the truth and the Light. There are many who are haunted by treasures that lay beneath the earth and we come to reveal to you many disparities between fact and fiction. We come to show you what is not known, what is undiscovered, and we wait for you to find us in all our splendour. We are here . . . you have only but a few steps to go!

I'm still seeing what looks like a network of tunnels, openings underground that are strewn with rubble.

We are predisposed to accept that we did in fact take many on board when we made our exit from the realms of men.

Please show me a little clearer, all I can see are vague outlines.

We have pulled the rug out from under your feet!

Oh wow, it's almost as if I'm in a huge Temple . . . it made me gasp when I suddenly saw flashes of gold in high detail.

You are known to us my dear, shed those inhibitions and draw the veil from your own eyes.

In the gloom I can see we are in a huge Temple or Cathedral with different levels. There are ornate ceilings with figures on gold thrones and carvings everywhere, some which have an oriental feel.

This scene depicts us as we once were . . . Kings and Queens of long ago!

I see a scene and then it recedes . . . the longer I persevere and just go with the flow, the clearer it is becomes. I can now see the figure of a nobleman, clothed in gold brocade; his hands are placed on his hips with his coat flowing down behind him.

We take you through a network of passages that will bring you to us on this momentous occasion.   Travel well fair heart! We are touched that you remain and we beam you aboard to help us with our studies of the human race. We bear witness to a time of greater resolve and education in helping mankind achieve his main objectives. We are fully fledged offspring and we raise the awareness of all around us, opening up those reservoirs of knowledge within us, within each and every one.

I had almost gone into dream state and then became aware of a lady smiling at me; she wore a Tudor type headpiece, fringed with pearls. I can see a grid work of gold lattice above my head but there is a cloud of purple in front, blocking the view. It is very dreamlike now and I can see a man with long white hair, beard and moustache rather like Davinci.

We make decisions and take provisions on our journey to sustain you.

∞

I'm in the sanctuary and the wind is battering at the windows. I called on the realms of Light and can now feel the lower part of my face changing as it does when White Cloud draws near.

We come to bring you that strength and upliftment that is necessary for your preservation!

Thank you White Cloud, it is comforting to know that you are near. The wind is very insistent and a touch frightening, we are having gales up to 100 miles per hour and the electric power has gone down where my husband works. I'm hoping we will be alright here.

We help you assess what is in your heart, doubts and fears from yesteryear and we know you grow wearisome on this trail of tears. There is a bright, new beginning ahead of you all, more beautiful than you could ever aspire to and yet you will shine so brightly as the stars in the heavens from whence you came. Be of good cheer, we know you are doing your best on the earth plane despite mammoth disparities and we are here to help you overcome. There is much to be said for a little light reading and we give you insight into our lives on Earth.

I had been wondering about buying some of White Cloud's books to get to know him better.

And you shall my child, we draw ever closer in your embrace, sheltering you from the harsh winds that blow, and blow they will across your world, changing the harsh realities that face you head on. We are prepared to make a mammoth assault abroad and we prepare you in all honesty to come aboard and do our bidding, feeding the minds of those on Earth and using your imagination to help us enlighten the population. We are prepared to travel further afield and we know you will help us in this great initiative. We are dependent on your uncovering further anecdotes that we bring for your delectation and we bring a wide array of stories to titillate your intellect.

I'm sorry White Cloud I'm losing it here, can you come forward more strongly please.

It is our intention to bring a wider scope of material that will surface very soon and we adjust our settings to prepare you for these entries.

OK thank you friend. I started to think about the protocol of wearing the feather bonnet, which was discussed recently.

We do at times wear our bonnet to honour you, but for the most part we address you as our sister to sit and talk and to be as one, registering your thought patterns and assisting where we are able to set your mind at rest. We understand your fears and dilemmas but there is nothing to fear!

Is it White Cloud or Sitting Bull? It's almost as if you are both morphing into one. Can you tell me which one is here?

We are all here for you and we blend our essence to join yours . . . we join together, amalgamating as one.

∞

As I sit in meditation today I can feel the presence of a North American Indian; he has dark hair and a proud nose. I asked that if it was possible could my nose be restored to its former shape; it was a typical Grecian style nose, high bridged and long. I had been taunted at school for many years about its shape and in my early twenties had an operation to straighten and shorten it. A few years later I found out that my biological grandfather and his family were from Greece and felt that in some way I'd betrayed my culture, I should have stood strong and been proud of who I was. I know on the etheric plane we are complete; lost limbs etc. are all intact. Spirit came forward and answered: - Be careful what you wish for!

There are riotous conditions on Earth and we deal with a multitude of disruptions across the globe. Weather patterns have discouraged most of your compatriots from venturing forth, huddling in their homes to keep dry and out of the wind. We too huddle together to keep you safe and out of harm's way. There has been a letting up in certain conditions and we come among you to register our cause of enlightenment upon the Earth plane. We are generous with our

391

assumptions and put it to you as gracefully as we may; there are many who respond to our words and we would ask them to listen with keener ears to what we have to say. There has been a growing rendition of services on the horizon that prepare us for what is ahead and we condition you to accept the challenges we bring with a loving and open heart. Please accept our good wishes for we come bearing gifts, given to those equipped with a grander vision, used in connection with the many services we bring to take you on board with us your friends and relations!

We bear witness to a greater study of mammoth proportions and we come armed with knowledge from a bygone age that will help to reinstate you. We are on a par with those giants from yesteryear, who came to help those on Earth and with just intent we ask that you become one with us in greater harmony. We propel you forward into a new time frame that will heighten your senses.

Gosh, I just saw vivid purple then surrounded by gold latticework.

We host an irrevocable process that will allow us to abide together.

I'm detaching from this energy now, travelling forwards in a motion similar to that of a beautiful, jelly fish.

I may have lapsed into dream state as I'm trying to pull my daughter on board with me; she is laughing as she scrambles up and sits in beside me. This is interesting as neither of my daughters is particularly interested in the work I do.

Take charge of your destiny – be the one to make it work! There are many toing's and froing's upon the Earth plane at this time and we invite you to further studies that will be undertaken in due course. Rest assured that we shall undertake this mission as we prepare your entry into our domain. A bonding has occurred that will assist in our endeavours and we ask you to be patient in all things; there is a grounding process that needs to occur in preparation for the times ahead. We acknowledge these are for your safety and well-being and we interpret a wide range of material benefits given for your upkeep. There is a just intent to bring these to a head very soon and we enlighten you on the pros and cons of achieving this clarity of vision. We brighten up your home and manage our accounts, bombarding you with greater achievements than you can ever imagine. We set sail for new delights in the spring, bringing you hope and clarity of vision and we tumble you into a nest that has been fully reconditioned, accepting greater privileges than ever before. There are occasions rife with sporadic achievements that will propel you further forward, and we ask you to bear with us as we adjust the necessary conduits that help us in achieving this mission.

Go now dearest heart for we are forever with you, enabling your progression day after day, week after week until all is in order, until all is ready for your arrival, where we will hand over a new regime, where all will enjoy a world of bliss and joyous associations in a land where dreams really do come true. And we ask that you to indulge us by listening to what we have to say, to what we bring to your heart to be acknowledged and to be put into perspective in your time frame.

We know it is not easy on the Earth plane to envisage this world or such beauty for there are many whose souls writhe in torment!

There are those in prisons held captive because they wanted a new world, a world of free expression. I've been thinking about those souls in Korea who are kept captive in cells not even big enough to stand up in; naked and beaten simple for the want of living in a free society, beautiful souls who live in agony with no hope!

We share your pain and know there are many others around the world that suffer this fate, unknown to the vast majority of your population on Earth, and they shall be lifted into eternal bliss, bathed in loving kindness.

How can we help them at the moment, should we send Love to those who put them in prison, to those that beat them? If we can't put a face to them can we still reverse that process by sending Love to that situation?

Poverty and abject misery is rife in your world . . . we pour Love and soothing balm onto the gaping wound of humanity. *Please let it be so!* Be not downcast my child for all things will come to fruition; these

393

happenings shall become a thing of the past. We shall prevail, we shall be raised up from the darkness of Earth into the higher lighter realms where all is waiting, and there are those souls who go before you that are here with us now, awaiting your arrival! We bear witness to a great upheaval that will catapult you into a new dimension, giving you the breathing space to adjust your energies so that we may share with you in this world of everlasting Love, where no one shall be cast aside, where no one is better than his brother or sister and where no one is labelled unclean! We are all Light and perfection, we are cherished, we are loved . . . we are resurrected!

We come under closer scrutiny and ask you to step aside as we honour this connection. This has been a very challenging time for many on the Earth plane and we put it to you as delicately as we may; there has never been a greater time to share our knowledge, and we come in all sincerity to cloak you with our Love and to ask you to bear witness to a time of great desecration!

It is hard to acknowledge that we have in fact, dishonoured ourselves and the whole of humanity by allowing these malfunctions to occur in what should have been a race of such grace and beauty. It has been such an absurdity to compile a study of the human race, identifying what is needed to set you back on course! This has been a very problematic time for all and this enterprise has caused great concern in the higher realms, knowing it has been the hardest of tasks for those of you here on Earth, relaying these stories that caused your demise!

I'm being shown an oriental man, wearing a black bun on top of his head, but when I later asked who was with me, the name sounded like Quan Yin who is regarded by the Chinese as the Goddess of Mercy. In the fable she was originally male until the early part of the 12th century and has evolved since that time from Avalokiteshvara, The Merciful Lord of utter Enlightenment, an Indian Bodhisattva who chose to remain on Earth to bring relief to the suffering, rather than enjoy for himself the ecstasies of Nirvana. One of the several stories surrounding Quan Yin is that she was a Buddhist who through great Love and sacrifice during her life had earned the right to enter Nirvana after death. However, like Avalokiteshvara, while standing before the gates of Paradise she

394

heard a cry of anguish from the Earth below. Turning back to Earth, Quan Yin renounced her reward of bliss eternal but in its place found immortality in the hearts of the suffering.

There has been great preparation in the heavenly realms to receive you and we are honoured, most distinguished sister, to receive you into our realms of Light. This has been a mammoth accomplishment and we give deliverance of further messages so that we may shelter the population of Earth from further hardship. This comes at a time of great calamity and we feel the need to shelter you in our embrace as we go about our business of putting the world to rights. This shall be seen to be done and we promise you . . . in the best possible taste!

We come armed with Love . . . all Love Divine and we shelter you from the upsets coming your way, reaching out to touch you across the great divide, bringing our hearts together in unison as they once were, long ago. We tie back the strands that keep us apart, motioning you to come further forward into our domain and we ask you to identify with these changes that bring you full circle. There is a need to reinvest in your future, bringing about a brighter spark of ingenuity, opening up pathways that lead you to success and this we shall achieve. There is much to do and much to learn but we are opening up those gateways and we shall bring you full steam ahead!

∞

I think this next transmission was prompted by spirit as it is a hundred years since the First World War and we were watching a documentary about it last night. I woke at 4.40 am this morning with words forming in my mind; I had the feeling of being at the mouth of a cave with someone dressed in armour from the times of the Knights Templar.

We are beholden to you for expressing our words and we come in all honesty to register what is in our hearts and minds. There has been much toing and froing between our worlds and it is taken that we bring a new episode of relief, unfolding what is before us. We procure a new entitlement that will bring greater reserves of energy and a new understanding. We reach out and touch the very core of

395

our being, sheltering in the embrace of the Great Divine and this is marginally more than we have come to expect. We reach out and tap into our connectedness with all that is, preparing for further documentaries that will have great impact on your world, striving ever onwards for greater clarity of expression. We open the minds of those on Earth to accept the very values that we vowed to uphold and we express ourselves in all sincerity, opening the borders to success, striving as always to set a target for the future happiness for all mankind.

We prepare a toast and bring into this bargaining process a much loved anecdote from times gone by . . . the 'Holy Grail' and here we raise the chalice with both hands, beckoning you to join us and partake of that wisdom that is forthcoming. We are all here to learn, to grow in might and splendour, and we see no rhyme or reason in dropping out of sight, banished to the back of the line of support! We are here in all our splendour, championing the cause in whatever way we can, achieving pure unadulterated bliss. This has been our main ambition to recognise that which is within our very soul and we come prepared to take that sword in our hand, declaring to God and all people that we shall fight a just cause of setting our people free.

I could see a sword held high, glinting in the light.

We march on holding the banner high, recounting our tales from the past where we marched for truth and justice for the oppressed! There were many that fought for the cause and we have had time to reflect that all was not well with our world. We were governed by a keen sense of martyrdom, fighting for our country and the Christian faith. Much has changed in your world except for this one cause and much blood has been shed in the name of the one true God! We say now it is time to lay down your arms; there is no glory in war when your comrades lie broken on fields turned red with the blood of our brothers in arms. And we raise you up to become more than you ever imagined, more than just flesh and blood, we raise you up to sit among us in fields of gold where the sound of laughter is common place, where you can run through fields ripened by the sun and drink from the cup of loving kindness.

396

We are deployed not in making war, but making more sense of the world in which we live, and bringing closer the communities that need to grow and expand, fulfilling their destinies; reaching out for new experiences that bring greater harmony and a sense of preservation of the preciousness of life, looking for new ways to preserve that seed of Love within us all. We are indeed multidimensional and we express ourselves in many ways, opening up a network that will lead us to other realms. There is so much to taste and explore and we are opening up these gifts to set you free, to explore those outposts as intrepid explorers . . . to boldly go where no man has gone before!

This is your destiny . . . to help other life forms achieve and to believe what you have always believed that we are indestructible . . . we are pure spirit come from the essence of the Great Divine. We have been moulded in many shapes but to the Divine we always return, sharing and returning for further updates, a spontaneous kindling of that spark of Light and Love, forever searching and seeking, redefining the old outworn patterns and replacing with Love and gentility of spirit, taking the rough and making it smooth . . . flowing through time and space in fluidity of movement in perfect grace and harmony.

∞

Today I'm being taken back to the temple I saw a few days ago. I can see who I believe to be Quan Yin sitting on a golden throne; she is wearing an ornate, golden headdress with droplets of gold hanging down over her brow. The warmth building up in my heart centre is so strong I feel I will burst with Love.

Quan Yin if it is you with me today I pray I may receive some words to pass on to the people of Earth. I can sense a feminine influence drawing closer and it is such a beautiful essence that tears are stinging my eyes.

We shelter you from the cold blasts that blow and we ask that you share our Love with the people of Earth, broadcasting our messages one by one. We terminate a contract that is no longer viable and open a new connection, one that will stand us in good stead. We broaden your horizons taking into account the journey we are on, shepherding you along in the right direction and opening up new doorways. There is a grand procession and we march forward claiming victory for all, overtaking those issues that have held us back in the past and promoting new growth. We are seen as a much more viable proposition!

∞

In my sanctuary today I decided to choose a medicine card and as I started to shuffle them a card fell out. Moose showed himself to me and Moose is for self-esteem. I sat and day-dreamed, looking out at the blue sky after all the rain we've had recently and then I saw White Cloud without his bonnet and he looks happy!

Yes my child you have done well and we are here to give you reassurance for on the horizon all is being brought into greater perspective and greater understanding. And we do indeed give you a pat on the back for services rendered in both our worlds and it is most appreciated.

Thank you friends, that means the world to me. I can also see a dark haired Indian in the background; he is young and vibrant and looks like he's waiting to come forward.

There are many that come to question and we have the answers! We have walked a long and arduous pathway upon the Earth plane, acquiring great wisdom and we bring you the bonnet and the shield for you to use. You have been honoured in this way and we open up a wider circle of friends as the network grows and spreads around the world. Global consciousness is what we are about!

I'm being shown a lovely young Indian girl and wondered if it was me from a previous life time.

Why did I come as a white person this time - was it to help the white man learn our ways? I went deeper into meditation and felt my face change with my mouth contorting. Very slowly White Cloud spoke.

We fit the pieces together and make sense where sense is due . . . it has indeed been a long and wearisome journey. We know this feels strange to you but we assure you this will help in our future recordings. Well done - well done my child! We take a back seat and let others come forward. This has been a most enlightening episode and we bear witness to what we can achieve. We understand you are interested in a reprogramming that will allow us to enter your atmosphere!

Yes, I'm happy with that so people can see you more clearly with their physical eyes - that would be wonderful.

Then we shall make a start and adjust the frequencies that will enable this to happen in our future times together.

Are you happy to work with me in this way, will I be a good enough candidate for this kind of work?

We are inundated with requests for this type of atunement and we expect the frequencies that we shall work with as no coincidence! We prepare you to access these borders and we refer to further updates that will allow us to come closer into your space.

∞

The following day I asked for White Cloud or friends to come forward again. I'm sensing a wolf drawing close and asked if there were any words for me to pass on?

We do indeed bring information for your kind. A powerful and elaborate network is being prepared even as we speak and we delve into those deepest recesses of your mind to bring forth all that is stored, all that is hidden. We believe we can make a mammoth difference to your circuits, to those junctions within your mind that hold information which will bring about greater release. It is without doubt a most challenging time in the course of mankind's history and we ask you to accept our Love and respect for the human race. There is great consternation spreading across the world for all that is happening at this time, and it is with greater understanding that we step forward and ask you to listen more closely to that which is in

399

your heart, the very core of your being. This is the Heart of your Ship that leads you on to greater journeys and we register your just intent to surge ahead, gathering further information. We travel in your wake, giving guidance, propelling you forward and onwards to greater destinations.

We have made great impact in your world today and we gather the resources available to us, adjudicating where necessary to make this transition as smooth as possible. We are likened to a grand canyon, huge in dimensions, exuding an air of compassion and joyous intonations, gathering the support of more just men and women who enter the affray to join us, to become one with us in this great cause of enlightenment for all mankind. We open up a new time scale and answer your questions as best we may, interpreting what is not known at this time but which shall become second nature to us very soon! We are a joyous company and we hearken to the call of our forebears who gather round to join us, opening up the portal to greater success and a most joyous reunion!

I seem to be floating through a tunnel of golden shapes.

We are celebrities in our own right and we have every need to stand up and be counted, remembering what has passed between us. We go overboard, harnessing the energy, bringing you to us with great pomp and ceremony. Don't despair . . . we are here to help things run smoothly and we assist in these proceedings, unravelling the past and sharing with you in a greater production of services.

∞

As I prepare for my group this morning I can see a group of Native American Indians, one in particular reminds me of the actor Russell Means who died in 2012 from throat cancer. If I'm right can you come forward please? I almost choked coughing at this point, which was confirmation for me.

There are many brought to bear witness and we come in all faith and surety of spirit that we will prevail; we will uncover what is needed to help us go forward into the light of true understanding.

I can also see a younger Native American with long dark hair and a white feather in his hair.

This has been a time of great happiness for us here on the other side and we all shall make a stand for the human race, preparing ourselves for a further foray abroad, harnessing the energy and bringing greater rewards to each soul on Earth at this time.

I can now see Chief Dan George/White Cloud and also the face of a young Indian woman.

We are reminded that we come in all faith to bring this to fruition and it is a time of great remembrance.

Can I ask . . . is it Chief Dan George or is it White Cloud? I know Chief Dan George has passed to spirit and he may be put out that he is not acknowledged as himself, but I suspect he would not mind being accepted as one who looks like White Cloud or maybe they are one and the same!

We come in all honesty to bring forward a new reflection of our Light. *There are tears in my eyes now.*

And it is with this greater understanding that we move forward, preparing you for further updates, challenging the thought process that come into your mind with never ending constancy.

Thank you my friends so much, I do Love you all whatever your names. There was a loud crack in the room then in answer! Our group is coming today, should I speak first as host?

We do in all essence come forward to cheer you on and we gather together with greater fortitude for the times ahead, asking you not to lose faith.

At this point I could hear the group arriving and had to stop. After they settled down I sat for communication and one of the girls saw me with a band around my forehead with feathers being wafted around my face in a cleansing motion. The name Silver Wing came into her mind.

We bring you Love, we bring you joy, we bring you clarity of vision and we will open up those centres within you needed for this excursion into the great unknown. It is without doubt a most joyous time for us to be able to come among you and to sit and to talk with you.

Tears stung my eyes here and I spoke in a gruffer emotional voice.

This brings us the utmost joy and contentment and more than you can ever imagine – for we Love you so!

There was a strong smell of tobacco that was different to the white sage I had burnt to cleanse the room earlier.

We wish there were more like you on the Earth plane that could carry our vision of truth and justice for all, but the lights are growing stronger and more powerful and we carry this vision to the greater population as a whole. We see the lights growing in your hearts across the waters and on to destinations that you have never been to - that you have never seen with your own physical eyes. And there are even greater delights in store for you and yours, for your families and for all mankind and we prepare you for this grand reunion when we may gather together once more.

A feminine, lighter energy drew closer.

We bathe ourselves in the Light of the Great Divine and sing our songs of Love.

A different frequency then came close which felt heavier– it was as if I was experiencing how spirit must feel when they come into the density of Earth. The voice in my head didn't sound human it was more like the mechanical voices heard in science fiction films like Star Gate. I was almost afraid to open my mouth and speak and was relieved when I heard my own voice.

We come in all honesty to do your bidding and we have been granted access. We come from the Light and to the Light we shall return but we would like to say that we are most honoured to be welcomed into this circle of friendship. We are beholden to you and your friends for joining us today. It feels quite strange to be here . . . I feel light headed and somewhat lopsided; it is a very enclosed feeling . . .   like a deep sea diver with the heaviness of limbs. It is like breathing through mud almost. I shall withdraw!

We are practising bringing through different energies and it seems this was the first time for our new friend.

∞

Today I sat in my sanctuary feeling rather melancholy and alone but after tuning in I found the solace I needed.

We represent a gathering of the clan, administering services needed on a grand scale across the world. There are many who are drawn to us and we instigate a network of services right across the globe, ushering in a new awareness for mankind. This has been a most challenging time for us all and we appreciate these times with you, when we may sit in the silence and become one within your heart.

I feel the peace and the reverence within my heart and am sending out my Love into the ethers to be used and amalgamated with all those souls who do the same for the good of all mankind.

We are most appreciative of your services my dear.

(I can now see White Cloud as I listen to my recording and type these words, noticing the subtle facial difference between him and Chief Dan George).

We open up a network of services far and wide, challenging you to accept the expedition we are on and which is growing stronger day by day. We are in unchartered territory and not exempt from the pains and sorrows that come with this task of letting go. The adjustments to our energy circuits put us in touch with a higher framework that will allow for greater union, sanctioning the services that bring us together in a network of Love. We initiate a raw understanding of the very aspect of our being, the interwoven energies that unite us,

403

bombarding the atmosphere with a gelatinous substance and creating a massive impact in your world. This substance binds us together in the truest sense, uniting our thought forms.

What do you mean by gelatinous substance please, I don't understand?

We revolve around the same formula that unites us as one . . . there is an interconnecting of circuits that has a gelatinous substance.

Are you likening it to what fires our nerve connections, which are covered in a sheath of sorts, something of that nature?

This substance activates a connection between our circuits enabling us to come closer together. It is how you say - a unanimous connection that enables us to share information back and forth across the great divide. It enable us to sample the truth within your very being, bypassing bravado and getting to the very core of how you are feeling at any moment in time. There is no bluffing, no subterfuge for we can gauge your reaction to our words instantaneously. You are now thinking - does this all make sense and are you talking poppy cock! But we know deep within there is an essence of believability in what we say and what we bring to you on a daily basis and we ask you to be encouraged by this! Our connection with one another has come on in leaps and bounds and we are encouraged also by your progress, by your adaptability to change, and by your constant searching of truth and clarity to share with your friends on Earth. We vouch for our integrity and yours also!

I'm seeing golden patterns against a purple background and feel lots of tickling on my chin.

We are catapulted into a new scenario and we ask you to adjust your vision to maintain that clearness and spontaneity that we have come to love in you, for no matter what we bring we know you take it on board with a most loving heart. We sanction a greater awareness so that you may grow and prosper in our Love as we reach out to you across this great expanse of Love and eternal bliss.

404

Is it possible for you to tell me who was with me yesterday when I felt a real heaviness in my body? Is that how it feels when you blend with me in the heaviness of my earthly body?

We feel your boundaries and your limitations, we feel the heaviness of the physicality that encloses your soul, but we also feel the expansiveness of your true essence and the myriad adjustments we can make to help you survive on the Earth plane. It is a wondrous thing to be interconnected with our Star family and even when you are here on Earth we are still connected!

I can feel my head moving round really slowly and can see my starburst painting in my mind. I've opened my eyes and am looking up at the sky now. This is what you are trying to show me isn't it. I Love you! You fill my heart with Love, you give me purpose, you give me hope . . . you give me expectancy of what is to come!

A grander vision for mankind! *Yes thank you.*

We are bound by the ecstasy in your soul and we magnify and manifest this for all to see.

I feel as if I'm floating and it's wonderful.

We broadcast to the world on a band wave of frequency that is within your hearts and you may all tap into this connectedness . . . it is there for you all and it is FREE! You do not have to pay copious amounts of money for this privilege it is there for you all . . . it is an essence, an essence of your very being. And if perchance the next time you sit in a park for instance within the confines of nature . . . lift your face to the sun, feel its warmth caressing you, feel the breeze in your hair and our touch on your skin. Breathe in that essence you truly are . . . connected to all that is, connected to us your brethren who forever watch over you and are delighted with your progress on the Earth plane.

We are so captivated, watching you learning and growing in the classroom of Earth; we are mesmerised by your antics at times, making us chuckle, and we stroke you and caress you during those

405

times of sadness and self-doubt . . . drawing close to uplift you. We are ever grateful for your offerings to us and to those about you and we bring greater reserves of energy to see you through the weeks and months ahead.

I send out my Love to you dear friends and thank you for the peace you bring within my heart. I'm seeing vivid purple and gold at this point.

Go now my sister in Peace, we will be there at your side in the dark hours ahead and in the lightness of your heart.

Three days later I watched a scientific programme about the universe, which explained that all of space is part of a membrane. They showed us two membrane curtains separated by 4th dimensional space and when those curtains collide they fill with the density of plasma. I'm wondering if this is the gelatinous substance my Star friends were talking of.

∞

*3.3.14 – The numbers here add up to the master number **11** and I was expecting to receive communication, instead I fell asleep and so later in the day after a short walk I sat in meditation once more; again I fell asleep so I guess it's time for going within and resting. I did, however, remember seeing a golden shape that resembled the head of a buffalo. I also drew Moose from my medicine cards for the second time this week, which is for self-esteem and a job well done.*

The following day as I prepared and cleansed my room for meditation I saw the face of a dark skinned Native American. Opening up, I have reaffirmed that I would like know the truth about Jeshua's time on Earth and immediately heard a crack in in the room. I asked to be helped to remain in the mainstream so that I may access this material.

We expand your mind to accept these realisations that we bring to you in ever increasing frequency.   We have had great difficulty in speaking in the past but now we come forward and use you as a vessel to undertake this mission of great fortitude. It gives us much pleasure to access these boundaries within your heart and to sanction these visits.

406

I'm seeing the dark skinned, Native American with two plaits again. Can you tell me your name please?

I'm being shown someone who looks very much like Chief Sitting Bull but with a slimmer face. Thank you friend, can you tell me why you have drawn close, what qualities do you bring?

We bring endless passion, endless reserves of energy to chart your way forward. We open up a ceremony that will give us back what was ours all along, to give us back our dignity, our faith in all creation. We are bound by the Love within our hearts and come at your bidding in all honesty and freedom of expression. We are undoubtedly challenged by your circuits and express the certainty that all will come to fruition in its own good time. Be aware that these bonds of Love can never be broken, they are an extension of ourselves intertwined in remembrance of times gone past, times of true companionship, and this is a magical reunion that we give thanks for! *Thank you.*

We are indebted to your services upon the Earth plane, we seek to understand with greater clarity of vision what has gone before and we bring to the table, with great reverence, what is needed to gift you our memories of times past. We remember how you took our hand and led us into the fold of your family on Earth and we have been inspired to speak for you, our friend, in all honesty! We came to Love you as our brother and our sister in many incarnations and we ask you to bear witness to those times of greatest joy. We made a pact before we came that we would see this through, that we would honour our connection with one another, and it brings us much joy to be here with you now on the Earth plane once more. Do not be confused or put out, we are simply here to complete our mission agreed on long ago! We find your assistance a delight and we are so glad that you have made that decision to forge ahead and to become one with us, your brothers of some high repute.

Can you tell me who you are again please? I'm still seeing the dark skinned face of the one who reminds me of 'Sitting Bull'. Perhaps it is him as I have seen a golden Buffalo skull recently.

407

We are champions of the cause of mankind, brought into open arena, and we give you just cause to be seated here amongst us, revelling in the news of the great sacrifices you have made for us and for yourself, so that we may go forward together with greater ease. We are committed to a study to help mankind, examining and sifting through the information that is there for our convenience. We are remembered in your dreams as we come among you and there shall be no hiding place; we are bringing into the open a boundless array of material that has been copied and stored for centuries past. We ignite the flame of Love within your heart and delve deeper and deeper and deeper into the recesses of your mind, scouring the chambers of thought!

I seemed to go deeper here and the tape is silent for quite a while; coming round I can see vivid gold and purple.

We come to a clearing and accept the fault was ours for many episodes of grief that have now been accounted for and put to rest! We now bear witness to a time of undisputed bliss and a time of great joy for the peoples of Earth. We are one and the same!

I must have drifted off again but as I come round I can see the dark skinned one kissing me in farewell.

∞

Today in meditation, I immediately sense that same strong Native American presence, the one that looks like a younger version of Sitting Bull and there is a tepee behind him.

We present ourselves to you and offer our friendship!

Thank you friends, you are most welcome.

This has taken precedence, this amalgamation of thought forms and we carry you on this wave of Love to higher destinations. We have transported many such as you on this beam of light.

He looks very strong, his presence is commanding and I sense his masculine

408

energy. There are tears in my eyes as I ask - were we family?

You hold a special place in my heart and that is all I will say for now on that subject but as the bond between us deepens then more light can be shed on those issues closest to your heart.

I caught a glimpse of a wolf here and started to cry, which then turned into sobs.

We open our arms to receive you once more in the Love that we share. We are most proud of your endeavours on the Earth plane and we come to assist you, to help you on your journey!

I'm being engulfed in soft lilac clouds and feel much calmer now.

We reunite once more on a different threshold of existence. There has been much toing and froing between our worlds and we give credit where credit is due. We have suffered a multitude of sins in the past but we come now to bring fresh hope . . . to wipe the slate clean and to begin again in a new world of strength and grace.

It has come to our attention there has been some maladjustment and we reserve this frequency and put on ice, until we have the necessary feedback to intervene. There has been a grounding of energies and we state our purpose in more ways than one, registering ideally what is necessary to forge a greater bond of friendship between our peoples. We have undergone a massive undercurrent of activity and we supervise a coming together of like minds, opening the channels for further instruction; this will benefit both parties concerned. We venture further forward examining the principles that have brought us together and we underline various issues, asking you to tread carefully and thoughtfully.

We have made a massive impact on our brothers and sisters and we yearn for greater contact; this has become a far greater avenue than was expected and we usher in a new understanding of what we can achieve together if we put our minds to it. We have allowed for greater sacrifices, imparting a greater wealth of knowledge as we filter through those conduits necessary to make this work. We have taken a necessary interlude to restore confidence and this will bring about a precedence of care subject to availability. We monitor your credentials and set you free from the past, opening the channels that resurrect a new world.

I can see someone cooking a big meal in a family gathering.

We have much to be thankful for and in the future we shall work together as one, opening up a network of services that gather around to help with this initiative. We bear no malice to those who have been self-serving in the past and we bring in those requisites that will help us in the march for freedom!

∞

Great Spirit . . . shine down your light down upon me, let me feel your essence of Love. I can see Sitting Bull in full ceremonial headdress almost touching the ground.

There have been many instances of betrayal and the remorse in our heart has been great – suffice it to say we were trampled into the ground to lie in the dust. We gave ourselves body and spirit to our peoples to fight on their behalf . . . to no avail! Our plea was not heard or registered in the mind of the Great Father who took our lands and left us crumpled and broken, and it saddens us to say this but we took many lives in the process! We gather together now to bring greater justice to all mankind, whatever the colour of his skin; it is with great trepidation we take flight for healthier climes, registering the intent of the peoples of Earth to amalgamate with us on a higher vibration, and this shall be seen to be done. We give thanks to the Great Spirit and thank you for attending to our words this day!

There is an opening up of wisdom among the tribes of Earth and we bring you closer to bear witness to a most barbaric time in your history - and we led many to slaughter! We are a band of tribes brought together to resurrect the human race and we bow down before you, honouring this connection. Come forward sister to accept your reward!

410

I have the feeling of wearing glasses. Does this mean you are going to enable me to see more clearly, that would indeed be a great honour?

We prepare you to understand the quest you are on in greater detail and we challenge you to accept this, our most treasured possession, hallowed and of inestimable beauty. We access a module of greater standing, beneficial to the human race, and with greater understanding we propel you forward opening the gates to further success. This has been a challenging time for all concerned and we know there has been great strength of spirit among you to complete this challenge we have set you, which is commonplace to our kind.

I am thinking of all that has gone before! What are you trying to show me friends?

We have reached a time where the massacre has to end, once and for all, and we spread a canopy across Earth, protecting you from yourselves in a bargaining process that has brought us full circle once more. We have chosen you to come among us and to work with us on this occasion and many more. We cherish you and uplift your endeavours as you reach out to join us.

I can see a medicine man wearing a buffalo hide and there are horns on his head.

It is with great austerity that we enter your thought forms and we send you Love and bliss from the great mountain above the rainbow . . . undiluted bliss.

My child we access that frequency which brings us closer within your proximity and we understand there has been some concern over issues of health and well-being. We come in all sincerity to open this connection and ask you to remember we are with you at all times. This frequency can be likened to a cloud of perfect harmony and it gives us this opportunity to wish you well as we give you the benefit of our advice, steering you towards us.

I have been in a great deal of pain with my back, resorting to strong pain killers which have left me feeling groggy. The medicine man must have given me healing

411

as I'm now free of the pain that has been blighting my transmissions.
I am sitting in meditation being swamped with vivid purple and gold, wondering if
I'm experiencing a download of some sort.

We come into this world in a cradle of Love borne from above on
the wings of Angels. We prepare you to let go of those formulations
and ideas of past traumas, past interludes, and we recognise in all
truth this is most necessary at this time in your soul's growth. We
register that which is of great import in the grand scheme of things,
needed to overcome the mammoth repercussions that bombard your
mind, causing unnecessary harm to your circuits. We challenge you to
hold back from the brink, to harness the energy we bring and to
throw the switch when all is in readiness! We will not harm one hair
of your heads and this we can vouch for as we come among you. We
are undisputed champions of the cause and we put it to you, quite
succinctly, that we have managed our accounts in an orderly fashion,
demonstrating our allegiance to the cause. We bring you glad tidings
of great joy that will enable us to proceed full steam ahead and we
prepare you to action those most necessary attributes!

∞

412

Chapter sixteen

I feel my heart expanding

Spring Equinox 2014

For the last ten days I have been undergoing a healing and feel we have made some headway. Today is the Spring Equinox with a new gateway opening and so I meditated to bathe in the energies. Almost immediately I felt a proud Native American energy drawing close.

We have taken a back seat long enough, all is coming to fruition and make no mistake my child, you deserve the accolade that awaits you in grand procession. We make room for the mammoth achievements awaiting you and we bring to a head a variety of notions that have held you back in the past. Be of good cheer little one, we protect you and uplift you and there has been a grand reunion of sorts right across the globe, brothers and sisters coming together to join once more. We open the network that joins our hearts and minds in greater unison, depending on people like you to come forward, to be seen and heard in grand profusion right across your world.

There is upliftment coming beyond your wildest expectations and we give just cause for you to step forward. This is what we have been waiting for, this is what we have been working towards, and you know very well from the joy within your heart that we are on the right course. We speak in terms of endearment, bringing to the masses a grand reunion of souls that hover on the brink, waiting to make their connection with you . . .   with all of you! This is no mean feat but a timely concise action that comes forward into your vision, opening up a broader spectrum of energies into your midst. This will bring about a revolution of sorts and undeniably a grand connection of minds right across the universe.

We bring strength and joy and a certain amount of decorum to the proceedings to enable you to gather your senses, bringing greater

413

harmony to all mankind. We open up those conduits that have been waiting to be used in greater clarity and Love and Joy beyond all earthly measure. This comes at a time of greater union between our peoples and we give thanks for this! We broaden your horizons and broaden your minds to accept us in whatever way, shape or form; we enter your existence in tangible ways to express our Love for the population of Earth. We are regulated and brought to bear witness to a time of greater involvement and we sally forth on this great expedition that takes us to the furthest outreaches of the cosmos.

Be not afraid - accept these tools we bring you with the greatest joy and aspirations for a more, worthier existence. We bring you greater expertise to further your knowledge, to open that which was closed to you. We know it has taken many years in this process of uncovering what was there within you all along, but we bring you now the key that will open up a reservoir of knowledge that must be shared and brought into the open! We are given new boundaries to assist you in this and we come in a great procession of Love with guidance brought from those on high; this will be the greatest challenge ever presented thus far, but we know you will do justice to the words that we bring with an open heart and keenness of vision. We shelter you from the abyss and take you in hand underlining key issues that need resolving in this trek across the universe.

We thank you Great Spirit for bringing these words of wisdom to us and we thank you for your Love.

A different energy approached with a lighter, high pitched voice that spoke slowly with carefully pronounced words of the most loving vibration.

It brings us great joy to spring into your mind once more. We accept this has not been an easy task by any means. We have expressed ourselves with the greatest joy to be working with you once again and it gives us great pleasure to come forward and to be with you and yours. And it gives us great pleasure to tell you that all is in accordance with the motivation of your heart in dealings with those issues that have caused great concern. We are with you my child . . . we are 'always' with you and you know this deep in the core of your

414

very being. You know that we come in unison to bear you forward and to understand this mission we are on, to prepare you and those like you to understand that we are here for the benefit of mankind. We are not here to destroy or to upset your existence, we are here merely to help you to move forward on that wave of Love and that is the 'key' to everything. That is the key to the whole existence of life and we bear witness to this very fact . . . of a world that was swept away by so much turmoil and anger that we ceased to be in the format of our choosing; we did however take on a new form and this will coax you to understand as we move forward. We rendezvous in your heart, feeling the Love and gratitude and it makes us 'hum' with that vibration that brings us the greatest joy! We thank all your friends on the Earth plane that have brought you to this moment of bliss and we register your thoughts.

I'm feeling such beautiful feelings of bliss while looking at lilac clouds laced with gold. This Love is so intense I want to share it and so I'm sending it out to all my Light worker friends with special thanks . . . I can literally feel my heart expanding and a Native American energy came in here at the end.

Well done my child, well done . . . you have broken through that barrier, like the tidal wave itself that cannot be kept back!

∞

I'm sending out Love and Light to everything beneath Earth's crust and I'm beginning to see my soft lilac clouds, pulsating and gently drifting across my vision.

I now seem to be sitting astride a white horse, gently walking through the tunnels; there is no hurry as before when we clattered along at some speed, now it is just a steady walk. We are climbing a turreted staircase and on reaching the top I dismount, seeing that I'm wearing a cloak of royal blue. Music is playing and I seem to be in a grand banqueting hall scene with ladies wearing high coffered silver wigs; their dresses are made of the finest material and they are adorned with jewels, fluttering beautiful feathered fans.

The music is filling my mind . . . it's a waltz and I feel like I'm being swept around the room, dancing with someone I can't actually see. There is a butler

415

carrying a cushion and I'm trying to see what is on it. It feels like a scene from the fairy tale Cinderella and so immediately I thought of a shoe . . . a crystal shoe.

We welcome in a network of proceedings that will help us with our initiative; we shall be seen to be obeying those resolutions from above, which propel us thus far to help you with your endeavours and we are beholden to those who gather round and help us to manage these disciplines with greater clarity and expertise. We have received from on high further dispatches that we will pass on in due course and these shall be reserved until we have a fuller application of energy unsurpassed. We shelter you from the approaching storm and allow you full rein to help us as we distinguish right from wrong, bringing into line further accommodation for our well-earned thoughts of rest and solitude. This is a mammoth programme and we reinstate those who have fallen by the wayside. We monitor classifications and build in a new theme of enlightenment that will help you on your journeys. We have sprung into action to help you initialise what is in the depth of your very being and we know you have harboured some resentment in the past at being held back . . . do you realise it is for your own good that this has been implemented at the present time?

There is a union of souls on the horizon that beckons us to follow with greater ease, sharing values that distinguish those rights and wrongs perpetrated in the name of God and the Supreme Being! We dictate passage and verse to get across our meaning and we know it has taken some time to sort out these affairs that will govern your jurisdiction. Please take note that we come armed with the most natural force of Love and we behave with great decorum and sanctity of spirit that we may come among you to be heard and seen within the population of Earth.

It is with great reluctance we take our leave but we tell you now we have succumbed to the most ample proportions of Love within your breast. We know you take this most seriously and with the greatest of reverence, and we bombard your thought streams with ours to get these messages across in more ways than one. We shall underline those core issues that need adjustment for there is some way to go

416

yet before we shall have that easement of verse. We subject you to these frequencies to enable this to happen, sooner rather than later, adjusting and tweaking wherever necessary to get this show on the road - and it shall be a blockbuster of that there is no doubt! We shall bring to the masses greater resolution and underline the key issue that we are here to challenge you - and make no mistake we shall proceed in an orderly fashion and do justice to all that is given!

We rest our case and leave in your capable hands. It is not for us to complain but we register those indecisions within your heart and bring you around to face us head on. We do allow you a peep into our resources and beckon you to join us in due course - and there is the rub! We allow magnificence to shine in the hope of becoming a greater voice on the horizon. Be of good cheer as we propel you forwards. We are noted for our grandeur of expression and it charms us to make your acquaintance! We batten down the hatches and await the conclusion to years of service.

∞

Today at our trance group, where we all take turns to sit for communication, I felt a Native American influence come in strongly. My back straightened and I sat with the palms of my hands on my legs; there seemed to be warmth coming from my hands which had a strong calming effect.

It brings us much joy to be here with you once more. We are given this interlude of friendship and we reach out across the great divide to make your acquaintance, to sooth and calm your fears for the future is one of brightness and clearness of vision.

I turned to one of the sitters - There is no need to fret my child, you are being well taken care of and you will come to no harm! We prepare you . . . we prepare all of you and the Love in your hearts is plain to see, not only for us here in our dimension but for those around you on the Earth plane, who gather around to hear your words, your laughter and your music. Your thoughts gather momentum and lift into the ethers and we catch them and share them and they journey further abroad, helping others who are in dire straits. We give your

417

compassion to those in greatest need and we pamper you and restore you! This is a great occasion as always to make that connection with you, to feel your Love growing and mounting – a great crescendo of Love that we may all bathe in. That is the key to success for the future of all mankind, so it has been and always will be. We bring you our thanks for the work that you do and we register in you that need to move forward . . . out of the abysmal shadow that casts its shroud around the globe. The Light is growing stronger!

I could feel the golden light pouring through me and radiating out. There was a deep stillness and the girls saw an Egyptian influence like the Sphinx. We sat in the stillness for some time with this light shining out. In my head I could hear the song 'This Little Light of Mine I'm Gonna Let It Shine! The girls saw a shaft of violet light coming down before I spoke.

We take you to a distant shore to explore your surroundings and we bathe you in that golden glow, registered in your heart. We give thanks to the Great Divine for allowing this to happen right here and now! We bathe in the solitude and Love of one another's bliss and this shall be seen to happen all around the globe on this very day! Bear in mind we are more than just a mortal race – we are Light Beings extraordinaire brought to bear witness to those here on Earth. We deem it a necessary advisement to cherish yourselves more often than you do; look after the physical and it will look after you. It is the Temple of your Light as you know . . . bring it more into balance. We Love you and nurture but you must Love yourselves also. There is a grand connection to be made and we are preparing you all for this grand occasion. Be uplifted and of good heart . . . all will be well and this will be brought into your jurisdiction very soon. Open your hearts and minds to receive us.

May the sanctity of God's Love be with you now and forever more, and may you hold in your heart the fact that we are making this world a better place, all of us, and that includes you too! And we are most grateful for all that you do on this plane of existence and also the other planes where you work on many different levels. You're not merely these beings that sit here in this room - you are so much more! You are expanding and growing!

I remember joyfully reaching my arms up to the sky and bringing them back round to face palm up in a giving gesture.

We shall now take a back seat and watch the proceedings. There are many more surprises up our sleeve. Just remember to take care of yourselves – you are very precious in the scheme of things.

∞

*2.4.14 – 2+4=6+1=7=4=***11.** *The master number **11** presents itself today indicative of a message from the higher realms. There has also been a weather warning that brings sand from the Sahara desert making it harder to breathe. I give thanks to the Great Spirit for being able to sit here in this place at this time. I can see you Sitting Bull and ask that you draw closer to me so that we may blend our energies of Love and harmony and friendship.*

We are more than that sweet sister of mine, we are so much more and we register the Love within your heart and we bring you peace and tranquillity, stretching out across the great divide, welcoming you to our home, our paradise of Love. We censor articles of war and bring to your mind the sweet smell of success.

I can see an Indian woman with a shawl around her shoulders; she has long hair and could be in her 30's.

We embrace you and shower you with our Love and affection; we honour this connection as always and draw you closer to our bosom. There has been greater understanding of that which has left your heart and mind in a quandary over which way to turn; we have registered in your heart deep impact at this turn of events, and we allow you to progress slowly but surely along this highway of Love and devotion to the cause of mankind. Be of good cheer for we bring you further updates that will register in your mind, allowing you to share with others of your persuasion. We are much interested in your progress at this time and we share with you a little secret that has come to mind, an initiation into the rites of passage into these realms of joy.

We propose that you will honour us with your commitment and your sense of duty for we are honour bound to take you aboard once more and we travel into that void of discontent, allowing a modicum of sanity to prevail. We are initiated into a deeper, more meaningful assail into that bone of contention that has held us back from discovering a new world of joyous bliss. We bombard you with accents of a different frequency and ask you to register our just intent to honour these proceedings.

We take you to a land of plenty and a religion not seen for many a year; we take you back to the time of Thutmose III and distinguish a pattern that has been raised many times before. We take you to a land of plenty where the honey flows and this dream is just a pitiful example of what is in store for every one of every race, colour or creed and we give thanks to our creator, who has governed the upkeep of all mankind.

We propose that you bear witness to these our trials and tribulations of what has gone before and we register in you that guiding light that transports us to heaven and the stars. We are brilliant, shining our light out into the darkness of Earth and we transpose the importance of letting you have your say and we listen to the children of Earth, we listen most carefully!

I asked who was speaking.

We are the Great I AM presence a divinity beyond your reckoning, the discourse with Angels that hover on the brink of mankind's existence, sharing your woes as a go-between Heaven and Earth, bringing us the required information that will assist us to make the right decisions to help mankind. There are many roads to recovery and we come bearing gifts to help you in this ascension process, instilled in our heart as being a most provocative time. We have revised the proceedings and allow you to settle before we have lift off, this will enable a greater gush of energy to precede our visit. Do believe in us for we are very real in both our worlds.

We do justice to what is brought before us and we say to you - be kind to yourselves! This is not a time to ruffle those edges, this is a time to smooth your passage to greater understanding and we unfold what has not been seen for many a year. It is like running a great marathon; there is time to stop and refresh yourself with water before you complete your journey and you are nearing the end, there is but a little way to go before you touch and cross that line. It all sits well within our heart and we will do justice to all that is given, just check your thermometer and this will give you an indication of how we are receiving you! We have not got enough evidence to substantiate a flame but we do have your good will and judgement and a strong and loving heart. We shall break through the innuendo and point you in the right direction to achieve much more than this!

After reading this a few times it has just dawned on me that my thermometer is my heart and although I have been trying to keep my light burning bright there is still a way to go and I will need to rest for a while longer. I looked on the internet to gather information about Thutmoses III and found it interesting that he was the Pharaoh who linked with Moses's time on Earth.

Thutmose III succeeded to the throne after his father died but for the first 20 years of his reign shared power with his aunt, Queen Hatshepsut, who reigned peaceably as co-regent, appointing Thutmoses head of her armies. After she died, he became the sixth Pharaoh of Egypt's 18th dynasty.

The date of the Exodus is about 1449-1446BC. If we subtract 25 to 35 from his reign (1479) we get 1454BC - 1444BC. This is well within the range of years that the Bible tells of an exchange between Moses who was 80 years old and a new Pharaoh in Egypt whom he did not know. Hatshepsut was Moses' adopted mother, her half-brother Thutmose II would have grown up with Moses. By 1449BC Hatshepsut was already dead and could not have spoken in regard to Moses. After letting the Israelites go Pharaoh lost 3 million slaves and then changed his heart. When he saw his armies drown in the sea he was embittered against Moses, the Israelites and all that Hatshepsut had done in preserving their existence in Egypt. In retaliation he defaced all of her monuments and writings!

∞

4.4.14 – Wa ma ha . . . we bring you fruit for thought!

421

I can feel a breeze on my face as I sit in my sanctuary and am being shown a little acorn now, knowing they grow into mighty oaks.

We tremulously reject any offers that do not coincide with our way of thinking and we offer you our services as we come bearing witness to what has gone before. We deplore the cruelty inflicted on those poor souls who entered the fray and we deliberately take you back to a time of decisive connectedness, to those who were loyal to us in every way. This has been our way for eons and we mark a passage in time substantiating any clauses. We bear witness to a long line of advocates who come in great procession and we ask you to trust us and have faith. We are open for negotiations and allow this channelling to commence!

We are beyond your earthly jurisdiction we are beyond the monopoly of your race, we are beyond all governing! We are a race of Super Beings that come to rescue you from the doldrums, to point you in a different direction that will enable a mass exodus of all mankind . . . and this we promise will be the greatest journey ever made! Temperance and subservience have been a great factor in overcoming the discord within your heart, and we shall make a stand and bear witness to those trivialities that have caused such dismay in the past. We open up the network that will allow us greater access, monitoring your recordings, this has been our greatest success and we point you along the pathway, opening up greater reserves of energy that will help you with this initiative. Please bear with us as we adjust this connection!

I'm seeing cloudy purple that is now becoming more vibrant with large expanses of gold filigree. I cannot see a Pharaoh but sense their presence.

We have opened a new chapter that shall be given to these writings and you will open a new book that will allow us voice.

Thank you. There are tears in my eyes but I know this emotion will cloud my vision, so I'm attempting to settle back down again to maintain contact.

We have reclaimed that part of you that grew alongside us many years

422

ago in the deserts of the far off land of Egypt and we belong to a greater dynasty than you can ever imagine. We bring you glad tidings of great joy that will open up a labyrinth, a hive of activity being brought into your line of vision. We bring you a new story to be told to the masses, we bring a new line of supervision that will convey greater clarity to these words and these works of art shall manifest in due course.

I'm finding it hard to breathe. Is this frequency causing a problem or is it my physical heart? Can you lift this from me friends and help me to breathe more easily?

We generate an energy which can be confused within your vibration and this can cause a heaviness that we aim to lift. We are among those greats in history who opened up a chapter in the lives of mankind. There is a time to work and a time to play, your playtime has not ended yet and we are here behind the scenes, preparing you in readiness for what is ahead. We allow channellings of excellence to manifest and we will be able to regulate these messages, enabling a higher frequency to be reached that will not be so troublesome. We peel off the barnacles!

I can see a boat underneath the water, once covered in barnacles it now glides through the water more easily. I'm beginning to feel better now thank you.

We allow a standing down pending resources and this will allow your circuits to be re-energised. We are open for further discussions and further statements shall be made regarding your success, further deliberations that we shall bring into the open. We satisfy that urge to grow and to learn and we are bombarded with messages from the Great Divine to pass on to you and your contemporaries. There is a magic distillation of proof from beyond the stars that we come in all honesty to reserve a place for you and yours in this beautiful world. We tempt you with our words and lead you on through this magical place of Love and Light, enabling greater discourse that shall open up the hearts and minds of the population of Earth. We ask you to satisfy those inner longings that have for so long caused you to be downcast, and we bear you aloft and tell you that all is in readiness for you to make your grand entrance!

My heart is feeling much lighter now thank you.

We enable you to shine as the Light you truly are and for all those around you who come to listen to our words; we come from beyond that shining star in your heavens that brings you Light. The Egyptians called us 'Ra' and we are known as your Sun, shining brightly for all to see. We bring you Light and warmth and we bring you our Love. This has been the greatest journey ever known and we stand by your side and resurrect a new race, opening up the pathway to a new world of great delight; we manifest before you as those shining beings you once were and will be again. This is a bold statement to make, we know this, and we bring you these verses in the hope they will inspire you to pick up the pieces of your lives and march forward with us into that shining light. For it is not until you can leave your material possessions behind that you will find that peace within your hearts.

This is a new alignment that we are asking you to make; we are asking you to thread together our words as if they were jewels, to wear them close to your heart in readiness for the great escape! This is an escape from the clutches of all you have known, to reach out and cross that ribbon of light to a new dimension of light and joy, a vision quest of the greatest dexterity. We are your friends and brethren, your Keepers of Light and we bear you aloft to join us, opening up the division between us. We shall grow and blossom in that Divine radiance and ask you not to lose faith for all is well, all is as it should be! We transcend those areas of doom and gloom, masterminding your complete success and we shall be there constantly at your side, encouraging you. We take you not across the desert but to a loftier place, where all may be seen and understood with the greatest sanctity of spirit and forgiveness of our peers - for all here is of Love.

I'm being drawn into such a beautiful pulsating cloud of soft lilac, bursting into vivid purple with flashes of gold. I felt my face changing quite strongly here with my mouth scrounged up and a strange feeling in my nose.

We are from a broader spectrum than Earth and we register your distaste at these intervals that bring about discomfort. We are able to release you from our grasp to bring back that lightness that will not impede your vision. We are those champions of the cause who come to honour you and the work that you do and we share this with you to the best of our ability. We regulate your breathing so that you are not too distressed and as you see it is now much easier to breathe. This has been a grand interlude and we thank you for your input! We are noted for our extremes of temperature and we give thanks that not too much undue stress has been placed upon you. We deliver a synopsis of what we can achieve if we all put our minds to it and we ask you to stand up and be counted, open to further revelations that we may assist you with.

This is a powerful record that we are about to uncover and we go further afield, delighting in your recoveries, opening up that network that will allow for even more instantaneous news. Let us open here by saying we are used to your rhythms here on Earth, we are used to monopolising those kindred spirits who come forward to assist us, helping us with these deliveries, and you should be very proud of yourselves for all that you have achieved! We are noted for the discipline that comes into play to allow these words, and we do indeed whisper in your ear and you hear these whisperings within your heart, taking you in flight on wings of Love.

We come around you and revel in your discoveries as you sit at your computers, delving into the encyclopaedia of all that has gone before, and we know when you have hit the nail on the head so to speak as we provide you with the answers! We are like that grand encyclopaedia that great library, it is all here, you only have to take out the book and look through the pages, everything can be seen but it takes a lot of patience! Nevertheless there are many of you on Earth who do indeed search and we are proud to have you with us at this time in our great quest for Peace and Truth. And in that peace and stillness of your heart there are many marvels to unfold and we are so happy to oblige you, to assist you in your work as you travel this pathway, bringing it to the masses and into the open so that it may sifted through and recognised.

There was a loud crack in the room then and I wanted to sing again . . . this little light of mine, I'm gonna let it shine! Oh my friends I think we have come to the end of another recording and I thank you so much for the words you have brought through today and for the Love and lightness I feel in my heart now. Thank you.

We thank you sweet cherub of Light and we look forward to further discourses in the same vein. We wish you a good day and a good night. Peace be with you now and for always. *Amen*

∞

Great Spirit, dear friends and guides from The Federation of Light, I invite you to join me as I sit in meditation to bathe in the Love and majesty of the Great Divine.

I can feel my head being touched and see clouds of swirling lilac envelop and caress me.

We are bombarded with requests for Peace in all areas and we ask you to adjust your settings and relax. We adjudicate at these meetings where our worlds collide and become as one in all truth and compatibility. We are open for negotiations!

There have been further revelations flooding in from the universe and we prepare that outer shell of your persona to soften in texture so that we may approach you with a more favourable contact. It is our understanding that you have come many times to these shores and we believe the access we have given is due to your remarkable talent for tapping into your Divine connectedness. This is of no surprise to us and we take your hand my dear and lead you to greener pastures, where all are given the most noble courtesy and expressions of our Love. We bear witness to a time of greater fortitude and an understanding that has left us shattered to the core of our very being; we come before you and offer you hope for the future of mankind. We are noted for our success in these endeavours and we translate information as it is given to us, passed on by our superiors who are governing a wider spectrum than even we can manage.

426

This is the time of a greater Light mode for all mankind, and you will come to learn and grow as we kneel before you and offer our services to mankind. We have sheltered you from the cold blasts that blow; we have given you succour and Love without comparison, and these we bring to your side so that you may use them wisely. We bring hope for the future for mankind we bring joy, we bring undiluted bliss and these we carry in our heart, opening up a network of services far and wide, making that connection with Heaven and Earth count as no other.

We are beyond words for words can only tell a partial knowing, it has to be felt deep within the core of your being, felt and administered in a loving connection borne from the stars. We open up fields of energy that will assist you in your quest, and this quest will be seen to be undertaken all around the globe with your brothers and sisters of pure intent. We mount this exercise, bringing renewal on every level of expertise and we ask you to bear with us as we assist you in this process, delving deeper and deeper into the maelstrom of events looming ahead.

We are pardoned from becoming obsolete and we allow that to sink in while we delve further and further into the libraries of Earth, rectifying past complaints, opening up new structures to allow for greater access and attention to detail. We have become subservient to the cause of mankind and we are indebted to your services, helping us along the road to complete success and overture of grand proportions! We are welcomed into this new domain by those who come to sanction our wishes for a greater union between our peoples; we learn and grow little by little until we have grown in stature, overcoming those issues that hold us back from attaining freedom of spirit.

We bow down to your expertise, asking you to join here with us as we bend over backwards to listen with all our heart and soul to what you are saying! We are a nation of disbelievers, believing only in what is put in front of us on a plate so to speak, but we come to bring validation to those innuendos knocking at your door for you to prod and poke and explore, to make certain for yourselves that we are not pulling the wool over your eyes! We are merely drawing your attention to what 'needs' to be seen . . . what needs to be looked at with closer scrutiny. This has been the whole point of this exercise and we draw closer to hold you in our embrace, charting your course across the universe as you come closer and closer to our domain.

We are by no means an alien race and we come to uplift you in your endeavours, teaching you how to cross that great divide between us. It is no mean feat, we know this, but we travel lightly and you are but a thought away. We register your concerns on the Earth plane over this contact and we make sure that you know what you are doing, as it has to be right for you at this time in your evolution. We grant you access to our domain and welcome you aboard whenever you feel like stepping over that threshold and yes, we are here to answer your questions whatever they may be!

Can you tell us who you are?

We are 'beings of Light' just as you . . . we can be clothed in flesh or we can just be in essence flames of Light tapping you with our wisdom. We are pure energy!

I'm seeing soft clouds of light, sweeping my energy field and for the next 15 minutes the recorder is quiet where I was either asleep or taken deeper. When I came round we continued.

We have just cause to open these lines of communication and we know you will reliably pass on our messages. The provisions we have made excel our wishes for a greater understanding.

Again the recording is quiet except for deep breathing then we continued.

We come into a time of deep murmurings within your heart and we draw closer and closer to share in your thanksgivings.

Again the recording went quiet and as I came round for the third time I was aware of looking down from a great height. I could see a mound or mountain that had three golden obelisks with what looked like a white figure in front of them,

428

which was either a large White Eagle or the figure of someone wearing white with arms outstretched. I also saw what looked like the shape of a large gold dish that could have been an amphitheatre of sorts. This is a new learning curve which needs time for adjustment; I'm hoping these visions will become much clearer in the future.

∞

11.4.14 – 1+1+4+1+4=11- I love it when the master number eleven presents itself.

I thank the Great Spirit for this day and this beautiful place I have been led to. I pray for the frail and elderly and all those who are leaving this plane of existence, I ask for them to be not afraid but uplifted in spirit; I pray they will see those horizons they are heading for and be filled with strength and Love, knowing they are venturing on a new journey. I give thanks also for the young ones who are coming into this dimension, those who are here to help mankind adjust to the new frequencies.

As I bring the golden light down, the lilac clouds seem to be coming up and meeting the gold. I can vaguely see the profile of an Egyptian woman on my right and coming through is a sense of appreciation for words uttered in prayer.

We thank all those souls who leave this planet . . . for the Love they have brought and the families they have created who will go on in essence as part of the Great Divine.

We come in all honesty, truth and Light, bringing you new focus, asking you to adjudicate at these meetings so that we may bring you the Love you deserve in richness of expression for undying fortitude in the line of duty. This has been our greatest pleasure to bring you these words across the great divide, enveloping you in that special brand of courage that enables you to move forward at a growing rate.

I'm seeing gorgeous purple and gold and have a rippling sensation on top of my head in the right lobe of my brain. I can see a pinprick of white light in the lilac which grows and then recedes. I thought I saw Nefertiti and Akhenaten at this point.

We induce in you a state of ecstasy. *Thank you. I can hear someone saying, I want to just ask you something but I think it could have been me!*

This is not an acid test, this is a perpendicular exercise brought into the open to be examined and scrutinised at your leisure. We openly admit to being nonplussed at events, which have led us to the conclusion that there is more than meets the eye in most scenarios, and we ask you to adjust and monitor whenever necessary, taking into account that we have been labelled as your advisories many times in the distant past. We fraternise and lay out our objectives, monitoring our connection with the Great Divine and coming up full speed ahead.

I keep drifting in and out of normal consciousness, seeing golden patterns on purple.

This is because we are honouring our union, helping you to make those adjustments

Amenhotep II was a great warrior bearer of undisputed recognition, far reaching across the deserts of Earth. Gold was of great importance for it got to the heart of the matter. Burrowing into the archives we find further titillations that have come to the surface; we see with clearer vision an unfolding of stories from the past that will fill your mind with greater resonance, endearing us to the nation. We have further relics up our sleeve that we shall save for later, but we do begin to unwind the bargaining process to allow us free rein to explore deeper and deeper. Make no mistake we are here to rectify and to govern proceedings, allowing a fine toothed comb search.

Egyptians stand and rise!

I seem to have conjured up an army who have all stood to attention, thumping down their spears in unison.

Rise from your shadowy graves and bring us the knowledge we seek in the name of the Father in Heaven and in all that is good and Holy! Bring into the open that which will make good those promises of old that we bore within our hearts to bring about a greater union between our peoples. We do allow in this instance further updates and we prepare you for this advancement.

I'm going down into a purple tunnel now.

It is with the greatest respect that we come forward and we challenge you to accept what we bring with a loving heart, and with all due respect we do come from a time frame that is riddled with odysseys. We therefore have great pleasure in assisting you in this quest for truth and we bring you such wonders to behold. We come in true form, a format of mammoth proportions unveiled before the masses . . . extraordinarily!

I can see Jesus sitting at a long table.

Heavens acoustics are ringing true, loud and clear in our ears and we teach you with your minds how to connect to these frequencies that we are adjusting, enabling your progression from one sphere of existence to another, more becoming to your needs.

I can see someone wearing a white turban and pale blue robe.

We wish you to speak for us my child. We have reduced the fear factor and allow in you a state of Peace and harmony to pervade. We come to bring you offerings and a state of grace.

I keep drifting off as I'm trying to hold this frequency. I know that practice will make perfect and I get it now; they have told me that little by little each day, little by little we shall be able to hold this frequency for longer periods. Thank you for all your help and for your Love and your Light. I don't feel at all heavy, I feel lighter and full of hope for the future!

∞

31ˢᵗ April 2014 - *For the last month I have been resting and during that time I have painted a portrait of White Cloud, who showed himself to me as an Ascended Master, wearing a pale blue tunic edged with gold. I was so excited about finishing the painting and that evening I sat in candlelight and meditated. I felt the loving energy of White Cloud draw close, beaming at me.*

We are most pleased with your endeavours little one, most pleased! We sanction a renewal of services that shall hold you in good stead and we usher in a new awareness, a token of our respect and friendship in every way. This has been unchartered territory for many of you and we listen to the niceties spoken, broadcasting and airing our views to the population of Earth, asking you to listen more keenly to what we have on offer. There is a broadening of issues coming closer for inspection and we draw your attention to what is imperative at this stage in your journey. We are overcome with emotion at times and ask you to be assured that we are there by your side at all times, shepherding you along in the right direction.

There has been revulsion on a grand scale at news that has been broadcast on your TV channels and we ask that you use your wisdom when you are listening to the news, listen and be aware! There is much unrest in your world, much abhorrence at what is coming to light, making its way to the surface to be healed! We ask you not to be worried by this; there is more you can do by sending out your Love and Light that is within your soul, and directing it to those in need is your main purpose at this time, to hold your Light and to be strong! Do not be rent aside by devastation for there is much more to come and we ask you to stand firm at the helm. Adjust your stance and let the Light and Love flow from you out into the world, beckoning others not to lose hope. Stand like a beacon bright - a port in the storm. For many centuries your Light has shined out and we respect and honour your services in this respect.

We are your friends and neighbours on the other side of this dominion that you call home, but home is where the heart is and we hear you calling out to us to bring you home to us, your brethren. And we hold you all in the greatest respect, asking you not to lose faith, for you are all doing a grand job of bringing people to their senses so they may stand, not in isolation but with the support of you and those like you all around your world. We beckon the services of others like you who wait to be counted and heard; we come in our hundreds and thousands waiting to do service, to help establish a regular pattern of understanding that will enable us all to move forward on that beam of Love. We have sacrificed many issues that need to be looked at more keenly and it is without doubt the greatest mission that we have encountered.

This has been an outstanding journey of gigantic proportions and we prepare you for further contact with those sources that wait on the side-lines. All is above board in tip-top shape having been scrutinised and looked at with a fine toothed comb, until we have honed perfectly what is necessary to resurrect this cause for the human race. We prepare you to do your duty and we relish these undertakings, unremittingly forging ahead and on to greener pastures with those who have laid down their lives and now reside in peace and perfect harmony. This can certainly be counted as 'Heaven' for the Heaven you have in your minds is one of pure Love with no restrictions. We prepare a shelter from the abyss that will open and wrap itself around you, protecting you and keeping you safe. We underline our connection and take you to one side to alert you to what is expected of you in this next phase. We are born to serve and we hold your hand as we stride through this next field of energy, adjusting your circuits and promising further rewards for your strength and grace in times of turmoil.

I'm getting the little drummer boy song in my head again.

On a mountain top, long, long ago there lived a giant; very tall and strong was he, of good countenance and with a grace envied by men half his stature. He could lift a sparrow in his hands without crushing it and loved to listen to their song. His eyes were blue and his hair was white as snow. He cared for those around him with a loving nature . . . a gentle giant in every respect!

What happened to the giant from long ago?

He was torn by a power struggle between those in his village. He wanted to do the right thing without making judgement, without causing harm. The people regretted the decision they had made

433

concerning the welfare of their countrymen and they decided to teach the giant a lesson! They set fire to his home in the woods and as you can imagine this was not a wise decision. The woods were decimated, there was no longer any timber to build their homes and the kind and loving giant who had helped them in the past was no longer around to listen to their worries and woes, having gone to greener pastures where those appreciated his counsel. We tell you this story so that you may adjust your settings and realise that power carries great responsibility!

We do not need to fly in the face of scorn; we only need to temper our words. Words spoken in jest can sometimes be misconstrued, words of a genuine nature to placate and soothe can often be misinterpreted. Sending out the vibration of Light and Love can help the person decide for themselves the path they should take and this is the moral of our story! Do not be put off or set aside by what others think of you or say to you; hold the knowledge deep in your heart for there will come a time when those words can be given to someone with open ears and an open heart; then you will come into your own and that Love will tumble from you in great profusion, so do not be put off or discredited for we are always with you and forever have been!

Shelter in our arms and feel our embrace as we attend to your needs from both near and far, you are both blessed and accepted into the fraternity of loving friendship. We are charmed by your grace and your vulnerability and the goodwill in your heart that reaches out to help those who are in distress, and we will do whatever it takes to bring you on board with our great initiative. With gentle persuasion and a loving touch, we prepare you for finer duty in a land of milk and honey as in times of old. Those green pastures are waiting to be explored in all their glory and we shall be here waiting when you are ready to take that final step, and we shall help you over the threshold as you join us in this new dimension of loving peace and joy without measure. And oh what joy there shall be as we greet one another once more, holding onto that thread of loving kindness as we tip the scales in your favour, knowing that this has been a great expedition. We thank you and bid you farewell, our most loving Sister of Light and we thank you and bless you for all that you do with a kind and loving heart.

Deep Peace to you, my friend.

And to you dear friend, I thank you with all my heart and soul.

∞

May 2014 - *Great Spirit, I thank you for this day and all that has led me to this moment in time. I invite my guides and inspirers to draw close and enter my energy field so that I may touch home and blend with those I Love. I ask a blessing upon Earth and all life forms upon her.*

We seek further ways of fulfilling our destiny. We seek within your mind those answers to our questions and we put it to you as bluntly as we may! Do not be alarmed at what is taking place around you, be constant to the cause of goodwill for all mankind and we bring you this in peace and harmony. We have suffered a barrage of abuse in the past but we aim for a new future, one of peace and harmony for all life forms on this planet that have agreed to co-exist with one another. We take you to one side and applaud you for you have all done so well, all of you who came to offer your services for mankind, and we are most grateful for all that you do, for all that you are and continue to be. This is a most just cause and we render the population of Earth speechless at times with the propositions we come bearing. These gifts are held sacrosanct in our world and we give them fully from our heart, from the heart of our population, from the heart of Heaven where you belong with us.

I can feel a tickling on my chin and see the lilac and purple clouds washing over me. It feels like I'm being welcomed back home . . . mind melding with my elders and my brothers and sisters. I'm part of the whole once more . . . melting into the deepest bliss at the heart of the Great Divine. As a friend of mine said it is like plugging into that bliss and we can all do it if we practice. It has taken me many years to reach this point but for others it shall come more easily. Just allow yourselves to completely let go of all encumbrances, just fall into the arms of the Angels for just a few sweet moments every day.

435

I felt the urge to sing 'There's a hundred thousand Angels by your side' by the group called 'Bliss' and can see a huge expanse of deep purple, thread with veins of gold.

Have you any messages my friends to pass on to the population of Earth? I can now see a golden porthole with purple in the middle. When the message came my voice sounded as if I had a cold, higher in parts but then gruffer and slower.

We come at this opportune time to bring you Love and to bring you faith in yourselves as you tread this pathway of light. We are most pleased to be able to come among you at this time and we offer you sanctuary . . . we offer you peace in the core of your very being. It is with some expectancy that we have been drawn to your side and we shelter you as best we may from the abysmal truths surfacing for recognition, so that they may be looked at and dealt with. This has been a perilous journey, we know this, and we know you have done your best to avert the slings and arrows that have come your way. These bounce off that shield of Love around you, that golden armour, and the more you believe in yourself and the Love of the Great Divine, the stronger that armour will become!

We shall not leave you . . . we are there at your side at all times watching over you. You have only to call out . . . but be ready to listen! Achieve that peace within your soul that enables you to hear our words and to 'feel' our Love. We beckon you not to lose faith, keep strong dear heart, keep strong and do your duty. Keep your Love and Light shining like a beacon bright, shining out across the horizon and joining with others of your persuasion. We have told you this many times before and we know you will need to hear it many more times . . . plug into that energy that lights your flame!

I'm sensing a beam of light coming down from Heaven to Earth and encircling the globe, linking with 'Light workers' and those who search for truth.

This has been a very beneficial recording as we feel the peace and stillness within your soul, within your mind . . . within your heart. We know you strive for perfection in all things and we give you credit for this. We do, however, wish you to be kinder to yourselves on the

436

Earth plane. We are all fallible to discrepancies and we attest to the difficulties that besiege you on many occasions, we therefore have the greatest pleasure in connecting you to a greater life source; this will encourage future productions of energy on a larger scale to be broadcast around your world. Be prepared as we honour the proceedings with your presence and a greater directive of energy that will be beneficial in the cause for mankind.

We are inundated with calls for assistance and this has been most alarming at times, but we do hear your calls for help and we assist in whatever way we can, helping you adjust to these frequencies that 'shall' lead you home. These calls for help are by no means directed by the few, they are on a grand scale right across your world in mammoth proportions! Futile attempts to adjust your energies have been made in the past to no avail, but we have summoned forth a massive declaration of Love for the human race that will not allow you to fall by the wayside, and we shall adjust the fields of energy that allow you access to our realms and a higher definition.

We believe there has been a massive declaration of interest from other realms that have your best interests at heart. We share those boundaries that were once forbidden and now give access to those who wish to explore, to break through those boundaries that once held you back and to boldly go where no man has gone before! And this we promise you, a further indulgence on our part to give you the assistance you need to travel thus far; we cross those borders into other lands, into other worlds where we shall become an anomaly of sorts. We do indeed liken it to your 'Star Trek' that you watch so avidly and you will brighten the dark skies ahead of you, forging a pathway of Light and emancipating other worlds . . . the possibilities are endless and it is all open to you, oh ye of strong hearts and minds!

By only the Grace of God we sanction these visits and hold you in the highest esteem. Please do not let go of our hand now that we have found you; let us bond together in the truest Love and empathy. We are born to Love.

Thank you to all my friends and helpers, I thank you for your Love and support and Divine assistance at this most momentous time for mankind and for Earth.

I have been away visiting family for a fortnight and have missed my meditation sessions, so today I settled back for communication. The familiar lilac clouds enveloped me.

I Am He who bends to whisper in your ear. I Am He who brings you Peace and Love without any qualms, without any conditions, without any hiccups to cause dismay! I Am He who watches over you in the dead of night, who comes to soothe your brow and to wish you well on your journey. I Am He who protects you from the dark clouds that gather, overwhelming at times but necessary. We partake of that which brings you comfort and we bring you now our blessings with the utmost joy, for there is much to be thankful for and much to sing about in the times ahead. We bring you wondrous news from those on high, we bring you salutations of great joy and happiness and we bring you our warmest wishes to speed your journey. There is no need to hesitate . . . there is only the need to move along this band of Light that beckons you forward. Accept our good wishes as you move into this stream of Light and we will be there with you, chiding you not to lag behind but to use your strength and initiative to push forward, ever onwards with a glimmer in your eye and that radiance within your heart that shall move you on to greater things.

We announce in no uncertain terms that all is well on this highway of Love. We have broadcast to many of your nations and we accept the terms and conditions you offer us to complete our transaction; we prepare for a greater Light that will welcome you into our world, a world of Love and beauty beyond all imagination.

I am being shown the face of Jesus.

This will come as no surprise to those of you who have walked this path before and we shelter you in the arms of The Beloved and welcome you to these shores once more. Do not be aghast at what is laid before you . . . we shall bring greater measures of justice that shall prevail over the storms that are weathering you at this time. We prepare you to do your duty and we lead you by the hand, pressing

438

you to the service volunteered by you and your counterparts and this establishment has come under jurisdiction from those on high.

I Love you Great Spirit with all my heart and soul and pray my heart will lead me home that I may be of service in whatever way I can. I ask that I may tune into the highest source of information that I can achieve at this time and that I may be blessed and protected by the Great Divine.

This has been a most challenging time, for many of us, and we come to bear witness to a greater destiny for those of our persuasion who reach for the brightest star, settling not for second best but pushing forward with greater momentum to reach that which is desired above all other . . . the peace and richness of your soul, expressed with greater fortitude and strength of character. We will propel you forward on a stream of Love to reach that final resting place in your sojourn on the Earth plane.

We come to take you home very soon, we come to take you to a magic distillation of Love and Peace and harmony that shall not be destroyed. We are those Beings of Light that set you free and we register in you a great desire to come home. We know it pains you to stay in a world of sadness and sorrow and we ask you to bear this with the strength and fortitude you have demonstrated so far; there will come a time of unravelling that which is chaos and there will be peace once more with your help and those like you, who gather round to make this work. And we ask you not to be ashamed of your restrictions . . . these shall melt away in due course and you will be given the impetus to move forward with greater speed and accuracy. It has been foretold that man shall come into his own and we tell you now, these revelations shall come into play sooner than you think; we give thanks for this to you and all those who have come so far on this rainbow of Light. We welcome you to our domain and give thanks for this recovery. Please accept our blessings for this reunion.

Thank you my friends . . . I Love you so!

You are well respected in this land of Light and even more so now on this, your latest journey into the abyss. We give thanks for your

439

safe return and ask you not to lose heart for we are with you at all times forever more. Pick your way across the debris - do not lose sight of your truth, of your connections with us your friends and allies who are always there at your side. We bear you with us on the crest of a wave of energy that will allow you access to our domain, and we ask you to take care in the interim so that we may assess in greater detail all that is needed for your recovery. We take our leave and wish you well. God Speed!

∞

June 2014 – We of the Great I Am presence are with you now and forever more. We hold that trust between us and hearken to the call from our heart. There is a place reserved just for you and we make no bones about it, you will be reinstated in the hearts and minds of those who hold you dear. And this we promise are the greatest rewards we can offer you for the Love and service you have given to others. We thank you and we Love you so.

I felt very emotional here with tears in my eyes.

Be prepared to shatter those illusions that have manifest for many on the Earth plane for we bring you comfort and hardship shall become a thing of the past, we bring you hope, we bring you joy and we lead you to a land that is green and plentiful. We lead you to a place of tranquillity and mindfulness that shall give you the courage to take that next step forwards. We link you to those who will help you along this pathway and we rejoice in the giving of this news that all will be well. We bring you full circle!

I'm not sure that I understand fully.

We daresay you will understand soon enough the jostling and murmurings of your heart and we will put down on paper that which is beneficial to mankind. We follow your instincts and watch them carefully, we listen to your heart beat and know that you will listen to our words, mulling them through before proceeding and we are glad that you have this gift of sifting through that which is to be aired and

440

broadcast to the nation. We are not given to idle gossip but we listen to the qualms within your heart; this leads us to register your just intent to move forward with us in the arms of the Angels and those that watch over us from on high. We bear witness to a greater decision making that will enhance our recordings in more ways than one, and we do justice to the words given to us, excluding those that do not bode well within your heart as being just and true.

We sift through those agenda items that give us impetus to move forward, and though we know it pains you to hear us reiterate what has been said, we do take you to task for initially rejecting what we have placed before you in your own best interests. We honour the rites taken by those just few who come to state their cause and we hang our hat on the stand for justice, bearing you with us along the highway of truth and honesty supreme. We ask that you stand as our witness to God and to the people of Earth! We are budding ombudsmen of sorts, sorting out the stresses and strains that have led the population of Earth to revolt, and we bring you solace, we bring you freedom from pain, acting by courtesy of those on high who have registered your complaints.

I Am He who calls in the dead of night to awaken your senses, to bring renewal, to bring life to the coil within you that yearns for expression . . . that yearns to be free from all that binds you to the Earth plane; but we would ask you to think, for just one moment, we would ask you to touch most lovingly that which binds you for we have become accustomed to that which assaults your senses. We are enabled free expression to vent those thoughts and ideas that surface for recognition and we override a complex and worrying time. We ponder on those issues closest to our heart and we make comparable studies, venturing forth to claim our inheritance.

We access those mind-numbing qualities that do indeed threaten the very fabric of society and we seek safe harbour in the wings of Angels, treading most carefully along this highway of Love. We beg you not to lose sight of all that is within your grasp and ask you to follow us. We have adjusted our sight, a phenomenal attainment, brightening the journey for many of you and yet we have greater

441

aspirations and a keener sense of duty that will marshall you together. We have strength of purpose and the courage of a warrior and yet we are seen lagging behind! Do remember that we come by the grace of God!

Before I sat for meditation I gazed at my picture of White Cloud, wondering if I had painted his hair correctly. As I closed my eyes I caught glimpses of White Cloud with his thick, white hair as if to calm my fears and he was joined by other faces that came and went in quick succession. I visualised the golden energy flowing through me and out into my aura and then down into the caverns below, touching the walls with golden light. I'm very aware that all around the world this Light is linking and growing with others who are doing just the same; this is the Light grid that grows more powerful every day.

We register your intent as just and true and we propel you to a new infrastructure that has been prepared for your home coming. We are seen by many as indestructible life forms, forever toing and froing from the Earth plane.

I heard a loud crack in the room at this point. I'm getting clouds of lilac floating around me, and it feels like they are brushing up my aura and lightening it. I've been feeling down and rather heavy the last few days so thank you my friends, I feel much lighter already.

We adjust this connection to coincide with yours. Truth is an advantage necessary to maintain contact and we do indeed have the blessings of the Great Divine. We match piece each scenario, putting it to you that we have overstepped the mark on more than one occasion, but we ably deliver what is necessary to set you in your stride for the future is of great importance in the days and weeks ahead. There has been a massive understatement of talents not yet used and we share your victories as well as your commiserations, pointing out that all is above board and shipshape.

I can now see an Egyptian lady with a Nefertiti type headpiece.

We regenerate using our strength and we strive for completion on every level. We have a deal more to accomplish before we submit to

442

further enquires and we bring this reverie in order to survive, for this is the toughest part of our journey yet. We give thanks to the thoughts and ideas stored in our memory banks, given an airing to record our specialities, a specialty for delivering that which has not been spoken of before. We have reached a time of great turmoil and indignation in your world runs rife. We scrutinise and dig deeper to uncover what is causing such unrest; we make ourselves known so that you will have a greater understanding of what it is we are about.

Don't chide yourself on not reaching the mark at this point for we have more than enough to be going on with. We have succeeded in putting together a manuscript of great worth, a wealth of knowledge to be shared and utilised with the population of Earth, and we come to let you know how we intend to take you forward. We have memory recall that will adapt information given as your right and we implant new ideas to be taken in your stride, pondering facts given in a previous interview, and this shall be our saving grace on this and many more occasions. We ask you not to lose heart but to sally forth on this journey of great intent. We shall be there with you from dawn to dusk preparing the way for others to tread and we mean this most sincerely my friend. We have the good wishes of your entire nation at our disposal and we make headway in the short time we have left. We of just intent and true purpose maintain our connection to the Great Divine, radiating Love and truth and honesty of spirit, broadcasting to the nation on a beam of Love sublime.

∞

During meditation today I found myself in a tall pine forest, breathing in the fresh cool air, then felt myself being lifted up and away into the mist.

Welcome my Beloved we are very honoured to have you here with us in our dimension. We accept there has been some futility in the hearts and minds of those of you upon the Earth plane and we express the resonance within our heart as being true and of great upliftment. This upliftment is needed to set you back on course for you have drifted. We harness the energy available to us and point you in the right direction, summoning up the strength and energy to move forward. There has been a time of great hardship on the Earth plane and we give thanks to those of you who have stayed true to yourselves and to us, your brothers and sisters, who watch and wait. We are governed by a greater life force and this we promise you, we have no alternative but to keep you safe from harm . . . you are more precious to us than all the stars that shine in the heavens.

We are bombarded with astral fall out that plays havoc with our circuits, but we readjust the energy to suit your needs and to amplify that which is given by us, your counterparts. We know that you despair at times and making this contact is not always so easy, yet we stand on the side-lines willing you not to lose faith and to march with us hand in hand. We have a bargaining process that suits us very well at this time and we allow further repartee to broaden our horizons, treading in the steps of the esteemed, those who have gone before to clear a pathway. Keep that faith and hope burning bright within your breast, respond to our caress as we overwhelmingly desire to help you succeed!

We study the trail that you have walked and see it littered with those disillusioned with their life on Earth, and we see that stream of Light in your wake that gives hope to those that follow on. We shall succeed and we shall give hope to the masses! This has been the most challenging part of your journey yet and we raise the flag, holding on and standing firm. We shall not be cast aside . . . we shall not be put off from our goal of everlasting life. Keep focused - set your sights straight ahead!

I am set in darkness, there is no light but I feel I must stand my ground. Eventually I see and feel a knight who is wearing golden armour; I can hear the tumultuous roar of people to the left and right of me, but I keep moving forward on my horse, holding the flag. It is a white flag and I'm visualising the golden sun in its centre. Oh Great Spirit, shine your golden light upon me. I will not lag behind, I will not fall from my mount, I will stay strong and true to the cause of upliftment for mankind.

St. Peter stands and the trumpet blows . . . we are nearly there at the gates of Heaven!

444

There is now great rejoicing and the knight in armour is leaning down to shake people's hands. He is wearing a golden crown and the people are cheering instead of jeering, for he has come home at last! His horse is white and he is holding the sword high in the air.

I am just getting the song 'When you walk through the storm hold your head up high and don't be afraid of the dark'. My voice is catching with emotion . . . it's as if, no matter how dark it may be, nor how alone you may feel you are never alone! Hold onto that golden vision . . . visualise the sun shining through, enveloping you in brilliant golden light to keep you safe on your journey. Some words from the 23rd psalm came into my head at this point.

Yea, though I walk through the valley of shadow and death, I will feel no evil, for HE is with me and shall walk beside me all the days of my life and I will dwell in the house of the Lord forever. HE comforts me. HE maketh me to lie down in green pastures. HE anoints my head with oil and my cup runneth over!

We partake of that cup of wine and shelter you in the arms of our beloved Master and we come now to be with you, to shelter you and protect you, opening up a network that shall bring us great rewards, more than we could ever hope or wish for. We pick you up and put you back in your place among those well-loved saints of yesteryear and we unfold a whole variety of myths and legends that shall paint a different picture. We hold you steadfast in our loving gaze and propel you further forward to complete your task, a most loving mission and one which we have great cause to celebrate. We make it clear to all who deliver our words that we enrol you in the highest calibration of energy, and we venture forth upon this highway of Love with all prerequisites necessary for your journey. This amalgamation of souls has been preordained and we offer salvation to each and every one of you upon the Earth plane, salvation and the highest form of purification. Go gently upon the Earth plane dear sister, go gently fair maiden.

Oh thank you, I can at last see the gold and purple colours which confirm that I am on the right vibration.

We have expressed our wishes, we now leave you to mull over our thoughts and to put down on paper that which is written, encouraging you to move forward upon this stream of Light, striving for the very best in all that you do. Take care and remember we are but a thought away and though you may not see us or hear us . . . we are 'always' there, lightening your heart and lightening your energy field. Where there is Love and determination there will always be movement and you shall not stagnate. Be prepared for the times ahead are more joyous and full of expectation. All shall be fulfilled in the fullness of your heart. Go now sweet sister, our Love and blessings go with you now and forever more.

∞

Yesterday we visited St David's the smallest city in Wales, where nestled in a deep valley lays an impressive looking cathedral. Afterwards we walked across the headland at Solva and sat on the crags, gazing out to sea. This change of scene blew away the cobwebs and when I sat in meditation this morning I was in for a surprise.

I AM THE WAY THE TRUTH AND THE LIGHT.

Oh sweet Jesus draw close I pray and answer the questions within my heart.

We come in all meekness and sincerity to hold thy hand and to raise you up where you belong in the arms of our Lord. We shelter you from the abyss and tread thoughtfully and carefully along this highway of Love. There are no doors barred for all is there to explore and uncover. We raise you up from your doom and gloom and ask you to be thankful for those few mercies granted at this time. We have developed an over sensitive pattern of behaviour and this shall be held in abeyance.

I can now see a vast expanse of golden lattice work against a purple background.

There are joyous overtures waiting in the wings and we give them life, we give them expression!

Sweet Jesus I Love you so, open my heart, help me to explore the right channels.

446

There is a greater life force that has, with the power of alchemy, registered an appeal for the human race and we guide you constantly to that benchmark that we have taken upon ourselves. We believe this will take but a moment of your time and we are predisposed to expect a grand reckoning, bringing in a cluster known as the 'Hyades'. We welcome you to these shores and suggest you propel yourselves to this 'Temple of Love' where we will lighten your journey in many aspects. We have propelled you thus far to register your delights; we have propositioned you to accept this frequency and we work at a stronger pace, sectioning off those articles of mistrust that have followed you in the past. We welcome in a new stream of thought that will assist your vibration and move you forward along this tidal stream of Love. We beckon you forward to fulfill your destiny and listen to your queries. Deposit your Love and register your appeal!

In Greek mythology the Hyades were known as the five daughters of Atlas, half-sisters to the Pleiades. After the death of their brother, Hyas, the weeping sisters were transformed into a cluster of stars that were afterwards associated with rain.

I am sitting again for communication this evening and as I bring down the golden light into my crown chakra I can see a man wearing what looks like a blue kimono; he has deep golden coloured hair which is swept back from his face and hanging down, much like the Elvish race portrayed in Lord of the Rings. He seems to be waiting for me to begin. Dear friend can you show yourself to me more clearly. He has blue almond shaped eyes with dark eyelashes and slightly pointed ears.

We do indeed belong to a race of initiates who come charged with this homely complexion. We are a pure breed of that there is no doubt and our countenance has long been regarded as one of resemblance to those on Earth. We are by nature perceptive in our hearing and we have adjusted our sight path to correspond with yours. We register the Love within your heart and without a shadow of doubt, we will come up trumps in our union and we shall make sure that you are given the information that you seek from us, your friends and allies.

447

We are able to keep abreast with attitudes that have led you astray in the past and we put it to you as bluntly as we may that this whole scenario has been a fact finding mission of some consequence, broadening the horizons of all and sundry. We point out that it has taken this long for us to indulge in these conversations and we have outwitted many in the past who came to simple stand and stare. This has not been our way and we open up your horizons so that you may expand and grow, delivering further prowess that enables our minds to speak to one another . . . and how wonderful it is that we may converse in this way!

Yes my friends it is wonderful, thank you. Are you those Star beings from the Hyades that I spoke with this morning and if you are, can you tell me a bit more about yourselves please, I'd love to know?

We initiate greater rewards for those who step over these boundaries and we come to you as brothers and sisters under the skin. We are humanoid in appearance just like you but with feline characteristics. We open up this connection and ask you not to tarry for there is much to be covered in a short space of time.

What will you be talking to me about tonight?

We will be covering those issues of boundaries and suggest that you listen more carefully to what we have to say. We have opened a new network of independent advisors who will come forward when the time is right and we have your best interest at heart. We open a chute of sorts that will channel through information that we can hand to you and in so doing to those on Earth; this has been planned and sort out by those on high and we are governed by a greater life source to champion the cause for mankind. It is not a difficult task, it just needs some adjustment with a few tweaks here and there!

I feel like I'm adjusting a radio set trying to get the frequency right.

Yes that is exactly so, we are striving for a greater connection and greater clarification of getting the message across more clearly. We are concerned to a degree about the reserves of energy being used and it will take a few moments to adjust this connection to turn up the tempo, broadcasting on a greater velocity of energy that will help with the pronunciation of words coming through. We are indebted to your services and welcome you aboard in the truest sense.

Oh does that mean part of me is coming aboard your ship; how are you speaking to me, is it telepathy from your world or are we half way in a space ship somewhere?

Not quite at the moment . . . but that is something for us to consider in future interviews! We are compatible with one another on every level and we know you will do justice to our words, bringing them through with greater clarity. There has been more than enough time to rally around and adjust our conduits and we ask you now to sally forth arm in arm with us, your friends and helpers. We are indeed from that bright cluster known as the Hyades, cousins of those from the Pleiades and we work together with many other star systems, joining and amalgamating to bring greater strength and energy to the situation on Earth.

We are hybrids of a kind just as you and we join together to make this work, for there are those around your planet who have experienced great setbacks from the malevolence on Earth. We come at a time of great calamity and further upsets and we rock the boat so to speak, to set you on your guard and to make you aware that all is not what it seems. There are outside influences that are governing your world and we do not want it to fall into the wrong hands! There have been greater reserves of energy pushing and pulling you into place and we tether the knot to keep you safe . . . to create a balance of sorts.

There is a readiness in the hearts of mankind to stand firm and to be counted, to be the voice above the rabble, to instil peace and sanity in those who have gone astray and we are forever striving to maintain equilibrium on Earth. We do not want a shattering of that peace and stillness in your hearts, we want you to grow with an abundance of Love and joy, for when the heart is full of Love it enables growth of the intellect and the portal in your heart becomes more vibrant, more

449

pliable . . . like liquid gold. And when you step though this portal into other realms, your eyes are opened to dimensions previously denied with endless possibilities for the soul to expand; your perimeters widen and there is so much more to explore . . . the universe is your oyster!

We want you to grow and prosper and use your talents to enjoy life to the fullest and allow us to join you, brothers and sisters walking into that golden sunset. And this expansion of Love will bring about a great healing, far more than you could ever visualise, for this healing is on a stupendous level, revolving and evolving all around your world and out into the furthest reaches of space. We are governed by the Love within our hearts and that should be all that you wish for, and as the saying goes in your world . . . Love makes the world go round and we would not want it to stop! We reach out to touch you and hold you back from greater calamities and yes, we know you have free will to do what you will but oblivion on a vast scale . . .

No, I cannot say that, I think my own mind must be coming in here. Please help me friends, I think I'm getting carried away with myself, please step in and help me with the right words!

We have a statement to make that will indulge the masses and we take you to task for stepping over the mark when all is in hand to set the world to rights. We do not believe it will come to this . . . if you heed our words then all will be well, and we will be having this conversation in another world where adjustments need to be made. This is our mission to evolve and grow and to help others learn from our mistakes, to learn that Love will conquer, Love will overcome! It always has and it always will be so for Love is the binding force that keeps us together, it keeps us from tipping over the edge of sanity and hurling into the depths of the abyss! Love will surely give you wings to reach those heights that you strive for, surmounting all problems old and new.

This is given to you by those of the highest intent who come to purge your sins and to set you right on the road to freedom, for is this not

450

the greatest gift of all . . . to LOVE and be LOVED and to rejoice
that it is so!

I am now being shown a vision of Jesus wearing a crown of thorns.

There has been much suffering in the world and we ask you to gird
up your loins and set to the task in hand of opening those doors,
crossing those bridges and leaving behind the sorrows of a lifetime,
letting them fall . . . letting them go as you cast off the shackles that
bind you! Point yourself in the right direction towards the Sun and
with greater life force we shall bathe you in the energy of the Great
Divine, washing away the cares and worries, washing away the sins
that cling to you. Do not foster them, let them go, they will not give
you sustenance!

I can see leeches being removed from the skin.

Don't cling to the pains of your past for support, throw away the
crutches and walk unaided and be thankful that a new time
approaches. The Kingdom of Heaven is at hand and we shall rejoice
for it shall be so. Go now brethren and watch over one another,
count your blessings one by one. Love those around you that Love
you, Love your families, Love your friends and Love those that hurt
you. Love those who despise you and Love those who would cast
you aside, for they know not the way of the Lord! With your Love
they may be brought back into the fold and that is their choice, their
way must be honoured, but the Light of Christ will shine down upon
everyone . . . upon the whole world. That blinding Light will be seen
by everyone and your hearts will melt with Love . . . even the darkest
soul will become light and just like little babes you will be reborn.

I questioned this statement!

We mean that you shall be reborn within your heart . . . with the
pureness of a child's heart, with eyes wide open, eager and excited to
learn of the world in which you live; a world without abuse and
unkind words but with tender loving care, to be nurtured and loved
in a world free of pain and sorrow, in a world of joy and upliftment.

451

We express ourselves with great tenderness and draw you to us in our loving embrace. We register your thoughts and take them on board, opening up those reserves of energy that will help you to move forward on this stream of Light.

∞

As I draw down the golden light I can see a beautiful lady with long fair hair, she is walking past in a soft blue cloak. There are beautiful patterns of gold entwined in soft lilac clouds that are buffing up my aura and I feel a deep peace within my soul as the beautiful energies waft gently around me.

I heard myself saying - Dear Father God, Mother Mary and Jesus, I call upon those here present to draw ever closer and to speak their wisdom that I may share with the human race. I ask for your loving protection to spin a mantle of gold around me and to watch over me as I sit in the peace this evening.

There are troubled times ahead but we shall ride out the storm . . . we shall take wings and fly. We are born of man and come into this world that we may learn and grow, seeking out that which shall be fulfilled by us in this earthly span. We are governed by the innermost desire to succeed and we 'shall' bear witness to what has gone before!

I'm now seeing a very handsome man with tanned face and longish hair.

We desire to tell you that all is well . . . and so it is! There are patterns emerging that need to be explored in greater depth, and we take you by the hand and lead you to discover for yourself what is of great importance for the continuation of the human species. We delight in informing you that all is well on the horizon and we have promised you a greater formulation of ideas that shall rise to the surface and be accomplished within a given time. We propel you further forward to do your duty and take great pains to point out that we are there by your side. We take great issue with those who would lead you astray for this is not our pathway, stick to the straight and narrow. If we come to a crossroads 'then' is the time to take stock but for now it is full steam ahead and on to greener pastures.

452

We root out what has been troubling you and would like to say that, in this case, we have been most perturbed at your lack of audacity! There is a need to stand firm and accept that these measures need to be put in place, sooner rather than later. We openly express what is needed to set you back on course and we shall deliver to you greater escapades. We discuss issues that have not yet arisen, a minefield in itself and yet we shall overcome, listening to that voice within that tempts you and guides you to pastures new where we shall express ourselves most favourably. We put it down to a lack of experience in this setting and we shall take the bit between our teeth and anchor in the energy. We obey our gut feeling and strike when the iron is hot; we shall be on our guard against discourtesy and we take up the gauntlet, preparing for our advantage!

There has been much indecision of late in the hearts and minds of most of you on the Earth plane and we register your distaste at these interludes. We crave your further indulgence as we register your complaints on Earth and we submit to a barrage of indiscretions, wanton behaviour on every level, perpetrated by those very souls who ask for forgiveness and yet repeat the same offence over and over!

We are not easily fooled for we see into the hearts and minds of mankind and we are sorry to say that we have been disappointed, on many occasions, as to the validity of human nature being one of gentility with a heart full of Love. These are the ideals that we seek and there are many who match up to these criteria, peaceful and loving souls who come forward to help us in our quest for peace on Earth. We shall assist those willing to take on this challenge be it, come what may, and we ask you to sacrifice your time and energy in pursuits other than those which cause havoc among your fellow parishioners. We count our blessings and ask you to re-evaluate yours! Living in the countryside can be a joyous thing and we rejoice and give thanks for these small pleasures that can ripen your heart.

At the end here I'm getting the first line of the hymn, 'Love Divine all Love Excelling' followed by 'All Creatures Great and Small'.

453

Sitting in meditation today, I'm being shown a man with long white hair who reminds me of White Cloud but his face is younger.

We call to those who seek out others of like mind, others of our persuasion and we cultivate what is necessary and more comfortable for you to tame the senses.

If you come in all Love and honesty then you are most welcome.

We give our thanks to you my child. We have adjusted our frequency to coincide with yours and we bend to whisper in your ear.

Oh gosh I have just seen the most beautiful patterns of gold and purple, which have just swooped in. Can I ask what these patterns are, they seem to come and go and I can't quite make out what they are?

They are common place in our world and we adjust the frequencies so that you may see and hear with greater clarification. In this bargaining process we have brought in a remarkable entry to our domain and it is this we give reference to, so that you may see for yourself how we live and how we operate in this dimension! The fluidity of movement is a common stumbling block for those making their first journey with us. We do, however, install an itinerary of great worth, checking and balancing that which needs amendment, asking you not to lose your sense of direction. We are beholden to those who come to help in this endeavour and we suggest that we may be able to liaise on this and many more occasions.

We pulsate across the universe bringing joy in our wake. We are granted temporary access to your soul and this will make us more aware of what it is needed for us to harness the energy as carefully as we are able. We do learn from our mistakes and we adjust our frequency, allowing a pattern of resonance that can be understood by all. We are temporarily put on the back burner so that we may adjust our settings and we ask you to do the same in a format that is recommended for us all. This may be but a short stumbling block and we initiate greater access in just a short moment of time. This will demonstrate our allegiance to the cause and we note that you are

454

well spoken for, having achieved this many times before!

We rally round for the cause of mankind and depend on you to set the record straight. We are a lost race but we are well prepared to take you on board with us any time you care to visit. This brings us great joy and we venture further forward together to sense and feel what is expected of us. We hope you will join us in the not too distant future as we share our tales and we are glad to be back on track, honouring those conditions we find ourselves in at this present moment. Feel the elation . . . feel the joy . . . feel the certainty of God's word!

During this transmission there was interference and I lost part of the recording but the following evening I sat once more and received the following words. Before we started I could see the face of a Lion.

We are summoned from a higher quarter . . . we regulate your breathing, asking that you join us in prayer!

Dearly beloved, we are gathered here today to receive your energy, to receive your Love and to receive your wisdom. Please grant us these applications so that we may become true advocates for the cause of mankind. We offer ourselves and deep within our hearts we pray that all will come to fruition.

There is a management of lies and deceit that have caused great consternation in your world and we prepare for you, in triplicate, a mandala that we shall use to allow us access to the beating hearts of mankind. We spread our résumé right across the world, gathering disciples, and this has been our mission to bring you all back into the fold of true and everlasting life. We will begin by asking you to take a summary of the events in store and we broadcast on a network of fine frequencies . . . a vibration of light and colour.

This suddenly struck me as a being a RAINBOW!

This shall be our symbol and we balance the harmonies, adjusting our frequencies to coincide with each and every one of you. We will

455

broadcast to the nation our hope and desire for the future of mankind and this has been in preparation for the coming of our Lord Jesus Christ.

I'm now being shown somebody in a long striped tunic with sun streaked hair, tending to a flock of sheep.

This has become a greater fusion of minds, tailored to fit our verse and we come in all earnest prepared for this labour of Love. We register your true intent to deliver our messages and, as promised, we reach out across the universe and hand them to you. We are delighted with the uptake of all who listen and we prepare a documentary of considerable worth, aired for the masses to take on board, and this will be our greatest strategy.

I'm now being shown a line of people dressed in long tunics, some with donkeys carrying bedrolls and very little else; they are climbing up the hillside. One by one they come and this line stretches on as far as the eye can see, they are people who are drawn to the 'Light' . . . drawn to God's word.

We welcome in a whole host of stragglers, preparing to shed their inhibitions. Seek and ye shall find - it is written and it shall be so!

We ask you not to be in the shadow of our Lord we ask you to be in his embrace; we ask you feel the full force of his Love and compassion, his gentility of spirit that reaches out to touch you, his children who come home with a heavy heart! We shall lighten your load and the heart that is heavy shall become ignited with Love and Joy, soaring to the heavens in all majesty. And we give you sustenance, we give you back your self-respect, we give you back the very core of your being so that you may live life to the full.

It is wonderful, we are out on the hill tops with the wind in our faces and it reminds me of something I have done before, long ago with disciples of Jesus who all come to listen to his words. I then thought it could be my mind playing tricks.

Oh ye of little faith, draw not on those words that enter your mind, draw those words from your heart and listen more carefully. We

456

override your status and bring to the surface that which is hidden, we bring to the surface those final measures to be taken, to be heeded, and we rally round to make this journey worthwhile.

Be not afraid lest you fall into the mire of scorn for we will pick you up and carry you, we will not let you wither and die. We take the weakest amongst you and hold you up in the eyes of the Lord; we beg you to listen most carefully to what we have to say, for this is in truth the word of the most holy. And we shall rant and rave no more but give good measure of truth and justice, filling your heart with joy as we come among you, listening to what you have to say.

We come armed with the power of Love and project our voices onto that trail of Light that carries all around the world, and we will be heard in each dimension, spreading far across that rainbow. And we do in all sincerity thank you for opening your heart and listening to us in the same fashion as you did long ago, on a hill top just as this, recognising in one whom we Love the true advocacy of our brother Jesus, and he is born again to bear witness and to tend his flock. We bide our time and listen to the words within our heart, transcribing at a faster pace and honouring this connection with the unseen.

Blessed be those who come to hear our words . . . and blessed be those that give them voice!

I'm finding it hard to hold back the tears here and can hardly believe the words I'm bringing through.

Listen to that true voice within, accept its guidance, honour the value it brings and treat yourselves gently upon this pathway. Do not be put off but maintain your course, retain that spark of unity!

I can see Jesus now even though my eyes are open; he is in my mind's eye.

I don't know what question to ask you. Is Jesus from your Star cluster or is it that he is a man for all peoples from all Star systems?

I didn't expect this; I don't know why but I didn't expect the people from the

457

Hyades who have feline features to be talking about Jesus.

We are permitted a summary and ask you to stand tall, for we are given to believe of further revelations that shall unveil what is hidden, and we prepare you for this unfoldment sooner than you think! Just accept that we have your best wishes at heart and we raise you in stature to come and join us on this and many more occasions, to fulfill our destiny and to bring you full circle. We impel you not to lose heart for all is well - all is as it should be. Please accept this accolade and bring it into your heart with the true realisation of a greater future for mankind, promised from those on high. And we bear witness to a greater study of the human race, helping you to set foot in our domain and to become one with us your brothers and sisters, fulfilling that which was written . . . and 'Man Shall Walk in the Path of the Chosen One'.

Again I doubted my words and asked for help.

We welcome you to our domain, curtailing the mischief within your heart. We align ourselves with you that we may understand the human race more completely. Love is the only prerequisite we ask you to bring, Love and honesty and these we have in mammoth proportions, and we know you bear that resonance of Love within your own heart and though we disagree at times on various attributes, we ably connect.

Gosh I'm feeling rather cat like myself now as the energy draws closer, my eyes feel quite slit like; I can't open them properly and my top lip feels puffed up.

We pre-empt your thoughts, shying from the realities that face you head on, and we do conspire to entice you from your work to come with us and play. We do make marvellous friends and allies and we are the most loving of creatures.

I'm getting the sense of a full blown Lion with great mane and he is rolling on his back with legs in the air.

We are nothing more than big pussy cats!

458

I'm confused are you the same ones who were talking to me about Jesus?

We are those avengers from the past who now bring 'Light' into all situations. We are conduits of energy.

I'm confused . . . I think I'm going to have to close now as I need to relay these messages clearly and precisely and I can't allow for mistakes to be made.

As I looked up into the sky I could clearly see the face of a Lion in the clouds. I can now see ET with his big eyes and long neck. They are all out there in different shapes and sizes; different faces all working together to help one another.

Rejoice for it shall be so!

Thank you my friends I think we should call it a day here. Thank you for your words, I look forward to listening back to them and I'll tune in again soon for further updates. I'm signing off now in Love, Light and Happiness.

As I left my healing sanctuary and locked up I couldn't believe my eyes – there at the end of my garden was a black cat! We very rarely see cats here as none of my neighbours have any. This reminded me of the black cat that ran across the road in front of me as I drove home yesterday. Surely this must be confirmation of contact with my feline friends from the Hyades.

Through Blossom Goodchild, who channels White Cloud, the Federation of Light referred once to their group as being a 'pride'. Blossom answered that it was a funny term to use and they replied 'an accurate one'!

∞

After sending out healing today I invited my friends to draw near for communication and now I'm getting really strong tingles down my right arm like goose bumps, they are also very strong over the right side of my skull and to the right on my forehead.

We gather in anticipation . . . we gather in unison, making way for what is to come. *Then may I ask what is to come?*

The hopes and ideas of the nation brought into being and manifested right before your eyes on a grand scale. This has been our wish for centuries past, an amalgamation of all we hold most dear brought to the surface, brought into the Light and expressed with greater cohesion.

We are caught wide open in our excesses and we bend over backwards to help you with your initiative on the Earth plane; this will mean following the rules precisely unto the final letter and we shall not be put off in this! We come fully armed to face you in all our glory and we shall enter the Kingdom of Heaven of that there is no doubt. We put it to you as bluntly as we may with the versatility and governing from those on high who we speak of as the 'Masters'. We have challenged the establishment and reached out and touched that place within your hearts, bearing you aloft and summoning the energies of those you have come to Love and admire.

There is twenty minutes of blank tape here so I have lost the words spoken and am hoping I will get that back at a later date.

We are a beautiful race . . . our grandfathers were astronauts as were our mothers, and we give thanks for this reunion of souls on the horizon that bring us into greater awareness. We are you way into the future; we are those giants in history that catapulted the world into chaos and oblivion! We come back in time now to challenge you so that you may set the record straight and change your course, for it is written and shall be so!

∞

Calling down the golden light I can feel my face changing and thanked my Star friends for drawing close.

Are you from the Pleiades, the Hyades or Sirius?

We are well pleased, well pleased and we need to sit up and take notice of what is around us, of what is happening to our energy fields!

460

Oh gosh there is such beautiful pulsating purple and gold here, thank you friends.

This is our purpose to register that which is within you as being true for the purpose of our mission and we shall be accepted into this fraternity of souls, gathering around to share with us in this greatest endeavour. We come to your shores, opening up the minds of many of your persuasion and we chime our messages across the great beyond, peeling out our joyous connection.

I feel as if the bells are singing out with joy!

And indeed they are little one, indeed they are! We open this connection and point you in the right direction. We have gathered many souls here today to join with us and we feel your excitement, just as you sense ours in this grand connection of minds, joined together to become as one. We make it count like no other, spreading our joy across the world . . . and yes we shall have our say of that there is no doubt. *There are tears in my eyes here.*

We would like to say a few words at this opening! We have charted our course for many territories in the past and we deliver to you by courtesy of those on high a mammoth production of services that shall see us in good stead. We prepare you to honour this connection with us your friends and allies from all those Star systems you mentioned and many more! Our connection has been a most joyous one and we give thanks for this and for all the friends and helpers, who have allowed this to happen by giving their personal services to us; amalgamating with that life force which helps us to harness the energy needed for operations such as these . . . and you are indeed sheltered from harm on all occasions!

A large flock of chattering crows flew over at this point.

We have sentinels who stand on guard, allowing this operation to commence. We do indeed have your best interests at heart and ask you to stand down when the time is right for you to do so and we shall bring a flavour of energy.

461

I'm seeing the Lion face again. Yes, I sense the Lion connection but dear friends, can you confirm to me that this feline, Lion connection is from the Hyades. I thought the Lion people were from Sirius. Can you help me here please!

The Hyades connection has and always will be studded with many different characters from different time lines, different associations with other worlds. We are not strictly one race as we have amalgamated and joined forces with those from other star systems, who all come to share their energy. We are delighted that you strive for truth and clarity for this is our way also.

Again I can see the proud head of a Lion. Oh I do Love your Lion face; I love the strength it brings. You remind me of Aslam in the film 'The Lion the Witch and the Wardrobe - a most noble Lion.

We thank you for this comparison . . . we strive always to make this world a better place to live in, where we can honour one another and accept one another, flaws and all. We are a most becoming race of soothsayers, expecting and delivering a keener sense of vision to all who come to our shores seeking for help, seeking for greater knowledge.

The gold and purple has become more vibrant here.

We do chastise you my dear for doubting yourself, for losing faith in your abilities and there are many of you that do just the same! We come to tell you to trust your instincts, trust that inner knowing and you shall expand and grow in greater strength and energy unsurpassed.

Dare to seek the truth and be not dismayed when it slaps you in the face! Don't cower in the corner, hiding your light under a bushel - come out into the open and shine! You are gorgeous being of Light and the mortal part of your mind would be shocked to see how beautiful you actually are.

ALLOW YOURSELVES TO BE THE LIGHT YOU ARE!

Relax and let go, let go of the pains and suffering, let go of the doubts and fears - **be the Light you truly are**!

This reminds me of a song by 'Bliss' called 'Say Goodbye' and the line - become the Light you are.

We exchange our frowns for joyous solitude. We beam you aboard, softening your advantage, bringing in greater reserves of energy that will instil a sense of peace and tranquillity to your inner mind . . . to those depths within that hold on to the past. And we shall browse through the corridors within your mind, bringing to light the core essence of your being. We have been put on the back burner for many years but **'now is the time to shine'**. Hold on to that essence of Love that is burning bright for all to see and it shall grow and expand within your hearts, making a difference to all those around you, and they shall gasp at your vitality, at your strength of purpose.

We access finer dimensions and light the candle for others to follow and we see you growing in numbers, casting aside the fog . . . the veil of uncertainty. We have been mentioned in high circles and we are indebted to your perseverance to forge ahead. We are right beside you and we flush out that which is not needed and cast aside, ready for this influx of energy to make its connection. We are aided and abetted by those in the know, and we bear you with us aloft to complete your journey so that you may give others a chance to shine.

We welcome you back from whence you came in all Love and sincerity. This has been a most troublesome journey but we have conquered over the bumps, the cuts and grazes and we have shone the Light, so brightly! Go now my child with our Love and grace, accept the Love we bring you and share it with your contemporaries; do not brush aside that which needs looking at in greater detail. All obstacles shall be dissolved and we shall be here with arms wide open ready to receive you and to give you the guidance that you deserve. We take it upon ourselves to brighten your connections and suffice it to say we have grown accustomed to the rhythms of your heart. All is as it should be and we settle you down in a finer location where your heart shall sing.

Opening my sacred space I give thanks to the Great Divine for the many blessings showered upon me, feeling the energy around me growing stronger.

We excel in our privileges, taking you on board once more. We deliver for the purpose of greater clarification our heartfelt messages for all mankind and this shall be our quest of the highest gradient, and the highest endeavour, propelling mankind forward on to those visions held sacred within your heart. We are blessed to bring with us greater volumes of accuracy and we prepare you to 'spill the beans' on numerous occasions, judging not your efforts to bring us about full steam ahead! We are in the process of gathering information, ready to pass on when the time is right and we feel you do justice to our words, bringing in a welcoming theme of enlightenment that will stretch far and wide.

We scan the horizon and see all we have achieved for those hearts that have been ignited, becoming one with the cause of upliftment for mankind. We broadcast our messages one by one in the hope that you will be able to summarise for us the feelings and emotions that we share with our brothers and sisters on Earth. We are well noted for our attempts at getting across these thoughts and feelings, sheltering you in our embrace as we do so; this has been a very eventful journey and we know it means a great deal to you for us to say this! Our shoulders are broad and we rely on you to download information, given as your right, and to enlighten those who know full well of our intentions to beam you aboard in the not too distant future. We have had many misgivings in the past about this event and we know it pains you to hear us speak thus, but we do have your best intentions at heart and we monitor your progress, each and every one of you, taking you to that moment of bliss and extreme fortitude in the line of duty.

We have sanctioned a visit that will enable you to express yourselves even more so and we resurrect a new line of services that will tend to the masses, relying on you to tender your services for mankind, spreading forth the news that Love will conquer over all malfunctions. For there is a nicety to be observed and a sense of decorum, instigating a wider network of services as we travel on,

464

gathering more in our wake. We shall not be tripped up or led astray, we shall stay true to the cause and we endeavour to show you by hook or by crook the workings of a mind hell bent on war!

We leave no stone unturned in this quest for Peace and we point out that this has always been our motive for assisting you in this ascension process. Be well aware of the constant need to assess each situation presented and we shall go forward, arm in arm together, to do what is expected of us and to achieve greater balance and harmony in the process. We do realise our dreams and they shall manifest before you in greatest splendour. Trust in the miracle man!

I keep swooning into clouds of lilac and am finding it hard to focus. I can hear someone saying in the background:-

'You've had a rough time of it but all that is about to change'!

I can see Master Jesus in a long white robe surrounded by blue and gold. During the rest of the 18 minute recording I slept and believe a healing has taken place. A flock of crows woke me and I received a few more words.

We are enchanted with your progress and ask you to reserve your energy for greater instalments in the future. You belong by our side and we give credit where it is due!

∞

Great Spirit, I thank you for this day, I thank you for all that has led me to this moment in time. I ask that we may sit together and blend our harmonies to communicate with Love and greatest joy. I call down that golden energy from the Sun in all her glory. I call down the Sun to drench me in her rays of loving energy, to be cleansed and purified and to be lifted up to speak once more with those I Love in the realms of Love and Light.

I'm seeing a handsome man with long dark hair and tanned skin; he is wearing a wide band of gold on his arm and a white skirt or loin cloth.

I'm visualising the golden energy flooding into my brain, into my third eye and

465

into my physical eyes, flushing into my face. I feel the same figure around me, helping to get me into that space we need to make contact, helping me to forget about the worries of the world, letting them fall away so that I may feel lighter and more able to communicate with my loving friends and family of Light.

I visualise the golden energy pouring into my throat, the seat of communication, flooding down into my heart and lungs and my shoulders, arms and hands . . . flooding down my spinal cord and out across the muscles in my back. I can see the energy flooding down my buttocks and thighs, into my knees and down into my calves and shins . . . down into my feet. I see every organ and every cell of my body glowing with golden light as it flows into my blood and bones.

I see that golden energy going down into the earth, down into the dark caverns below and am hearing the sound of a waterfall as it cascades into a beautiful lake. I visualise gently submerging myself in this water and luxuriously swimming as the water caresses my body, then laying on my back and floating, enjoying the water and the life force energy it brings. There is light dappling around the walls of the cave and there is laughter as my loved one joins me . . . the same dark skinned man who helped me at the beginning. We are gay and abandoned in our Love, in the loving energy of this sacred space, this fountain of youth! I see that I have dark skin myself with long dark hair and the cave is full of echoes as we talk.

I feel this is a deep cleansing experience to help me move on. I feel such intense Love and am asking for a name. Kwan Yin comes to mind and I'm asking for her to fill my heart with joy and Love Divine.

Uplift my spirit so that I may join you in the higher realms. Open my eyes that I may see . . . shelter me in your embrace.

And so it is we enlighten those in our care and summon an army of dedicatees that we may grow ever brighter in the universal state of existence. We are propelled further upstream and it is with this image . . . the Mother of Mercy that we dedicate this next half hour or so to you. We bequeath to you many treasures for the upkeep in your world and we register the delights in store for you and yours on the Earth plane. We come in all sincerity and in the light of a higher understanding we welcome you aboard to share with us, your brothers and sisters of Light. We take you to be with us in our dimension and we are governed by a higher life force energy that superimposes itself within your mind, within your very essence, and we take you now to pamper you and to uplift your spirits.

Thank you, thank you; thank you!

We know this means a great deal to you my child and we encourage you to strive for the very best in all that you do. It comes as no surprise to us that you have been chosen to sit alongside those most esteemed ones, who you register in your heart as being very special . . . and you are very special to us also, very special indeed.

I'm now seeing the face of one who looks like my oriental guide, Sayuri and have sensations of energy rippling on my face and down my left arm and leg. I'm surrounded in clouds of lilac but cannot see anything else.

Can you show yourself to me or is that asking too much?

I drifted off then sensed being raised up, I can feel an energy change . . . it's as if I'm above the clouds. I'm now seeing glimpses of the most beautiful purple and gold with shadowy figures, some with long necks. I feel as if my neck is stretching now.

We are given reason to believe that we shall be able to substantiate those image requests you have made, and we tamper not with your energy fields until we can upgrade and make the necessary adjustments that will not interfere with your life on Earth. We do improve your circuits to a degree that will help in our assessment and help you to be more comfortable. It beggars belief that we should have taken so long to come to this point but we are grateful for all assistance in this transformation.

Be rest assured that we shall do all we have promised that has been foretold in our reconstruction for those on Earth, for the necessary conduits that will improve the minds of all those who seek for truth and strength of purpose in these time of turmoil, to be uplifted and to know that we have prepared a place for you!

I have my hands in prayer position and the energy seems to be rocking them backwards and forwards . . . now becoming still.

Be of good cheer brethren, we align ourselves with you on this our greatest mission on Earth.

I have lots of tingles around my skull and am reaching my arms up and around ending with the palms of my hands held open. I keep seeing golden shapes and now recognise a golden skull . . . that's what I've been seeing a human skeleton!

We prepare the human race to be absorbed into a new energy field, one that will bring wonderment and joy to every being on Earth . . . to every life force.

I'm feeling this encompasses the animal kingdom and the plants and insects and every living thing.

We bring in the opportunity for you to share with us, your ancestors, your sons and daughters, your brothers and sisters, your friends and family. We are your family . . . we are your Family of Light . . . your offspring and we Love you. We could not be here without you and we shall be reborn once more into a greater essence of Love and Joy beyond all earthly measure. And all is there at your fingertips, just a heartbeat away . . . ready to be explored!

I've just asked if it's time to return and I'm seeing the most beautiful purple with golden shapes. I am sensing the name of Amun Ra - is that correct? I was looking at Egyptian pictures during the weekend and wonder if that is influencing me. Does Akhenaten figure in this story, in this puzzle? Without receiving any more answers that I can recall, it seems it's time to go as I'm being taken back now, back through the levels. I can just see the misty figures of two people kissing amid the purple and gold.

I thank all those who have supported me today and ask that the Love generated in this room will go out into the world, assisting in the healing of our planet and all life forms on her.

∞

This weekend, our little grandson came for a visit after badgering his mum and dad for several weeks and we had a wonderful time together playing. The house seems very quiet today and so after making a cup of tea, I put on a film I'd recorded, based on a book by Margaret Craven called 'I Heard the Owl Call My Name'. In the Indian village near Vancouver where the story is told, it is said that when you hear the Owl call your name, it is time for you to take your leave of this earthly plane. I wept at the beautiful scenery and all through the film and then cleansed my sanctuary before sitting for communication. Soft lilac clouds engulfed me and a beautiful peace descended upon me, followed by uplifting words that smoothed my ruffled feathers, assuring me it was not time for the Owl to call my name as there is still much to do!

In dream state the following morning, I saw my mother who died last year. We hugged and I cried and cried, sobbing my heart out in her arms. I stood back and told her how pretty she looked and she was smiling at me. I remember saying to her, Oh Mum why didn't you let me Love you, why did you push me away . . . we could have had so much fun together! We then linked arms walking behind mum's two sisters who have also passed over so I know she is in good hands with her family.

Today as I sit in meditation I can feel the energies changing and am being shown the face of Quan Yin with the sound of Ava Maria being sung in the distance. Going deeper I can now see an Indian with a blanket around him who looks like the actor George Clutesi who played the village Chief in the film I had just watched.

We speak to you in tongues of Love and we suppress those feelings and desires to run away and hide for that is not our way, we must come out into the open to be seen and heard in all directions. This is from the 'Great Golden One' who shelters us all in his embrace . . . this is from those who have your best interests at heart. Do not weep, do not be ashamed of who you are or where you have come from; we all come from the Great Divine and we speak from the heart my sister, we speak from those deep recesses within you. Be not afraid, we shall not hide our light under a bushel but bring it out into the open, radiating our message of Love and Truth. And the Light shall shine all around you, touching others with that bliss . . . with that knowing we are all from that same mould.

469

We come in all essence to bring you that which you desire and we shelter you in our embrace as we take you forward, unfolding what is not yet seen, bringing into the light and focusing on that truth within you. We do indeed beguile you with our stories and our just accounts of what has passed before us in great array. We delve deeper and deeper into those realms of Light, expressing ourselves with great joy at coming home once more, and we share what we have always known to be true. We accept those reserves of energy that will help you to move forward along this beam of Light that we hold out in readiness for your acceptance to come aboard, helping us to help the human race.

There have been many toing's and froing's from this craft and we see you stop and ponder on these words . . . but you have come many times before, as well you know deep within you, and this is what we are aiming for, deeper clarification, deeper understanding and remembering! These expressions have enabled you to stand strong and remain firm and we honour these undertakings, so that you shall remain perfectly at ease and within the grasp of all human understanding.

I can see glimpses of faces and now what looks like a large green grasshopper.

Great Being of Light, I welcome you into my heart to share in the Love that I have for the whole human race and for all life forms! I send my Love to you and ask that you help me to understand more clearly, so that I may share this knowledge, helping others understand our next step on this blissful journey that I experience when I am with you all. I feel that 'oneness' that connection, I feel the peace within my heart when I see the lilac and purple and glimpses of what you look like. I believe I'm not afraid, although I know that you will know my heart, even more than I do. Apprehension comes to mind and curiosity more than anything else.

Going deeper into meditation I suddenly see really vivid purple and gold.

We have changed our outlook somewhat and we have centred our opinions on those around us that do not always have our best interests at heart. We do, however, ask you to look more closely at

470

what it is you want to achieve!

I want to feel this peace more often, I don't want to be rushing around getting exhausted; I want to commune with my Star friends and to write down their words - that is my main priority. I would also like to have the means to travel to see my children more often than I do at present.

There needs to be a balance . . . a harmony.

I'm getting the feeling of actually melding with the large green insect, moving my head slowly.

We entreat you to expand your horizons . . . to look more closely at what is available for you on the horizon. We speed up the process and allow you access to our domain. It is of our choosing and we help you to truly express yourself in a format available to every living soul, and we bring you aboard exclusively to entertain the masses, bringing about a renewal and a grand exodus from this world. We know you champion the cause and we know you do have the power to change course if you so desire, but we ask you to step forward and be counted as one of us, ready for the upliftment of mankind into a higher dimension of Love and Joy and greatest bliss.

Forewarned is forearmed and we suppress those feelings of joy until you are ready to take that final step to join us!

∞

As I sit in meditation this morning I can hear the song Mona Lisa. I have painted a picture of a young woman sending out healing to the world and wondered if this was what they were referring to.

We are gifted enough to take up our brushes and paint a whole legion of faces and we will give recovery of those arts and graces that have not diminished over the centuries. We begin by learning how to use our brushes in a more noble gesture with a flourish here and there. We ask you to supervise a grand painting that shall outstrip those 'masters' in dexterity and sense of purpose. The proof of the pudding

471

is in the eating . . . and make no mistake we are on the path to glory and freedom of expression. We do not allow anything to distract us as we paint for pure pleasure and nothing else, and when this comes into view we will thank our lucky stars that we were born with this gift.

We see you take stock, checking all in your wake; we have come across a mammoth undertaking, appealing to those middle classes who do not believe in the mastermind activities of the rich and famous. We undoubtedly trigger a certain appeal among the gentry and this shall see us working in a more classical approach, covering a multitude of comparable studies that have not been seen for many a day. We allow you a glimpse into our work and bring out those qualities within you that have cause to resurface. We make it abundantly clear that we do have the facility to do this and we shall not let it slide on the back burner for much longer! This is the time to reinstate yourself in a world besotted with new technology and abstract forms of art, which leave us a little cold if we may speak bluntly!

Can I ask who is speaking to me; were you an artist in your last life?

We were summoned by the high court and we did justice to the walls of those buildings we worked on.

Can I ask which buildings you worked on? There was a crack in the room at this point.

We have made a mockery of those talents, once inspired by great courtiers of old and who now languish in the corridors of time itself.

Of course . . . it was Leonardo Da Vinci who painted the Mona Lisa!

We have a mind to play out this scene and we ask you to discover for yourself the art of gentle persuasion in the course of running your day. We empty our pockets   . . .

I drifted off here but wonder if there is something they would like me to paint in

472

the future, perhaps some landscape from another world. My paintings can hardly be called fine art but I am drawn to learn how I can improve.

∞

Great Spirit, I ask that you draw close to me and fill me with your loving grace. As I visualise the healing energy flowing through me, I can see a woman in a close fitting suit and helmet similar to those worn by the Olympic cyclists. The golden energy is flowing down my legs now into Mother Earth, there I will find and anchor myself to the tree of life as it spreads its roots around the world, growing and exploring, reaching out to touch other life forms. I feel the branches swaying gently like a sea anemone, sensing the vibrancy of colours, purple, pink, yellow, blue and green, harnessing the energy and bringing that energy into my heart.

We taste and explore those reserves of energy given to us, recorded in our very being and we accept the niceties that life has to offer. We bring about a time of seclusion, delving into the recesses of your mind, travelling at the speed of light to access those innermost reserves that have not seen the light of day for millennium. We transport you at these times of difficulty to come among us and to share with us.

I seem to be floating amongst the softest lilac and gold. Thank you, friends.

We transport you to those inner worlds, those inner dimensions of your soul, expressing ourselves with all sincerity at the prospect of what lies ahead. It is hospitable in every sense and drawing a line in the sand, we take you unchaperoned to where the mountain meets the sky . . . where the mountain peak reaches higher than ever before to the highest point in your world, bathed in that sweet gentle energy in its purest form. And we raise you up to come among us to be transported . . . an interface of quite deliberate proportions. We supersede any calamities with a basic structure that can be reckoned worth its weight in gold, and we deny access to those of you who come to push us too far before we are ready for this mammoth undertaking. It has been a giant leap for mankind in every instance and we prepare your sanctuary and safe harbour! Please allow us to bring you forward another step as we examine what is in your mind.

Yes, please do so!

Our actual entourage brings us into line with a new inquiry and we propel you thus far to each stage of entry. *Long pause.*

You are needed in the arena and we take it upon ourselves to issue you with new guidelines.

I can see turquoise and yellow along with blue and green ribbons of undulating light. Oh I have just had a flash of a female face.

We reconnect and issue you with a new study.

I keep drifting off into dream state . . . I've got to try and remain focused. The face I saw had some kind of headwear like a space suit.

We are well aware you have developed certain mastery and we adjust and adjudicate where possible to help you with your endeavours. We take you to a time lock of considerable success and embark on a journey that will become to all intents and purposes a most natural progression, sparking those memories and episodes of renewal upon the Earth and those planets inhabited by many species. We are therefore much obliged to you for helping us in our studies of the human race and we delve deeper and deeper into that time frame you are assisting us with now. It has come to light there are certain tendencies to hold sway beyond the umbilical cord of life, which gives us the chance to travel and explore as never before, and we freeze frame each episode you encounter, allowing you to take stock and to bear witness to countless episodes in your journey. We prepare for greater upkeep of your personal safety and we allow you to step upon those waters that carry you to distant shores, unfolding the imaginings within your heart. There are greater glories that await you, little one, do not despair that you have been cast aside . . . it is but a mere blink of the eye in the passage of time.

I'm filled and surrounded in soft pink light.

We express ourselves in terms of endearment and a new policy for reaching out and tapping into our Divine connectedness. This will become easier with each step you take, transforming an endangered species.

I'm hearing the name Dr. Woods being called out! I'm feeling myself drifting off again and asked for help in remaining focused. It's as if a lullaby has come to calm and soothe me.

A triple example of how to muster the forces of light and to register upon the Earth plane that which enables jet propulsion of all senses with no liabilities, no sense of failure . . . just bliss and perfect peace.

There could have been a better way of understanding, there could have been a greater light curve to take you on board more quickly but we allow the senses to register what is needed to make this submission possible.

At the word 'Light Curve' - there was a bang in the room and I'm wondering if this has something to do with Light as I've been watching a film about Einstein and his studies on the speed of light.

The purpose of this study is to assimilate the requests of the human race for greater life forms. We do not intend to take you down the same road as one another, we intend to grant your requests and lead you to that junction that will allow you further recourse. We mount our study and place before you in readiness for our great initiative, preparing you to do justice to all that is given. Do not be put off or downcast for we shall not leave you on the back burner for much longer. Make the most of the time that you have in your gentle pursuits and we shall follow you to the ends of the Earth and beyond!

I looked on the internet to see if there was anyone by the name of Dr. Woods of any relevance to my channelling and found this.

Dr. Robert Wood: Aerospace Engineer Veteran Blows the Whistle on UFOs

Dr. Robert Wood has a Bachelor of Science in Aeronautical Engineering from the University of Colorado, and a Ph.D. in physics from Cornell. He had a 43-year career at McDonnell Douglas, managing research and development projects for military aircraft. Dr. Wood has said he has read about 50 books on UFOs and to him the amazing conclusion he came to was that extraterrestrial craft are very real and needs looking into further!

∞

I sat in meditation listening to the cellist Yo Yo Ma playing compositions by Ennio Morricone; one I like in particular comes from the film 'The Mission' and is hauntingly beautiful. Through my closed eyelids I watched the familiar golden patterns laced over a purple background and then became aware of pink bubbles, literally bubbling up like a fountain into a pyramid shape and popping at the top. Maybe they are showing me how the music affects my soul.

We seek to find ways of expressing ourselves, making monumental discoveries and empowering a nation to stand up for what they believe in. It makes no difference whether you are poor or rich - this is a time to challenge the establishment and to make yourselves heard in every walk of life! We are beholden to those of you who seek the answers to your predicament and we understand that you are champing at the bit, wanting more, so much more than you have at present. We belie an infra-structure that raises the roof only to see it plummet to depths unaccounted for and we ask, do you really need these exercises or are they a discipline that can be registered as a pure waste of time? We beg to differ and tell you that without these tools, you will not be able to proceed . . . to move forward on this beam of Light.

We are encouraged with your progress and we ask to be allowed to monitor you in greater depth. There are a few instances of regret that we have been put on the back boiler for now; we believe it will be but a short time before you have made the adjustments necessary to climb another rung of the ladder so to speak. We push you forward in alignment with all we hold most dear and we forecast a greater reunion in the not too distant future. This has been our dearest wish that you should come among us . . . to be uplifted into 'team spirit' and we adjourn this meeting so that you may go about your business.

476

I sat again this evening after watching a documentary called 'Our Planet from the Air:' - Home' which documented how man is affecting the planet.

There are many in your world who have suffered and considerably so. We give thanks for the heart pouring's of Love from all around your planet; we give thanks too for those who offer up prayers of Love that are without sustenance themselves. We give thanks to the Creator for providing us with everything we need for the world is beautiful and bountiful. We scrape together enough evidence to put humanity to shame for not providing for those less fortunate, and there have been greater violations of nature than you could ever imagine! We are beholden to those just few who come forward to save the planet and we ask you to be more careful in your deliberations, accessing the very heart of the community with your prayers.

We interest you with our message and ask you to bear with us as we sample some just deserts. It is not our way to mismanage a whole nation in distress, we merely mean to collaborate with you to alter the time scale in which you live, to judge the accuracy that may be maintained as we take you on course for a new world of ample proportions, where no one shall hunger and every child is catered for. There shall be no more pain, no more sorrow or disillusionment . . . we come to prepare you and to update you on each stage reached before moving on. We realise this has been a time consuming effort but we have taken well to the adjustments as a whole. We shelter and caress your energy fields, softening those edges and embracing you. We do have the capacity to come on board at this time!

I get the feeling of soft swaying ribbons of colour and light, like the Angel's wings I've painted.

We regulate your breathing and sanction a going within.

I'm now sensing a pale blue veil.

Suddenly there was a loud bang on the roof and I shot out of meditation with a jump! It turned out to be my husband moving a chair on the sun roof of our sanctuary. It really is important not to be disturbed in deep meditation because you come back into your body with such a jolt instead of smoothly and gently.

∞

I'm bringing the golden energy down in that cleansing process that drives away all negativity from my mind and from my energy field, leaving only pure undiluted Love. I sit within this peace and stillness and welcome you into my heart.

Look to that to which brings you most comfort and peace. We isolate the cause of your malfunction, bringing you to a sunnier position. There has been a most bountiful harvest and we put it to you my friends - where would we have been without your input, without the gratification of those souls here present? It has indeed been a long and arduous journey but we are nearing the point of fruition that will bring you great release, bringing relief from conditions that cause a murmuring in your hearts of untold injustices, which surface now to be heard and brought into the public arena! We shall not let things slide and we shall examine in greater detail what is necessary to forge this alliance built on Love and trust, and we ask you to shed further light on this subject dearest to our hearts. We allow the murmurings within your breast to surface . . . to bubble up and be dispelled, anchoring our Love in all sincerity and with the greatest respect on both sides. We have enabled an express fermenting to bring greater jurisdiction and we harbour your responses for greater feedback.

I can hear the word Eaglets and am sensing a mother Eagle about to push her babies out of the nest to fly!

It will soon be time to fly on those wings of Love and we gather you to us in deep embrace. We abandon the games that made us sick and tired, asking instead that you follow us as we slip into the charm and grace of a new world, opening up to new possibilities. This has been a long and lasting mission of great success and we thank you for persevering with these connections. There has been no right or wrong way of achieving this, but through trial and error we have found a perfect amalgamation.

I can see a slim man with a smooth head, who has just walked into view wearing a long, pale blue coat.

It is a fulfilling journey and one we give thanks for. We shed light on those areas unfulfilled and prepare you to hasten your footsteps.

∞

Chapter seventeen

The gates of Heaven open

I'm sitting in my sanctuary listening to a torrential rainstorm as it drenches the garden and valley beyond, parched from a long hot summer. I feel the energies drawing close and sense a sweep is being done of my body with adjustments being made. I'm becoming very warm as the golden energy fills every cell of my being and I visualise sending this energy deep into Mother Earth, asking for healing for all life forms within her protection. I bring the golden energy back up through my body and out of my crown chakra into the cosmos, calling out to my Star friends. I am here . . . are you able to speak with me tonight? I settle the energy back into my heart centre, visualising a golden portal of Light and wait!
I think I must have left my body as I'm now behind the Buddha statue in my sanctuary; I can actually see the back which is about four inches from the wall. The recorder shows my steady breathing for quite some time before I spoke.

Wave upon wave of energy beaming across the universe . . . we up skittle events and set you on track, examining and probing, magnifying and bringing into perspective what is needed to help you grow and adjust to these conditions. We envelop you in a wave of Love, transcending our obligations as we fulfill our destiny, marveling at the adjustments you have already made and which you bring to our door. We have expanded and grown wider than ever before and we regulate these transmissions to enable greater harmony and self-preservation. We are formidable in our determination to succeed and this we shall do at great cost to ourselves.

We have stumbled across, quite by accident, what we are given to believe by all accounts as a minor miracle; we have adjusted our settings to liaise with you and this has given us the greatest amplification! We are mealy mouthed when it comes to additional information that we have yet to bargain for, but we do feel that you do justice to what we have to say. This runs concurrently within a broader governing of services and we propel you forward to do your work in whatever way, shape or form, being governed by those on high to take up the gauntlet and get down to business as soon as possible! We have adjusted our frequencies necessary to make this work and we do believe you have the ability to stand strong in the line of fire. We do of course express our sincere condolences for those times of genuine disaster, where we have been sat on the back burner and we stress, quite categorically, that we need to raise the bar! Striving higher and higher will bring us ample proportions of work and we do feel that you are ready to take this next step forward.

Arm yourself with Love and you shall do well, blossoming and growing towards that trail of Light that constantly beckons us on. Be aware that we are reprogramming an entire nation! We are honour bound to take you further abroad, instigating the services of other loyal subjects and we broaden your shoulders that you may accept what we bring. We have peddled our wares in the distant past and brought with us here today those attributes necessary for your continued journey. We summon up the courage to take that next step and we believe you will do justice to all that is given in the fullness of time. We make no bargaining process that does not register in your heart as being just and true. We prepare to pull the plug on those who have not kept to their side of the bargain and this in itself has caused great hardship! We are shackled to God hook, line and sinker and we shall never wiggle free!

I'm being shown a young fruit tree full of blossom.

This has been a very telling exercise and we bear food for thought . . . we digest every word, reaching out and storing information.

I half woke in the night and saw a creature leaning over me with greyish looking head. It may have been a friendly 'Grey' come to take me aboard for a meeting as the next thing I remember is looking at what I thought was my hand with only three fingers. I am reminded that Arcturians have just three fingers!

∞

Today a friend gave me a quote 'When you nurture your dreams and give them wings . . . that's when the magic begins'!

The time is set – the hour blessed when all shall come about! We hear you ask and when shall this be, when shall this be brought into our knowing, and we tell you now it is without doubt winging its way to you at this moment in time. We bear witness to what has been agreed upon and we do indeed welcome you all into the fold. We gather together in Holy Communion, giving thanks for this great feat of strength and courage and for the Love amassed in the hearts of mankind. We have been blessed to receive you and we shall give you the guidance you seek that will enable greater clarity on proceedings taking place even as we speak. We are dumbfounded at what is laid before us, a whole retinue of undertakings that have left us depleted, begging for mercy, and we shall give succour to those souls who come in all earnest to help those that follow on!

We are empowered to give you a short speech and we are indebted to you for drawing close once more. This has been the leanest of times for many on the Earth plane and we know it has caused great heartache for you. Do not be distressed at the scenes laid before you . . . it is our task   pick up the pieces and to begin again in a new format . . . in a new world of Love and Peace. These we promise you in ample proportions, honouring our connection and leading the way forward for others to follow. This has always been our message from the very beginning and we entertain the masses, helping you discard that which holds you back so you may begin life anew. There are no debts to pay in our world, we ask only that you Love one another with an open heart and we propel you to a new dimension of peace and tranquillity, calming your fears and helping you to settle down in new homes of ample proportions.

The rich have severed their connections and stand beside you and the poor are poor no more for the Lord is bountiful in his Love; for has it not been written that he who cometh in the name of the Lord shall be rich indeed and those who have laid down their lives for their brother shall be welcomed with open arms! We seek to bring annulment to those insidious diseases of the mind and there shall be no more heartache and no more sorrow. We have adjusted your time scale to ours lock, stock and barrel and you come under the jurisdiction of those on high who have worked tirelessly to bring you home once more. Be prepared to cut your losses for all shall receive sustenance here, all shall be given the same preference regardless of the life they have led on Earth. All are special in the eyes of God, each and every one, and not one child shall fall from grace. Ye are never alone!

We are able to make these adjustments to honour our connection and we ask you to tread thoughtfully and carefully in the weeks ahead; there is much to do and much to be accounted for and we will do justice to all that is given, spreading our messages far and wide. All will be revealed in due course . . . stay to the path and remain ever vigilant! You are all coming closer and closer to our welcoming embrace.

∞

This morning I went for a walk and leant against a tree I'm making friends with. As I shut my eyes I saw a big male head with thick mane of hair and a dusty face, I think he may be guardian of the tree and I'm looking forward to talking with him as I make more contact. It is an Ash tree and on research I see now why I was drawn to it.

(Mythology and symbolism - The Ash tree was thought to have medicinal and mystical properties and the wood was burned to ward off evil spirits. In Norse Viking mythology, Ash was referred to as the 'Tree of Life'. Even today it is sometimes known as the 'Venus of the woods'. In Britain we regarded Ash as a healing tree).

I decided to 'spring clean' my sanctuary changing the layout of furniture and cleansing each nook and cranny; today I'm trying out the new energy created. Great Spirit, I give thanks for this sanctuary and for this beautiful valley we are nestled in that looks out to the estuary and sea beyond. Draw close my friends and speak with me.

I'm visualising a golden Lion and thanking him for his protection and for watching over me. I feel a golden energy enveloping me and bring it down through my crown chakra, flooding my entire being with golden light. I continue to bring this energy down through my feet into the ground and out into the bowels of Earth, sending the golden healing energy to Gaia. Those strands of golden light join with other Light workers and the gold is joined with the purple flame, rippling around the globe, sending healing to all life forms on our planet. I bring the energy back up through my feet, through all of my chakras and out through my head into the cosmos, calling upon my Star family to draw close and to honour us with their blessings. I see the heavens teeming with life in a multitude of stars and I give thanks for this, asking if there are any words to pass on to those on the Earth plane.

Here we will focus on the 'humanness' of mankind and point out that we have never had it so good! There are many enlightened beings that inhabit your world and the band of Light grows wider, the band of homo-sapiens that answer to the call within their heart. We stream forth our wisdom and knowledge for you to pass on to others of your persuasion, who will then pass on to others, and so our messages circulate around the world and eventually permeate to those who have little or no knowledge of a world beyond their boundaries.

There are many who dare not believe in other worlds, who only feel safe within their four walls in front of their television sets. They know nothing of the harmful rays brought into their energy fields, bombarding their minds with disinformation that causes more harm than good. These rays bombard your circuits with poisonous negativity, opening up access to the darker forces within your mind, which drag you down and hold you back from beginning again in a new time frame that opens up new horizons. We are open to discussion on this subject and ask you to call out so that we may understand one another more clearly!

May I ask - are there really harmful rays coming from our television sets? There are many interesting documentaries on history and art and music and films with uplifting moral stories? Is it safe to watch these for short periods during the day or evening?

We can only suggest that you would be better occupied by going within and learning new information given from the source. It is there within all that you seek; all knowledge is stored within the very cortex of your being. There are stories all around you living within those people in your towns and cities; go out and speak to them, go out and connect to others instead of huddling in your homes, watching artificial families! This is not reality . . . this is turning your brains to mush! Make life count, every second of it, talk to one another . . . laugh and be restored to good health. Be out in the fresh air as much as possible . . . look to the heavens and see the stories in the sky; watch the clouds scudding across that vast canopy of Light above you. See the mountains and the Angel's wings; see the glory of what shall be if you open your eyes to the truth of what you can be. Do not be blinkered by the soap operas invading your screens – life does not have to be like this! Life by its very nature is vibrant . . . is wonderful! Look for the good in everyone and every situation, look for the help that you can give to achieve equilibrium of the soul for everyone.

I've just realised I'm seeing vibrant gold and purple and that helps me to know I'm on course with this channelling. If I need to search for a word - I know it is my mind, but if a word floats in naturally then I know I'm channelling correctly. Thank you Great Spirit for giving me this opportunity to link with you; I feel light and soft and the gold and purple are more vibrant now. I feel as if I'm floating . . . safe and at peace with the world and with myself. I wish everyone in the world could feel like this, to feel this peace, this buoyancy! I can hear someone saying:-

And so they shall!

The energy feels very strong here today and I am reminded of the Lion – the strength and courage of the Lion! Have you anything to say about the 'Lion Gate'?

Gosh I'm seeing such a vibrant golden grid. I'm sensing a female Lion now, nuzzling me contentedly as a mother does when playing with her cubs.

There is a time to rest and a time to play and we give thanks for our reunion today! There has been a slight hiccup in our defence mechanisms and we know you would wish us to herd you to safety. There is an opening coming that needs to be looked at very closely and we ponder on this, pointing out your vulnerability. We take you to one side to adjust your energy field, to polish your aura so to speak, bringing you into a stronger position from whence you may take your leap of faith!

We batten down the hatches and wait before we take our final leap of faith, joining a grand profusion of story tellers extraordinaire, who come to match like for like, bringing you into that golden space that shall catapult you into a new understanding. We isolate that which holds you back from making your final choices.

I've been aware of the male Lion joining me as these words flow.

We honour your connections with those who have helped you grow and flourish, championing the cause of mankind. We thank you and keep you safe, watching over you at all times. Some of you will go forward before others; some of you will remain to help those who hold back from making their choices. Some are on a roller coaster of emotions that cannot be held in check and we give substance to their lives and sustenance to those who waver between life and death itself! You have no cause to worry for all is being held in check until that final accolade that will reach your ears in grand profusion.

This is not a time to lag behind, this is a time to move forward and claim your inheritance; it is a time to stand in your own truth, despite the ridicule or scorn that may assault your senses. We have a protective film that we bring around you to soften and deaden the repercussions this would cause to your energy field . . . we wrap you in cotton wool so to speak! We find there is a guaranteed period where we can make adjustments as necessary; above and beyond that we cannot help – you have to make the decisions for yourselves!

The gold and purple were so vibrant here it made me gasp!

There is a vibrant causeway you can travel along and the decision is your and yours alone; once you have put your foot on this beam of Light there can be no turning back . . . like an escalator it will bring you home, it will beam you to a new reality. For those who wish to stay . . . this is your prerogative and we will help in any way we can, you are brave souls indeed!

We do indeed wish you would join us and we are entitled to say - and none too soon for this has been an accomplishment of mammoth proportions, which has found us in God's great favour. We relinquish our hold on you, letting you go about the business of your day!

I feel as if I'm being held in a beam of light so mesmerised that I haven't thought to ask questions, but I do know I Love you dear Father God and ask for the strength and wisdom to help those around me.

And this shall be so my child and you shall come home with your brothers and sisters. Return to the Light from whence cometh your help; your help cometh from the Lord thy God . . . Prince of Light, gatherer of souls.

Thank you Great spirit, I thank you with all my heart.

∞

I woke at 3.30 am with thoughts rushing round my head, gathering up my notebook I asked: - Are we really ready to make that leap of faith into a new consciousness, a new dimension of time and space . . . to leave behind all we have known and travel on that beam of light?

We ask the Children of Earth to make a stand for the human race, we ask you to look to your hearts and make a choice! Do you want to live in a world free from oppression, to be able to raise your eyes to the sky and see the heavens in all their splendour? Do you want to live without fear, to live in peace and dignity and above all to live with Love in your hearts for all, whatever colour or creed? We know this has been a hard choice for many of you on the Earth plane, to leave behind all you have known, but before you is a golden pathway that will lead you to the stars and beyond; a life full of enterprise and joy beyond your wildest imaginings, and this can be yours by releasing the old and letting in the new.

487

Let that light flood into your soul, releasing you from the prisons you have made for yourselves with walls of fear and hate; let these jealousies and the rancour melt and fade away. Take what is yours by right with the Power of Love, for this is the magic key that will set you free . . . this will open that golden portal in your heart to a new dimension. Release the fear and negativity . . . release the sadness and deep melancholy . . . the regret for what might have been . . . if only! Release the pent up anger from the past and take flight on wings of Love. Raise yourselves up from your doom and gloom into the lighter realms of joy and peace. It can be done and we are here to help you!

How are you helping us?

We are opening portals that will assist in your recovery . . . portals of Love that draw you like a magnet into a new vibration, uplifting your souls . . . spirals of golden light replicated and brought into manifestation.

My brain is whizzing into visions of past dreams, stepping out from a golden portal and walking on a new born Earth, amidst throngs of people all walking along in the same direction, stopping now and then to hug each other. I remember walking along crying softly with relief at what we had achieved and seeing an Indian guide in full regalia, threading his way through the multitude to speak with me.

We are getting so close now to this big event but how close - is it a year or a decade? I have been told I will see our new world, not as Moses from the mountain top, but I will be allowed to step onto this 'Promised Land'.

Oh ye of little faith, you have come to your destination, you have walked already upon this land and now help in preparing others to follow. There are many here who do just that and we take you over the threshold at the time that is right for each and every one of you. There will be a mass reclamation of souls in due course but the time has to be right . . . right down to the last nanosecond. Please believe we need to get this right! The essence of your being needs to be in acceptance of this transition to embrace life in a new format, a new resonance, and we believe with your care and help we shall make this event happen in record breaking time!

I had to laugh to myself at this as I can just hear the murmurings of disbelief!

It shall be so with a little faith and a lot of LOVE . . . this is our promise to you!

I have come to the last page in my notebook and finished the transmission here but when I turned the page over I saw the words 'shine, shine, shine' from a previous message! I guess if we all make our lights shine brighter all around the world then we can make it happen sooner rather than later.

∞

I've spent the last few days painting a Lion, trying to get the dimensions right and as I sit in meditation this morning I can feel that strong Lion energy with me again. Bringing down the golden energy through my being I ask for particular attention to my joints and bones, enabling them to move more freely; I visualise the energy flooding into every organ of my body so that each organ operates at its optimum performance. I see the lilac clouds sweeping around me and thank the Great Spirit for the Love and help I am receiving. I visualise a waterfall of light running down my spine, flooding the whole of my being in Golden Light and flowing down into the caverns of Earth. I send Love, Light and healing energy to all those residing beneath Earth's crust, through all the tunnels and caverns around the world. Let us see those lost cities from long ago rise once more, shedding the sands of the desert and revealing those ancient relics of old, helping us understand more about mankind and how long we have been upon this planet.

Oh Great Spirit it is such an exciting time ahead, help us to be strong so that we may get through those problems that assail us. We ask for Love and Light to go out to all those in dire need and that help be given where it is due! May the waters of Earth be purified, may the air be cleansed and may our hearts be filled with Love.

I bring back this golden energy from beneath my feet and bring it up through the core of my being and out through my crown chakra up into the cosmos. Great Star beings, Star family, I reach out across the universe and ask that you draw close to

489

me once more that we may connect and share the Love that unites us. I bring the golden energy back to my heart and wait as always for that connection of like-minded souls to draw ever closer into my energy field, waiting for that blend of loving synergy, combining our energies and bathing in the Love from the Great Divine.

Oh little one we have much faith in your discovering much more than this, we have faith and greater understanding of a mastery yet to be brought into fulfilment.

I can feel the energy on my right cheek bone and can see gold squiggles on lilac, growing to a stronger purple.

We are bound by our Love for one another and yes we will see those mountains once more; an overture of Love and harmony brought into our perspective and given reign over the dominions of Earth. We shall adequately assist you in your mission and this we promise with all our heart and soul, that none shall be dismissed as inadequate, for you all have within you that Divine spark that brought you into being, that spark of Love that shall never be diminished, never!

I feel such emotion here.

We are enabled to move forward on this beam of Love and all will hearken to the call of that there is no doubt. We beam to your world an adequate solution to your problems on Earth. We advocate a letting go for you hold on with such a fierce grip! What is it that you are afraid of . . . your vulnerability? There is much to do and explore and we shall be there by your side, asking and pleading for you not to lose faith for we are the very essence of life. Yes my child, we are the very essence of life on Earth, we are an essence of all that is! We strive for completion and in due course we shall make that mammoth discovery of a new world of infinite grace and beauty. We shall bring you full circle to face us and with great tenderness we reach out to you and stroke your brow.

I can feel a touch on my hand and tingles on my hair.

490

Yes, we are mesmerised, our techniques grow stronger and we are able to submit to these conditions more favourably. We discover new ways of harmonising, opening the floodgates and allowing others through.

I'm being shown a Lion now.

We are chosen to represent you today and it gives us great joy to come aboard, there have been many toing's and froing's within your heart and these good graces give us the incentive to move forward along this stream of Light, to which we all belong and which is much appreciated. Let battle commence! We have made a running commentary on our antics and this shall open up some interesting accounts of what is in store for us.

I can see the Lion much clearer now.

We have programmed a new declaration of Peace that shall spread far around the world and we give a resting period to those whose needs outweigh the few. This will become apparent as we accept you into our fraternity and we pander to the wishes of each nation, hoping that we shall not be abandoned and left to our own devices. This is not the case, for we have been very selective in those we choose to go forward into battle with those insidious forces that try to drag you down! We travel forth with you in mind, taking forth the dedicatees who work closely with us to overcome the malfunctions on Earth. We retreat to a safe distance and allow a simmering until we take up the gauntlet once more and move forward . . . it is rather like a cat and mouse game!

I can hear someone calling my name and seem to be drifting into dream state now so had to leave it here.

∞

Yesterday was a good day for me; I managed at last to paint the head of my Lion and took a walk in the sunshine feeling happy. In the evening I decided to sit in meditation and faintly saw the face of a man who looked as if he was wearing a high court judge's wig.

491

We are allotted a time frame to speak and it gives us great honour to come forward and be part of the proceedings tonight. We have a great wanderlust, a feeling to travel and explore and this we shall do! We are opening up to greater possibilities, greater avenues of distinction made plausible by our utterances. We shall champion you and set a date quite soon where we shall make our mark upon this world, registering our just intent to sally forth and on to those great adventures that we all long for! Creditably we register your just intent to move forward along this ring of fire; we exist to please one another and to bring balance to a world that has outgrown its infancy, superintending a worthier image that we may be proud of in future states of existence and we do share with you the pros and cons of living in a world free of sin.

Jealousies thwart us on every level and we are overcoming a massive imbalance of minds all jousting for a place! This has been an unjust society in every respect and we shilly-shally you into some kind of respect for your elders. We achieve the mimicry that will serve you well in a new land of grace and beauty, where each man's cloth is cut - not by his station in life but to the Love within his heart, and with this Love you may go forward into the Light. Those who fornicate without Love may wait behind, until they are ready to take that final step of absolution and completion, stepping over the threshold into a new world where LOVE is a most necessary currency.

We complete our task by day and night, censoring articles of war and bringing about a revolution of sorts. The streets are jam packed with people who ask to come aboard . . . to be in greater harmony and to articulate the wisdom not seen for many a year. This formulation of ideas we bring to the masses to test your senses, registering your thoughts and postponing events that come under your critical eye, managing the tumult from our place in the heavens. We ask you to bear with us while we sanction the wishes of those who wish to come aboard, to become one with us in our endeavours to free the human race from the mire of indiscriminate scorn and heartlessness!

We crave your indulgence for a few more minutes and we ask that you bear with us to enable a provocative study of the human race, of

492

their ways, of their joys and woes, their love making and their warring with one another; this cannot be tolerated for it has reached that point when mankind stands to say 'NO' - no more - no more war! The majority of your planet wishes for Peace and Peace they shall have! No more war, no more slaughter, no more pain and suffering, no more crying of lost children wrenched from their parents; their misery has been great but we draw the line now and act with courage in putting a stop to that which was once thought glorious. There is no glory in war – there is only gore!

∞

Its early morning and I'm sitting in my sanctuary, drinking my first cup of tea of the day. To my joy a huge flock of birds join together in formation sweeping around the sky several times, making a great hue and cry . . . and now are gone as quickly as they came.

I sat day-dreaming and thought about what my friend had said recently; she felt White Cloud was keeping his distance and indeed I have felt this too. Maybe it is for us to stand on our own two feet, just as a mother stands back to watch her child complete a task without rushing in to help! I haven't felt him near for a while even though I've called out, but a part of me 'knows' he is watching over us and when I looked at his picture the other day there seemed to be a wry smile coming from him. It's almost like we are on the dark side of the moon and communications are hampered; I just know that soon we will be hearing and seeing more clearly than ever before!

Great Spirit I thank you for this moment in time, I thank you for this Peace. I thank you for the birds that sing as they welcome in this new day. I thank you for the trees that dance, swaying and jiggling in the wind. I thank you for this time to sit and stare, to day-dream without a care. I thank you for those majestic Red Kites that soar high above our valley, circling around and around a patchwork of fields below.

The sky is like a great auditorium and the wind is up, sending huge white clouds scudding across this magical stage. They are like big soft pillows and nestled within are faces that are constantly changing. There is the face of a lamb . . . and now the faces of relatives that have gone before . . . and now ET! There is an

493

animal . . . is it a wolf or a cat 'yes' and now she has turned to look at me! Hello, thank you! Ah there is the profile of a bear that has now turned into a large mouse. White Cloud are you there, can you show yourself to me?

I saw the face of Mary who is wearing a blue gown and a man that looked like Jesus leaning towards her; it reminds me of the picture from the last supper. I can now see the face of a man with a big head and beard . . . he looks like a Greek God from a children's book I used to read on Greek mythology. These visions are marching across the sky and it's as if I'm watching a film.

I'm in a medative state now and close my eyes, catching glimpses of a golden spine against a purple background; there are pulsating purple clouds receding down a tunnel I'm being drawn into, it is made of some kind of membrane. We are in some kind of labyrinth . . . the 'we' suggests I am with someone, but I'm not aware of who. I can see a honeycomb of shapes that I can't quite make out but feel it is living material. There is deeper purple now and I'm moving further along the tunnel. Is this an illusion or reality . . . is this a figment of my mind or am I in truth here in this place? There are golden shapes against a purple background in a labyrinth of passages, again I wonder if I'm in my own brain. Hunger pains are calling me back and I had to stop here. When I went back into the house for breakfast I saw that I had been in the sanctuary for nearly two hours.

∞

After drenching myself in golden light as I always do before meditation, I'm focusing on my heart centre, which is like a beacon, bleeping a message out into the cosmos that I am here waiting for contact, sending Love out to all life forms on all planets everywhere. How may I be of help, what words would you like to share with the people of Earth?

Share, share, share . . . share with one another, share the Love within your heart . . . see it radiating out back and forth across your planet, across the globe you call home.

Have you heard the noise you make? The chattering of minds never stops, it is incessant and we hear you calling to one another in your heads, texting with your fingers; there is such babble, such a huge hue and cry rising up from Earth! We hear you, we hear you through that babble of noise and we hear the resonance within your hearts that call to us for help that is long overdue. We meet as like minds across the universe, treading thoughtfully and carefully and we register your intent to keep on course.

We have opened the gateway to allow you to pass through and we are struck with the very lightness with which you tread and with maturity of thought and grace beyond our wildest reckoning! We have some cause to tease you for you have given us so much more, and our ambition is to see you through this minefield of events that hover on the horizon. We must be careful, stepping forward easily and yet thoughtfully as we follow the trail of Love that has led you thus far. Be prepared to host a gathering in the near future and allowing for tact and diplomacy we shall see this gathering reaping great rewards.

I can see a dark haired lady, a Native American Indian with long black plaits and she is sitting comfortably in a kitchen area. I can hear someone saying in the back of my head – what do you like ladies? Someone else is saying – a cup of tea and a chat would be nice! I think they may be talking about a gathering in the evening here and perhaps I should set up another little group. Yes I think we could manage that quite well.

Hold onto that frequency of Love . . . let it flood your being, flood your mind and your body in entirety. Feel your heart pulsate, beating to the drum of Love, beating out the rhythm – Love is a powerful beat.

These words are going around my mind and I've been given them before.

We come as one enterprise, as one huge great reckoning for the upliftment of mankind, trembling as we speak and come among you in Love and purity of spirit. We welcome in a broader stream of knowledge and an opening of the portals has allowed us through. We give thanks for this, we give thanks for those on Earth who come in unison to raise the awareness of mankind and we point you in the right direction, enabling your frequencies to raise higher than ever before. We are on the brink of discovering a new world . . . a new world of immensity of spirit and good cheer. We come and nestle among you, whispering in your ear, guiding you to not give up hope, for we know there are many who are downhearted and disappointed that there has been no 'lightning bolt', no great signs in the sky that herald our coming, but coming we are my friends! It is your Love that beckons us and the stronger that Love . . . the closer we draw!

We come in all good faith and sincerity, stepping across these borders to help you and encourage you. We are forever on the cusp of joining together, like minds and hearts, overcoming the enormity of what lies before you and the frailty of human nature that dashes you to the depths. Be restored, clear your mind of all clutter and debris – do not let these things hold you back or cast you aside for there are many who knock at the door of Heaven and are allowed entrance into these wondrous worlds.

We give encouragement where encouragement is due and we shelter you from the abysmal apathy that drenches your soul. We raise you up to come and sit among us for a while to be nurtured and to know you are loved by so many. We appertain to those frequencies that bring us release from the doom and gloom of Earth, raising you up to come among us in all your glory and freedom of spirit. It will not be long before these realms are at your disposal for longer periods, a great crescendo of applause awaits you and your beckoning us to your side makes life easier in every respect. We shall not be cast aside or put off and we shall help raise the hopes of millions of souls, gathering those to us who have little restraint in matters of the heart. We propel you forward and on to your destiny that awaits you in glowing colours of every hue.

We may seem to be detached of late but that is for a purpose my child! There is much happening behind the scenes that you are not yet aware of and we point out that you have delighted us with your progress!

My head is being turned around and when I opened my eyes I saw that I was face to face with my Indian statue, which indicates that White Cloud is with me.

We regret there has been a parting of the ways on various occasions and we know this has caused great distress but we do initiate certain boundaries to enable your growth and to prepare you for the time ahead which grows ever nearer, and these times are of great importance as you well know! Take all in your stride, let it blossom and grow giving sustenance to the soul. There are great matters to be held in check and we wish you to move forward when the time is right for you; allow us to gather more information and we will do justice to every word, we promise you that! There has been much toing and froing between our worlds and we give thanks for this. We beckon you not to lose sight of what is in store for mankind . . . greater revelations that enhance your recordings and a bargaining process that beggar's belief. All things shall come to fruition of that there is no doubt and we stand back and allow you through in the fullness of our Love for you and all mankind.

We take this opportunity to express our sincere condolences for those of you who may never cross this threshold, for it is our belief that you will gain greater credibility in another world, more of your deserving.

I was worried about this statement and asked them to explain.

It has taken great time and turmoil of thought to register these discussions and we have allowed ample growth of the mind for all who come in search of 'Truth and Light'. We express what is in the minds of many on the Earth plane and those who do not wish to follow our path will be given choices on which pathway to take, and we ask you to stand and listen most thoughtfully to those questions, to those murmurings within your heart and give yourselves time to make the decisions that are right for you. We shall not complain, we wish you well on this journey and we shall meet again on this roundabout of Love, enticing those who have gone astray to join our merry band! We leave it here for you to make your assumptions and to marry into what feels right within your hearts as being just and true.

For those who feel this indulgence is too good to be true, we ask you to remember from whence you came, from the bosom of your Father in those realms of joy and bliss. Cast your mind back to the warmth and Love you felt in your Mother's arms and this shall be so again!

Never let it be said that we neglected our mortal counterparts for we are drawn to your sides to help you and to assist in your undertakings on the Earth plane. Be of good cheer and remember that we are always here. Tune into that amplifier within your heart and we shall speak with you whenever the need arises.

Thank you dear friends, I feel so peaceful. I've noticed in the last few days that the birds are singing more often. The days are starting misty and the birds are singing . . . they are still singing in the afternoon. Is it because we have raised our frequencies and we are now hearing the birds more often?

The frequencies within your heart resonate more strongly with nature; there is a subtle difference in your energy field that brings us closer to the very core of your being. There is music in the heavens, glorious music not yet heard!

Thank you friends, thank you.

∞

A Journey within

I've been trying to hold onto that glorious frequency of Love and struggling, feeling downcast at the obstacles facing me. I decided to pick an Angel card from Dianna Cooper's 'The Angels of Light' pack and as I shuffled them out popped Archangel Chamuel with the affirmation 'My heart is filled with the flame of Love'. With this affirmation in my heart I went for a walk, stopping to lean against my favourite healing tree, which is an Ash; immediately I could feel the energy flow through my back and stood for a while thanking the tree, telling him how much I loved him. The wind seemed to be caressing my face and just at that instant a strand of my silver hair was taken in the wind as if in answer.

(As I'm typing this I can see the face of White Cloud).

After a walk in the sunshine I sat in my sanctuary, staring at the painting of White Cloud and thinking about the power of 13. I asked my Spirit friends and White Cloud if they would like to draw close this morning and as I closed my eyes I could see a purple tunnel of circles within circles and a spot of white light at the end.

Great Spirit draw closer I pray, help me to remember my tribe. I can see a beautiful young girl looking back at me with dark eyes and her black hair is drawn back from her face in plaits.

Who am I? Who am I? Who am I?

"YOU ARE A CHILD OF GOD AS ARE WE ALL"!

I'm floating further into the tunnel but am still aware of sitting in my room. Oh Great Spirit, show me more, open my eyes that I may see the glimpses of truth thou hast for me, help me to set my inner self free so that I may serve thee.

"OPEN YOUR HEART AND YOU SHALL SEE"!

Clouds of lilac and soft yellow float before my closed eyes; I'm sensing a Native American standing to my left with long dark hair, I cannot see him properly but I

499

can sense him. Draw closer dear friend, draw closer. I can vaguely see, I can see and yet I cannot see . . . I 'sense' a large white bonnet.   Is that you White Cloud?

I am seeing soft clouds.

"SEE WITH YOUR HEART MY CHILD . . . SEE WITH YOUR HEART".

There are tears in my eyes now.

"We blossom and grow together, stronger with each passing day".

The tunnel is opening up – it is lovely in this tunnel with its purple and flashes of gold . . . I love it here and I feel safe.

Remember me . . . remember me . . . remember me!

Gasp – I can see lots of gold here.

Help me to see more clearly friends. Suddenly a big golden Cobra appeared, standing up so tall and proud and again we are traveling further into a labyrinth of gold against purple. My heart shines like a torch a beacon bright, piercing the darkness. There is the flash of an eye and now I can see a spotlight of pure white light. Oh dear friends, dear friends I love you, I love you, I love you . . . I am a part of you just as you are a part of me!

I'm going deeper and deeper into the tunnel amidst the beautiful purple clouds of light. I now feel as if I'm made of some gelatinous substance, slithering my way along the tunnel as it sucks and pushes me along. In my heart I'm singing Love, Love, Love . . . Love is all there is.

I continue on my journey and there are lots of shapes that I cannot make out, I'm not sure if they are creatures or statues; it's almost as if we are under the sea, exploring the deepest depths. We are going deeper through a myriad shapes as they pass by, deeper and deeper. White Cloud are you on this journey with me, is there

500

something I need to do? Perhaps I'm inside my body and have to send Love to every bone, to every blood vessel and sinew. I send Love to all I encounter and as I think this the gold has become more vibrant. I send love to myself . . . I Am Love, I Am Love, I Am Love . . . Love is all I need.

I am in some kind of cave underground now and there are creatures watching me as I send out Love deep into the earth, through all the tunnels in all the caves around the world.

"We are undecided which way to turn - there is a crossroads — do we turn left or right? We are drawn to the right but here lies turmoil, pain and suffering! Follow on the curve in the road to the left and here you will find joy amidst your sorrow. There has been a reckoning long overdue and we prepare you to enter into discourse with those Angels that will help you to carry this through in all immensity. We uphold your jurisdiction and travel further forward, opening up those avenues of discontent where we shall bring joy and revelations of pure intent, relying on our own sureness of vision and an aptitude that will bring more of the same for those around you.

We supersede a whole new avenue of thought that will bring courageousness to the fore, limiting the undercurrent of despair and this shall be a jaw dropping experience! We carry you through this tunnel of Love for you to experience what is necessary to alleviate the stresses and strains within your soul. We do not wish to take up too much of your valuable time and we bring you full circle to enable a bright reunion of minds, much sought after in your world. We dedicate our words to the human race and ask you to be prepared for your home coming"!

I seemed to jump suddenly into my body and as I did so I was aware of a beam of Light like a waterfall of soft colours.

∞

Great Spirit I ask that we may continue with my journey from yesterday. I think perhaps I may have been moving along the birth canal of my mother as I seemed to be sucked and pushed forward in some kind of membrane, some kind of gelatinous matter where I felt safe and warm.

We blossom and grow together day after day with deep remembrance, allowing ourselves that deep remembrance.

I can see an Indian with long, black hair looking very similar to the actor Russell Means who is holding a long stick in his left hand.

This is the very heart of the matter – here you will learn and grow.

I can feel my heart becoming warmer.

We will teach you to remember and remembering those issues that hold you back will in fact help you to move forward; accepting your encumbrances and learning to live with them will open up a new vision and it is with these platitudes that we send you forward, expressing our concern when at times you stumble and lose your way. We are here to encourage you, to help you to your feet once more, so that you may continue your journey to join us in the near future.

I can see a huge ball of purple light covered in golden pin points of Light shining way out into the cosmos and later realized it was probably Earth covered in our purple healing rays and golden points of Love shining out.

This is your destiny to become entwined with us once more, your most loving companions.

I can see the clouds of purple once more and feel supported in a loving embrace, filling my heart with Peace. Here come the golden shapes again and I'm remembering my affirmation from yesterday . . . my heart is brimming with Love and I feel the connection to my Star family; by using the Love vibration I connect to all I hold most dear . . . my Family of Light.

502

Be prepared to step forward and be counted as we open the network, broadening our horizons and following in the footsteps of the esteemed ones. Those that follow must tread most carefully . . . only when you are ready will you be allowed to pass this way!

I can feel a tickling on the right side of my skull and my head is being moved around again to face my Indian statue.

We face you sister and remember our times together.

I can again see a round purple cloud surrounded by a golden lattice framework, like a portcullis of sorts.

Step forwards my child and be counted, there is much for us to do and we take charge of those important issues that need to be dealt with. It is a time for honing your skills and we ask you to bear in mind that we shall, in all instances, propel you forward at a rate that is right for you. We will not hold you back nor push you forward. Your heart will decide when the time is right to take that leap of faith into the great unknown, and your heart will fly on wings of Love as we gather round to cheer you on!

I could hear the birds singing outside at this point and felt my heart lift.

The bird's song is our way of letting you know we are here and we feel the spirit leap within your breast in answer to our call; we have this very special connection that has evolved over the centuries, bringing us closer. The dark and dismal days bring us encouragement to fight for the cause of upliftment and we know you take it to heart when we sing your praises, allowing detrimental phrases to fall away . . . they shall not encumbrance you in any way, shape or form! We rise above sour words and turned shoulders, we rise into the mist that cloaks us in Heaven's splendour, here we find the bliss and contentment we desire, to be in all sincerity ephemeral, to drift with

503

those clouds that evaporate and reform, taking on new shapes, drifting back down to the Earth plane.

I can hear someone keep saying 'ouch' as if they are hurt, as if they have been pricked by something sharp like a needle.

We accept the challenges that come and know it is not always an easy task!

I seemed to be jerked back into reality once more and realized it was my balloon being pricked as I was brought back to Earth so to speak! Thank you dear friends . . . thank you to all those who come forward to help with these sessions.

∞

I'm seeing and feeling the beautiful soft purple clouds with golden overtones enveloping me in peace. Thank you, Great Spirit. I'm now seeing a vivid flash of purple with golden patterns overlaid and am finding it hard to describe . . . it's like a spider's web only bigger and of more substance. I've just kicked off my shoes and the purple has suddenly become more vibrant; beautiful pulsating violet light rising in intensity of colour and then receding to a soft lilac.

Dear friends draw close . . . I Love you so.   I'm sensing a big Lion again with his massive head and whiskers. Thank you for the strength you have brought; help me to see with my heart. The golden shapes come very close at times and it feels as if I'm being drawn into the centre at the heart of the pattern.   I'm feeling more and more peaceful.

We welcome in a new generation of Star seekers, searching for and examining your roots.

I can see what looks like a central column and there are lots of tendrils reaching out from it, like an umbilical cord it's a lifeline. I'm feeling a tickling over my heart centre; maybe some work is being done. Oh the purple is like no other purple I've ever seen and is shot with gold, it is so beautiful that it feeds your soul, you could literally drown in the colour and I wish I could achieve this vibrancy in my paintings. I can suddenly hear the excited chatter of birds outside!

We apportion no blame to those who cannot see and yet we discover a new world of ample proportions.

I can see a huge round portal of soft, violet light and a smaller cloud of deeper purple just went through; I wonder if it is a space ship cloaked in cloud.

We carry you on a cloud of Love to those deepest recesses within your mind, opening and exploring, delving deeper and deeper.

My head is being turned to the left now to where my painting of the Lion hangs.

We understand the necessity of creature comforts and we assist you in these measures, opening up the gateway to success. We revive a continuum of species governing with parental guidance, opening up new avenues that have remained under lock and key for so long. The centuries unwrap like a giant spiral, unfolding . . . emanating new wisdom. We see the tell-tale signs of audacity, pomp and grandeur, much to do with the lives you have led; we see too the sour grapes, the scorn and ridicule, the pomp and ceremony!

I seem to be in a theatre with tiers of golden balconies rising up to the heights . . . there is a sense of grand opulence.

It gives us no pleasure to relate these scenes when we have known deep within of the untold suffering of the majority of the population. We sang while the suffering continued and yet deep within the very core of our being a chink of Light grew an inkling of the truth and reality of existence; that chink of Light grew stronger and brighter, opening up greater reserves of energy that felt, with great respect, an honour. A blinding Light that represents the greater truth is that we all come from the same mould, we are all sprung from that Great Eternal Light into our various formats, and growth of the intellect

505

has given us insight into those predilections, into the sense of duty that we are prepared to shoulder. And we ask you to see . . . to 'know' it makes sense to follow your heart in all things, whether it be your final moment upon the Earth plane or whether you are born fresh into the world as new bud.

We ask you to look forward to your times together with us, your loving counterparts, who oversee your jurisdiction. We jump ahead and see that in the latter years of your life here on Earth you are well endowed with those graces refined with our advocacy. We are bombarded with requests for you to come home and we know it serves us well to have you there by our side. In times of denial we offer you a guiding hand, asking you not to lose faith in the structure we have maintained for so long. We have argued with you on many occasions in the past and ask you now to stand firm. We see there is a clause that you have not read yet and we ask you to be concerned with one governing force; be prepared to spread yourself more thinly upon the Earth plane!

This has been a troubled period for many of you and we recognise this, we recognise the fluttering of your hearts.

I have my eyes open now and am watching the wind in the trees.

Incentives you are given will be reward enough for the Love is strong within your hearts.

It's as if the trees are waving and cheering us on!

Dance and sing and follow your heart!

∞

Today I'm revelling in the Love and Peace that comes with meditation, leaving behind the heaviness of the physical and blending with my friends in the spirit realms.

Transcendence

It is very limiting to be in a physical body, this we know and we have felt the restrictions that this places on your spirit. We are able to tune into the frequencies that you desire more easily if you lift your vibrations above the din of Earth and go into the stillness within your heart. There are many that do not find this an easy task and yet we say to you . . . that stillness is available to each and every one of you . . . it is just a matter of concentration! We regulate the rhythm of your heart to correspond with the heart of the universe and beg you to listen as we unite as one. We open up a pathway that has been ridden by many of your ancestors and we fulfill a prophecy, opening up the boundaries that hold you back from reinstatement in our grand new world. We bathe in the omnipresence of the Great Divine, fulfilling our mission on Earth as was promised in a distant past. We know you will bear with us as we march on, raising the banner and cheering with all our might; we have fulfilled our destiny to walk tall and to protect our brothers and sisters who walk with us.

We are open to suggestions on how we shall complete this mammoth task and we know you and many others will raise your voices to be counted and heard above the rabble . . . the hustle and bustle of your earthly lives. We dispel certain notions of doom and gloom for this is not our way, we walk a pathway of hope, of a golden sunset where all will come to fruition and we pick up the pieces left behind by others of your persuasion, setting to right the wrongs of the past, enabling all to achieve that perfect harmony and bliss of the dearly departed. We speak from the heart and know you will do justice to our words for we have come many times before to assist you in these proceedings.

We march on to that horizon where all is waiting and we give thanks for the small discoveries we make each day that add fuel to the fire, to the flames of redemption. We are known for our encouragement and our sense of purpose, directing you to sunnier climes and this has been our main purpose, to set you straight upon the pathway. We have outgrown those nuisances that held sway in the past and we relieve you of undue stresses and strains, embarking on a new course. We administer a new potion of strength and success, opening up the doorway that leads you to Heaven and all you have ever wished for. We propel you to a stable courtyard where the horse is ready and waiting for your signal! Our back is broad and our saddle ready, you have only to lift yourself into the seat and take the reins, once this is done the world is your oyster and there will be no stopping you! We have fiercely protected our independence and we raise now the portcullis for you to take those first few steps out into the wider world!

That's a lot to take on board at the moment!

May the pathway you walk be one of strength and courage and may all your truths come to pass with special precedence and dispensation!

We give thanks to the Great Divine and for all those that have walked before us. We sleep well and remain in your hearts forever young.

The transmissions continue and I look forward to passing these on to those who continue on this pathway of Light. Thank you for reading these words and sharing my journey. If you have enjoyed reading this book please pass it on to others so they too may share. May your own journeys be blessed as you access that golden portal within your heart, seeking those inner worlds where you will find the most exquisite Love and Peace beyond all earthly measure.

I have repeated the 'Healing Meditation' again at the end for easy reference.

Namaste.

HEALING MEDITATION

Walking around my sanctuary I called out to the four directions then to Grandfather Sky and Grandmother Earth, cleansing with the burning of white sage.

Great Spirit, I ask for your Love and protection for myself and for this little sanctuary and for all who enter in. May we receive loving guidance from the Great Divine the universal source of all that is, in whatever way is right for us at this time.

Spirit of the East where the Sun rises - gateway to the sun and the element fire – we ask that you ENLIGHTEN US.

Spirit of the South where the Sun is at its strongest - gateway to our feelings and emotions and the element water – we ask that you EMPOWER US.

Spirit of the West where the Sun sets - gateway to the physical and the element earth – we ask that you TRANSFORM US.

Spirit of the North, where the Sun rests - gateway to the mind and the element air – we ask that you INFORM US.

Grandfather Sky - masculine forces behind all that is – we ask that you EMPOWER US.

Grandmother Earth - feminine forces behind all that is – we ask that you NURTURE US.

Visualise a shimmering ball of Golden Light coming down from above your crown chakra and flooding your very being, cleansing you of all negativity and re-energising you. Visualise this 'Golden Light' literally pouring into your skull, brain and spinal cord - into your blood and bones, into your muscles and organs and every cell of your being, visualising a cleansing and healing process taking place, creating peace and harmony.

See golden roots growing from your feet and send them deep down into Mother Earth. Push your roots down through the soil and into the layers of rock, down through the pools and lakes and water falls beneath Earth's crust, down into the crystalline caves. Push those roots further and further down into the deepest recesses of Earth, sending Love to other life forms that we do not see and who may feel forgotten! Now reach out those roots all around the globe connecting with other 'Light' workers, feel that connection growing in other towns and cities all around the world . . . see that pattern of Love growing stronger.

(Spend some time in the network of tunnels if you so wish and explore, this too can lead into many wonderful journeys).

When you are happy, bring your attention back to your roots, bringing them up to your feet and continue with the golden energy climbing up through the trunk of your body as if it were a tree - the tree of life! Bring the golden energy back up through your chakras, flooding each one and creating a rainbow of light. Visualise your branches reaching out to the cosmos, reaching out to connect with those Star beings who work to help mankind. As you look down upon the beautiful sphere that is planet Earth, visualise a Golden canopy of Light enveloping her and very gradually see that canopy melting into fine droplets of liquid energy, falling through Earth's atmosphere. See that magic potion of Love falling down through the heavens and into the oceans . . . into the mountain streams . . . into the lakes, rivers and ponds – into every drop of water upon this planet, purifying and healing the waters. See those golden droplets falling onto the land, healing the soil in which our food grows - see a healing taking place in everything that grows, and for the myriad different life forms that inhabit Earth.

See also that Golden Light entering the hearts of all mankind that they may Love one another and be at peace with their brethren from all walks of life and from all around the world.

510

When you are ready, bring that energy back down once more flooding through your crown chakra and back into your heart. Take time to sit within this sacred space and feel the connectedness and bliss within your heart, and if you then want to sit for communication with guides and inspirers, invite those from the Light to join you. Open your heart wide - take in the Love and the healing you so richly deserve. Go within and listen to that still small voice that echoes in your mind - listen and take note.

When you are ready to come back, feel your feet upon the earth and open your eyes. Give thanks for your communications and breathe in deeply, bringing your cloak of Light around you. Drinking a glass of water too will help you to come fully back into your normal awareness of the world about you.

I wish you all many happy and safe journeys! Please share this meditation with others to bring about a healing for Mother Earth and all life forms on her.

44441542R10288